Crime, Crusades and Corruption

To my mother and the memory of my father

Crime, Crusades and Corruption

Prohibitions in the United States, 1900–1987

Michael Woodiwiss

Barnes & Noble

© Michael Woodiwiss, 1988

First published in the United States of America in 1988 by
Barnes and Noble Books
81 Adams Drive, Totowa, New Jersey 07512

First published in Great Britain in 1988 by
Pinter Publishers Limited
25 Floral Street, London WC2E 9DS.

ISBN 0-389-20796-9

Library of Congress Cataloging-in-Publication Data
Applied for

48069

Printed in Great Britain

Contents

Foreword

As the wise man said, there is very little wisdom among the governors of the world. Fortunately human society is so resilient that so far it has survived even the worst blunders of its rulers. We can still afford to laugh at follies which we see little chance of correcting. And the story of morality laws in the United States, of the attempts, continuous since the arrival of *The Mayflower*, to impose arbitrary standards of conduct on ordinary, decent, sinful human beings, has been endlessly diverting, providing perhaps the surest of all themes for the brilliant artists of American humour.

But it would be a cold heart that found nothing save mirth in the chronicle here presented by Michael Woodiwiss. The grotesque parade of the criminal, the corrupt, the hypocritical and the plain idiotic which he marshals before us certainly has its ridiculous side; yet the cumulative effect of so much folly is deeply saddening. It undermines faith in the human capacity for reason and justice. If the efforts to build a vice-free America had merely been ineffective they might be pardoned; but they have been counter-productive, as Michael Woodiwiss shows. Attempts to stamp out commercial gambling drove it finally to its stronghold in Nevada, where it became big business. Prohibition of alcoholic drinks increased the number of drunks; prohibition of recreational drugs has increased the number of addicts; and all three crusades have generated wholesale murder and official corruption and political persecution.

Just as the Soviet black market is at once a parasite and a searching critique of official socialism, so the American black market in gambling, sex, drink and drugs is a parasite and critique of capitalism and democracy. And just as the Soviet black market is the inevitable outcome of the Soviet-controlled economy, so the American black market in so-called vice is the inevitable outcome of a politically enforced moralism. It would be nice if the two societies made the obvious inferences.

It must be difficult for them to do so, for these points have been made often enough, with little result. So it is tempting to read Michael Woodiwiss's book simply for its history, which is thoroughly up to date. The temptation should be resisted. This is history for application, application to an urgent current problem. When Ronald and Nancy Reagan are seen to have failed in their war on drugs (it may well become clear at about the time the next President of the United States takes office), it may be possible to face the facts of life at last and, as Michael Woodiwiss suggests, to bring the laws into line with human reality. Until that time this study will do excellently to remind us what are those facts of life and, especially, what is the relationship between the law and the human condition it professes to correct.

Drug use can be a personal and medical calamity; but it has become a leading social problem largely because American politicians have called in the criminal law. The result has been disastrous, so much so that even an adjustment so slight as the decriminalization of marijuana (the consumption of which only became a federal crime as late as 1937) would have a hugely beneficial effect, not least by making it impossible to send young men to prison for thirty years for such a trivial action as handing a marijuana cigarette to an *agent provocateur*. It would free the police for useful, uncorrupting tasks, and weaken the power of organized crime. The thought must arise that bolder reforms might have even better consequences.

Admittedly, it is hard to be optimistic in view of the story of general stupidity so carefully unfolded by Michael Woodiwiss. It was not the impossibility of stamping out gambling which gradually brought about the decriminalization of that pastime: it was the need of state governments for a new source of revenue. It was not the palpable failure of Prohibition to save America's soul, or at least make the country teetotal, which ended the experiment noble in purpose: it was the discovery by big business that its taxes had been increased so as to pay for Prohibition enforcement, that its markets were no larger, and that organized crime was using its new wealth to compete with legitimate business. The legions of the intolerant, the lobbies and the lawmakers, have never been compelled to see where the root of so much evil lay: in legalized prejudices which exacerbated the problems they pretended to abhor, ensured the corruption of the police and federal agencies, and opened vast fields of bribery, kickbacks and profitable hypocrisy to the politicians themselves. According to Al Capone, it took him $30 million a year to make all the necessary payoffs in Chicago, 'and his own payroll needed to include nearly half of the police force. "When it comes down to cases," Capone said, "nobody's on the legit"' (p. 74).

Where crime and morality are concerned, Americans have long been fed a diet of legend; and they have clung to their fairy-tales fervently. Thus, Michael Woodiwiss is not the first, and presumably will not be the last, to expose the myth of the Mafia; but it will probably retain its hold on the American imagination for along while yet. Federal Prohibition was a dream associated with the Progressive reform movement in the early years of the twentieth century: perhaps reformers need illusions (concerning the perfectibility of human society and of clear and present dangers) if they are to achieve anything in the face of social and political inertia. Such illusions, unhappily, can be lethal. Lyndon Johnson's Great Society bred its own Prohibition movement in the shape of the war on drugs; it is not over yet. Indeed, it has institutionalized a new hypocrisy. When it turned out that one of President Reagan's nominees to the Supreme Court had occasionally smoked marijuana in his youth he was instantly forced to withdraw his candidacy. This went one better than the 1920s: it is not recorded that nominees to the Court in that decade had to have been total abstainers all their lives.

Yet one of the duties of a democrat is to believe in the ultimate efficacy of reason. This faith is at times almost impossible to sustain; but if it is valid, we may hope that this admirable study will bring the day of successful reform a little nearer. If it does not, at least the supporters of the present system will not be able to plead ignorance: Michael Woodiwiss has set down the consequences of their moralism plain and black.

This book does not cover all the ground of problems related to drugs; indeed it is not really about drugs at all; but it implies the case for reform by showing what a mess the present legal situation is, and, by appealing to the historical record, how inevitably the mess arose. By taking stock so masterfully it becomes an essential preliminary to legislative, executive and judicial action. As such it should be read by every judge in Britain and America, by every member of Parliament and Congress, by the British Home Secretary, and by the President of the United States.

Hugh Brogan

Acknowledgements

Researching and writing this book has taken a number of years and many people have helped me bring it to completion. As a historian my main debts are to Patrick Renshaw of Sheffield University and Hugh Brogan of Essex University. It must also thank my brother, Anthony Woodiwiss, also of Essex, not least for the original idea for the book, and Dr Frank Pearce of Wolverhamptom Polytechnic for sharing his insight into the nature of crime in America. My debts to other writers are, I hope, acknowledged in the notes.

I have also benefited from conversations with John Dombrink, Ramsey Clark, Aaron Kohn, Bill Lambie, C. Stanley Hunterton, Richard Evans, Paul Hoyles, Nigel South, Kevin Zeese, Harry Shapiro, and other knowledgeable people.

I owe a great deal to the staffs of many libraries, notably the Rare books, Manuscripts and Archives Section of the University of Rochester's Rush Rhees Library, the Howard-Tilton Memorial Library of Tulane University, New Orleans, the Special Collections Departments of the University of Tennessee, Knoxville and the University of Nevada, Las Vegas, and the Library of Congress. In England, I must thank the staffs of the Official Publications and the Newspapers Sections of the British Library, Elizabeth Ziman and Valerie Ransom of the University of London's United States Library, and John Witton, Information Officer of the Institute for the Study of Drug Dependence.

My research has been made possibly by grants from the British Academy, the Twenty-Seven Foundation Awards, the British Association for American Studies and the Department of Education and Science.

Finally, I would like Andrew Lownie, Graham Barbrook, Gerry Dermody, Peta and Tessa Wolpe, Hilary Cole, Anna Kuczmierczyk, Min Cooper and Bob and Sue Morgan to know how much I have appreciated their support.

Michael Woodiwiss
London, 1988

Introduction

Nothing can be more certain than that numerous written laws are a sign of a degenerate community, and frequently not the consequences of vicious morals in a state, but the causes.

Oliver Goldsmith

In the twentieth century the United States has had on its statute books the most thorough oversight of personal behaviour in the Western industrial world. Tens of thousands of federal, state and local laws have attempted to enforce morality by prohibitions on alcohol, gambling, prostitution and drugs, plus strict censorship and a host of more trivial restrictions. Compromise proposals to control and regulate such behavior were swamped in a wave of righteousness that came in with the new century. The intention was to end all behaviour that a Protestant culture defined as sinful and nonproductive. Persuasion and education were not enough: Americans had to be coerced by law into a virtuous and healthy way of life.

The laws failed to make the United States a better nation and, instead, fostered, facilitated and sustained a level of crime and corruption far in excess of more tolerant societies. Corrupt networks, often including police and politicians, ensured that prohibited activities continued. The profits were immense, and often worth killing for. The laws were ignored or selectively enforced, filling the prisons with transgressors who had run out of luck or failed to make the right connections. Americans continued to drink, gamble, fornicate or take drugs whether or not it was against the law.

Rather than acknowledge failure and pursue rational policies based on regulation and control, the country persevered with unenforceable, crime-breeding and corrupting prohibitions. In the process many civil liberties were undermined to produce arrests and convictions. Unofficial forms of regulation and control were imposed by intimidation and deception by criminals, many of whom had been elected or appointed as public servants. Simple greed ensured that morality could not be imposed, but hypocrisy and ignorance ensured that the crusade to impose it has been perpetuated.

By the middle of nineteenth century, local and state legislatures had already passed numerous anti-gambling and anti-prostitution laws in most parts of the country. Few city governments, however, consistently directed their police to enforce these 'vice' laws. The politicians, in effect, licensed vice, enabling talented and ruthless entrepreneurs to build up bookmaking, lottery and policy syndicates, operate strings of gambling houses, or run houses of prostitution. Enforcement was purely for show or to crack down on those operators who failed to pay enough protection money. Much nineteenth-century crime was systematically and profitably organized.[1]

Periodically genuine attempts to enforce the vice laws were made in the belief that the arrest and punishment of some transgressors would deter others. Scapegoats were required and some intrinsically immoral methods of law enforcement evolved to supply them. Vice crimes involved cash transactions between willing parties; therefore, there were no complainants to act as witnesses. From the beginning law enforcement had to rely upon espionage, eavesdropping, the use of informants and entrapment to get results. This provided innumerable opportunities for the abuse of power not only for simple financial gain.

A notable pioneer of intrusive enforcement methods was Anthony Comstock. Comstock's favourite target was sex which he described as 'a vulture which steals upon our youth, silently striking its terrible talons into their vitals'. After intense lobbying he persuaded Congress to pass a bill in 1873 banning 'every obscene, lewd, lascivious or filthy book, pamphlet, picture, paper, letter, writing, print or other publication of an indecent character' from being sent through the mails. Because birth control literature was included in the above definition it became Comstock's practice as a volunteer postal inspector to write letters to physicians imploring them for contraceptive advice in the name of a fictitious woman whose health would not permit another child. If any physicians responded they were arrested.

Comstock's New York Society for the Suppression of Vice was later endowed with police powers by the state legislature and Comstock himself was granted the right to carry a gun. The Society was no more than a network of spies, eavesdroppers and informers which subjected prostitutes, in particular, to a reign of terror. Some fifteen women, for example, who were accused of immorality, chose to commit suicide rather than face trial, and many more were entrapped and convicted with undercover methods. Once Comstock and five male helpers visited a brothel at 224 Greene Street, paid three girls fourteen dollars to strip and then arrested them for indecent exposure.

Towards the end of his life Comstock's excesses were ridiculed, particularly his crusades against art galleries and museums which displayed nude statues and paintings. One cartoon in *The Masses*, for example, took his crusade a stage further and depicted Comstock dragging a woman in front of a judge and complaining, 'Your Honor, this woman gave birth to a naked child'.[2]

The idea that fundamental human instincts such as gambling and sex could be totally suppressed was conceivable to Comstock and many others who shared his rigidity of mind. But in the towns and cities most politicians were more realistic and tended to ignore vice laws or exploit them as much as possible. The police were instructed to control vice, not suppress it. Gambling and prostitution operations were allowed to function as long as they paid off and stayed in segregated districts.

Towards the end of the nineteenth century, however, America's moral crusade gathered momentum. In part this was a response to the disruptive processes of rapid industrialization and urbanization, and the influx of millions of migrants and immigrants into the cities. Native-born Americans were horrified, in particular, by Catholics from Europe with their relaxed attitude towards gambling and liquor. Any illusion that Protestant moral values could be maintained with existing legislation was shattered. Many reacted by forming or joining anti-vice or temperance societies, and lobbying energetically in state capitals and city halls for more laws and real enforcement.

For the crusaders evidence of moral decline was everywhere. New styles of clothing, 'suggestive' dances, 'titillating' movies and 'salacious' stage productions were all examples of the 'deadly moral poison' sapping America's strength or the 'germs of licentiousness' contaminating national morality. Illegal gambling houses, from the lavish to the most basic, operated in every city, and turned 'promising' young men into 'slothful idlers'. The use of alcohol and other drugs was said to have reached 'epidemic' proportions. Whole libraries of lurid subliterature predicted degradation and disgrace for the country's youth if exposed to liquor, in particular. Boys were doomed to be profligates and degenerates and girls would inevitably meet with seduction and 'white slavery'. One book, for example, characterized liquor and lust as 'the Devil's Siamese twins': 'The saloon is the arch destroyer of men, the brothel the arch destroyer of women. A sort of hellish blood-relationship exists between them.'[3] Such propagandists ignored appalling working and living conditions; their only concern was the threat to Protestant values of thrift and self-denial. Only total suppression of vice would do; the idea of regulating and controlling gambling, prostitution, recreational drug use or saloons was as unthinkable as licensing murder, robbery or other crimes.

In order to spread the prohibition message, the crusaders were prepared to exploit the endemic racism and xenophobia that pervaded every part of the country. In the West, prejudice against the Chinese was behind state and local legislation prohibiting the smoking of opium which began to be enacted in the final quarter of the nineteenth century. The propaganda behind these campaigns spoke of 'yellow fiends' or 'yellow devils' enslaving white women and children with their 'seductive poison'. According to the San Jose *Mercury* the practice of opium-smoking had to be 'rooted out' before it could 'decimate our youth, emasculate the coming generation, if not completely destroy the whole population of our coast'.[4]

In the South, fear and hatred of black Americans were used to bolster the case for the banning of all intoxicating substances. A popular anti-liquor argument was that white women had to be protected from drink-crazed black men. In 1908, for example, *Colliers' Weekly* related that 'the primitive negro field hand . . . pays his fifty cents for a pint of Mr. Levy's gin' and:

> absorbs not only its toxic heat, but absorbs also the suggestion subtly conveyed, that it contains aphrodisiacs. He sits in the road or in the alley at the height of his debauch, looking at that obscene picture of a white woman on the label, drinking in the invitation which it carries. And then comes—opportunity.

'Everyone knows,' added another commentator, that the saloon fed the 'animalism' of blacks and was 'a debauching agent let loose upon them'.[5] Stories were also circulated that blacks achieved immense strength and cunning when under the influence of cocaine, which in the late nineteenth century was a popular and legal ingredient of medicines and soft drinks. Many gullible people were even led to believe that the drug made blacks capable of withstanding .32 calibre bullets, and some Southern police departments felt it necessary to switch to .38 calibre bullets.[6] The campaigns to prohibit intoxicants in the South were a part of a wider movement to keep blacks passive and subordinate and to keep poor whites united only in racist hatred. Recent research has shown that the campaigns to disenfranchise and repress blacks and the campaigns to prohibit liquor were often led by the same people from the dominant political and economic cliques.[7]

In the Northeastern and Middle Western states the most usual scapegoats for America's alleged slide into degeneracy were the new arrivals from Europe, in particular the Jews and the Italians. Ethnic conspiracy articles were churned out and ethnic stereotypes established in people's minds. In 1909 *McClure's* magazine, for example, informed its readers that 'the acute and often unscrupulous Jewish type of mind' was behind the liquor business and that the 'Jewish dealer in women' had done most to erode 'the moral life of the great cities of America'. The Dearborn *Independent*, a newspaper owned by motor manufacturer Henry Ford, went further and described Jews as 'vile', 'lewd', 'erotic' and 'criminal' conspirators intent on softening up Americans for the kill with alcohol and sex. Italians were described by *The Outlook* in 1913 as an 'aggregation of assassins, blackmailers, kidnappers, and thieves that have piled up a record of crime in the United States unparalleled in a civilized country in time of peace . . .'. Other publications talked of Italians as 'vermin' and 'desperadoes' and circulated stores about how they had transplanted secret criminal societies such as the Camorra and the Mafia into their adopted country. Crime and vice could thus be neatly explained to a gullible public as the work of alien and sinister rings, despite the fact that Jewish and Italian criminals had few opportunities to engage in lucrative illegal enterprises before bootlegging in the 1920s.[8]

Manufacturing and business interests provided crucial financial backing and political pull in the campaigns to put morality on the statute books. Working-class morality and abstinence made dollar-sense. Drinking, gambling, prostitution and drug-taking, for example, were seen as diverting wages from the purchase of manufactured goods and if wages were not spent on wasteful activities there would be less demand for wage rises. Alcohol decreased work efficiency at a time when most managements were searching for ways to get more productivity out of their workers. Business interests could also use their alliance with prohibitionists and America's preoccupation with vice and crime to divert the reform element away from attacks on the trusts and other economic evils. Finally, businessmen believed that the way saloons had become the principal focus of working-class political and economic activity was simply not in their interests. The saloon vote often decided the outcome of city elections and many of these went against the candidates most favoured by business. Even more significantly labour unions were clearly using the saloons to recruit and organize workers, and American businessmen had no greater fear than that of a strong trade-union movement. For such reasons business found America's moral crusade an increasingly attractive investment, and no anti-vice organization was better financed than the Anti-Saloon League.[9]

By the beginning of the new century America's moral crusaders had the finance and organization, as well as the commitment, to persuade, cajole, bribe and bully enough people to ensure that virtue and abstinence became official state policy. Their first intention was to enforce existing anti-vice laws. Pressure was brought on state and municipal authorities to close down red-light districts such as the Tenderloin in New York and the Levee in Chicago and end openly tolerated gambling wherever it existed.

Some apparent success in the suppression of prostitution was soon achieved. By the First World War most red-light districts had been closed down. This, however, did not lessen the problem and merely dispersed it. The immediate increase in street-walking and soliciting was noticed in most American cities. Moreover, without recognized districts or brothels prostitutes could not longer receive customers in a relatively protected environment, and the search for custom made them vulnerable to both customer violence and police shakedowns. Pimps also benefited from the new conditions as they moved in to fill the legal, physical and emotional needs formerly met by madams and other prostitutes. Prostitutes paid a high price in financial terms for this protection and could be subject to indiscriminate beatings. Customers were also more prone to be beaten and robbed as the prostitution business adapted to its new conditions.[10] After 1900 the system of open gambling was also under sustained attack. One impact was upon horse-racing which depended on the non-enforcement of the gambling laws to attract spectators. Even the threat of enforcement could force the race-tracks to close down, and from a golden age in the 1890s racing declined so that by the First World War only six states, New York, Maryland, Kentucky, Louisiana, Colarado and Nevada, still had tracks. In the cities lavish and conspicuous gambling houses gave to way to dark, smoky rooms reached through discreet entranceways, as law-enforcement campaigns made their mark.[11]

The moral crusaders were not satisfied with more fines and prison sentences for gamblers and prostitutes, however, and their second intention was to enact more and more laws governing personal behaviour. By 1910 more than 16,000 such laws were on federal, state and local statute books, governing not just gambling and prostitution but cigarette-smoking and the length of skirts and size of bathing suits in some states. Censorship laws were so strict that it was a federal crime to send birth-control information by mail or across state lines and occasionally local legislation went so far as that in Norphelt, Arkansas, which prohibited 'improper and lascivious sexual intercourse', even among married couples.[12]

The peak of the crusade was the passing of three major Federal acts, the Mann Act, the Harrison Act and the Volstead Act. In 1910 the Mann Act made it an offence to transport a woman across state lines for 'immoral purposes'. The framers of the Act claimed to have struck the death blow against the brothel and, in particular, the white-slave traffic that was thought, at the time, to sustain prostitution. Although the abduction of girls and women into forced prostitution was a problem then as now, it did not at any time sustain prostitution. The vast majority become prostitutes for purely economic reasons and the Mann Act could not change this fact of life.

In 1914 the Harrison Narcotic Act was passed. Although the intention of the Act was chiefly to prohibit the use of drugs for recreational purposes, Treasury agents exploited its ambiguous wording to prohibit certain drugs totally. There was an intense campaign to prevent doctors treating drug users: between 1914 and 1938 some three thousand doctors served penitentiary sentences for this offence. Doctors were effectively prohibited from dispensing heroin or morphine to addicts or to ease the pain of the terminally ill. A major black market soon developed as criminals moved in to supply both addicts and users with a variety of the new illegal drugs.[13]

In 1919 the Volstead Act was passed, providing for enforcement of the 18th Amendment to the Constitution. The Amendment prohibited the manufacture, transportation, sale or importation of intoxicating liquor within the United States. At midnight on 16 January 1920 millions of Americans said farewell to legal liquor and prohibitionists rejoiced. The Reverend Billy Sunday organized a mock funeral for John Barleycorn and crowed: 'Goodbye John. You were God's worst enemy. You were hell's best friend. I hate you with a perfect hatred. I love to hate you.' Sunday then predicted that: '. . . the reign of tears is over. The slums will soon be a memory. We will turn our prisons into factories and our jails into storehouses and corncribs. Men will walk upright now, women will smile and children will laugh. Hell will be forever for rent.' The Anti-Saloon League announced the beginning of a new era of clear thinking and clean living in a prosperous and moral country.[14] Part I of this book describes how this ideal was shattered. Prohibition merely took the legitimate income of brewers, distillers and saloon-keepers and gave it to criminals and corrupt public officials. Rumrunners, bootleggers, gunmen, speakeasy operators, graft-seeking politicians, corrupt judges and bribe-taking cops and coastguards all shared in this immense new potential for easy money. The 18th Amendment was repealed on 5 December 1933 and the federal government's first serious effort to enforce morality was over.

America's moral crusade did not end with repeal and the local crime crusades examined in Part II were part of a continuing effort to control personal behaviour. The burden of enforcement was back with the cities and the states but the public's demand for such illegal activities as gambling, prostitution and drug-taking ensured that corrupt networks would continue to prosper. Any honest efforts to enforce the vice laws were outweighed by hypocrisy, political opportunism and corruption. Illegal methods were routinely employed to secure convictions and scapegoats were produced to confirm people's fear and ignorance and, at the same time, to assure them that something was being done. No financial interests emerged to sponsor the repeal or liberalization of the remaining vice laws, and few politicians or newspapers had the courage to draw attention to the futility of the effort. Millions of dollars of potential revenue from the legalization of gambling, in particular, went instead to those in a position to circumvent the laws. Police, prosecutors and judges were consistently more responsive to the laws of political expediency and pressure, plus the attractions of graft, than to the official laws against gambling.

Although the vice laws were treated with contempt, the institutions which moulded public opinion, such as newspapers, churches and chambers of commerce, had set themselves against any more tampering with the morality legislation after repeal of Prohibition. Part III describes how proposals to rationalize the laws against gambling and drugs were countered by misrepresenting the problem of organized crime. Tabloid journalists, Senate committees, and drug enforcement bureaucrats sold the public the notion that a mysterious alien conspiracy known as the Mafia controlled organized crime in America. During the 1950s Americans were led to believe that the Mafia super-criminal organization had virtually taken control of the illegal economy and parts of the legal economy as well through its control over police and politicians—a bizarre explanation but one that was more convenient than the more prosaic truth of combinations of American businessmen, police, politicians and criminals getting rich by supplying the constant demand for illegal goods and services. By dulling the critical and analytical faculties of commentators and investigators, the Mafia interpretation of organized crime became the conventional wisdom. Since gambling, in particular, was thought to be the 'lifeblood' of the Mafia, there could be no rational response to the problem of organized crime while the Mafia interpretation held sway. The fight against gambling and the fight against organized crime became one and the same thing. Stricter and more efficient enforcement of the laws remained the almost exclusive approach, but the law remained relatively easy and immensely profitable to exploit.

The conception of organized crime as a united entity transcending state lines was vital. It could then be plausibly presented as many-faced, calculating and conspiratorial, relentlessly probing for weak spots in the armour of American morality. Compromise was therefore out of the question—the only answer was to defeat the alien menace with more laws and increased law enforcement capacity. In the 1960s the federal government again became seriously involved in attempting to enforce the morality laws. The FBI vainly concentrated its resources in the pursuit of gansters with Italian names and achieved negligible results against gambling networks at an enormous cost in manpower and surveillance.

Since the early 1970s, when a series of police scandals revealed that gambling was as much police business as bookie business or syndicate business, a very low priority is given to gambling law enforcement by city administrations. The crusade against gambling is rapidly being abandoned in the United States. The trend towards decriminalization and legalization of some forms of wagering is now clear.

At the same time, however, another crusade is still gathering force. The war on drugs represents the final serious attempt by the federal government to eradicate an aspect of personal behaviour, and is already on a scale far in excess of the attempts to prohibit alcohol and gambling. Part IV explains how federal, state and local drug law enforcement was expanded massively from the 1960s as politicians used the fear of drugs to further their careers. In an irrational response to the problem of addiction and recreational drug use a massive drug enforcement bureaucracy was created whose only success has been self-perpetuation.

Like the wars on liquor and gambling, there is no feasible prospect of success in the war on drugs. Smuggling, manufacture and distribution is simply too easy in such a hugh country; too many sources of supply already exist or can be developed. Inevitably corruption and power abuse have characterized drug law enforcement and attempts to eradicate drug use and trafficking in the United States have been as counter-productive as the earlier crusades. Successful investigations are isolated, costly and consume law enforcement time which could be better spent. Illegal drugs can be bought anywhere. The harsh penalties for drug possession and sale have merely guaranteed high prices for drugs in the richest and most easily accessible market in the world. Acknowledging continued failure, US drug-control policies have been modernized; education, treatment and prevention pro-grammes were added in the early 1970s to the policy of bare repression. But still policy continues to be inflexible and unrealistic and the old illusion that with relentless enforcement worldwide a drug-free America could be achieved continues to be disseminated. Numerous other countries have been persuaded to adopt the American model of drug control as their own. Approaches which acknowledge the limits of the criminal sanction and suggest that the fight should be against the harm that drugs do rather than the drugs themselves continue to be discredited.

This work will trace the efforts of the United States to enforce and sustain an excessive body of legislation governing personal behaviour and the lawless consequences of these efforts.

Part I Losing the war against liquor, 1920–1934

A national prohibition amendment to the Federal Constitution will be adopted against the views and practices of a majority of the people in many of the large cities and in one-fourth or less of the States.

The business of manufacturing alcohol, liquor and beer will go out of the hands of the law-abiding members of the community and will be transferred to the quasi-criminal class.

William H. Taft, former President of the United States, 1919

This law will be obeyed in cities, large and small, and in villages, and where it is not obeyed it will be enforced . . . The law says that liquor to be used as a beverage must not be manufactured. We shall see that it is not manufactured. Nor sold, nor given away, nor hauled in anything on the surface of the earth or under the earth or in the air.

John F. Kramer, Prohibition Commissioner, 1920

Prohibition is here to stay. The illegal liquor traffic is under control . . . The control becomes more complete and thorough with each passing day.

Roy Haynes, Prohibition Commissioner, 1923

There is as much chance of repealing the 18th Amendment as there is for a humming-bird to fly to the planet Mars with the Washington Monument tied to its tail.

Senator Morris Sheppard, 1930

1 Making crime pay

There was no need for abstinence during Prohibition. The number of illegal drinking outlets soon approached and then overtook the number of pre-Volstead saloons. By 1925 there were at least 15,000 'blind pigs' in Detroit, and by the end of the 1920s at least 32,000 'speakeasies' in New York.[1] Countless establishments, such as grocers, drug stores and tobacconists, sold liquor as a sideline. Rural drinkers continued to concoct their own alcoholic beverages. The rich had liquor delivered to their homes. The poor drank beer which was close to water, or spirits which were close to poison. Prohibition simply made consumption of alcohol more of a challenge. Drinking became more expensive and secretive, and much less selective.

Prohibition immediately made the problem of crime and corruption in the United States considerably worse. Within hours of the Volstead Act taking effect at midnight on 16 January 1920 there were liquor robberies and hijackings. On 19 February the first of many federal agents were arrested for liquor law corruption. By June it was estimated that physicians in Chicago alone had issued about 300,000 phoney prescriptions for liquor; also the dockets of Chicago's federal courts were congested with over 500 prohibition cases awaiting trial.[2] City authorities had already shown no inclination to enforce the new law honestly. Corruption rapidly became more routine, crime more profitable.

There were many ways to slake the country's thirst. Not only doctors profited from the provision that permitted alcohol as medicine. One enterprising bootlegger[3] from Ohio, George Remus, bought up chains of drug stores so that he could order truckloads of medicinal liquor and then arrange for them to be hijacked. By 1924 Remus had enough capital to purchase seven distilleries and their warehouses, ostensibly for the production of industrial alcohol. From the bonded warehouses liquor was diverted in railroad-car lots. To continue operations, however, Remus estimated that he had to pay around $20 million in bribes.[4]

Industry was one of the most prolific sources of home-produced alcohol. There was so much need for alcohol in the legitimate manufacture of products ranging from shaving cream to rayon that large amounts could be siphoned off without arousing suspicion. The government required that industrial alcohol be 'denatured'—that is, poisoned—but it could easily be put through a process which, sometimes successfully, removed the poison. However, not many bootleggers were concerned about the purity of the product they sold. Governor Gifford Pinchot of Pennsylvania indicated the extent of diverted industrial alcohol in 1924 when he complained that 150 of his state's firms authorized to purchase denatured alcohol to manufacture perfumes and hair tonics had ordered enough to fulfil the needs of the population of the entire world.[5]

Direct distilling and home brewing also became organized on a massive scale. 'Alky cooking' became the cottage industry of numerous ghettos where the smell of fermenting mash was permanent. Stills were installed in thousands of warehouses, garages and tenements. People were supplied with the ingredients and operating instructions and paid generously to keep the fire burning and the alcohol running day and night. The product was collected every few days and sold to speakeasies or to nationwide distributors at a handsome profit. The Gennas, a gang of six brothers on the south side of Chicago, were thought to make around $150,000 a month from this enterprise even after the police had been paid off.[6]

Some pre-Volstead brewing and distilling interests formed alliances with criminals not only to organize successful robberies of existing stocks, but also on a long-term basis. One major Chicago brewer, Joseph Stenson, made an estimated $12 million out of such an arrangement. He escaped prosecution even though this activities were well enough known for the Chicago *Tribune* to note that:

> Mr Stenson has not been convicted of being a twin king of commercialised vice. He is the silk hat for the crowd. There are avenues into the federal building that he knows well. He furnishes the money, buys the breweries, and makes the connections necessary to undisturbed brewing. Having financed a brewery, he installs as president, secretary, and board of directors a number of healthy, good-natured young men. These gentlemen operate at a high price and in return they take the fall when there is trouble.
>
> Taking the fall consists in being defendants when there is prosecution. Of course only the officials of a brewery are legally responsible. Which lets Stenson out.[7]

To distribute his illegal beer, Stenson needed the services of gangsters, most notable of whom was John Torrio. Torrio, formerly of New York, had been involved in various Chicago gambling and prostitution activities since 1909. With Prohibition, Torrio was at first successful, buying sufficient official protection and persuading his fellow gangsters that cooperation was more likely to yield profits than violent competition.

Torrio's position was undermined when a new administration under Mayor William Dever took office in 1923. The old protection system broke down and in May 1924 police raids established enough evidence to indict Torrio, some of his associates, and several pre-Volstead brewers associated with Stenson. The brewers had enough influence to avoid facing trial, while Torrio and two others were convicted and sentenced to short spells in jail.[8] Torrio was shot by rival gansters while free on bail and decided to bestow the leadership of his gang on Al Capone, whose fate will be examined later. However, the important aspect of the Stenson–Torrio relationship was that while 'respectable' businessmen had illegally enriched themselves *and* stayed out of jail, gangsters had proved to be vulnerable to a change of government.

The demand for beer continued to be supplied throughout Prohibition, sometimes by breweries operating quite blatantly in major cities, but usually more discreetly in rural areas. The Anheuser-Busch Company in St Louis, of Budweiser fame, had hopefully spent $18 million converting their plant to the manufacture of legal near-beer, only to discover that it could not compete with bootleggers who were selling the real thing.[9]

Prohibition created a vast new market for illegal goods and services, and a brand new illegal industry. Along the coasts, rivers and the Great Lakes, fishermen, tugboat operators, shippers and dockworkers gave up their normal occupations and entered the smuggling trade. Apart from smuggling, the illegal liquor trade made thousands of new jobs and executive positions available in the multi-ethnic American cities. Young men graduated straight from the juvenile gangs and were able to avoid the drudgery and long hours of their parents' occupations. Bootlegging was so much better paid.

Cars and trucks made for easy and fast transportation, and telephones aided organization; city-wide and state-wide criminal networks multiplied. Local, regional, national and international ties soon developed among bootlegging entrepreneurs. One reason for this, as the historian Mark Haller has pointed out, was that a large urban market could absorb not just great quantities of liquor but also a large variety of types: beer, Scotch, bourbon, gin, wines, champagnes. No distributor of illegal beverages to speakeasies, roadhouses and other outlets could possibly manufacture or import such a variety. Therefore, some organizations specialized for good economic reasons, and any large organization necessarily had ties with other organizations.[10]

Middle- and upper-class Americans constituted a lucrative market for properly distilled and blended spirits. Along the Eastern Seaboard and the Great Lakes the big money came from smuggling liquor into the country. It was a complex and costly undertaking requiring a great deal of organization: contracting for the liquor in many countries, getting it past the Coast Guard and the Customs, landing it on the docks, loading it on to trucks, carting it to warehouses and delivering it to the retail outlets. Hijacking was always a threat. Any systematic smuggling or bootlegging operation routinely hired gunmen to protect shipments from hijackers; a few tough, armed men could seize valuable cargo in transit to the warehouses, and sell it for the same price with none of the overheads.

As in the early days of other American industries, competition for markets and territory was fierce and expensive. In New York and Chicago, it took savagery, shrewdness and luck to survive the bootleg gang wars. On 11 May 1920, Jim Colisimo was shot twice in the lobby of his own restaurant and thus became the first of Chicago's gang bosses to be assassinated. The murder of a minor bootlegger became so ordinary an event as to be worth not more than a paragraph or two on the inside page of a newspaper. Police conducted cursory investigations and never obtained convictions. Murder became routine. Rival gangsters were pistoled or machine-gunned, taken for rides on the front seats of sedans and their brains blown out from behind, lined up and shot by firing squads, packed in cement, tied up in sacks or pinioned with wire and then dropped into lakes or rivers—any way that was convenient or would serve as a warning to others.[11] Thousands died simply because both the liquor trade and the gun trade were unregulated.

To a great extent during Prohibition, bootleggers and speakeasy operators took the risks while public officials took the money. In the country's two largest cities, police and politicians were far more concerned with being paid off than with the accumulating numbers of dead gangsters on the streets. Violent and prolonged gang warfare was, moreover, limited to New York, Chicago and a few other cities, and represented poorly organized crime. The public officials of San Francisco, Los Angeles, Philadelphia, Pittsburg and many others ensured that fortunes could be made with the minimum of fatalities.

From the beginning enforcement agencies were integral parts of the organized distribution of alcohol. The Federal Prohibition Unit (renamed the Prohibition Bureau in 1927) was a small group of low-paid and inefficient agents, numbering only about 1,500 for the entire country. Many of these proved to be incompetent and venal, their only qualification for the job being political affiliation. Many had criminal records, and some were former bootleggers. Stories of dry agents escorting liquor trucks, protecting smugglers and even helping them unload their cargoes, accepting bribes for information about raids, allowing real beer to be shipped as cereal beverages, dealing in withdrawal permits for alcohol, and in general sustaining the illicit liquor traffic, appeared in newspapers daily. Once, it is said that the chief of the New York office of the Prohibition Bureau asked his men to put their hands on the table and then fired anyone wearing a diamond ring. He lost half his staff.[12] Such clean-ups, however, were exceptional and, on salaries averaging less than $3,000 a year, prohibition agents bought country homes, town houses, real estate, speedboats, expensive automobiles, and a host of other luxuries.

Hundreds of agents were accused of corruption, scores were arrested and indicted, and many of these were convicted and sent to prison. During the first four years of Prohibition, 141 agents were jailed. During the first ten years of Prohibition, the Bureau employed 17,816 agents of whom 11,926 were separated from the service without prejudice and 1,587 were 'dismissed for cause'. The latter were the ones against whom the evidence was lacking to justify court action. Proportionately, the turnover was about the same in the higher ranks of the enforcement service. There were four national commissioners during the first five years and New York and Pennsylvania each had six different state directors in less than four years. In each of these states one director was indicted for conspiracy. The Pennsylvania case against State Director William McConnell involved a conspiracy to withdraw 700,000 gallons of alcohol and to share a corruption fund of about $4 million. McConnell was tried against the express wishes of Attorney-General Harry Daugherty. At the trial government attorneys announced that most of their documentary evidence against McConnell and his associates had disappeared. The charges were dropped.

Corruption spread to every government department with dry law responsibilities. At the 1925 trial of Big Bill Dwyer, an enormously successful rumrunner, it was shown that numerous coastguardmen were on Dwyer's regular payroll. Often Dwyer's motorboats, loaded with liquor, were escorted into port by coastguard patrol ships, and coastguardmen helped unload the cargoes. Similar helpful service was given for a price to other rum syndicates on both the Atlantic and Pacific coasts, on the Gulf shore and the Great Lakes.

The most extensive corruption found in the Customs Service was at Detroit. In 1929 a grand jury revealed that smugglers paid off an average $2 million a year to operate. About 100 agents were involved in the 'graft trust', and their monthly take averaged $1,700 each. The customs men also received lump sums for 'free nights' on the border, when smugglers were permitted to run in as much liquor as they could handle, and were also known to bribe rumrunners to give them information leading to the seizure of liquor shipments on which the graft toll had not been paid.[13]

The most significant criminal network uncovered during the first years of Prohibition consisted of members of President Warren Harding's government, popularly known as the Ohio gang, and including Harry Daugherty, the Attorney-General. Although the best known of this group's many crimes was the multi-million-dollar oil swindle—Teapot Dome—Prohibition's potential for illegal enrichment was also exploited. Extortion was especially profitable. A file from the Department of Justice listed convicted bootleggers who could be sold pardons. In 1924 Special Agent Gaston Means told a Senate committee that he had collected around $7 million from bootleggers for his political bosses and the aforementioned George Remus (see p. 11) also testified that he had paid more than $250,000 to Jesse Smith, a member of the Ohio gang, to stay in the liquor business. For a price the government gang would drop prosecutions, sell federal enforcement jobs and permit the illegal withdrawal of bonded liquor.[14]

Innumerable state and local officials emulated the Ohio gang. In every large city it was common knowledge that the police and politicians were in collusion with bootleggers and speakeasy operators, and periods of genuine enforcement were exceptional and temporary. In January 1924, for example, an aggressive campaign by Philadelphia's police chief, General Smedley Butler, closed 600 speakeasies and resulted in 2,000 arrests. The response to the campaign was sabotage. High-level police officials warned speakeasies of impending raids, politicians and city officials interceded for violators, and magistrates dismissed charges with monotonous regularity. 'Trying to enforce the law in Philadelphia', General Butler said, 'was worse than any battle I was ever in.' Of more than 6,000 arrested for liquor violations in his second year of office, only 212 were convicted. 'Enforcement,' according to Butler 'hasn't amounted to a row of pins after the arrests were made.' An additional problem was that liquor held as evidence tended to disappear. As the historian Herbert Asbury pointed out, immediately following these losses a number of policemen resigned from the force and opened up speakeasies. Others found it more profitable to stay put. In 1928 it was revealed that Philadelphia policemen, on salaries less than $4,000 a year, had bank accounts ranging from $40,412 to $193,553.[15]

Pittsburg's graft system was just as well organized. Among those implicated by a federal grand jury in 1928 were two police magistrates, two members of the state legislature, five Republican ward chairman, the superintendent of police, fourteen police inspectors, five patrolmen and a constable. Before 1926 the Pittsburg system had provided for the sale and distribution of a moonshine whisky, locally known as 'mooney'. It could be bought at countless restaurants, soft-drink bars, former saloons and sandwich counters. In 1926 the new city government under Mayor Charles Kline was accompanied by a new and inferior form of 'mooney', called 'administration booze'. Retailers had to pay $4 a gallon, twice the previous amount, and passed the increase on to the consumers who now had to pay 25 cents a drink, 50 cents a half-pint, and a dollar a pint. The new drink was unpopular. It was not only foul-smelling but if left standing for a few days, a greenish scum was likely to accumulate. However, retailers who tried to reintroduce 'mooney' were promptly raided by the police and put out of business. The terms of the new system required that a fixed weekly quantity of the new brand be taken by all retailers whether they could dispose of it or not. All that mattered was the continued profitability of the system.[16]

Overall during Prohibition, police and federal agents made a huge number of arrests for liquor law violations, but any genuine accomplishments they made were frequently undermined by the courts. Many thousands of cases were plainly 'fixed'. When protected bootleggers stepped in front of judges, assistant district attorneys suddenly found they had 'insufficient evidence' or witnesses failed to show up, or police officers admitted that they had overstepped themselves in the performance of their duties. The blatant fixing of cases caused Assistant Attorney General Mabel Willebrandt to complain that she spent more time prosecuting prosecutors than the people they should have prosecuted.[17] Judges were also more prone to the pressures of corruption and anyway were forced to dispense an assembly-line justice to relieve the congestion of the courts. Criminal justice in the United States had never been more of a misnomer.

In the years since Prohibition government officials, as well as many crime writers who accept their information without analysis, have given the public the false impression that organized crime is somehow alien and distinct from the mainstream of American political and economic life. During the Prohibition years, however, there were no such delusions. Liquor-related organized crime was seen clearly as combinations of producers, distributors, politicians and law enforcement agencies working together to make crime pay. No one tried to pretend that organized crime was an alien conspiracy.

2 The dangers of enforcement

The scale of the country alone made effective prohibition of alcohol an impossible dream. The borders with Canada and Mexico were several thousand miles long. There were more than 12,000 miles of Atlantic, Pacific and Gulf shoreline, abounding in inlets. Smugglers won the battle against the Customs Service and the Border Patrol without problem. A population of over 100 million inhabited a land mass of around 3 million square miles. Only a huge standing army would have made an impact on distribution. The very idea of true enforcement was mocked. Representative Fiorello La Guardia estimated that it would require a police force of 250,000 men to dry up New York alone, 'and a force of 250,000 men to police the police'. Diligent state enforcement in New York, according to Governor Al Smith, would require one-third of the state's citizens to apprehend another third who were violators, while the remaining third would be tied up serving on juries.[1]

Dry law enforcement, such as it was, alienated rather than endeared Prohibition to the public. The rough handling of the public and the shooting of innocent bystanders, in particular, caused many people to wonder whether the ideal of abstinence was really worth the problems which accompanied a show of enforcement. At the end of the first year of Prohibition, one federal official and one civilian had been killed in the process of enforcement. By 1930 the body count had risen to eighty-six federal agents and 200 civilians These figures did not include killings by numerous non-federal groups—state enforcement agents, sheriffs, deputy sheriffs, town marshalls, constables, undercover men, special squads appointed by local authorities, citizen volunteers employed by federal officials; and local, state and highway policemen. In December 1929 the Washington *Herald*, after a survey of the entire country, estimated that 1,360 people had been killed, and at least a thousand more wounded.

Many of the killings were justified self-defence, but many others were as a result of the carelessness or criminal recklessness of enforcement officers. Some civilians were killed by officers who invaded their property without search warrants. Others, stopped on lonely roads by armed men with no distinguishing uniform, were shot down when they became frightened and tried to escape. A few were innocent bystanders, struck by stray bullets. In many parts of the country, particularly along the Canadian and Mexican borders, there was so much indiscriminate shooting by prohibition officers that people were afraid to drive their cars at night. A popular car window

sticker during the 1920s was, 'Don't Shoot, I'm Not a Bootlegger'. Frequently squads of agents set up road-blocks and searched all cars, without
warrant or authority; many civilians who resented such illegal and high-
handed procedures were in danger of being shot. Sometimes an agent who
had killed a citizen was convicted in a local court and sent to jail or fined, but
if a federal officer was involved, the government intervened and transferred
the case to a federal court under a writ of habeas corpus. If brought to trial at
all, the agent was generally acquitted. The Chicago *Tribune* of 11 November
1928 listed twenty-three civilian killings for which government agents had
been indicted by local grand juries. All the cases were transferred, and all the
agents escaped punishment.[2]

Dry leaders were unsympathetic when the casualties of liquor law
enforcement were reported. On one occasion dry congressmen loudly
applauded when it was announced that a young man driving a liquor truck in
Washington had been shot dead by a policeman. Senator Smith Brookhart of
Iowa articulated this attitude when he made this point in a 1929 Senate
debate:

> When we get senators in this chamber talking sense, instead of all this gush stuff
> about murders by men who make mistakes once in a while, we will have a better
> attitude toward the bootleg question.[3]

Until the end of Prohibition police continued to shoot bootleggers or
bystanders while the suspects were, for example, reaching for hip pockets,
running away, stooping to the ground, or warning companions. One of the
last fatalities was a youth who was shot dead by the Sheriff of Durant,
Oklahoma, when running away from the location of a still. The official
justified his action on the ground that he was a dry and that it was his duty to
kill to enforce the law. He faced no charges for the act.[4]

More resentment of liquor law injustice was caused by the disparity in
sentencing according to wealth, influence and locality. In most cities, young,
affluent and vicious gangsters faced mostly fines for repeated liquor law
violations, while the poor in rural areas could face long terms of imprisonment for repeated offences involving mere possession. One victim was Etta
May Miller, a mother of four in Lancing, Michigan, who was sentenced to
life in 1929 for possessing a single bottle of gin.[5]

The one federal government policy which caused the most controversy,
however, was the denaturing of industrial alcohol. Deadly poisons, capable of
causing paralysis, blindness and sometimes immediate or lingering death
were added to industrial alcohol under government instruction to deter use.
By the mid-1920s thousands had died. Some children were even poisoned
because their mothers had fed them a spoonful of 'whisky' as a cold cure.
Senator James Reed condemned such results of government refusal to
abandon the policy of denaturing and asked whether this 'was not as near an
approach to murder as possible'.

The historian Richard Hofstadter has made the point that this was just one of the tragic ironies of Prohibition:

> Before Prohibition became law, the prohibitionists decried alcohol as a form of deadly poison. After Prohibition was law, they approved the legal poisoning of industrial alcohol, knowing full well that men would die from drinking it. Excess had this way of turning things into their opposites: an amenity became a crime; the imposition of controls led to loss of control; the churches created gangsters; reformers became reactionaries; purifiers became poisoners.[7]

By passing Prohibition the government was attempting to extend its jurisdiction to every individual and every home in the United States in order to stamp out the long-standing custom of millions of Americans. Some of the methods used in the attempt were necessarily devious and intrusive. To entrap violators dry agents often posed as customers in search of a drink or even persuaded people to buy drinks in order to arrest them. One prohibition agent who resigned when he could no longer stand the deception involved in enforcement cited, in particular, the entrapment of bell-boys in hotels:

> The scheme usually pursued is for a prohibition agent to take a room in the hotel, go to bed feigning to be recovering from a spree, and plead with the bell-boy to get him a drink. He frequently succeeds in inducing the bell-hop to do so. Then a raid follows, the hotel is 'pinched' and the bell-hop is arrested—a most glorious achievement by the officials of the great United States.[8]

Such entrapment techniques were developed and elaborated and by the middle of the 1920s. Prohibition agents were even setting up phoney speakeasies to snare bootleggers. One such was the Bridge Whist Club in New York, where a dictograph was concealed and connected by wires to an adjoining room where a stenographer transcribed every word uttered within range of the machine. In six months, despite the enormous expense of this operation, only a few bootleggers had been successfully trapped.[9] Today, such 'scam' operations are a common police tactic.

The practice of tapping into private telephone conversations to gather incriminating evidence also began during Prohibition. Former police lieutenant Roy Olmstead, who became Seattle's richest bootlegger, was convicted with wiretapping evidence in a case that was fought all the way to the United States Supreme Court. The court upheld the verdict by a five to four decision and declared that wiretapping was not unwarranted search and seizure. In the opinion written by Chief Justice William Taft, the court ruled that no element of force had been used in obtaining evidence and that the element of force was the essence of unreasonable search and seizure.

Two of the four judges who dissented from the majority verdict issued warnings of the inherent dangers involved in undermining constitutional rights. Justice Louis Brandeis took the ground that:

> When the Fourth and Fifth Amendments were adopted, the form that evil had theretofore taken had been necessarily simple. Force and violence were then the

only means known to man by which a government could directly effect self-incrimination . . . Subtler and more far-reaching means of invading privacy have become available to the government. Discovery and invention have made it possible for the government, by means far more effective than stretching upon the rack, to obtain disclosure in court of what is whispered in the closet.

To protect the right to be 'let alone—the most comprehensive of rights and the right most valued by civilized men'. Brandeis felt that 'every unjustifiable intrusion by the government upon the privacy of the individual, whatever the means employed, must be deemed a violation of the Fourth Amendment'.

Justice Oliver Wendell Holmes opposed the new police practice even more vehemently:

> It is desirable that criminals should be detected, and to that end that all available evidence should be used. It is also desirable that the government should not itself foster and pay for other crimes, when they are the means by which the evidence is to be obtained . . . We have to choose, and for my part I think it a less evil that some criminals should escape than that the government should play an ignoble part.[10]

The warnings of the two justices were not heeded since the country persevered with the misguided attempt to impose morality even after the war against liquor was declared lost. The laws prohibiting gambling, prostitution and drugs remained on the statute books and devious and intrusive methods gradually became accepted as necessary to produce the quotas of arrests and convictions that create the illusion of success and justify futile and counter-productive policy. Constitutional safeguards could never prevent large-scale abuse and injustice.

The city of Denver and the state of Colorado experienced some of the worst abuses during Prohibition. In Denver's 1923 election Benjamin Stapleton was elected mayor with strong Ku Klux Klan support, having pledged to wage war on crime and vice. Much of the Klan's appeal during the 1920s lay in its promise to restore law, order and morality to American communities and fight any possible threat to God and country. Klan violence—whippings, torture, castration and murders—was directed at WASP transgressors as much as Catholics, Jews and black people. In order to repay political debts Mayor Stapleton's police department included numerous Klansmen, including the Chief of Police, William Candlish, several officers and dozens of patrolmen. Chief Candlish used the department as an instrument of the Klan's will, intimidating political opponents and labour leaders, and attempting to impose morality by terror. In April 1925, however, a flaw in the Klan's own commitment to morality was revealed. Bypassing Chief Candlish, the Mayor secretly deputized 125 American Legionnaires to execute a series of raids. Around 200 bootleggers, gamblers and prostitutes were arrested, and a complex network of tip-offs, graft and protection controlled by the hand-picked men of the Klan's vice squad was exposed. Candlish was fired and twelve Klan policemen were dismissed.

Colorado State's 200 prohibition agents were almost all Klansmen, also appointed to repay political debts. On 19 June 1925, agent R.N. Mason, the Exalted Cyclops of the Trinidad Klan, led a raiding party on a random search for liquor. Mason's men battered in the doors of fifty homes without identifying themselves, drew revolvers, and lined up the frightened men and women for search. No convictions were obtained. The following day another contingent of state agents staged a night raid in Weld County. Armed raiders, lacking criminal or search warrants, ransacked several suspected residences and arrested twelve men. The presiding justice of the peace levied fines for possession of liquor which he subsequently divided with the dry agents. The search for liquor in both city and state also covered harassment of Catholic, Jewish, black, labour and other anti-Klan leaders.[11]

Although for many Americans liquor law enforcement meant abuse, corruption, brutality and futility, dry politicians continued to run the nation's affairs. Public outrage over the worst scandals was short-lived and irrelevant. Prohibition was not the overriding political issue of the 1920s. Prosperity and industrial expansion ensured Republican national government throughout the decade. Not even the rampant corruption in the administration of President Harding, nor the torpidity of his successor Calvin Coolidge, could threaten the Republican ascendancy. Generally lax liquor law enforcement and the fact that growing numbers of people could afford to pay inflated bootleg prices meant that the demand for alcohol could be satisfied while the country remained officially dry. The American people showed they accepted this situation in the 1928 presidential elections. Herbert Hoover, the Republican candidate, declared his intention of enforce the 18th Amendment efficiently, and comfortably defeated Al Smith, who wished to repeal it. As Will Rogers said of Virginians, Americans would vote for Prohibition as long as they could stagger to the polls.

Hoover proceeded to do everything in his power to enforce the 18th Amendment, strengthening federal enforcement and criminal justice wherever he could. The Prohibition Bureau, in particular, was drastically improved in honesty and efficiency, multiplying the amounts of illegal liquor and apparatus seized or smashed and the numbers of prison sentences imposed.

The most dramatic evidence of the strong federal response to liquor law violations under Hoover, however, was provided by the highly publicized arrests and convictions of major bootleggers, most notably the subject of the next chapter, Alphonse Capone.

3 The fall of Al Capone

Capone was born in a Brooklyn slum at the turn of the century. He graduated from New York's juvenile gangs to join another New Yorker, John Torrio, in Chicago and help run some of the nation's most lucrative racketeering operations. In 1924 Torrio left the city and Capone was in control of a large and growing business. Bootlegging profits enabled him to expand and diversify operations; illegal rackets were complemented by semi-legal and legal enterprises. Breweries, distilleries, speakeasies, warehouses, fleets of boats and trucks, nightclubs, gambling houses, horse and dog racetracks, brothels, and numerous small but legitimate businesses together produced a yearly income of hundreds of millions of dollars.[1]

Capone was supported by an army of thugs and assassins, 700–1,000-strong with allied gangs, which was motivated enough to withstand the nation's bloodiest gang warfare. Among the hundreds who died were Capone's most dangerous competitors. On 10 November 1924, three men walked into the flower shop of the leading North Side gangster, Dion O'Banion. While one shook hands with O'Banion the others shot him. On 11 October 1926, O'Banion's successor, Hymie Weiss, was hit by at least ten bullets and killed instantly in front of the Holy Name Cathedral, which still shows signs of the shooting. A few weeks before Weiss's death Capone himself had been lucky enough to survive a spectacular attempt on his own life in Cicero, the Chicago suburb where his operations were based. As journalist Frederick Lewis Allen described it, the attack came in broad daylight from scores of men pouring machine-gun fire out of eight touring cars.

> The cars proceeded down the crowded street outside the Hawthorne Hotel in solemn line, the first one firing blank cartridges to disperse the innocent citizenry and to draw the Capone forces to the doors and windows, while from the succeeding cars, which followed a block behind, flowed a steady rattle of bullets, spraying the hotel and the adjoining buildings up and down. One gunman even got out of his car, knelt carefully upon the sidewalk at the door of the Hawthorne, and played one hundred bullets into the lobby—back and forth, as one might play the hose upon one's garden.[2]

Capone survived, flat on the floor of the hotel's restaurant.

Such luck and his own fire power alone would not have ensured the survival of his syndicate. More important was an intricate and enormously expensive linkage with City Hall, involving officials at all levels. This determined that not only were Capone and his partners virtually immune from arrests on serious charges but that the police cracked down on the operations of rival gangs.

Capone became the world's most famous criminal because he was the first of the racket bosses to attract saturation treatment in the Press, and not because of his criminal success. In fact, in relative terms Capone was not a success; his power and freedom in Chicago were short-lived. His downfall was a direct result of receiving too much publicity.

Capone actively encouraged the Press, often feeding reporters with a quotable remark and justification for his operations. Bootleg liquor was obviously in such great demand during the 1920s that few could argue with Capone when he said, 'Somebody had to throw some liquor on that thirst. Why not me?'[3] or when he elaborated:

> I make my money by supplying a public demand. If I break the law, my customers, who number hundreds of the best people in Chicago, are as guilty as I am. The only difference between us is that I sell and they buy. Everybody calls me a racketeer. I call myself a businessman. When I sell liquor, it's bootlegging. When my patrons serve it on a silver tray on Lake Shore Drive, it's hospitality.[4]

He violated the dry law but, as he said, 'Who doesn't?'[5]

Capone was a millionaire many times over before he reached the age of 30. In many ways he represented the American ideal by going from rags to riches by taking business risks and continuing to expand his operations. Unfortunately for him, however, the new federal administration was committed to a show of effective liquor law enforcement and someone had to take a fall. Capone's national notoriety ensured that only he could fit the bill properly.

Capone's wealth showed too clearly that crime paid. In particular, his violent and ruthless methods in fulfilling the American Dream became too blatant, particularly on 14 February 1929, St Valentine's Day. At a garage at 2122 North Clark Street, headquarters of the North Side gang of George 'Bugs' Moran, seven of his associates were waiting for a shipment of liquor. A Cadillac drew up and five men, two dressed as policemen, got out and entered the garage. They disarmed the Moran men, who assumed it was the inconvenience of a routine raid and did not object. They were lined up against a wall, as if for a search, and then suddenly sprayed with machine-gun bullets. One man briefly survived to tell police, 'Nobody shot me'. But the police, the newspapers and Moran himself had no doubts that the Capone gang was responsible for the massacre. Seven more had been added to Chicago's total gang-death tally of 703 during Prohibition, and it was the ultimate warning to Capone's dangerous competitors.[6]

The St Valentine's Day massacre, more than any other single act, made it politically necessary to 'Get Capone'. Little credibility was given to the predictable bluster of Chicago's Police Commissioner, William Russell who said,

It's war to the finish. I've never known of a challenge like this—the killers dressed as policemen—but now the challenge has been accepted. We're going to make this the knell of gangdom in Chicago.[7]

A deputation of Chicago business interests chose to ignore Russell's reassurances and went to Washington to ask President Hoover to intervene. Hoover than directed the law enforcement resources of the federal government against Capone.

A coordinated attack was launched. Eliot Ness of the Prohibition Bureau made sudden, unexpected wrecking expeditions on Capone operations and destroyed valuable equipment and merchandise. The intention was to wreck Capone financially and to undermine his prestige. Ness was the first of a wave of crime-fighting personalities to achieve national prominence in the 1930s. He loved personal publicity, keeping the Press informed of his battle plans, and often when he beseiged a Capone brewery or warehouse cameramen would be there to record the scene. Although these raids caused Capone considerable financial loss they were melodramatized both at the time in the Press and, years later, in the successful television series *The Untouchables*. The raids did not, as Ness claimed, dry up Chicago, with its 20,000 drinking places, nor do any lasting damage to the Chicago rackets. This did not matter to the Press, who presented Ness as Capone's nemesis, the representative of Good in a triumph against Evil. Yet Ness did not exploit such a potential gold-mine of political capital to the extent of those who followed in his crime-busting footsteps. He settled eventually for private practice.[8]

Any criminal organization, pursued by the law like Capone's and unable to finance political protection, would fold up rapidly, bloodily helped on its way by rival gangs. In this case, however, the federal government wanted Capone's scalp, and his ultimate arrest and imprisonment for tax evasion in October 1931 was the result of the persistence of the Intelligence Unit of Elmer Irey, chief of the United States Treasury Enforcement Branch. A fair trial, unintimidated witnesses and jurors, and the refusal of the federal government to accept a $4 million bribe, finished Capone as a criminal power. The only defence his lawyers could offer was that Capone had not known that money received from illegal businesses was taxable. He was sentenced to eleven years in a federal penitentiary.[9]

As a news event Capone was all but finished in 1931 but law enforcement authorities and politicians had an abundance of public enemies and criminal 'Mr Bigs' to replace him in newspaper columns across the nation. With the conviction of the world's most notorious criminal the federal authorities withdrew from Chicago law enforcement. Capone was gone but syndicate operations were left intact, and most of his partners and rivals had learnt not to draw attention to themselves. The continued success of politically protected crime will be examined in Part II.

The Capone syndicate represented an old American phenomenon which was given a new name during the 1920s—organized crime. Ruthless entrepreneurs had been combining with thugs and government officials to carve out illegal fortunes since colonial days. Capone and his equivalents in other cities took their cues from American models and not, as many writers have suggested, from ancient criminal fraternities in semi-feudal parts of Europe, such as Sicily. The United States was built and shaped through organized criminality, as Gus Tyler has concisely described:

> Land grants, covering the acreage of full states, were gained by bribery of colonial legislatures and governors. Original accumulations of capital were amassed in tripartite deals among pirates, governors and brokers. Fur fortunes were piled up alongside the drunk and dead bodies of . . . Indians. Small settlers were driven from their lands or turned into tenants by big ranchers employing rustlers, guns, outlaws—and the law. In the great railroad and shipping wars, enterprising capitalists used extortion, blackmail, violence, bribery, and private armies with muskets and cannons to wreck a competitor and to become the sole boss of a trade. In time these 'robber barons' became the very models of a modern major gentleman, writing laws and appointing law-enforcers to establish legal dominion over their illegally won gains.[10]

The production and distribution of illegal goods and services also long preceded Prohibition. Syndicates, often run by politicians, controlled large-scale gambling and prostitution enterprises from before the Civil War. Until the 18th Amendment these rackets were tightly controlled, usually by native-born or Irish-Americans. The more recent arrivals from Europe were kept strictly in subordinate positions. Bootlegging suddenly presented second-generation Jews, Italians, Sicilians, Poles, Slavs and others with an opportunity to climb up the criminal hierarchy, which many eagerly accepted.

However, like Capone, all significant gangsters were Americans first, complete with the worst American values and the worst American business ethics. Organized crime developed in the United States not because of some mysterious alien conspiracy but because it exploited easy opportunities to amass wealth for a select few in a corrupt system.

4 The end of one prohibition

Federal triumphs against major bootleggers included not just Capone but the successful convictions of Morris Kleinman in Cleveland and Waxey Gordon in the New York/New Jersey area. But signs of federal enforcement effectiveness could not stem the pressure for repeal of the 18th Amendment. President Hoover himself had made an accurate prophecy in 1929 when he suggested that, 'if the law is wrong its rigid enforcement is the surest guarantee of its repeal'. By the end of his administration more than 40,000 liquor law offenders overstretched federal prisons and Hoover had undertaken the building of six new institutions. But more arrests, convictions and incarcerations cost ever-increasing amounts of money and Senator Robert Wagner of New York caught the mood of the nation when he asked what purpose would the hiring of more men and the spending of more money serve, 'Why heap more sacrifice upon the altar of hopelessness?'[1]

The Volstead Act itself was made more severe and oppressive in 1929 by the passing of the Jones Law Amendment. Under this new addition to the law anyone who bought a bottle or a drink, or who had seen a bootlegger or a speakeasy in operation, could be charged with a felony if he or she failed to disclose what he knew to the authorities. This created innumerable felonies which could be associated with the Volstead Act and its absurdity and injustice brought a clamour of protest from the public, the Press and many politicians.[2] The nation's mood of benign tolerance and contempt for an unworkable law during the 1920s had rapidly altered. The Hoover years produced a surge of support for the 'wets' who favoured repeal.

Crucially the wet cause was now supported by most businessmen. Aside from pre-Volstead brewers and distillers, many manufacturing and commercial interests had discovered that the promised beneficial effects of enforced abstinence were illusory. The deficiency in government revenue from losing the liquor tax had been made up by a tax on the wealthy and the corporations. The increased consumer market promised by the prohibitionists had not materialized and finally businessmen looked on in horror as non-WASP gangsters, made rich and powerful by bootlegging, were buying and muscling in on other industries. This was not the controlled working class and expanding market that some had hoped for in originally supporting Prohibition. The vast resources of publisher William Randolph Hearst plus those of several dozen millionaires including T. Coleman and Pierre Du Pont, John J. Raskob, and Edward S. Harkness were used to further the repeal cause. In declared expenses alone more than a million dollars yearly was spent to further the wet cause after 1926. Even the oil magnate John D. Rockefeller, who had been the Anti-Saloon League's most generous backer, withdrew his support and funded research into more effective liquor control than Prohibition.[3]

Henry Ford was one of the few big businessmen who remained a committed and loyal supporter of Prohibition. He even threatened to stop manufacturing cars, 'if booze ever comes back to the United States'. 'Production would drop,' he explained in the Anti-Saloon League Year Book of 1928, 'if men were slowed down by a return of alcohol.' He thought that there was little chance of that and made the claim that enforcement conditions in Detroit were adequate, 'we manage to get along well enough'. He managed to write this at a time when it was universally acknowledge that Detroit was one of the wettest cities in the nation, with speakeasies doing a roaring trade and with the bootleg industry ranked by federal agents as second only to car manufacturing in the state of Michigan. Ford did admit to his Anti-Saloon League readers that smuggling from Canada was a problem and suggested as a solution turning out the Army and Navy to stop violations. But the United States was not ready for this constitutional deviation until the 1980s.

Ford's hypocrisy did not end with outrageous threats and claims. Control of the workforce was the overriding concern at his plants and sacking workers whose breath smelt of liquor was only one method. Throughout the period Ford Motor Company employed a private army of thugs and gangsters to suppress unionization. Most notable among these was Detroit's equivalent of Al Capone, Chester LaMare, whose bootleg enterprises along the city's seventy-mile waterfront amassed hundreds of millions of dollars each year. LaMare's usefulness to Ford ended in 1931 when he was assassinated, but the company's labour control methods stayed the same long after Prohibition had ended. Ford did not carry out his threat to stop manufacturing. In 1940, The National Labour Relations Board stated bluntly that Ford's labour control methods were 'organized gangsterism' and cited numerous beatings, maimings and suspected killings to support this verdict.[4]

Hypocrisy was epidemic during Prohibition and publishers and writers made sure that the public knew. Examples were legion: legislators who voted dry and had their own personal bootleggers; judges who imposed tough sentences and then drank moonshine to anaesthetize their consciences; police and prosecutors who made selective arrests and convictions while their bank accounts expanded; innocent people who suffered injustice and even death through incompetence or worse. The wets had only to report the news to win the propaganda battle. Moreover, the economic disaster of the Depression which followed the Great Crash of October 1929 gave even more force to their arguments. Prohibition deprived men of legitimate jobs, deprived governments of revenue, contributed to the continuing economic problems and only succeeded in enriching a few murderous and corrupt individuals.

Many more people began actively to resent Prohibition for the first time.

Matthew Woll, vice-president of the American Federation of Labour, articulated this when he said in 1931:

> Certain great employers supported Prohibition so that the workers might be more efficient to produce, to produce, to produce. Well, we have produced and six million are unemployed. And Prohibition has produced, too. It has produced the illicit still, the rumrunner, the speak-easy, the racketeer, graft, corruption, disrespect for law, crime.[5]

The same year Will Rogers's comment was:

> What does Prohibition amount to, if your children are not eating? It's food, not drink is our problem now. We were so afraid the poor people might drink, now we've fixed it so they can't eat . . . The working classes didn't bring this on, it was the big boys that thought the financial drunk was going to last forever.[6]

In 1931 also, a national commission, named after its chairman George Wickersham, issued its long-awaited report on the workings of Prohibition. This, in the words of newspaper columnist Walter Lippmann, 'evaded the direct, explicit official confession that Prohibition is a hopeless failure', but could not conceal the rotten effects of such an unpopular law on American society and, in particular, on American law enforcement.[7] The commission found, for example, that:

> When conspiracies are discovered from time to time, they disclose combinations of illicit distributors, illicit producers, local politicians, corrupt police and other enforcement agencies, making lavish payments for protection and conducting an elaborate system of individual producers and distributors.

'Organized distribution,' the report added, 'has outstripped organized enforcement,' and, 'As to corruption':

> it is sufficient to refer to the reported decisions of the courts during the past decade in all parts of the country, which reveal a succession of prosecutions for conspiracies, sometimes involving the police, prosecuting and administrative organizations of whole communities; to the flagrant corruption disclosed in connection with the diversions of industrial alcohol and unlawful production of beer; to the record of federal prohibition administration as to which cases of corruption have been continuous and corruption has appeared in services which in the past had been above suspicion; to the records of state police organizations; to the revelations as to police corruption in every type of municipality, large and small, throughout the decade; to the evidence of connection between corrupt local politics and gangs and the organized unlawful liquor traffic, and of systematic collection of tribute from that traffic for corrupt political purposes.[8]

In sum, as few commentators failed to point out, although the report recommended that there should be no repeal of the 18th Amendment, its findings were that Prohibition had created or worsened a situation of widespread and systematic lawlessness in the country's cities and states. A popular poem of the time made this point best:

> Prohibition is an awful flop.
>> We like it.
> It can't stop what it's meant to stop.
>> We like it.
> It's left a trail of graft and slime,
> It's filled our land with vice and crime,
> It don't prohibit worth a dime,
>> Nevertheless we're for it.[9]

By the early 1930s most Americans could see that there was no logic left in Prohibition; the remedy for the evils of drink had proved worse than the original problem. Wet pressure finally secured the passage of the repeal of the 18th Amendment on 5 December 1933. The legalization of alcohol provided legitimate employment for over a million people in brewing, distilling and related jobs, from serving drinks to making barrels and pretzels. Federal, state and local tax and licence receipts exceeded a billion dollars yearly by 1940. There was no noticeable increase in drunkenness and alcohol-related problems.[10] The dry experiment was soon regarded by most people as a ridiculous and costly mistake, and an unacceptable intrusion by the government into personal behaviour.

Bootlegging continued to be a flourishing but localized business in the few Southern states that preserved anti-liquor laws. In such states as Mississippi and Oklahoma, the temperance lobby could always rely on the covert support of bootleggers whose businesses required that the attempt to impose abstinence continued.

In most states, however, bootleggers could not successfully compete once the legal liquor trade was fully established and soon folded up or adapted to the new conditions. Some successfully legitimized smuggling operations to become importers and others of the more thuggish variety were employed by companies to 'persuade' retail outlets to sell particular brands of legal liquor.[12]

Prohibition was dead but the Anti-Saloon League had accomplished one of its primary objectives—the old type of saloon did not reappear in most American cities. One of the reasons for this was that licence regulations in many states prohibited screens, upstairs rooms and back rooms in the new type of drinking places. The inside of bars had to be visible to policemen from the street because, so the argument went, behind the blinds of the pre-Volstead saloons 'degradation and vice were fostered'.[13] Although such restrictions proved irrelevant as far as vice in America was concerned, they could prove useful to any authorities wishing to curtail trade-union or political activity within bars. Those who supported Prohibition as a crude means of social control did have this important victory. After repeal, few drinking places were saloons either in name or form. They were called bars, taverns or something else, and their function was restricted as much as possible to the consumption of alcohol.

Many of the leading wets had attacked national Prohibition on constitutional grounds, arguing that the states should make their own laws to meet different needs and conditions, and advocating repeal as a protection against excessive, distant federal power. They therefore rejoiced when the Prohibition Bureau was disbanded in 1933 and federal policing power was primarily confined to inter-state crimes. However, they failed to take account of the long-term potential of the Federal Bureau of Narcotics (FBN) in the Treasury Department and its Commissioner, Harold Anslinger, to create and use the fear and ignorance about drugs by public and legislators alike. Until 1937 the FBN's task was restricted to the suppression of opiate and cocaine use—neither of which it could accomplish—in that year marijuana was added. The Marijuana Tax Act, and state laws passed around the same time, lumped marijuana together with other very different and much more addictive drugs, making possession or sale of a mild intoxicant subject to draconian penalties.[14]

The propaganda accompanying this legislation was little more than an update of the hysterical themes of the earlier moral crusades. Fantastic stories were circulated as 'proof' of scientifically preposterous claims that marijuana made users homicidally and suicidally insane. Anslinger orchestrated the propaganda campaign and himself testified before Congress that marijuana use was linked to violent crime, insanity and sexual degeneration. Just one marijuana cigarette might cause 'homicidal mania', as he told one Senate committee.[15] The following advertisement was widely circulated by a group supporting the Bureau's campaign to prohibit marijuana:

Beware! Young and Old—People in All Walks of Life! This [picture of a marijuana cigarette] may be handed to you by the *friendly stranger*. It contains the Killer Drug 'Marijuana'—a powerful narcotic in which lurks *MURDER! INSANITY! DEATH!*[16]

The same irrationality is reflected in two Hollywood films released in 1936 to exploit public interest in the new threat. *Marijuana—The Devil's Weed* and *Reefer Madness* have messages which are basically the same. Nice, well-brought-up kids smoke marijuana. This experience is quickly and inevitably followed by sexual depravity, rape, crime and murder. In fact very few whites used marijuana at the time, and since the drug was used almost exclusively by Mexican immigrants and black Americans at the time, there was a racist aspect to its prohibition. By 1938 the law was in operation and a quarter of the Bureau's arrests were for marijuana. The extra burden was thereafter stressed in Commissioner Anslinger's budget requests.[17]

The FBN had been created as a separate agency within the Treasury Department in 1930 in the wake of a scandal involving the Narcotics

Division, which until then had had responsibility for federal drug law enforcement. A New York grand jury had found that there was 'gross dereliction and incompetence' within the Division. Agents had not only been routinely falsifying their records by reporting city police cases as federal cases, but also colluding with prominent drug traffickers. Small-time offenders were arrested while the higher-ups went free. One revelation particularly embarrassed the head of the Division, Levi Nutt. Both his son and his son-in-law had been employed by Arnold Rothstein, a businessman who was also thought to be the organizer of the country's largest drug-smuggling organization. Nutt was soon replaced by Anslinger as head of the Division which itself, in September 1930, was reorganized to become the FBN.[18]

Anslinger remained in control of the country's policy on drugs until his retirement in 1962. He insisted that there was no alternative approach to the drug problem to strict law enforcement and harsh penalties for both users and traffickers. He successfully limited public education and discussion on the grounds that this might stir up curiosity among potential new victims and thereby aggravate the drug problem. His agency poured out statistics designed to mislead Congress and the public that the flow of drugs into the country was being successfully curbed and the spread of addiction checked. Until the 1960s there was an almost complete absence of non-official information about addicts and so even the most outrageous estimates could go unchallenged.[19] The ineptitude of FBN agents was also successfully disguised until after Anslinger had left the agency, as was an endemic corruption problem.

Meanwhile traffickers exploited the fact that drugs are less bulky than liquids and therefore easier to smuggle, transport and distribute. Importation was also aided by the worldwide network of business and political contacts established by bootleggers. Although the drug traffic was, of course, much smaller than the traffic in alcohol, the profits were probably greater for those involved and the chances of disruption by the authorities just as slim. The Bureau's authority was based on the taxing provisions passed by the Harrison Narcotic Act of 1914 and the Marijuana Tax Act of 1937, not a constitutional amendment, and the basis of federal police authority in the drug field was therefore questionable. Yet this Bureau, which was small in 1930 and for three more decades, eventually spawned a drug control bureaucracy of a size never contemplated for the larger task of prohibiting liquor. But even by the end of the first decade of Anslinger's tenure, the main features of drug prohibition in the United States were already present in outline: distortion and statistical deceit covering up a reality characterized by futility, corruption and more opportunities to organize crime as a source of regular and, for some, spectacular income.

The aforementioned Arnold Rothstein was much more than a successful drug smuggler—he pioneered many other ways to make crime pay on a long-term basis.

As a young man at the turn of the century he worked as a collector for a bookmaker. By 1909 he was taking bets himself and owned a gambling house on West 46th Street in New York's Tenderloin district. Rothstein's establishment was protected by Tim Sullivan, a prominent city politician and was therefore one of the few Jewish-owned casinos in the area to operate free from police interference. In 1912, however, the casino was closed down after the murder of another gambler, Herman Rosenthal, had led to a scandal which forced the authorities to take gambling law enforcement more seriously. For a while Rothstein had to make his money by running 'floating crap games' as a substitute for stationary gambling houses. But in a few years he was back to the covert operation of plush casinos catering to a wealthy clientele. Rothstein also profited by first providing a service that was essential to bookmakers. Those who felt themselves dangerously over-extended could, through Rothstein, lay off bets with other bookmakers in different parts of the country.

Rothstein was also one of the first to spot the potential of the 18th Amendment and have the capital and connections to exploit it. He arranged for associates in Britain to buy up quantities of Scotch whisky. This was then shipped to points beyond US territorial waters and transferred to small, fast boats to avoid customs and coastguard patrols. The liquor was then distributed to restaurants and nightclubs in which Rothstein had an interest. These included such famous resorts as the Cotton Club, the Silver Slipper, the Rendezvous, and Les Ambassadeurs, as well as numerous clip joints and speakeasies. Rothstein ended his direct involvement in bootlegging as the business got more bloody and competitive but he did continue to 'bankroll' or finance the operations of others. The most notorious of these was Jack 'Legs' Diamond, a gunman who found it more remunerative to hijack the contraband of others than trouble with the more complex operations of bootlegging.

Rothstein also began to traffic in drugs in the early 1920s. The business was not as crowded as in liquor and yielded a better and quicker return on capital invested. Two Rothstein associates, Yasha Katzenberg and Dan Collins, bought drugs in Europe and Asia; these were smuggled into the United States and then sold to retailers in New York, Chicago, St Louis and Kansas City by more Rothstein associates. One of these was Charles 'Lucky' Luciano who was unlucky enough to achieve a great deal of notoriety soon after the Prohibition era.

Rothstein's connections with gangs of thugs also enabled him to provide strong-arm services in industrial disputes, particularly in New York's garment industry. For the right price he was prepared to back both sides in the same dispute. At one time employers had the services of Legs Diamond and his men as strike-breakers, while the unions countered with the services of Jacob 'Little Augie' Orgen to protect pickets and beat up 'scabs'. Both sets of gangsters received their payment from Rothstein. By 1926 both employers and unions had been severely weakened by years of conflict in the needle trades. In this situation racketeers, notably Lepke Buchalter, moved in to become much more than mere hirelings.

Rothstein had legitimate and profitable covers for all his illegal activities. Apart from restaurants and nightclubs, he owned real estate, an export–import firm, and a bailbond firm that provided bail of $14 million in liquor prosecutions alone before 1924. By that time also he had built up unrivalled political connections and this gave him leverage in the district attornies' offices and with the minor judiciary. He could therefore provide not only capital but protection for numerous illegal enterprises; cases could be 'fixed', prison sentences could be shortened.

Rothstein was shot and killed in November 1928. He was 46 years old. Many New Yorkers felt that the police and politicians did not try very hard to find his murderer. They were sceptical when the authorities reported that some of the 40,000-odd papers in Rothstein's office files had been mislaid. None of the remainder contained anything that was too embarrassing to top politicians. The murder was never solved.

The essential ingredient of Rothstein's success was, according to his biographer Leo Katcher, knowing the price of every man—whether politician or killer—and having the money to pay for it. Most significantly he pioneered techniques and organizations which effectively nullified the prohibitions of gambling, alcohol and drugs.[20]

By the time of his death a formidable array of professional criminals was challenging Rothstein's ascendancy over New York's rackets. Thanks largely to Prohibition many more had their own bankrolls, organizations and local political protection. Few, however, survived long unless they could distance themselves from actual criminal activity and establish bases for themselves in the mainstream of American economic life. Gangsters had two instruments for this: the infiltration of the labour movement and the ownership of legitimate businesses. The first often led to or complemented the second and both have been profitable in their own right apart from serving as fronts for other activities. However, there was no intrusion in any real sense during the 1920s and 1930s. Bribery, kickbacks, pay-offs, shakedowns and violence had long been part of American business. The profits from the supply of prohibited vices and other illegal enterprises simply enabled the more ruthless representatives of recently arrived ethnic groups to play a larger part in a business system that had made its own rules.

Repeal immediately cut off an immense source of illegal income. However, corrupt networks, consisting of gangsters businessmen and public officials, continued to supply the demand for such illegal activities as gambling, prostitution and drug-taking. Gambling returned to its pre-Prohibition position as the most lucrative source of illegal income.

Downtown areas of the cities supported dozens of illegal gambling houses running roulette, blackjack and dice games. Illegal slot machines were set up in bars, clubs and stores. Policy or numbers games, which had originally been played exclusively by black Americans, were rapidly becoming city-wide, million-dollar operations. The most important form of illegal gambling from the 1930s was, however, off-track bookmaking. Many states had legalized wagering at horse and dog tracks as a means of raising revenue during the Depression. More races and better long-distance communications enabled bookmakers in virtually every city and state to turn a substantial profit in defiance of the laws against betting. Independents and syndicates, with their political and police protectors, capitalized on the duplicity of the state legislatures; these allowed those who had the money and leisure the privilege of gambling legally at the tracks, while the majority of the gambling public were officially denied the same privilege.[21]

The laws against off-track bookmaking were treated with as much contempt as the laws that prohibited alcohol. For example, newspapers in cities thousands of miles from the tracks provided details of form, weight and the state of the going, details which of course were only relevant to gamblers. In 1936 Moses Annenberg of Chicago hit upon the idea of providing bookmakers all over the United States with a specialized race service, from almost every race track in the country as well as those in Canada, Mexico and Cuba. This included the practically instantaneous communication of highly technical items, such as the changing odds on the tote board and the *pari mutuel* prices paid at the track. Again, the information was only relevant to gamblers in a country were gambling was, for the most part, a crime. Acording to Internal Revenue Service agents investigating Annenberg for income tax evasion, the operation was 'one of the largest rackets ever developed in this country'. At Annenberg's trial, records were introduced to show that his operation was the American Telephone and Telegraph Company's fifth largest customer. In 1940, Annenberg was sentenced to a three-year prison term.[22] He left the wire-service business which immediately became less centralized and more bloodily competitive.

The prohibitions of gambling and prostitution were not federal. Instead a myriad of state laws and local ordinances made wagering and commercialized sex subject to criminal sanctions in every state except Nevada which legalized gambling and prostitution in selected areas in 1931. The enforcement of these laws was left to the state and local governments with their limited, conflicting and overlapping jurisdictions and with networks of corruption sometimes inherited from even before the Prohibition era.

The nation's top policeman, J. Edgar Hoover, the Director of the Federal Bureau of Investigation (FBI), refused to contemplate enforcement of the vice laws—well aware that his agents would be just as susceptible to the pressures of corruption as other policemen. He therefore also avoided tackling the problem of organized crime until forced to do so in the 1960s, while at the same time establishing for himself the reputation as an unmatched crime-buster. In 1934 his agency was given additional jurisdiction over a variety of inter-state felonies, such as kidnapping and auto theft. Hoover immediately exploited the publicity value of his new powers by directing his agents against bankrobbers, who had been avoiding capture by crossing state lines. Freelance outlaws, such as John Dillinger, Bonnie Parker and Clyde Barrow, and 'Pretty Boy' Floyd, were built up by the newspapers into major threats to society and then shot down with clinical efficiency by Mr Hoover's agents. Books, films and magazines echoed a new theme: 'Crime Doesn't Pay' so long as Hoover's elite 'G-Men' were around. The FBI's failures and, in particular, its avoidance of organized crime did not reach the public's attention, who for the most part believed that the FBI was unrelenting in its war on crime.[23]

Many cities hardly took the trouble to pretend to enforce the vice laws. Ruling politicians tended to appoint judges, prosecutors and police chiefs who posed no threat to the regular pay-offs. They were fully aware of the political realities of illegal enterprises in urban America. Handbook and lottery operators, for example, constituted the nucleus of a political bloc that included the votes of families, friends, employees and customers. Vice operators made large contributions to campaign funds to ensure that whatever administration was elected would be friendly. Political ambitions often depended on the political and financial support of vice operations, directly for campaign funding, and indirectly because ward leaders constituted the essential parts of political machines and they often had their own interest in maintaining the supply of prohibited vice. Graft was the grease that kept these machines running. State politicians only took an interest when they decried these conditions at election times, and this interest rarely lasted long.

The organization of vice varied from city to city with their different forms of government, but personal greed was always the common denominator. In Jersey City a top official of the dominant political machine of Mayor Frank Hague had a full-time job screening applicants for unofficial bookmaking licences. Those successful were given a 'location', usually the house or store of a loyal precinct worker. They paid a grossly inflated rent of which a high proportion was 'kicked back' into the machine treasury. In order to stay in business, no one worked harder for the Hague machine than the city's one thousand-odd bookies and their landlords. City policemen and officials had an equally valid reason to keep Mayor Hague in office; their meagre official salaries and wages were supplemented weekly with the money collected from vice interests and others would benefit if the status quo was altered.[24]

Hague's control over the city was absolute for more than two decades, from the 1920s to the 1940s: in his own words, 'I am the Law'. Politics for him was business. He never received more than $8,000 a year in salary, but at the end of the 1920s the Internal Revenue Service ordered him to pay nearly two million dollars in delinquent taxes and penalties. His rule was not only characterized by graft. An army of spies was employed to keep track on dissenters; political opponents found their mail tampered with, if they received it at all; their telephones were tapped; property owners opposed to Hague were harrassed by building department officials, had their licences revoked and their property unfavourably reassessed. Hague also kept the city virtually non-union. Organizers were denied access to public halls, beaten up by police and often bodily thrown out of town.[25]

San Franisco experienced one of the most complete investigations of gambling and prostitution during the 1930s. Edwin Atherton, a former FBI agent, was brought in by the city after the Internal Revenue Service had revealed that a police captain had amassed a fortune 'presumably, in part, from pay-offs from houses of vice'. Atherton found numerous brothels operating quite openly. They were so plentiful in the North Beach area, for example, that tenants found it necessary to put signs on their front doors announcing the fact they were private residences. He also found that bookmaking was the most important form of gambling in the city. There were at least 150 establishments where handbooks were actually maintained and many more where bets could be placed with agents. In all, Atherton's report estimated 'very conservatively' that the annual graft toll from gambling and prostitution operations at around $1 million annually, and this figure can probably be multiplied. Atherton specifically implicated sixty-seven police officers and twenty-four city, state and federal officers in the running of what was known as 'the business.' More significantly he named the bailbond firm run by Pete McDonough and his nephew Harry Rice. 'No one,' the report stated, 'can conduct a prostitution or gambling enterprise in San Francisco without the direct or indirect approval' of this firm. 'Anyone engaged in these activities, who incurs the firm's disfavor, is sooner or later forced out of business.' A police officer who defied the graft system to enforce the law honestly was regarded as a 'snake in the grass' and his career sabotaged. Most policemen cooperated with the firm which the report described as 'the fountainhead of corruption' in San Francisco, 'willing to interest itself in almost any matter designed to deflect or circumvent the law'.

Atherton stressed that his investigation was not 'a moral crusade in the sense that it should bring about the closing of unlawful businesses'. He recognized that most San Franciscans were tolerant of these activities. In fact the report recommended that 'legal bars' against gambling and prostitution should be removed. Such activities 'should be licensed and subjected to close supervision and regulation by some agency separate and apart from the Police Department'. The argument supporting these recommendations was clear:

> We learned through the experience of Prohibition that people's morals and habits cannot be changed by legislation.
> . . . persons who think that prostitution and gambling are stopped because of prohibitive legislation, must be likened to the ostrich of popular repute . . . .
> The system at the present time, is in effect a form of licensing with the beneficiaries being a few private individuals and a number of police officers.[26]

Atherton's views were shared by August Vollmer, the foremost police reformer of the day. Vollmer had drastically improved the efficiency and organization of several police forces and no one was better informed about the problems of city policing. For Vollmer the policeman's duty was to protect society from criminals and not try to control morality. Any other approach was dangerously counter-productive, distracting the police and fostering crime and corruption. He wrote that:

> The only safe and sane method of handling the problem of gambling . . . is by licensing, regulation, and control, through a state agency established solely for that purpose and empowered to enforce the regulatory provisions. No municipal, and no county or state police . . . should ever be permitted to play any part in the enforcement of gambling regulations.

He considered also that the problems of prostitution and drug addiction could not be solved by regular policing. On the drug traffic he wrote:

> Stringent laws, spectacular police drives, vigorous prosecution, and imprisonment of addicts and peddlers have proved not only useless and enormously expensive as a means of correcting this evil, but they are also unjustifiably and unbelievably cruel in their application to the unfortunate drug victims. Repression has driven this vice underground and produced the narcotic smugglers and supply agents, who have grown wealthy out of this evil practice and who by devious methods have stimulated traffic in drugs.

He also warned that addicts were forced to resort to crime to pay inflated black-market prices and stressed that the profit motive had to be taken away by medical dispensation of drugs to addicts before any progress could be made in dealing with the drug problem. He concluded:

> Drug addiction . . . is not a police problem; it never has been, and never can be solved by policemen. It is first and last a medical problem, and if there is a solution it will be discovered not by policemen, but by scientific and competently trained medical experts . . .

In general Vollmer favoured a flexible approach to alcohol, drugs, gambling and prostitution, based on regulation, control and education. He knew that the prohibition approach was only in the interests of gangsters and corrupt police and politicians and would undermine even the most professional police forces.[27] Rationality, however, was to have little to do with the making of crime control policy in the United States. The country persevered with counter-productive prohibition policies and therefore maintained the economic underpinning of organized crime.

America's moral crusade did not end with the repeal of the 18th Amendment. The local crime crusades examined in the following chapters were part of the continuing attempt to enforce moral ideals. These campaigns in the 1930s and 1940s concentrated on securing the election of politicians who promised to make the police and the courts do their duty. The institutions which moulded public opinion, such as newspapers, churches, chambers of commerce and civic associations, were set against any more tampering with the morality legislation and backed appropriate candidates. People were presented the issues in terms of black and white; attention was focused on the bad guys, who made financial capital out of crime, and the good guys, who made political capital out of crime. There was no suggestion that a large part of the problem was in the laws and in the system.

In New York, Chicago, Los Angeles and elsewhere crime, vice and corruption were major issues at election time. Voters were told time and again to express their indignation at government corruption and rampart racketeering by voting the ruling party out of office. The victorious politicians would then, they claimed, get on with the job of cleansing the government and, in particular, making the law enforcement machinery more efficient. Criminals would be imprisoned and, theoretically, that would be the end of the problem.

Unfortunately in the United States neither of the two main parties, nor factions within those two parties, has had a monopoly of honesty and incorruptibility, and the profitability of systematic, protected crime was not significantly affected by changing administrations. Local and state efforts to enforce the vice laws were as ineffectual as the federal attempt to enforce alcohol prohibition. These efforts were futile because only one answer was considered—better law enforcement. Honest and effective efforts were always outweighed by hypocrisy and political opportunism; scapegoats were found to confirm people's fears and ignorance and, at the same time, to reassure them that something was being done. No financial interests emerged to sponsor the liberalization of the laws against gambling, prostitution and drug-taking, and politicians continued to follow the lines of least resistance. In such conditions crime and corruption thrived.

Part II   Crusades and corruption in the cities, 1930–1950

Before we can settle any other question, before any other question is worth settling, we must get a decision on who is the Big Shot in the United States—the criminal or the Government.

Saturday Evening Post, 1931

We have purged the city of gangsters, hoodlums and racketeers.

Mayor Edward Kelly of Chicago, 1934

We've broken the most powerful ring that ever had an American city in its grip.

Mayor Fletcher Bowron of Los Angeles, 1941

We shall pursue, and have constantly pursued, a policy of strict law enforcement. There is no possibility of the return of slots, books and lotteries.

Mayor deLesseps S. Morrison of New Orleans, 1949

This thing is so large and it is Nation-wide. This is no fiction about organized crime—it is a reality, and it extends from one end of the Nation to the other. In some respects, it is in its organizations rather loosely coordinated, and yet there are certain definite persons who give the orders and who make the policy. This thing is too big.

Mayor Fletcher Bowron of Los Angeles, 1950

5 New York's gangbusters

During the 1930s New York made a highly publicized attempt to enforce the morality laws. Increased police activitiy against gamblers and prostitutes and the downfall of a succession of gangsters and their political protectors made headlines in newspapers across the nation. A young Manhattan prosecutor used his courtroom triumphs as a springboard to advance politically, almost to the White House itself. The city was held up as an example of what could be achieved if the laws were strictly enforced. It seemed to be a triumph for the forces of law and order against the forces of evil and corruption but this impression was misleading. The New York vice crusade was not an unambiguous victory in the war on crime.

A series of investigations headed by jurist Samuel Seabury had revealed much about New York City government in the early 1930s. The system was organized for profit from top to bottom. Top politicians used their influence to make enormous profits in real estate and other business deals or by accepting kickbacks from firms doing business with the city. The criminal justice and law enforcement systems were riddled with corruption, expediency and incompetence. Political loyalty and financial contributions qualified people to be judges, prosecutors and police officials. Speakeasies, brothels and gambling enterprises enriched the politicians whose concessions they were. And even traffic tickets and marriage licences were used as instruments for extortion.

Early revelations concerned the Vice Squad whose ostensible function was the suppression of gambling, prostitution, and the liquor and narcotics traffic. Seabury reported that the squad had two types of arrest with regard to prostitution—the direct and the indirect. In the direct, the police officer approached the victim and arrested her after she had accepted money for prostitution. In the indirect, the police informer or 'stool-pigeon' was the customer and at any given moment the officers broke in and made the arrest. The Seabury report then detailed a number of ingenious traps for innocent and guilty alike, contrived to inflate arrest quotas and extort graft. One of these involved the informer renting a room in a small hotel, paying for it with marked money and bringing in a woman purporting to be his wife. Almost immediately the police broke in and arrested the landlady for maintaining a house of prostitution. Landladies tended to pay off to avoid court costs and bad publicity. More commonly, innocent housewives and working girls were framed as prostitutes and, if they could not raise the cash to buy their freedom, served prison sentences. The Seabury report indicated that the police and their informer were just a part of a cabal which included court clerks, magistrates, bondsmen, defence lawyers and prosecutors.

> The picture of the Ring is complete. The stool-pigeon or the officer framed the woman, the officer arrested her, the unlicensed bondsman bailed her out at an exorbitant charge and usually recommended a lawyer, the lawyer gouged her savings and either he himself, or through the bondsman, 'fixed' the arresting officer and the District Attorney.

Five vice squad detectives had accumulated bank accounts each exceeding $500,000 through these methods.[1]

Seabury also revealed to New York the spectacle of the 'tin box parade'. According to reliable testimony, Thomas M. Farley, Sheriff of New York County, Michael J. Cruise, City Clerk, Harry Perry, Chief Clerk of the City Court of New York, and James A. McQuade, Registrar of Kings County, all district leaders, had been protecting professional gamblers, allowing them to operate games in their clubhouses. Protection was undoubtedly the reason why out of 514 people arrested in gambling raids in 1926 and 1927, only five were held for the Court of Special Sessions. Farley, Cruise, Perry and McQuade were shown to have accumulated an amazing amount of wealth within a relatively short time for men on small salaries, for which they gave extremely unlikely explanations. Sheriff Farley banked $360,000 in seven years on a total salary of $90,000, and explained in public hearings that the money came from 'a wonderful tin box' which he kept in his house. McQuade saved $520,000 in six years on a net official income of less than $50,000, and explained that he had borrowed the money in small amounts to support his many poor relations. He repaid his loans with further borrowings, and neglected to keep any records. Farley was eventually removed from office by Governor Franklin Roosevelt; McQuade received the Brooklyn Sheriff nomination from John McCooey, Democratic party boss of Kings County.[2]

Seabury's final quarry was Mayor James Walker who had banked nearly a million dollars in his first five years in office. Walker had accepted money from contractors interested in municipal legislation, held stock in companies with city contracts and generally exploited his office for personal enrichment. Although it was difficult to prove that the mayor had accepted bribes, the disclosures were enough to force Walker to resign on 1 September 1932.

Walker was a product of the Democratic party organization in Manhattan, known by the name of its headquarters, Tammany Hall, which had dominated New York City politics for over a century and usually only lost control in the wake of a scandal. The remainder of Walker's term was filled by John J. O'Brien who then stood for election as the Tammany Hall candidate in November 1933. He faced a Bronx Democratic candidate, Joseph McKee, and Fiorello La Guardia in what was unusually a three-cornered fight for the office of Mayor of New York. La Guardia ran on the Fusion ticket which was

a newly formed combination of Republicans, disaffected Democrats, independent reformers and moral crusaders, who had rallied behind La Guardia
because he had consistently promised an efficient and clean administration.

Voting was conducted in the city's time-honoured tradition—as the *New
York Times* election results issue described it:

> Blackjacks, brass knuckles, lead-pipes, bricks, stones, and hob-nailed boots
> played an important part in the elections yesterday.
>   The Lower East Side, parts of Greenwich Village and parts of Harlem were
> overrun with roving groups of thugs and strong arm men who intimidated,
> slugged and booted voters.

La Guardia was an experienced street politician, whose supporters guarded
polling stations and in many cases gave as good as they got. The candidate
personally rushed about to challenge 'floaters'—who were intending to vote
up to a hundred times. At one point he came into contact with the Lower
East Side gangster, Charles Luciano, who was working just as hard for the
Tammany Hall candidate. Fists were thrown before police broke it up and
escorted Luciano away—with La Guardia allegedly promising to 'get' him
and shouting 'I'll see you in prison'.[3]

The split in the Democrat vote allowed La Guardia to win the election. He
began his term of office on 1 January 1934 with the promise 'The party's
over! No more graft', and to the best of his ability kept it.[4] He balanced the
city's budget, drastically improved administrative efficiency, and used federal funds to good effect to alleviate the worst effects of the Depression. He
also did what he could to see that the vice and gambling laws were enforced.

La Guardia had no jurisdiction over the district attorneys and minimal
influence over the courts, but he literally bullied his police into action. His
abrasive approach caused Police Commissioner John Ryan to resign after
only nine months of the new administration. The new Commissioner was
Lewis Valentine, chosen partly because his zeal had made him unpopular
with previous administrations. In December 1928, Valentine had been
demoted to captain in a suburban backwater as punishment for raiding
gambling games in Tammany clubs. Valentine remained Commissioner
throughout the entire twelve years of La Guardia's tenure.[5]

The new administration's first crusade was against slot machines—a
novelty that had become so popular that more than 25,000 stood in the city's
stores, bars and restaurants. The fear was that they might be a corrupting
influence on the young who might become addicted to gambling and steal to
finance their play. La Guardia ignored a federal court decision which
restrained the police from interfering with slot machines unless it could be
proved they were used for gambling and ordered the mass seizure of the
devices. Soon afterwards the Supreme Court reversed the previous injunction
and the police were free to seize and destroy the machines legally. On some
occasions the machines were piled up and La Guardia personally began
destroying them with a fireman's axe for the benefit of newspaper photo-

graphers. At the same time the administration fought against the establishment of pinball machines, which La Guardia called the 'big brothers of the slot machines', and railed against the demoralizing effect they also had on the young. By the end of his administration both slot and pinball machines had been effectively barred in public places in New York City.[6]

At the beginning of 1935 the administration began to come under pressure to suppress policy or 'the numbers racket'. In Harlem, the East Side, the Bronx and parts of Brooklyn numerous New Yorkers bet small amounts of money on a daily number in the hope of a 600–1 pay-off. On 20 January the Reverend George Drew Egbert, head of the Society for the Prevention of Crime, a long-established moral crusade organization, demanded action against gambling in general and the policy game in particular. Egbert argued that play on policy removed poor people's money from the 'channels of legitimate trade', money which should have gone 'to the landlord, the baker and the butcher'. He admonished the administration to crack down on the game in excessive and antiquated language:

> Once in a while the City of New York is rotten with evil. Once in a while a dirty band of plunderers fasten their filthy claws on the vitals of the city and exploit the poor. Once in a while the police and the courts stand helpless, or at least seem to, before a robber gang that is bloated with wealth filched from the meagre funds of the hungry and the cold. Such a time is now.[7]

Egbert's speech received a great deal of favourable publicity and La Guardia responded to it by ordering a concerted drive against policy. He pointed out that there had been a great increase in policy arrests in his administration and suggested that policy was especially vicious because it was linked to commercialized vice and narcotics, without supporting such a statement. The mayor also admitted that it was difficult to get convictions in any kind of gambling case, and hard to convict even 'small fry collectors' unless they were found in possession of policy slips.[8]

The La Guardia administration's attempt to enforce the laws against all forms of illicit activity inevitably led to abuses as police resorted to intrusive tactics. Once, for example, after the police had invaded a private poker party, Magistrate Anna Kross chided them severely for 'lawless law enforcement'. An editorial in the *Daily News* of 12 March 1934 attacked the anti-vice crusade in even stronger terms. Referring to the experience of Polly Adler, New York's best-known madam, the newspaper stated that

> The police tap this woman's wires, set spies on her, and in other ways keep her under surveillance as if they suspected her of being the Lindbergh kidnapper. [The baby of America's aviation hero, Charles Lindbergh, had been kidnapped in 1932.] They seize, without any vestige of the right to do so, her 'little black book' containing the names and addresses of various well-to-do patrons of her establishment. Thus they obtain opportunities for blackmail for anyone who can get a peek at this book.

The newspaper concluded that

> It is this crusading against personal and private habits and instincts—the sex instinct, the deep-rooted human fondness for gambling as shown by the prevalence of policy gamesters—which is futile and sickening, just as the prohibition of drinking liquor was.[9]

Such a liberal view of human behaviour, however, was becoming exceptional in New York newspapers of the time, and most acquiesced in any police methods which got results and therefore supplied copy. Constitutional rights began to diminish in importance as the ballyhoo surrounding the anti-vice crusade increased.

La Guardia exploited the anti-crime mood of the city, frequently claiming victories in the war to end gang power: 'We have driven the so-called big punks out of the city . . . they can't come back because we'll run them right out again.'[10] He rode on his reforming and vice-crusading reputation and was re-elected mayor twice, in 1937 and 1941. His Italian origins, however, prevented him from progressing politically beyond the boundaries of cosmopolitan New York City. No such handicap held back Thomas E. Dewey, a young Midwesterner of impeccably white, Anglo-Saxon, Protestant origin, who made an immense amount of political capital out of a series of 'gangbusting' prosecutions during the 1930s.

Dewey's prosecuting career was blessed with fortuitous timing. His legal talent and hard work made him Chief Assistant United States Attorney by March 1931, when he was only 29 and five years out of law school. In that post he first came to the public's attention as the prosecutor of two gangsters who rivalled Al Capone for national notoriety, Dutch Schultz and Waxey Gordon. As in the Capone case, tax evasion was the weapon used by the federal authorities. Schultz had a virtual beer-bootlegging monopoly in the Bronx and had muscled in on several Harlem policy games by the early 1930s. He escaped conviction but his legal difficulties and Dewey's part in them made headlines for months. His criminal career was ended in October 1935 when he was shot down by unknown assassins. Waxey Gordon had built up an immense illicit beer industry around the New Jersey town of Hoboken, and owned three breweries, a fleet of trucks, hotels and a Broadway nightclub. Dewey secured his conviction after an intense two-year investigation and the murder of two witnesses. Gordon was sentenced to ten years in a federal penitentiary. The popular press hailed the verdict as 'another telling blow against large scale lawlessness', and were fulsome in their praise for young prosecutor Dewey.[11]

Soon after the Gordon trial Dewey left the US Attorney's office to set up his own law firm. However, in 1935 he was presented with an opportunity no politically ambitious individual could refuse. In response to the pressure from New York's moral crusaders, a grand jury was impanelled in March to sift evidence of vice and gambling. The jury soon came into conflict with Manhattan's District Attorney, William Dodge, and refused to cooperate until he was replaced. To resolve the impasse Herbert Lehman, Governor of New York State, issued a call for an extraordinary term of the Supreme Court, with a special grand jury to investigate vice, racketeering and other crime in Manhattan and the relationship, if any, between them and the law enforcement system. Lehman offered the high-profile post of special prosecutor to Dewey, after four more senior Republican lawyers had refused to abandon their lucrative private practices.

On 29 June 1935, Dewey was sworn in as a special prosecutor, and the much trumpeted 'anti-vice' and 'anti-rackets' drive began. The New York *Post* reflected the high hopes of newspapers when it claimed that an 'iron fist' was to be clenched over vice during the Dewey regime, and Mayor La Guardia pledged his total support and the cooperation of the New York Police Department.[12]

In a city-wide radio address the evening after his appointment Dewey described the scope of the investigation:

> We are concerned with vice . . . where it exists in an organized form. We are concerned with gambling or numbers games operated on a large scale by criminals, for the profit of the criminal underworld. Any criminal operation which pours money into the coffers of organized crime is a continuing menace to the safety of the community . . . Organized crime has the means of corrupting public officials and buying immunity from punishment. This flow of revenue to the criminal underworld must be stopped and that is one of the objects of this investigation . . . We will prosecute every crime which is part of an organized racket, where we can get evidence. However minor the crime may be, we will prosecute if it is part of organized crime . . . When we have developed cases, we will present them in court. Until then, we will work hard and quietly. I am confident that with your help we can stamp out racketeering in New York. We can make this city too dangerous for organized crime.[13]

Dewey had accepted the job on the understanding that he would have an absolutely free hand and be able to choose his own assistants. He selected a special squad of hand-picked detectives from the police department and his own staff consisted of twelve experienced veterans plus seventy-five 'bright, ambitious' young men whom he insisted had 'no bad habits'. He chose the 14th floor of the Woolworth building as the base of his investigation and gave a great deal of thought to the plan for converting this space into an efficient, leak-proof office. Elevator operators, porters and cleaning women were investigated. A special untappable cable was connected directly with the main office of the telephone company. All stenographic work was done in one large room under constant supervision. These and other precautions were emphasized by Dewey, in press releases, to reassure potential witnesses.[14]

During the first year of the investigation Dewey concentrated on bringing about the downfall of Charles 'Lucky' Luciano, the man Mayor La Guardia was calling 'Public Enemy No. 1' after their election day confrontation. In early 1936, with Luciano in mind, Dewey had discreetly asked the State Legislature to pass a new law of dubious constitutionality. The law authorized the 'joinder' of similar offences in a single indictment. In effect this law made it legal to try Luciano, against whom there was little evidence, and convict him by joining his trial with his alleged associates, against whom there was much evidence.

Having got this legislation passed, Dewey directed simultaneous police raids on forty-one brothels in Manhattan and Brooklyn on 1 February 1936. Over 100 women and seventeen men were arrested and many of these were held in custody for months as material witnesses for the forthcoming trial of Luciano. During this time some of these witnesses, as they testified later, were offered immunity and other inducements, and were coached by Dewey and his staff to tell convincing stories. They were held incommunicado, set impossibly high bails, and also threatened with prosecution unless they cooperated. In relation to this, one prosecution witness came close to ruining Dewey's case during the trial itself. Frank Brown, assistant manager of the Brabizon Plaza Hotel, had been expected to identify several defendants as having visited Luciano's suite. Brown, however, said that although he knew Luciano as a tenant he could hardly identify any of the other defendants as visitors. When Dewey attacked Brown for changing his testimony, Brown replied:

> I never identified them positively. They tried to force me to identify these men. One of Dewey's men kept telling me, 'You must have seen this one, and this one.' The man persisted in telling me so. He warned me about jail if I didn't tell the truth. There were about three or four in the room. They were insistent about me identifying the pictures.
> When I said I couldn't do it honestly, they threatened me. They hinted that Mr Dewey was very powerful and could do as he liked.[15]

The trial lasted five weeks, from 11 May to 6 June, during which time Dewey based his case on building up the impression of Luciano's guilt in the minds of the jury. The most important prosecution witnesses were Joe Bendix, a burglar who was then serving a fifteen years to life term in state prison, and three prostitutes, Mildred Harris, Nancy Presser and 'Cokey Flo' Brown. Bendix hoped to have his sentence reduced, and thus had a vested interest in supporting the prosecution's case. The women, because of their illegal profession, were in a vulnerable situation. The evidence they gave was, anyway, not conclusive. Bendix testified that he had met Luciano, and that Luciano had offered him a job as a collector for several brothels, but that he had been arrested just before taking up the post. Mildred Harris's testimony amounted to an assertion that she had been told that 'Luciano is the boss'. Nancy Presser testified that she had been Luciano's mistress for about six months and claimed that she had heard many details about his prostitution racket. However, on cross-examination, she was unable to describe Luciano's hotel suite or even to remember whether the bed was twin or double. Cokey Flo had offered herself as a prosecution witness after the trial had commenced and merely repeated the testimony of other witnesses. In sum, the testimony of these witnesses amounted to no more than hearsay and unsubstantiated assertions that Luciano ran a centralized prostitution racket in New York.[16]

Luciano fared badly in his four-hour cross-examination by Dewey. The account of this in the *Dail News* is representative of the way the popular press reported the trial. Three lines of headlines announced:

Dewey Riddles Luciano on Stand
Luciano cringes on stand, admits record under fire
Dewey bares his past in Rum, Dope rings

The opening sentence of the story was similarly melodramatic:

Halting and stammering, his usually warm, broad grin replaced by a sickly twist of the lips, Charles Luciano proved by far his own worst witness yesterday. He fell an easy victim to the snares of cross-examination set for him by Special Prosecutor, Thomas E. Dewey.[17]

Luciano's defence was that he had nothing to do with prostitution and was only a crap-shooter and racetrack man. But he was trapped in so many lies about his past and his criminal record that he left the impression that he would lie about anything—including his role in the prostitution racket. Dewey's final address to the jury concentrated on Luciano himself without dwelling too much on the evidence:

I am talking about the act, that sanctimonious, lying, perjurious act on the witness stand, at the end of which, and I am sure every one of you had not the slightest doubt, there stood before you, not a gambler, not a racetrack man, but stripped stark naked, the greatest gangster in America. You know it and I know it . . . and gentlemen, the racket, the rotten vile racket of ruling prostitutes and taking money from their bodies by guns, which is the effect of this case, will go on . . . unless you are willing to convict the top men . . .[18]

The defence counsel, George Morton Levy, objected on the ground that this was an 'inflammatory and prejudicial address, with a desire to seek and elicit a conviction by unfair means', and was not based on the evidence. He was overruled.[19]

On 6 June after a short discussion, the jury returned the verdict that Luciano was guilty of the charge of compulsory prostitution. The judge imposed a thirty- to fifty-year sentence, unprecedented for such an offence. Both judge and jury considered the case less on its merits and more on the dramatic assertions and hyperbole of prosecutor Dewey. The righteous temper of New York at the time demanded a scapegoat and Luciano fitted the bill.

The New York *Daily Mirror* greeted the verdict with absurd but typical claims, calling Luciano 'the czar of chain store vice', and announcing that:

> The 100% verdict was the most smashing blow ever dealt the organized underworld in New York. It was, moreover, hailed throughout the country as the definite beginning of the end of gangsterism, terrorism, and commercialized criminality throughout the United States.
>
> Not only did the fearless decision of the 12 stalwart jurors make the smirking Luciano a beaten king of the underworld, but it blasted open the road to clearing the country of the terrors of gangsters everywhere.
>
> Prosecutor Dewey, the 34-year old master of the long battle against Luciano and his vice barons, regarded his hour of triumph as 'only the beginning'.[20]

Much similar bombast accompanied the verdict in the popular press and there was no room for comment about prostitution as a social and economic problem. Luciano was undoubtedly a criminal, but making him a scapegoat for the problem of prostitution in New York misleadingly gave the impression that law enforcement alone provided the answer. Dewey had satisfied a need to blame specific targets for problems which law enforcement could not solve and, in the process, advanced his own career. The Luciano verdict was a triumph of manufactured criminal justice but a set-back to a more intelligent approach to the problem of prostitution.

The *New York Times* welcomed the verdict but also reported the comments of Magistrate Anna Kross. Kross advocated a separation of the entire question of prostitution from the criminal jurisdiction and a change to a medical–social technique for handling it. She drew attention to a chart Dewey had shown the jury which revealed the large number of cases in which vice combinations had provided bail and legal advice and in which defendants were dismissed, and commented:

> The community is indebted to Mr Dewey for his vivid demonstration of the stupidity of handling a social question by criminal-legal procedures. The machinery of the Women's Court has created a group of shyster bondsmen and lawyers who make a speciality of these cases and are in cahoots with procurers.[21]

She concluded with a plea for rehabilitation programmes and a demand that police go after the pimps and not the prostitutes. Dewey regarded Magistrate Kross's statement as 'an amusing attempt to gain publicity', and the corrupt enforcement of the laws against prostitution continued. So long as prostitutes were committing a crime they could have no recourse to the police and were subject to intimidation and extortion from pimps and, at times, the police themselves. The Luciano case was exploited to justify the retention of that same system. Pimps and shyster bondsmen and lawyers were therefore still in business in the Women's Court of New York.

Dewey's melodramatic prosecution vastly increased Luciano's notoriety, which for a number of expedient reasons kept on increasing after his conviction. Before the trial Luciano was an important Manhattan racketeer, but not known beyond the boundaries of New York. During and after the trial he became the nation's most famous gangster, credited with almost unlimited power and influence across the entire United States. Undoubtedly Luciano was a New York gangster who knew and cooperated with other New York gangsters, but no criminal has ever been more overrated. His career was fictionalized to fit a simplistic conspiracy theory. How this happened will be explained later in this chapter.

Apart from convicting Luciano and a number of loan sharks, Dewey's two-year term as special prosecutor was devoted to an assault on industrial racketeering, the type of organized crime that most concerned businessmen at the time. Thugs and gangsters, particularly during the 1920s, had been employed not just to break strikes and emasculate unions but to control competition and fix prices. The gangster's function was, in effect, to stabilize market conditions, which was particularly necessary in service and small-scale industries such as garment manufacturing and trucking, food distribution, laundries and dry-cleaners. In the early 1930s, however, legalized price-fixing by the New Deal, through the NRA, undercut this stabilizing role of the industrial racketeer. In the words of sociologist Daniel Bell: 'What had hitherto been a quasi-economic but necessary function now became outright and unnecessary extortion.'[22] Business associations, therefore, put increasing pressure on the authorities to act and stamp out this kind of industrial racketeering. Dewey was the personification of the authorities' response in Manhattan. He investigated and secured convictions in the poultry and restaurant rackets and began an investigation into the bakery trucking and garment trucking rackets which eventually broke the hold of Lepke Buchalter and Jacob Shapiro, whose organization employed hundreds of thugs, as well as a staff of accountants, bookkeepers, and professional killers.[23]

Although Dewey's action against industrial extortionists was excessively praised in the Press at the time and in published works years later, it did nothing to stop unions being infiltrated by gangsters with the compliance or collaboration of employers, nor to prevent gangsters controlling the same kind of small-scale industries as before.

The rackets probe had brought Dewey city, state and even national acclaim and proved to be an unmatched vehicle for political advancement. On 14 August 1937, Dewey accepted the Republican nomination for New York District Attorney in the November municipal elections on the same ticket as La Guardia. His subsequent political rise was rapid.

Dewey fought his political campaign on two fronts. Firstly, he pointed to his achievements as special prosecutor, claiming in one speech: 'The underworld is desperately afraid. The structure of organized crime in the city is about to break up.' Secondly, he attacked the Democratic party by stressing that the city's criminal justice system, under Democratic domination, enabled racketeers to operate at will. He described the incumbent District Attorney,

William Dodge, as a man who 'would not, dare not and could not lift a finger' to stop racketeering. The Dewey campaign peaked a week before the election when he made a sensational speech on the radio in which he charged that Albert Marinelli, a top Democratic politician on the Lower East Side, was the 'political ally of thieves, pickpockets, dope-peddlers and big-shot racketeers'. Dewey spoke of Marinelli's links with Luciano and other gangsters, and of the criminal records of thirty-three of Marinelli's county committeemen. Marinelli resigned to save face and Dewey won his own election comfortably.[24]

Dewey had obtained his information by ordering his men to shadow Marinelli and tap his telephone for at least a year before the election. No charges resulted from the investigation, which was primarily for political purposes. There is little doubt that Dewey's allegations were accurate, but the use of intrusive law enforcement powers to throw dirt at political opponents was a dangerous precedent. Dewey could have targeted politicians from his own Republican party and got similar results.

As District Attorney, Dewey went for his next political quarry through the courts. On 25 Mar 1938, the headline

Dewey arrests Hines!

was spread across the front pages of newspapers in New York and across the country.

Jimmy Hines was the Democratic boss of the Upper West Side of Manhattan and the political overtones and implications of this were immense. Hines was charged with complicity in the numbers game and selling protection to the Dutch Schultz gang, but, in effect, Democratic machine control of the city was on trial.

The trail opened in August 1938 with Hines as the only defendant. His former co-defendants, Richard 'Dixie' Davis and George Weinberg, were associates of Dutch Schultz in the numbers racket. Davis had been Schultz's lawyer, right-hand man, and allegedly his liaison officer with Hines. Both had been persuaded to turn state's evidence and become the chief witnesses for the prosecution. Numerous other witnesses were produced to link Hines with Schultz's numbers operation and to show how Hines influenced police and magistrates. Dewey intended to show how Hines was involved with the aiding, abetting and protecting of the Schultz gang felonies in connection with the numbers game.[25]

During the trial Dewey was given the Republican gubernatorial nomination to contest the November elections. The New York governorship, as many politicians had shown in the past, was also a useful springboard for anyone seeking the presidency.

The *American Mercury* reported that Dewey's handling of the Hines case had been regarded by leading members of the bar as 'competent only from the point of view of melodramatic stage-setting'.[26] Dewey at one point asked a witness a question which linked Hines with the poultry racket. In the court's opinion, the question had prejudiced the case and a mistrial was declared.

This left Dewey free to concentrate on the state elections. He fought his campaign for the governorship on the issues of Democratic political corruption in New York City and the upstate cities of Buffalo and Albany, and in November 1938 came within 70,000 votes of unseating Herbert Lehman, a popular and respected governor. Dewey clearly threatened to break the hold of the Democratic party on the state that had the most electoral votes in the nation.

The Hines case was brought for retrial in the last week of January 1939, but it was something of an anti-climax, lacking the vast crowds and excitement of the first trial. The *New York Times* reported that this was just another court case:

> Mr Dewey says what he has to say without the dramatic flourishes, the barbed words and intonations and without imparting the vague sense of hurry that he gave in the first.[27]

Nevertheless, as in the first trial, much was revealed about the way the laws prohibiting gambling led to selective law enforcement. The 'nub of the case' for Dewey was his effort to prove that Hines had had policemen transferred for raiding numbers banks. Tammany leader, John F. Curry, testified that when Tammany controlled the Police Department, prior to La Guarida's election in 1933, Hines had asked him to transfer policemen. These requests were then forwarded to the Police Commissioner, who invariably granted them. Former Chief Inspector John J. O'Brien described how overzealous raiders of Schultz's numbers banks had been speedily transferred or demoted.

But Hines was convicted mainly on the testimony of Dixie Davis and George Weinberg, the associates of Dutch Schultz. They testified that the gangster had paid Hines an average of $750 a week to protect his numbers operations. Davis was rewarded for his cooperation with a light sentence for a career that he admitted was entirely criminal and an easy time serving his sentence. He spent less than a year in prison, and the newspapers enjoyed suggesting that the frequent visits from his girlfriend, Hope Dare were for more than the officially stated reason—'a change of clothing'.[28]

In his final address to the jury Dewey charged Hines with accepting money from the Schultz gang and being the reason behind the drop in numbers arrests and declared:

> There couldn't be organized crime for five minutes in this country if the paralysing hand of a crooked politician weren't available to break an honest cop or tell a magistrate what to do, or to use gangster funds to elect a public prosecutor who is under his control . . . The important thing is that you declare to the people of New York, the police of New York, that they are free; that they

will no longer be betrayed by a corrupt alliance between crime and politics . . .
We want to keep the kind of system we have in the country and we don't want it
polluted by a betrayer. We don't want protection of gangsters by political
leaders.[29]

Hines was convicted and sentenced to four years in prison. Dewey had once
again produced a scapegoat to justify the retention of useless laws. The
numbers game remained popular, illegal and protected in New York City.
Dewey did not appear in court during the remaining two years of his district
attorneyship, thus ensuring that his prosecuting career ended on a high note.

Dewey's publicity machine was slick, thorough and had a flair for the
dramatic. Dewey himself was without equal as a Press manipulator and the
Press were more than willing to be manipulated for the sake of good crime
stories. In all his major trials the newspapers were supplied with a maximum
of dramatic and sordid detail, and morsels from his investigations were
continually leaked, after a thorough vetting by Dewey's staff. His staff in the
District Attorney's office were used openly to promote his political career,
preparing a great amount of material for release to the Press, including
advance notices and briefs of speeches, feature or background stories and
special statements on specific topics. Most journalists did little investigating
of their own and lazily adapted material provided for them by Dewey's staff.
Dewey's dramatic trials had made him an ideal subject for popular national
magazines such as *Time*, *Collier's*, *True Detective*, the *Saturday Evening Post*
and *Woman's Home Companion*.[30]

The most significant image-making articles were published in *Collier's* in
1939, under the series title, 'Things I Couldn't Tell Till Now', by Richard
'Dixie' Davis, the man who had turned state's evidence in the Hines case in
exchange for a light sentence. Davis's direct references to his benefactor,
District Attorney Dewey, go from the admiring, 'Dewey was a bad guy from
our standpoint, for I had seen him operate as a prosecutor in federal court', to
the grovelling, 'I knew I was in the presence of a great guy'. Indirectly Davis
enhanced Dewey's reputation by grossly exaggerating the importance of
Lucky Luciano, adding spurious substance to Dewey's claim at the 1936 trial
that Luciano was 'the greatest gangster in America'. The articles describe
Luciano as 'swarthy', 'hard-eyed' and 'sinister', the 'dark Sicilian' who took
control of a secret society of his fellow immigrants, the Unione Sicilione, after
a mass slaughter one night in 1931. The Unione Sicilione was, according to
Davis, the 'mysterious, all-pervading reality', which organized the 'underworld' on a national scale during and after Prohibition. Its leader was
Salvatore Maranzano who was shot dead on 10 September 1931, 'at the very
same hour', according to a hearsay story that Davis repeated, 'there was
about ninety guineas knocked off all over the country (a guinea is a slang term
of abuse for an Italian). A fantastic story and, if it were true, proof of
Luciano's nationwide power. In fact it was the only substance Davis offered

for his repeated assertions that Luciano was the most important gangster in America, the man who 'set up a system of underworld co-operation that spread from coast to coast', and who he compared to 'Hitler developing the system of axis powers'. Countless writers have been gullible or expedient enough to repeat Davis's unlikely and unsubstantiated assertions as fact and to build on them to concoct organized crime 'histories'. We shall return to them later. For the present it is sufficient to note that Davis's stories were widely read and believed at the time—although he himself had admitted that he had spent his life telling lies—and that they all reflected well on Dewey. Since Davis was still in custody at the time the articles were written, it is difficult not to suspect that they were turned out with the active assistance of Dewey's publicity machine.[31]

Dewey's crusading image and political advance was also aided, both directly and indirectly, by motion pictures. A documentary film, called *Smashing Crime with Dewey*, was produced for the 1937 District Attorney's election, and similar films were used in his campaigns for the governorship. Hollywood also helped present Dewey's crusading image to a mass audience. *Marked Woman*, directed by Lloyd Bacon in 1937, was based on the Luciano trial. A District Attorney, played by Humphrey Bogart, convinces 'cabaret hostess' Bette Davis and four of her girlfriends to testify against their brutal boss. Fictional District Attorneys, but thinly disguised personifications of Dewey, were also the heroes of several other popular films, including *Racket Busters* and *Smashing the Rackets*, both released in 1938.[32]

In 1940 author Rupert Hughes produced a biography based on Dewey's extensive scrapbook collection of news clippings and interviews with Dewey and his staff. Before it was published the staff carefully deleted anything that might be construed as reflecting Dewey in a bad light. On release the author claimed that it was not a campaign biography, but the final sentence is indicative of the eulogistic tone on the book: 'High as his destiny may call him, it will not find him unprepared or undeserving.'[33]

Also in 1940, however, two magazines, the *New Yorker* and the *American Mercury*, printed articles which were important correctives to such uncritical praise. Woolcott Gibbs and John Bainbridge in the *New Yorker* recalled how Dewey, to convict Luciano, had held 125 witnesses incommunicado, set impossibly high bails, traded freedom and overseas travel for testimony, and used threats of tax prosecution as a club with which to compel cooperation. The article quoted an unnamed attorney as saying: 'He could lock you up in a minute if he wanted to. He's potentially more dangerous to constitutional freedom than Mayor Hague (a reference to the undisputed power of the corrupt boss of Jersey City). The conclusion was that Dewey was 'just another guy we have to watch'.[34]

Benjamin Strolberg in the *American Mercury* criticized Dewey's methods in greater detail. Dewey had used wiretaps, 'a technological extension of illegal search', in all his major investigations and had even abused this power to tap the telephone of an attorney for the defence. Dewey was also a strong advocate of the Blue Ribbon jury, before which all his important cases were tried. These juries were drawn from a special panel of citizens who 'by and large came from the . . . better dressed layers of society'. Dewey defended this system on the ground that the normal jury is not 'intelligent enough'. But to any prosecutor, 'intelligent juries are of course convicting juries'. Strolberg pointed out that juries composed of 'squash racqueteers' from the Upper East Side were not appropriate to try working-class defendants from the Lower East Side. The article also argued that the 'joinder system' legitimized to convict Luciano could 'become a sinister weapon in the hands of an ambitious prosecutor' and that Dewey's practice of offering immunity and other inducements to prosecution witnesses in order to build cases on purely circumstantial evidence was also a threat to due process. Dewey's conception of criminal justice had no place for constitutional rights and instead resembled that of 'a psychologist who builts a labyrinthian trap for rats, to learn whether or how soon they can get out of it'.[35]

Dewey's 'war on racketeering and vice' was a period of effective head-hunting that established dangerous precedents for civil liberties. Dewey's methods were presented to the nation as the answer to the problem of vice and organized crime. Films, books, newspapers and the great majority of magazine articles sung his praises and put over the false message that the answer to organized crime lay exclusively in the prompt indictment and vigorous prosecution of all law-breakers. Dewey's success only camouflaged deficiencies in the laws and the law enforcement system. The convictions of Luciano, Hines and others were gestures which ultimately made no difference to organized crime in general or the businesses of gambling and prostitution in particular, Federal organized crime control methods have since been modelled on Dewey's pioneering tactics: close and prolonged surveillance and wire-tapping, inducements for criminals to become prosecution witnesses and convict their associates, and laws which facilitate conspiracy convictions. The methods are fine for pyrrhic victories in the war on crime but obviously inadequate as an answer to the continued success of organized crime in general. Another problem is that the people with these powers are often also criminally inclined.

Dewey's righteous image helped elect him Governor of New York State in November 1942. His state machine got him re-elected in 1946 and 1950, and was the power base for two unsuccessful campaigns for the presidency, in 1944 and 1948.

Mayor La Guardia continued to try and enforce the unenforceable vice laws until 1945, his final year in office. His crusades to stamp out gambling and prostitution inevitably failed. Slot and pinball machines were successfully barred from stores, restaurants and bars, but New Yorkers could still bet if they wanted to and, as the war put more money into their pockets, they bet more. Numbers and bookmaking continued to be lucrative operations, and illegal casinos operated across the river in New Jersey. The courts viewed gambling as a trivial offence and, accordingly, imposed light fines or occasionally short jail sentences.

Remarks he made in 1935 indicate that La Guardia resented the state anti-gambling laws which he was obliged to try and enforce:

> You can't break people of the habits formed over generations either by law or by constitutional amendment. Men and women will gamble. If they don't do it one way they will do it by another. Some play games, others speculate on the stock market . . . and some play bingo, wingo, jingo or stinko—anything they can put a dime or a quarter down on . . . .
>
> In other countries lotteries are regulated and run honestly and a winner is sure of his money. But here they are in the hands of racketeers, gangsters, pimps and punks . . . We have to use a large part of our police force in the supervision, discovery and apprehension of the gentry who run these lotteries. If the lotteries were legalized, it would free these officers for other police duties.[36]

Although he realized the futility of the effect, La Guardia persisted. In 1943 his strict interpretation of the law was criticized by the *Daily News*. He was 'too zealous a crusading evangelist' and alienated many voters by his campaigns against 'bingo, burlesque and bookmaking'.[37]

La Guardia in the end admitted defeat. On one occasion during his final year of office, he declared on the radio that he had received 'tens of thousands of letters' complaining about gambling with such accurate information that he could not help wonder 'what the police are doing!' He admonished the police to 'Go on and act now. Snap into it. Clean them out!'[38] It was an impotent gesture. Gambling was the perfect racket, for, like drinking alcohol during Prohibition, it was socially respectable, popular and not considered a crime. The main effect of New York's period of 'heat' was to increase the amount of 'ice'—protection money—that bookies and numbers operators had to pay the police. New York remained a lucrative market for illegal goods and services and any vacuums created by law enforcement successes were soon filled. For all La Guardia's efforts, corruption and inefficiency remained in the criminal justice and law enforcement systems and the vice laws were still not enforced.

La Guardia's anti-gambling crusade had failed because the problem was beyond the capacity of individual politicians to solve. When, however, gambling re-emerged as an issue in the post-war years, La Guardia's supporters made much political capital out of blaming his successor, Mayor William O'Dwyer, for the continuing problem—this will be examined in Part III.

La Guardia was never a mindlessly righteous moral crusader. As mayor he simply felt that it was his responsibility to see that all laws were obeyed. On the marijuana issue, for example, he did try and encourage a rational approach, in contrast to the irresponsible scare stories being circulated in the Press and other media by the Narcotics Bureau. He appointed a committee of physicians, psychologists, sociologists and pharmacists to investigate marijuana smoking by New York's Latin and black population. The committee issued its report in January 1945 which concluded that the 'practice of smoking marijuana does not lead to addiction in the medical sense of the word', and the drug was 'not the determining factor in the commission of major crimes'. The report emphasized that 'the publicity concerning the catastrophic effects of marijuana is unfounded', and that marijuana use did not lead to morphine, heroin or cocaine addiction, was not associated with juvenile delinquency, and its use was 'not widespread among school children as some alarmists had reported'. The report called for an intelligent approach to marijuana which did not materialize.[39]

Instead the Narcotics Bureau and sympathetic members of medical profession launched a publicly effective counter-attack. In April 1945 an editorial in the *Journal* of the American Medical Association joined the Narcotics Bureau in condemning the La Guardia report as 'unscientific' because it 'minimized the dangers inherent in addiction to the weed'. The editorial backed its condemnation of the 'unscientific' report by citing an example of the 'harm' it had already done:

> One investigator has described some tearful parents who brought their 16-year old boy to a physician after he had been detected in the act of smoking marijuana . . . The boy said he had read an account of the La Guardia committee report and this was his justification for using marijuana.[40]

This method, which plays upon the fears of middle-class parents in particular, has proved effective in maintaining the prohibition of marijuana. Marijuana remained another prohibited pastime that was socially acceptable and popular amongst certain sections of the population. And therefore it also remained a drain on law enforcement and prison resources, a source of friction between minority populations and the police, and finally another illegal source of income.

People voted for Thomas Dewey in state and national elections during the 1940s and 1950s on the understandable assumption that a man who had made his name as a 'racket-buster' and scourge of corrupt politicians would continue this work in higher office. Dewey took pains to encourage this assumption, exuding righteousness in all his speeches, and specifically pledging to continue his crusade against organized crime as Governor. However, Governor Dewey accepted political realities as he found them, in the same way as the Democratic politicians he so often attacked. Graft was still the grease that kept New York's political machines running, although Dewey's state administration was not found out until his final year of office in 1954.

As Governor, Dewey took complete control of the state Republican party. As Warren Moscow noted: 'County leaders who opposed him were broken by cold, hard-bitten use of the patronage powers of the governor's office. Legislators suffered a similar fate. He brooked no interference.' Dewey ran for President twice. In 1944 he was beaten easily by Roosevelt; in 1948 he was beaten unexpectedly by Harry Truman. He consistently avoided using his greater powers against organized crime and rarely mentioned the subject except in unsubstantiated slurs on political opponents.

Dewey's career is usually considered in two distinct phases: 1935 to 1942 as the nation's best-known 'racket-buster' and 1943 to 1955 as a competent governor who nearly became President. His failure to respond to the problem of organized crime as Governor has been given little serious attention, although it is more representative of the country's response at the time than that of briefly effective local prosecutors. Dewey's image as a hard-hitting foe of organized crime has largely stood the test of time because it is what people wanted to believe. But this image needs re-examining in the context of his whole career.

The following sections examine in turn three aspects of Dewey's response to organized crime as Governor: firstly, the release of Charles 'Lucky' Luciano; secondly, his handling of the affairs of New York's corrupt waterfront; and, finally, the discrepancy between his pompous public condemnation of off-track bookmaking and the corrupt enrichment of his closest associates from on-track bookmaking on harness race tracks.

Governor Dewey's first significant public action in relation to organized crime was, ironically, the release of Lucky Luciano, the man he had called the 'greatest gangster in America', in his most famous courtroom triumph. On 2 January 1946, Dewey commuted Luciano's sentence conditional upon his deportation to Italy. Dewey's message to the State Legislature justified the decision on the grounds that Luciano had contributed valuable assistance to the war effort, but did not specify what this assistance was. Dewey persisted in being less than frank about the reasons for Luciano's release and thus allowed crime writers unlimited scope to speculate. Those with a vested interest in exaggerating Luciano's power and influence claimed that Luciano had ordered New York's longshoremen to safeguard the waterfront from sabotage and, much more fancifully, provided meaningful assistance to the Allied plans to invade Sicily in 1943. Other crime writers have seen Luciano's alleged assistance to the war effort as a convenient fabrication to justify his release which was much more prosaically purchased with massive campaign contributions to the Republican party.[41]

Dewey was not allowed to forget his leniency towards Luciano completely and the controversy simmered away during the remainder of his governorship, always threatening to boil over but in the end failing to inflict serious damage on his reputation. His Democratic opponent in the 1950 election, Walter Lynch, brought the matter up and charged that the release had been a response to pressure brought by Frank Costello, who by then was considered by New York tabloids as America's top criminal. However, 1950 was a particularly dirty election year and Lynch's charge was just one of many. Dewey responded with charges of his own against the Democrats and was re-elected without trouble. The following year the issue was picked up by the

Kefauver Committee, which was investigating organized crime. The committee expressed doubts that Luciano's release could be justified by his alleged aid to the war effort but, as Dewey refused to appear before the committee, no more light was shed on the matter.[42]

Dewey could have let the controversy run its course but in June 1953, for reasons only known to himself, he ordered William Herlands to investigate Luciano's release. Herlands examined scores of witnesses from coast to coast in an exercise that was described by crime reporter George Martin, in a private memo to Senator Kefauver, as a 'whitewash', which only amounted to 'an *ex post facto* justification of Dewey's position of nearly nine years before, that Luciano had contributed valuable assistance to the war effort'. According to Martin, Herlands for all his effort had not turned up any evidence of a specific act on the part of Luciano that was a valuable contribution to the prosecution of the war with the exception that, sitting in prison, he sent out 'the word' to his criminal associates 'to co-operate'. Luciano had been incarcerated five years before the United States entered the war in December 1941. Given the opportunity he naturally endorsed the Navy's collaboration with waterfront gangsters, but was unable to help in any other way. In Martin's opinion, the Navy 'was suckered into what now appears to be a clever scheme to lay the groundwork for the freeing of Luciano from prison, and it worked'.[43]

Dewey's motivation for spending the taxpayer's money on the Herlands investigation is not known, but at the time, June 1953, he was approaching a time of decision about his future career. He faced the choice of standing again for Governor, accepting a post in President Eisenhower's administration or returning to private practice. He chose the latter, but it is quite possible he still had aspirations towards the presidency particularly because Eisenhower's health was thought to be failing at the time. In any case the Luciano business was an embarrassment and the Herlands investigation appears to be an attempt to vindicate his decision.

Herlands' report was never released, but its contents were made available to author Sid Feder, who used the material to give some authenticity to a book called *The Luciano Story*, published in early 1954. Immediately after the book appeared Joachim Joesten, its co-author, made a public statement repudiating the book and disavowing any responsibility for it. The book, as published, eulogized Dewey, and justified his release of Luciano with the version of the affair that became standard in poorly researched crime books. In essence this version stated that Luciano rendered the United States war effort invaluable service by remote control from prison. Joesten complained that this in no way resembled the work he had delivered to the publisher in June 1953 and charged that Dewey had been shown the manuscript and then immediately appointed Herlands to conduct his investigation which was the basis for Feder's complete rewrite of the book.[44]

Dewey left public office on 1 January 1955 and the Luciano affair was effectively at an end. Just in case, by September 1955, Senator Kefauver had in his possession George Martin's analysis of every defect and misrepresentation of the Herlands investigation to use in a possible contest with Dewey for the presidency. A potentially dirty presidential election was avoided when Adlai Stevenson got the Democratic nomination to challenge President Eisenhower, whose full recovery of health before the election ended any lingering hopes Dewey might have been entertaining. Neither he nor Kefauver gained anything politically from the affair. The only beneficiaries were Luciano who gained his freedom and William Herlands who was rewarded for his loyalty with a judgeship.

While his name was being bandied about by politicians. Luciano himself was helping to establish a major drug trafficking network between Italy and the United States. Luciano's importance, however, was greatly exaggerated by the Narcotics Bureau which promoted him once again—from the 'greatest gangster in America' to 'the new boss of the current international gangdom of the world'. Luciano was simply one of many who benefited from America's draconian drug laws which inflated the value of products which were far less bulky than liquids and thus far easier to smuggle. According to one of Luciano's better biographers, Tony Scaduto, the Narcotics Bureau view of Luciano as an autocrat of the drug traffic was nonsense. Luciano may have provided capital and advice but he was as completely detached from actual criminal involvement as it was possible to become. For Scaduto, Luciano was more likely the 'contact man' who

> worked on the greed of owners of major drug houses in Italy, so that these men would divert large amounts of heroin into the illicit market . . . and established the distribution network to bring narcotics from Italy to his friends in New York City and Canada.[45]

Luciano remained in exile until his death in Naples in 1962.

Whatever Luciano's involvement, there is no doubt that Naval Intelligence did solicit and get help from the gangsters who controlled waterfront labour. The help consisted of a network of contacts and informants and such things as the union authorization necessary for agents to work undercover on the piers. Wartime sabotage was prevented but the collaboration did set a malign precedent. In post-war Italy, US Army agents helped indigenous gangsters—mafiosi in Sicily and camorrista in Naples—back to positions of power in local government as bulwarks against communism. The same cause justified an early 1960s conspiracy between the CIA and such gangsters as Sam Giancana, John Rosselli and Santos Trafficante which planned to assassinate Fidel Castro. And although this plan was aborted, the agency continued to promote anti-Castro Cuban groups whose main business was divided between terrorism and drug trafficking. In the final analysis, despite the rhetoric, the war on crime always occupied a lowly position on the list of the nation's priorities.[46]

Dewey's image as a dynamic righter of wrongs and foe of corruption is less than apt in relation to his handling of New York's corrupt and murderous waterfront during his tenure as Governor. Ignorance of waterfront conditions is no excuse in his case. In the early 1940s, as District Attorney, Dewey had begun, but did not complete, an unprecedented inquiry into the affairs of the Port of New York. Also, by signing Luciano's release Dewey was acknowledging that gangsters controlled waterfront labour. Dewey was either incapable or unwilling to provide the strong executive leadership needed to reform the waterfront.

The Port of New York during the 1930s and 1940s was the richest in the world. Each year, cargoes worth between $15 billion and $16 billion passed across its piers, including more than a third of the country's foreign trade and about half of the furs, jewels, watches and other luxuries. The port or ancillary occupations employed one in ten New Yorkers. The fictional corrupt union boss, Johnny Friendly, in the 1954 film *On the Waterfront*, used appropriate imagery when he demanded his cut of 'the fattest piers in the fattest harbour in the world'. The disorganized and exploited workforce was unionized in name only. The International Longshoremen's Association (ILA) enjoyed what amounted to a closed-shop agreement with the shipping and stevedoring companies. The union leaders had set-up thirty-one semi-autonomous locals in New York which effectively and systematically undermined its bargaining position. The ILA was, in effect, a company union run by gangsters. It made no pretence of maintaining a defence fund because its function was to prevent the men organizing and to break strikes. The union gangsters only drew a nominal salary from the treasury—they were regularly paid off by the companies and allowed to operate any pierside rackets they chose. These included wage kickbacks, numbers, bookmaking and larger-scale operations such as hijacking cargo and exorbitant fees for the loading and unloading of pierside motor trucks. On all but a few piers the longshoremen were hired on a casual basis by gangsters because gangsters had demonstrated to the stevedoring firms that they made the most efficient foremen.

The only way longshoremen could improve pay and conditions was through 'wildcat' industrial action. Beginning in the late 1930s and continuing through to the 1950s, rank-and-file movements of longshoremen fought both the bosses and the gangster union of ILA president Joseph P. Ryan. The gangsters used violence or murder to maintain the status quo, while politicians ensured, through either corruption or faint-heartedness, that the normal rules governing law and order did not apply. The occasional gesture of the law enforcement agencies was treated with contempt. Conscientious police and prosecutors were rare in waterfront areas and, if necessary, cases could be 'fixed' through political influence or by terrorizing or murdering witnesses. The longshoremen had no protection from the law.[47]

Longshoremen who were considered a particular threat to the status quo were murdered. Pater Panto, for example, organized a rank-and-file movement of some 1,200 Brooklyn longshoremen against the ILA and, in particular, kickback and extortion rackets. In July 1939 he disappeared and was later found dead. No waterfront murder was solved until 1949 when John

'Cockeye' Dunn and Andy Sheridan were convicted of the murder of Anthony Hintz, an uncooperative hiring boss. The waterfront murders which appeared on the record were only a small percentage of the actual total. A Catholic priest, Father John Corridan, testified that not all accidents on the docks were accidents, heavy dockside paraphernalia provided plenty of opportunities for planned mishaps. Corridan also knew of policemen who were aware of murders which went down on the record as heart attacks. Rank-and-file strikes were crushed with systematic brutality; Joe Ryan's 'goon squads' administered beatings while the police looked on.[48]

Ryan and his gangster allies were used by the employers to keep the labour force docile and cheap and to keep profits healthy. The enormous wealth of the waterfront interests effectively ensured that no politician interfered with this situation. Every year until 1952, the Joseph P. Ryan Association gave a testimonial dinner which dramatized the corrupt complicity of business, union, criminal and political interests. The title of Chairman of the Committee on arrangements for the annual dinner was usually held by William McCormack, a friend of Ryan's and the businessman generally considered to be the most powerful single individual on the waterfront. Ryan and McCormack presided over a gathering of district attorneys, judges, magistrates, state legislators, city councilmen, police, bankers, shipping and stevedoring entrepreneurs, AFL functionaries, usually the Mayor and always waterfront gangsters.[49] This annual get-together of vested interests was far more representative of the reality of organized crime than the periodic, clandestine meeting of Italian–American racketeers that crime writers have used to build their conspiracy theories around. Not all of those attending the functions were corrupt but by attending they were accepting political realities and the corrupt conditions on the waterfront in which organized crime thrived.

In 1950 after the publicity of the trial of 'Cockeye' Dunn and a series of revelations by *Sun* newspaper reporter, Malcolm Johnson, Governor Dewey found that he was unable to attend the annual dinner, but felt obliged to send Ryan the following letter:

Dear Joe:

    I would surely be delighted to come to the annual affair of the Joseph P. Ryan Association on Saturday, May 20th, if possible. As it happens, Mrs Dewey and I have accepted an invitation to the marriage of Lowell Thomas's only son that weekend and we just can't possibly make it.

    It is mighty nice of you to ask me and I wish you would give my regards to all the fine people at the dinner.

    On behalf of the people of the entire state, I congratulate you for what you have done to keep the Communists from getting control of the New York waterfront. Be assured that the entire machinery of the State of New York is behind you and your organization in this determination.

With warm regards,
Sincerely yours,
Thomas E. Dewey[50]

The Communists had little influence on the New York waterfront but Ryan used to manufacture 'red' scares to justify brutal strike-breaking. In this letter Dewey gave his explicit seal of approval of gangster control of the waterfront.

However, more revelations about violence and corruption and frequent wildcat industrial action brought a belated response from Dewey in November 1951. He issued an order to his State Crime Commission to investigate waterfront conditions. Although the commission somehow steered the hearings away from political explanations for the continued existence of waterfront corruption, it did expose the venality of Ryan and the ILA and could not disguise the fact that the employers were the chief beneficiaries of gangster control of the union.[51]

In the summer of 1953, acting on recommendations of the State Crime Commission, Governor Dewey and Governor Alfred Driscoll of New Jersey obtained state and federal legislation enabling establishment of the Bi-State Waterfront Commission with dictatorial powers to regulate longshore hiring. The bill provided for state-controlled hiring halls and permanent registration of all dock workers. This became the basis for a blacklist of union militants and any suspected Communists; in other words, it did legally what gangsters had been doing illegally for years.[52]

The Bi-State Commission did not end organized crime and corruption on the waterfront, but merely confused the issue. The longshoremen needed an honest union but the ILA emerged victorious from a jurisdictional battle with an AFL rival, the International Brotherhood of Longshoremen (IBL). The election to decide between the two unions in December 1953 was marked by knifings and beatings and by gangster foremen herding workers to the polls in buses to vote for the 'right' side. On the eve of the election an independently minded foreman, Michael Brogan, who had expressed a preference for the IBL, was murdered. The police asked for information from longshoremen on the dockside itself in full view of gangster foremen, apparently to ensure that the murder investigation was bungled from the start. Dewey's executive initiative did not change the situation on the waterfront; labour was still controlled by gangsters. The ILA, however, now had the Bi-State Commission as a ready-made opponent and could appear militant while remaining in cohoots with the employers.[53]

Dewey had tried to keep the waterfront at arm's length. He, like Ryan and his gangster allies, was basically on the side of the employers and because of this his response was slow, reluctant and ultimately inadequate. It shows that in the context of his whole career the description 'racket-buster' is very misleading. Everything Dewey did was consistent only with advancing his political career. During the 1930s, as prosecutor in Manhattan, his way forward was simple: convict star-name gangsters and destroy their political protectors, who were also political opponents. As Governor he was faced with a new set of political realities, including debts to power brokers and generous campaign contributors who had sponsored his career. The best way for government executives to repay their debts is often to do nothing to disturb the status quo and refuse to see wrong-doing, however obvious.

Dewey provides further evidence of expediency and hypocrisy in his response to the gambling controversies that marked his tenure. So as not to threaten the Protestant up-state vote he refused to countenance state regulation of off-track betting, charging the Democratic proponents of the idea with all manner of sin. After detailing Dewey's public attitude to gambling and corruption, an examination of the harness track scandals will show that his own administration exemplified successful corrupt money-making.

In April 1949 Dewey vetoed a bill appropriating $50,000 for a legislative study of the feasibility of legalizing off-track betting. It was estimated that such betting could raise $100 million in state revenue instead of enriching gambling syndicates, police and politicians. The following year Dewey reacted with outrage to a request by Mayor William O'Dwyer of New York for legalized betting on sports events. Dewey said that O'Dwyer's proposals were 'shocking, immoral and indecent' and elaborated:

> It would be immoral of government to make available to all of its people a statewide gambling apparatus with the implied assumption that the games of chance are a fair substitute for or supplement to the income of ordinary work.

He added that he thought it 'an indecent thing for government to finance itself so largely out of the weaknesses of the people', and that he had reservations about the 'wisdom and morality' of the state's receipt of revenue from betting. He concluded that the legalization of all types of gambling might result if O'Dwyer's suggestion were taken seriously, putting the state's 'imprimatur of approval on the morals and decency of wholesale, universal betting of every kind'. During this implicit attack on the Democrats and their hold on New York City, Dewey made it clear that the enforcement of the gambling laws in the city had been extremely lax.[54]

In the November 1950 state and local elections, Dewey found further opportunity to rail at the corruption of the Democratic rulers of the city; this was particularly necessary since, for the first time, his own integrity was also being seriously questioned. To begin with, Dewey had come under attack from a member of his own party. A Republican congressman, Kingsland Macy, embarrassed Dewey by making public the contents of a letter he had received from Lieutenant-Governor Joseph Hanley. Hanley, in failing health and deeply in debt, had wanted to run for Governor, but when Dewey announced for a third term he agreed to contest Herbert Lehman's seat in the Senate. To ease Hanley's disappointment, Dewey had promised him that if he agreed to oppose Lehman he would be guaranteed financial security for life regardless of the outcome of the election.[55]

The Democrats added to the embarrassment of the illegal proposition contained in this letter by first, as mentioned above (see p. 60), raising the

Luciano issue, and, secondly, countering Dewey's charges that gambling enforcement was lax in the city, by pointing out that illegal casino gambling was blatant in up-state Saratoga during the racing season. Casinos owned by such organized crime notables as Willie Bischoff of Detroit, and Joe Adonis and Frank Costello of New York operated openly and illegally, just as casinos had been operated in Saratoga since the previous century. The suppression of gambling was ultimately the responsibility of Governor Dewey's state police. Instead it was common knowledge that the local police were on the gambler's payrolls, 'steering' tourists to the casinos and guarding the day's takings on the way to the bank. It was inconceivable that Dewey was unaware of Saratoga's customs.[56]

However, in this particularly dirty election, Dewey had the advantage of his 'racket-busting' image and the fact the Democrats had long been associated with corruption and involvement with organized crime. In particular, Dewey took advantage of New York's favourite political football of the time, Frank Costello's known influence in Manhattan's Tammany Hall organization. In 1943 this influence had been illustrated when the following extract from a wiretap on Costello's telephone was released to the Press:

> When I tell you something is in the bag, you can rest assured.
> Right now I want to assure you of my loyalty for all you have done. It's undying.[57]

The man pledging his loyalty was State Supreme Court nominee Thomas Aurelio, and the man who put things in the bag was Frank Costello. Costello attained his influence in Tammany Hall in the same way that businessmen, bankers and gamblers had attained influence in United States political organizations for generations: campaign contributions, cultivation and sometimes outright bribery. Favours done for aspiring young politicians, prosecutors and judges would in time pay dividends. However, in the public outcry that followed the publication of the conversation there was no indication that it revealed a flaw in the whole political and criminal justice system, just a flaw in Tammany Hall. Politicians, prosecutors and judges should not owe favours to gamblers or anyone else, but the need for political endorsement and financial support to get elected ensured that they did owe favours. The Republicans had no interest in examining such flaws, but used the indication that Tammany was in Costello's pocket to good political effect.

'Costelloism' (see also pp. 124–125 and p. 128) for the Kefauver Committee's use of 'Costelloism') was still an issue in 1950 and Dewey stretched Costello's alleged control of Tammany Hall to the whole Democratic party in New York City and State. On 25 October, in a speech broadcast on a state-wide television network, Dewey made full use of the Costello allegations and other unconnected, minor scandals to discredit his opponents. The following day the *New York Times* gave the speech front-page prominence and noted that it was reminiscent of 'the Governor's racket-busting days'. Dewey began by charging that his opponent, Walter Lynch, was 'Costello's man' and pleaded with the voters to keep 'clean, decent and honest government' in Albany by voting for him. He appealed to the voters to defeat Frank Costello both as 'Mayor of New York and as Governor of the State', because, he explained, Costello had been reported as saying that he had never been a junior partner in any enterprise. Dewey concluded:

> We are engaged in a mighty struggle to keep decency in the government of New York . . . I invite you all to join me in that job—in keeping their dirty hands off the fine, clean, progressive government you now have in Albany.[58]

This type of tirade was effective and it was a bad election year for the Democrats. Although Herbert Lehman retained his seat in the Senate, Dewey was re-elected Governor and Vincent Impellitteri, a disaffected Democrat, was elected Mayor.

In 1953 a scandal began to break that eventually showed that at the same time as Dewey was pompously sermonizing about the evils of his political opponents and the 'immorality' of off-track gambling, his closest associates in the 'clean, decent and honest' government in Albany were making millions of dollars exploiting loose state regulation of legalized betting at the harness tracks to cheat the public out of tax revenue by systematic political chicanery.

The harness track rackets were varied and complex, stretching from the employment of gangsters to control and exploit the workforce at the tracks to complicated business and legislative deals that led William Keating of the New York Anti-Crime Committee to describe the tracks as a kind of 'trough':

> the story of their growth was replete with wheels within wheels, fantastic stock deals and transfers, the use of legislation to squeeze out competition, the enrichment of legislators and political bosses who pushed the desired laws. Few people could make sense of all the corporate and legislative convolutions, but nobody could miss noticing that the whole thing stank of corruption . . .[59]

The harness track scandals began to unravel on 28 August 1953, when a Bronx union boss, Thomas Lewis, was shot and murdered. His assassin was killed minutes later by a policeman and so it was impossible to prove who commissioned what looked like a 'hit'. Lewis was a small cog in a massive racket but his death enabled sections of the Press and the independent New York Anti-Crime Committee to attract the public's attention to the mess of corruption surrounding harness track racing.

Tommy Lewis ran the labour force at Yonkers Raceway and, although like Joe Ryan and many others he operated under a union banner, his function was to prevent labour trouble and his motivation was to enrich himself. He accomplished this chiefly by deals with his members' welfare insurance funds. Lewis, instead of placing the insurance with the lowest bidders, awarded the business to agents who paid off the most and this resulted in the membership getting less insurance for more money—a widespread practice then as well as now. Among the companies Lewis bought policies from were two owned by William Bleakey, Republican leader of Westchester County, and this might have been part of the pay-off Lewis made for being chosen to run the labour force at Yonkers. One favoured insurance company also happened to be owned by Lewis himself, and in five years he and his partners had accumulated $412,000 in commissions and service fees.[60]

After the disclosures about Lewis and Yonkers Raceway, the newspapers delved into the affairs of Roosevelt Raceway in Nassau County, Long Island. In charge of the labour force there was an even more enterprising union gangster, William DeKoning, an AFL boss. DeKoning did all the labour hiring at the track, represented the employees in union negotiations and owned stock in harness track associations—a not uncommon conflict of interest. Keating described how DeKoning collected money from every angle:

> As stockholder in the track, he profited from the labour of his members. As union official, he collected a salary. As shakedown artist, he extorted kickbacks from the members, requiring them to buy ads in the phony programmes he published, and insisting, as the price of employment at the track or on house-building jobs, that they show up at least once a week at his bar, the Labour Lyceum, and spend at least $8 a visit. Meanwhile he took graft from housing contractors. One of his pet devices was to accept $8 a day from contractors who did not care to observe the union regulation calling for employment of a $16-a-day cement-mixing operator. Nobody will ever know how much he took from contractors who did not use union labour at all, but the sum must have been considerable because DeKoning never so much as picketed certain non-union projects that he could easily have shut down.[61]

Trotting associations regularly gave both Tommy Lewis and William DeKoning high-priced help in their capacity as 'labour trouble shooters'. At Yonkers Lewis's partner, Joseph Pizzo, was paid $96,000 and a convicted bank robber, Laurence Lynch, $2,000 monthly, for helping to 'avert strikes'. At Roosevelt Frank Costello was employed to sort out a little difficulty with independent bookmakers. George Morton Levy, who as president of the Nassau Trotting Association was responsible for Roosevelt Raceway, testified before the Kefauver Committee in 1951 that he had called in his golfing companion, Frank Costello, to help sort out a problem that had arisen in 1946. Levy had been receiving persistent complaints from the head of the New York State Harness Racing Commission that independent bookmakers in large numbers were frequenting the race meetings and thereby endangering the licence of the Trotting Association. Levy then turned to Costello whom he knew had 'the reputation of having influence with gamblers', and the problem ceased. Costello testified that he 'didn't do a damn thing, I just spread a little propaganda in bars and restaurants'. For this Costello was paid $60,000—at the rate of $15,000 a year for four years. The payments ceased after 1949 because the Internal Revenue refused to allow Levy to continue claiming the payments as business expenses.[62]

These payments for services rendered were dwarfed by the profits of politicians. Top of the list was Dewey's close ally, J. Russel Sprague, Republican leader of Nassau County and a member of the GOP National Committee. Dewey had given Sprague what amounted to a licence to print money by appointing him Trotting Commissioner. On one deal alone, involving Roosevelt Raceway, Sprague invested $2,000 and profited by $195,000. Levy, who worked closely with Sprague, used his position in the Nassau Trotting Association to collect about $3 million from stock transfers and legal fees. The value of trotting stocks was enormously increased by favourable law provisions passed by the State Legislature and so it is no surprise that the leaders of both parties in both houses were also substantial stockholders. Other key party bosses and their associates showed remarkable returns on small investments. A representative level of profit was that of Arthur Lynch, who had been a deputy New York Treasurer under Mayors La Guardia and O'Dwyer; he made $400,000 on a $12,000 trotting stock investment.[63]

Dewey's closest associates were not only running an industry with the help of thugs and gangsters but were also swindling the taxpayers out of millions of dollars of revenue by not, for example, going for a bigger *pari mutuel* take. (*Pari mutuel* is a form of betting in which winners divide losers' stakes, less a percentage for management.) In the context of the harness track disclosures there must also be a suspicion about Dewey's outbursts against proposals to legalize off-track bookmaking in 1950 (see p. 66). Racetrack interests have traditionally been antagonistic towards proposals to legalize off-track bookmaking, fearing dwindling attendances and a lower volume of betting. Governor Dewey's moral outrage in 1950 helped block legalization proposals and, at the same time, safeguarded the profitability of the racetrack stocks owned by members of his political machine. However, although it stretches credulity that Dewey was unaware of the plundering of his friends and allies, his personal reputation emerged virtually unscathed from the mess. The newspapers were careful to absolve Dewey from any responsibility, although the *New York Post* dryly remarked, 'we look forward to the Governor's next sermon on Democratic sin'.[64]

The harness track scandals did result in more effective state regulation of the sport, and miscellaneous gangsters and politicians were forced to dispose of their stock and find new ventures. The politicians had ensured that the graft was legal and so no one went to prison over the track scandals. In the wake of the scandals Averell Harriman, a Democrat, defeated the Republican candidate, Irving Ives, in the 1954 gubernatorial elections. Harriman made crime his principal campaign issue and in one speech declared: 'the story of the harness-tracks has punctured for all time the myth of the integrity of the present day leadership of the Republican party of New York'.[65] Harriman was wrong and the 'myth' of Dewey's integrity was not significantly affected.

The key to Dewey's success as a prosecutor was that the righteous and hysterical temper of the 1930s in New York allowed him to ride roughshod over civil liberties in order to obtain convictions. As Governor he was no longer a threat to organized crime: he stood back and watched while gangsters were cynically employed to break legitimate unionism and his term of office was marked by the rampant conflict of interest and mercenary corruption which is necessary for organized crime to thrive or even to exist. The machine that kept him in power and just failed to get him the presidency was oiled by graft in the same way political machines had always been oiled by graft. And yet none of his biographers questioned the claim that Dewey was a foe of organized crime. His courtroom triumphs in the 1930s provided dangerous precedents for civil liberties and made no substantial difference to organized crime activities in New York. To look at his courtroom triumphs in isolation from the reality of his terms as Governor misrepresents the history of organized crime.

The fate of William Keating, a genuine foe of organized crime and the protective alliances and political expendiency which sustain it, is much more revealing about the county's response to organized crime. Keating, who had prosecuted and convicted John 'Cockeye' Dunn for murder, was counsel to the New York Anti-Crime Committee and had been instrumental in bringing the waterfront and the harness tracks to the public's attention. In June 1955, Keating was convicted by the office of Manhattan District Attorney, Frank Hogan, for refusing to identify his informers and thereby endangering their lives. Keating had been investigating the corrupt underside of New York City and State for thirteen years, refusing to be influenced and intimidated by political pressure. After serving a short spell in jail he had had enough of being 'The Man who Rocked the Boat', which was the title of his auto-biography, and returned to private practice. The New York Anti-Crime Committee was rendered ineffectual without immunity to protect informers and soon folded up. The fight against politically protected organized crime was therefore left to politically appointed or elected District Attorneys, whose policy is often dictated by political expediency or sensitivity and sometimes by outright corruption.[66]

After 1954 Thomas Dewey never again held public office, but he remained an important backstage power in the Republican party. His protégé was Richard Nixon whom he had helped win the 1952 Vice-Presidential nomination and then keep his place on the ticket after the private-fund uproar that climaxed in the famous 'Checkers' speech about the Nixon family dog. As we shall see in Part IV Nixon was another 'law and order' crusading candidate who had little time for civil liberties or honesty when they conflicted with political advancement. Dewey returned to private practice in 1955 and his firm prospered particularly during the favouritism-riddled conduct of the public business by the Eisenhower administration. Newspaper columnist Jack Anderson cited one 'extralegal intervention by T.E. Dewey's law firm that swung the awards of airline routes and earned legal fees as high as $110,000 for Dewey'.[67] Dewey died in 1971 worth more than $3 million.

Barry Beyer's biography of Dewey was published in 1979 and, at times, it reads like the excessively laudatory campaign biographies of the 1940s. He concluded:

> That he failed in 1948 to achieve the coveted symbol of political expertise and statesmanship—the presidency—was his personal tragedy, and perhaps that of his party and nation as well.[68]

Richard Norton Smith, Dewey's latest biographer, stretched this analysis for over 600 pages and he concluded:

> He would undoubtedly have made an abler president than candidate, and the history of his country might have been profoundly different had he succeeded in articulating a compelling vision contrary to that of FDR or Truman.[69]

A more concise and astute analysis of the man came from one of his contemporaries, a New York hostess: 'You can't help liking Tom Dewey until you know him'.[70]

6 Chicago: corrupt and content

'First in violence, deepest in dirt; loud, lawless, unlovely, ill-smelling, irreverent, new; an overgrown gawk of a village, the "tough" among cities, a spectacle for the nation', was how Lincoln Steffens described Chicago at the beginning of the twentieth century, and the city continued to live up to its reputation.[1]

Between 1830 and 1930 Chicago had grown from a village to one of the world's largest cities—second only to New York in the United States in trade, industry and population. In 1930 Chicago had over three million inhabitants, and millions more visited or passed through the city annually. The second city's attitude towards illegal enterprise was always tolerant. Corrupt alliances between politicians, police and gangsters had been exploiting this immense market for illegal goods and services for decades before Prohibition but the 18th Amendment provided an important addition to Chicago's institutionalized illegal commerce in bootleg liquor.

In 1927 the city's electorate delivered their verdict on the one genuine local attempt to enforce Prohibition. They turned out Mayor William Dever, whose police had been invading private homes in search of liquor, and replaced him with William 'Big Bill' Thompson, a former mayor who stated categorically 'I'm wetter than the middle of the Atlantic Ocean'. Thompson, in effect, promised and delivered an open city for bootlegging, gambling and prostitution, regulated in a haphazard way by the city's police. Scarcely concealed corruption characterized all aspects of the city's business. Public officials prospered while gangsters killed each other for the privilege of paying them off.

Despite the claims of some writers, Al Capone did not run Chicago in the late 1920s. One of his contemporaries gave a better analysis when he described Capone and the other gangsters as 'technicians' and emphasized that:

> The city was being run by the politicians and by City Hall, and the big bosses weren't interested if the gangsters killed each other providing they kept delivering the money.[2]

Capone himself estimated that Chicago required payoffs of around $30 million each year, and his own payroll needed to include roughly half of the entire police force. 'When it comes down to cases', Capone said, 'nobody's really on the legit'.[3]

Mayor Thompson convincingly demonstrated the limits of Capone's power in 1928. Briefly under the illusion that he might be in the running for the presidency, Thompson decided that harbouring the nation's best-known gangster might be an electoral liability. He therefore gave the word to his Chief of Police and a campaign of harassment commenced. Capone men were arrested on tenuous charges, breweries, brothels and gambling houses were repeatedly raided, and the boss himself was kept under continuous supervision. Capone left the city, grumbling to reporters about people's lack of gratitude. As soon as Thompson realized the hopelessness of his ambitions Capone felt safe to return home and resume operations.[4]

By 1931 Capone was finished as a criminal power and jailed for evasion of income tax. His reign at the top of the Chicago rackets had been brief, hard-fought, immensely expensive and totally dependent on the sufferance of the local authorities. In 1931 also the Republican administration of Mayor Thompson was defeated at the polls, discredited by years of corruption, gangsterism and financial mismanagement. The newly elected Mayor, Anton Cermak, had helped reorganize the Democratic party into the efficient organization that has ruled Chicago ever since. The Chicago *Daily Tribune* hailed the election as 'an ejection, a dirty job' and claimed that Chicago had 'washed itself and put on clean clothes'. The newspaper added that for Chicago Thompson had meant:

> filth, corruption, obscenity, idiocy and bankruptcy. He has given the city an international reputation for moronic buffoonery, barbaric crime, triumphant hoodlumism, unchecked graft and a dejected citizenship . . . He made Chicago the byword for the collapse of American civilization.
>
> He is not only out, but he is dishonoured. He is deserted by his friends. He is permanently marked by the evidences of his character and conduct. His health is impaired by his way of life and he leaves office and goes from the city the most discredited man who has ever held place in it.[5]

The much more perceptive *Nation* noted that Chicago had 'simply swapped one evil for another'.[6]

Cermak's campaign pledge was to purge the city of organized crime and he announced his victory by advising gangsters to 'pack up and leave or prepare for long terms in jail'. Cermak, however, was much closer to organized crime, to the gambling and liquor interests in particular, than Thompson ever was. According to Virgil Peterson, the main authority on Chicago crime, Cermak's aim was to rationalize and control the city's gambling operations in order to sustain an immense amount of financial and political capital for the Democratic machine. In the autumn of 1931 Cermak appointed James Allman as Commissioner of Police and convinced the Press that the police would thenceforward be independent of politicians. Allman's brief, however, was that policy on gambling would emanate directly from the Mayor's office.

On the West Side, Cermak's political power base, William Johnson was to be given ironclad protection to increase the scale of his already large gambling operations. William Skidmore, Johnson's partner in several lavish gambling houses, was to continue to be the chief intermediary between the local Democratic politicians and the gambling syndicates. Each week policy operators, bookmakers, and other gamblers and their representatives came to Skidmore's junkyard to make their graft payments. On the North-West Side, Martin Guilfoyle, whose gambling concessions had derived from the Republican machine, was marked for replacement by a pro-Democrat gangster. On the North Side, Ted Newberry, a former partner of Bugs Moran, was slated to receive important gambling concessions at the expense of the former partners of Al Capone, notably Frank Nitti and Jake Guzik. Years later, Roger Touhy, a North Side bootlegger, maintained that Cermak promised him and Newberry police support for a gang war against the former Caponites.[7]

The bizarre sequence of events that followed Cermak's election supports Touhy's contention. There was an immediate upsurge in gang killings, nearly 100 in two years, and most of these were Nitti's men. On 19 December 1932, a special police party led by Cermak's personal bodyguards, Detective Sergeants Harry Lang and Harry Miller, broke into Nitti's office in the La Salle-Wacker building and arrested him. The Press were informed that this was part of Cermak's anti-crime drive and that Nitti had pulled a gun and tried to shoot it out. Headlines announced that Lang had been wounded but had also shot Nitti in the chest and neck. Lang received a $300 award for bravery, Nitti survived and was placed on trial on charges of assault with intent to kill Lang.[8]

Fragments of the true nature of the assignment came out at the trial to the embarrassment of Cermak's administration. Police Officer Chris Callahan, a member of the raiding party, testified that Nitti was unarmed and defenceless, and that Lang had shot him twice and then shot himself in the arm to make it look like self-defence. Lang's partner, Harry Miller, added that Mayor Cermak had given Lang the office address where they had found Nitti. The case against Nitti collapsed and Lang faced trial in September 1933 on the same assault charge. Before facing the court Lang threatened to 'blow the lid off Chicago's politics' and to tell enough to 'wreck the Democratic party', but at the trial itself he remained stubbornly uncommunicative. An arrangement had been made; Lang was found guilty but went free on appeal because Nitti conveniently failed to appear in the retrial.[9]

By this time a new administration ran City Hall because Cermak has been assassinated. On 15 February 1933, at a rally for President-elect Franklin Roosevelt in Miami, a spectator jumped out from the crowd, fired five shots and hit Cermak from close range. Cermak died three weeks later and within a week Giuseppe Zangara was sentenced to death for attempting to assassinate Roosevelt and hitting Cermak in the attempt. Ten days later Zangara was executed. There is little doubt that Zangara was a fanatic who intended to assassinate Roosevelt but it has been speculated that another gunman could have taken advantage of the panic produced by the shooting. Cermak himself expressed this belief on his deathbed. No conclusive evidence was ever uncovered.[10]

Chicago's potential for organized looting by its public servants is well illustrated by the career of Cermak's successor, Edward Kelly, and his political sponsor Patrick Nash, the powerful chairman of the Democratic party in Chicago. During the 1920s Kelly had been Chief Engineer for the Sanitary District and had awarded contracts worth over $12 million to firms owned by Nash and his relatives. In 1933 Kelly admitted an income of $724,000 between 1919 and 1929 although his salary totalled only $151,000 for the same period. To appease the Internal Revenue Kelly paid $150,000 in back taxes but declined to divulge the source of his income, Nash paid back a similar amount. Kelly had owed his Sanitary District position to Nash and both had thoroughly exploited this conflict of interest.[11]

Kelly was inaugurated Mayor in April 1933, pledging to support State's Attorney Thomas Courtney in 'driving out the hoodlums'. Courtney had promised to crush organized crime and crack down on kidnapping, in particular; kidnapping had become the most popular crime target since the abduction of the Lindbergh baby in March 1932. Kelly remained Mayor until 1947 and the first ten years of his tenure did coincide with a period of stability in organized crime operations unknown since before Prohibition. However, this period of stability was achieved by organizing corruption on a large scale and by enforcing the law on a very selective basis. After Cermak, William Johnson and William Skidmore maintained their position as key gambling bosses, but accommodation was also reached with former Caponites, notably Frank Nitti, Jake Guzik and Murray Humphries, who were not to be denied their slice of Chicago's organized crime pie. Accommodation and the exclusion of mavericks and undesirables became the new order, while Chicago's internecine gang warfare declined to such an extent that in 1942 there were only two gang-connected murders.

Roger Touhy, one of the supposed beneficiaries of Cermak's attempt to reorganize the city's organized crime, was removed as a threat to the new order by covert means, which strongly suggests collusion between the prosecuting authorities and favoured criminal interests. (The other supposed beneficiary of Cermak's reorganization, Ted Newberry, had been removed as a threat by more conventional means. He was shotgunned and left in a ditch in December 1932.) On the night of 30 June 1933, John 'Jake the Barber' Factor was allegedly kidnapped by Touhy and his men. Factor, an associate of Nitti, Guzik and Humphries, was at the time under threat of extradition to Britain, where he had swindled $7 million from stockholders and then fled to the United States. On 12 July, Factor was found by Police Officer Bernard Gerard and claimed that he had just been released after twelve days of 'unmerciful torture' in a filthy and bug-infested basement. He said that his kidnappers were Roger Touhy and his gang, and that he paid $70,000 ransom. Policeman Gerard later testified about Factor's appearance after his '12 days' in the 'bug-infested basement':

> Well, his tie was in place . . . and he was wearing a light linen suit, which was clean . . . his shoes were quite clean, no marks of dirt on them . . . His nails and hands were perfectly clean, cleaner than mine and I have just washed them . . . The cuffs of his shirt were pressed and clean. His collar was straight, in place and—well that is about all.[12]

Nevertheless, on Factor's word, Touhy was arrested and brought to trial in a blaze of publicity. According to journalist Milton Mayer, who covered the trial, all the tabloid newspapers began referring to Touhy as Roger 'The Terrible' Touhy, and Factor as John Factor, 'wealthy speculator', in spite of the fact that Touhy had no sobriquet before the affair and crime reporters had always written 'Jake the Barber' Factor until the trial.[13]

The city prosecutors were determined to convict Touhy at any cost. The British Consul in Chicago had insisted that the kidnapping was a hoax designed to prevent Factor's extradition and demanded that Factor be sent back to England to face his charges. To prevent this State's Attorney Courtney travelled to Washington and persuaded the federal authorities to withhold execution of the extradition warrant and then permit it to lapse. During the course of the trial Courtney's prosecutors, aided by a sympathetic judge, were able to paper over gaping holes in Factor's story with respect to identification, location and the existence of a plot involving Touhy. Finally, Courtney's Chief Investigator, Dan Gilbert, was later found to have forced two witnesses to perjure themselves.[14]

The trial was held while revulsion at the crime of kidnapping was sweeping the country in the wake of the Lindberg baby kidnapping. Touhy was therefore sentenced to ninety-nine years in prison despite all the inconsistencies in the case, despite the fact that nobody was hurt, and despite the fact that Touhy had never been convicted of a felony before.

Touhy was paroled twenty-six years later, fully exonerated by a federal court. The ruling read in part:

> The courx finds that John Factor was not kidnapped for ransom, or otherwise, on the night of 30 June 1933, though he was taken as a result of his own connivance . . . The court finds that Roger Touhy did not kidnap John Factor and, in fact, had no part in the alleged kidnapping of John Factor . . . The evidence discloses and the court finds that Factor, the State's Attorney Office and the Department of Justice, once the publicity and notoriety originally set in motion by Factor started to avalanche, worked and acted in concert to convict Touhy of something, regardless of his guilt or innocence.[15]

Touhy was released but still had enemies in Chicago. On 16 December 1959, three weeks after his release from Stateville prison, he was shot dead.

No doubts were raised about the Touhy conviction in 1933, when the Press hailed it as a triumph for State's Attorney Courtney. Mayor Kelly referred to it in the 1934 campaign and boasted that the 'underworld' had been driven from the city by the firm action of the administration: 'We have purged the city of gangsters, hoodlums and racketeers'.[16] The reality behind Kelly's empty campaign rhetoric was that Chicago's criminal justice and law enforcement systems had rarely been closer to favoured criminal interests and that Chicago's successful rackets could not have operated without the approval of the police and the prosecutors, in particular.

Gambling was Chicago's most lucrative racket during the 1930s and 1940s. In the 1943 election campaign Mayor Kelly reiterated the official fiction when he said, 'we have succeeded in stamping out organized gambling in Chicago', while at the same time there were over 100 bookmaking establishments surrounding City Hall itself. In all there were over 7,000 protected gambling operations in the city, mostly policy shops and bookmaking establishments.[17]

Policy was such an important source of graft that during the 1938 strike of policy runners, police guarded the policy shops to protect the customers from picket-line violence. Play on the policy wheels of the South Side amounted to millions of dollars every year, as around 60–70 per cent of the mainly black population of this densely populated area bet on the numbers. The placing of bets was handled by hundreds of low-paid runners or commission writers who at election time also served as campaign workers for the polticial machine. The policy racket was an immense source of patronage to the ward politicians as most positions were filled on their suggestion. It is therefore not surprising that when, in January 1942, twenty-six key figures in the policy business were indicted, policemen and other officials successfully thwarted the prosecution, and all went free. Usually fines for policy offences amounted to a few dollars which were routinely absorbed as business expenses.[18]

Gambling on Chicago's scale could not exist without official sanction. The whole law enforcement machinery was geared to provide a healthy climate for a flourishing gambling industry. Virgil Peterson of the Chicago Crime Commission linked ward committeemen, judges and policemen in a conspiracy to deceive the public:

> Many of the arrests in gambling cases were the products of phony raids. It was all a big game to fool the public and protect the gamblers. The testimony of police officers in court usually made it easy for judges to dismiss the cases on the grounds that the evidence was illegally obtained and therefore inadmissible in court.[19]

Around 70 per cent of the cases were dismissed without a trial. Day after day the same police testified about the raids and the same small clique of lawyers made the motion to suppress. The routine became monotonous.

Throughout the 1930s William Skidmore remained the major political coordinator of the city's gambling. With his partner, William Johnson, he operated the largest and most lavish casinos in the city, and most of the city's gamblers still attended his junkyard each week to grease the machine. A former investigator for the State's Attorney office acted as Skidmore's master of ceremonies. He would call out, 'You're next'. The gambler indicated would then enter Skidmore's office, report the location of his operations, pay the necessary protection money and then depart—assured of continued immunity from police interference.

In 1939 Skidmore was indicted and convicted of tax evasion, but while out on bail continued to show that he had the right connections. In August 1941 Police Chief Laird of Cook County began a 'crusade' against illegal handbook operations within the city limits. The hypocrisy of this was soon revealed when, on the night of 21 August, a *Chicago Tribune* reporter found Chief Laird and Skidmore dining together in the fashionable Drake Hotel. A picture was taken before Laird beat a hasty retreat through the kitchen and was featured in the following morning's paper. Laird's resignation was promptly accepted. On 20 March 1942, Skidmore began serving his sentence and was still in prison when he died of heart failure in February 1944.

William Johnson was also indicted in 1939 but stayed out of prison until 1946 while his case was repeatedly appealed. Johnson had taken the precaution of making liberal donations to churches and charitable organizations, and numerous local dignitaries were prepared to extol his virtues to the court. Johnson served a short stretch in jail, and then moved out to Florida where he bought a number of race tracks.

Until federal prosecution broke up the Johnson–Skidmore combination the control of gambling in Chicago had been relatively centralized and stable. However, from 1943, an upsurge in gambling-related killings indicated that this stability had broken down. Dozens died in the space of a few months, including Ben Zukerman, a precinct captain and gambling boss on the West Side, Estelle Carey, a dice-game operator, and Paul Kare, the gambling boss of the Greek community. Bombs were also thrown by warring gambling factions, competing to fill the vacuum created by the breakdown of the old order.[20] After some problems of their own, former associates of Al Capone, became the dominating influence.

These temporary problems were also caused by federal prosecution. On 31 December 1943, Louis Campagna, Paul DeLucia, Francis Mariote, Ralph Pierce, Charles Pierce, Charles Gioe, John Rosselli and Louis Kaufman were convicted of conspiracy to extort more than $1 million from the Hollywood film studios. Frank Nitti had been indicted on the same charges but had committed suicide. The other Caponites were sentenced to ten years' imprisonment and fines of $20,000 each. They were released on parole twenty months later in circumstances suggesting a federal fix.[21]

In the meantime their associate, Jake Guzik, was continuing to extend the influence of the Chicago syndicate. By the 1940s this group had a monopoly on the distribution of racing information in the Chicago area, an interest in numerous policy operations, and several flourishing casinos, particularly in the downtown business district.

During these years also, gangsters such as those already mentioned and Joey Glimco, Angelo Incise and Murray Humphries had taken over numerous local unions with the tacit approval and sometimes active assistance of the local authorities, represented by persons in key positions such as State's Attorney Thomas Courtney and his Chief Investigator, Dan Gilbert. Many city businesses secured labour peace by using both gangster and police muscle and intimidation. Employers paid off handsomely in return for low wage settlements, and the union funds, which were not protected by local, state or federal legislation, were freely looted. The workers belonging to gangster-dominated unions had to settle for less money and poor conditions, and there was not much future for those who complained about it.[22]

Courtney remained Chicago's chief prosecutor until 1942 and during that time tried to advance politically like his contemporary 'crime-buster' in New York, Thomas E. Dewey. Before the 1939 elections for the Democratic mayoralty nomination, for example, Courtney suddenly began an aggressive campaign against gambling. His chief aide, Dan Gilbert, directed squads of police, armed with axes, to smash up bookmaking premises and arrest customers and attendants. About 600 raids resulted in 12,000 arrests. No convictions were obtained since the raids were without warrants and therefore illegal. Courtney put the blame for the gambling situation squarely on his opponent, Mayor Kelly: 'The fact that Kelly permits a hoodlum syndicate to control gambling in itself establishes that he is part and parcel of it. The fix is in at the top'. The voters, however, decided that 'Fighting Tom' was an opportunist; some probably thought that he was as much part and parcel of the syndicate as Kelly. The Mayor was once again chosen to fight the Democratic ticket. After 1942 Courtney settled for the less taxing role of state judge.[23]

Chief Inspector Gilbert held his position between 1932 and 1950 and prospered as a middleman in Chicago's political–criminal network. His official duty was to gather evidence for criminal prosecutions of felonies, but his actual role was described more accurately by crime writer Ovid Demaris:

He worked as a labour organizer for the syndicate in a score of unions; he kept his eye on the gambling and handbook joints. He was a wheelhorse for the Democratic party—when Courtney was elevated to the bench he raised $30,000 from among the hoodlum element for the campaign of William Touhy. He visited the Criminal Courts Building almost daily, where he wandered in and out of courtrooms and chambers, conferred with runners, fixers who worked directly with judges, and bondsmen, spending considerable time in Felony Branch, where tens of thousands of felonies are reduced to misdemeanours each year. He was interested in vending machines, jukeboxes, slot machines and a variety of vices including prostitution.[24]

In 1950 Gilbert testified before the Kefauver Committee and admitted that his net worth was about $360,000 and that dividends on stocks and bonds he currently held were bringing him in about $42,000 a year. He told the committee that he was a lucky gambler and that this explained his wealth. When asked if it would not be natural for the public to lose confidence in a police officer who amassed such great wealth, Gilbert replied earnestly: 'The failure of human nature is that we are prone to believe evil about our fellow man, and especially about a peace officer.' During the hearings the newspapers finally got hold of the Gilbert story and dubbed him 'the world's richest cop' after Gilbert had been playing a crucial role in organized crime operations for eighteen years. Just after the hearing Gilbert stood as the Democratic candidate for Sheriff of Cook County with the campaign slogan of 'I put Roger Touhy in prison'. Because of the bad publicity he lost and retired from Chicago politics to move to California.[25]

The great wealth of Gilbert and several other key police officers, and the relative stability of organized crime operations during most of these years can only be explained in terms of endemic corruption. The conclusion is inescapable that the agency most responsible for law enforcement in Chicago, the State's Attorney office, controlled and protected organized crime. Gilbert and Courtney were simply parts of an intricate system of selective law enforcement on which organized crime depends. The convictions of Roger Touhy and other lesser criminals had nothing to do with impartial justice and everything to do with control and providing the public with scapegoats.

The price for protection was so great that gambling in Chicago, as in other cities, could be described as much as police business as gangster business. Gambling remained a popular pastime in the city and few people really cared if the laws were ignored. Attempts to legalize gambling in the city were vetoed by successive governors during the 1940s and millions of dollars of potential revenue went instead to those in a position to circumvent the laws. Police, prosecutors and judges were consistently more responsive to the laws of political expediency and pressure, plus the attractions of graft, than to the official laws against gambling. The public were content with corruption.

In both New York and Chicago corrupt alliances between politicians, police, businessmen, union officials and criminals controlled vice, gambling and labour racketeering. These alliances adapted to changing times and conditions but the profitable demand for illegal goods and services was always met. In Los Angeles, the city examined in the next section, an attempt was made to emulate the New York example, and the political sponsors of this effort were applauded as crime crusaders in the Dewey/La Guardia mould. A closer examination of this effort, however, reveals that this too was only superficially successful. As in New York, hypocritical manipulation of people's fears and prejudices to advance political interests outweighed sincerity and honesty.

7   Los Angeles: city of fallen angels

The population of Los Angeles in 1900 was 102,479. By 1930 it exceeded a million and was still increasing at a phenomenal rate. The initial expansion was based on the migration of small-town Midwesterners and did not, at first, threaten the dominant Protestant morality of the city; Los Angeles, for example, was the only major city outside the South to vote for Prohibition. In the dominant value system gambling, prostitution and the drinking of alcohol were all anathema because they tended to conflict with such sanctioned values as hard work, self-denial and the accumulation of money. However, although legal sanctions against vice were taken seriously by campaigning politicians, the vice laws were no better enforced in Los Angeles than in other cities. There was always a sizeable minority who did not share the official morality and this section is chiefly about attempts to impose it on them.[1]

The local newspapers boasted about the city's virtue and proclaimed it the 'white spot of America', free of the crime and civic corruption rampant in other cities. In reality gambling and prostitution were openly available in the business district of the city and in segregated districts around Los Angeles County while, during Prohibition, alcohol was plentiful and cheap. Numerous conflicting and overlapping law enforcement jurisdictions made the laws impossible to enforce consistently in such a sprawling city. The forbidden services were provided by white, native-American syndicates, working closely with police and politicians. The police control was such that one former bootlegger declared that for years he had brought liquor into Los Angeles, paid a dozen or so police officers about $100,000 a year for protection, and was finally forced out of business because the officers demanded more than he could afford.[2]

In 1929 the city's moral crusaders won an apparent victory at the polls when Frank Porter was elected Mayor, but the new 'reform' administration did not seriously interrupt bootlegging, gambling and prostitution. There were an estimated 1,700 gambling and prostitution 'joints' operating in the city and Porter's administration came in for increasing criticism, especially after it was revealed that ordinary vice-squad detectives had assets of over $100,000. The vice squad reacted to the criticism by increasing its activity against petty acts of gambling, ludicrously creeping up to windows to spy on people's living rooms and catch out any wagering in card games. The squad confiscated sums of cash which rarely exceeded $10 while protected illegal gambling casinos were pulling in a lucrative trade.[3]

Porter's discredited administration was defeated at the polls by Frank Shaw in 1933. As Mayor, Shaw soon made powerful enemies, who seized on the continuance of protected vice and made it the issue that, in 1938, brought about his downfall. Shaw had antagonized elements of the business community, first of all by being pro-labour and supporting the New Deal policies of Franklin Roosevelt, and secondly by the elimination of all private utility companies from within the city limits. Public ownership and federal interference in local affairs, even in the form of assistance for the unemployed, were bitterly opposed by those who had prospered in the pre-Roosevelt days of unfettered capitalism.[4] Shaw was also opposed by the city's moral crusaders who launched a recall campaign against him in his first year of office on the false charge that the new Mayor was responsible for 'more vice, more crime, more debauchery, more graft in this city than there ever was before in its history'.[5] The Reverend Roy Smith, president of the Anti-Saloon League, was particularly incensed by Shaw's refusal to close down the beer parlours which the repeal of Prohibition had allowed in 1934. Smith's objection was quoted in the *Los Angeles Times*:

in those sink holes of vice, Mexicans, Negroes and white men and women drink and dance together with scores of children watching at the door.[6]

Shaw had no racist objections to beer parlours and, in fact, wanted to keep the support of both the Mexican and black communities. He therefore ignored the objections of the morality lobby and got on with the task of governing the city.

The 1934 recall campaign was unethically supported by Fletcher Bowron, the judge responsible for impanelling grand juries. Bowron had ordered the 1934 grand jury to delve into Shaw's finances, hoping to discover evidence of a rumoured campaign contribution by a prominent casino operator, Guy McAfee. The contribution, even if proved, would not have been illegal, but the linking of Shaw's name with McAfee's was politically damaging. McAfee was, at the time, melodramatically described in the newspapers as Los Angeles' answer to Al Capone. Bowron's political use of the grand jury was thwarted by the State Supreme Court, which ruled that Bowron's methods of jury selection was unconstitutional because he used his own views on such matters as Prohibition and communism as criteria.[7]

During the following years Bowron continued to select jurymen with views similar to his own and in 1937 succeeded in getting restaurateur Clifford Clinton on to the grand jury. Clinton proved to be a flamboyant showman with a flair for the dramatic, bringing political expediency and moral crusading closer together. He was also anti-union, forcing his workers to sign 'yellow dog' contracts (private agreements between the worker and the company which prevented the formation of unions) before these were outlawed by the Norris-La Guardia Act of 1931.[8] Clinton and Bowron were the key figures in the loose alliance between business interests and moral crusaders which brought about the downfall of Mayor Shaw.

Clinton first attracted attention to himself in June 1937 with the announcement that he personally had discovered '1,800 bookies, 600 houses of prostitution, and 200 gambling houses' operating within the city limits. At the same time he helped to set up the Citizens Independent Vice Investigating Committee (CIVIC), a committee of fourteen businessmen and religious leaders claiming to represent 500 organizations in Southern California, and demanded that Shaw grant them vigilante authority to drive the underworld out of town. Shaw refused with good reason. The state had legalized teletype bookmaking in 1935 and the courts condoned other forms of gambling unless they were specifically outlawed. Prostitution was a simple misdemeanour and, like gambling, did not warrant vigilante action.[9]

The hypocrisy of Los Angeles in the 1930s was used to the advantage of an organization called the California Republicans Inc. (CRI). The operators of gambling enterprises and brothels went in constant fear of exposure by moral crusaders and 'reform racketeers' could extort money regardless of protection bought elsewhere. The CRI were particularly successful in this racket because they used the winning combination of 'muscle', organization and a highly respectable 'front'. The front was Evangelist Rheba Crawford, whose popular radio programme was used to berate the city government and those 'merchants of sin' who refused to enrich the CRI, mainly slot-machine and pinball operators, and liquor law violators.[10]

Clinton failed to impress a majority on the 1937 grand jury with his charges, and the jury was dissolved without serving any indictments. However, with three others he insisted on filing a minority report which he later had printed and distributed. The report named twenty-seven local gang leaders and charged that vice was centrally controlled by the Democratic administration of Mayor Shaw.[11]

The majority on the grand jury did not accept this account of organized crime in the city for two main reasons. Firstly, Clinton neglected to find evidence to support his assertions; his leading witness, for example, was found to be a 'constitutional psychopath'. Secondly, Clinton's report was plainly politically motivated. The official Final Report of the grand jury described Clinton's investigation as nothing more than 'malicious, unbridled, reputation-smearing gossip', and declared these tactics 'Public Enemy Number One'. Clinton's financial resources, however, secured a much wider circulation for his own document.[12]

The purpose of all CIVIC investigations into vice operations was to discredit the Shaw administration. After Shaw was re-elected in 1937, CIVIC's objective was to secure enough signatures on recall petitions to force another election and the weapons it used were protest meetings, radio talks, handbills and pamphlets. Clinton kept himself constantly in the public eye and received a great deal of favourable publicity when both his house and restaurants were bombed. Investigating police declared that the bombings were 'advertizing stunts' by Clinton himself and later revelations about the man make this a distinct possibility.[13]

At the end of 1937 the business community and the city's moral crusaders moved closer together in the movement to oust Shaw. Clergymen throughout Los Angeles joined the open-shop campaign initiated by the Chamber of Commerce to break the power of the city's labour movement. On 29 December 1937, the City Council yielded to pressure and passed a stringent anti-picketing ordinance. A few days later the pro-labour Shaw vetoed the ordinance and became even more the man to get rid of.[14]

On 14 January 1938 another bombing incident occurred which ultimately caused the downfall of Mayor Shaw. One of Clinton's investigators, Harry Raymond, had been loudly proclaiming that he was going to 'blow the lid off this mess of corruption'. Instead he pressed the starter on his car and set off a bomb attached to one of the spark plugs. He survived after it was announced that 122 slugs had been dug out of his body.[15]

After Clinton charged that a police 'spy squad' had been shadowing Raymond for several weeks prior to the bombing, Police Captain Earle Kinette and two other members of the squad, which was officially the Intelligence Unit, was arrested and charged with attempted murder and conspiracy. During the trial District Attorney Buron Fitts, who had been actively campaigning against the Shaw administration for several months, made the unsubstantiated charge that Joseph Shaw, the Mayor's brother, had ordered Kinette's unit to intimidate the Mayor's political enemies. This and other charges gained a great deal of credibility when Kinette was convicted in June 1938.[16]

Meanwhile a recall campaign launched by Clinton at the beginning of the year gained momentum as the trial proceeded. By June the public had signed enough petitions to put the recall on a September ballot already called on another anti-picketing proposal. The Chamber of Commerce had secured this in the immediate aftermath of the Raymond bombing on the pretext that the bombing was in some way related to labour violence.[17]

The Republican party chose Judge Fletcher Bowron to face Shaw in the recall election, and Bowron's candidacy was endorsed by most newspapers, business and church organizations. The election was dirty on both sides. The opposing sides denounced each other as Communists, fascists, radicals, 'blue-nosed busybodies', political racketeers, union busters and machine politicians. Some ludicrous tactics were employed. For example, in black neighbourhoods canvassers identified themselves as Ku Klux Klansmen and solicited votes for their political opponents. Clinton led Bowron's campaign and made a series of effective radio broadcasts on Station KEHF. Daily the Clinton programme, 'The People's Voice', painted Los Angeles as a hotbed of vice and iniquity. Shrieks, screams and a simulation of the Raymond bombing were followed by malicious tales of the Shaw administration, many of which were completely fabricated. Joe Shaw was accused of smuggling $500,000 in vice profits to Mexico, and 'Eastside Orientals' were said to be planning to assassinate Bowron.[18]

The candidates themselves were more restrained. Bowron concentrated on his own honesty and decency, while Shaw complained of the 'hubbub of prejudice, presumption, gossip, vilification and judging without evidence that goes under the name of civic reform'. In the face of all the publicized dirt, however, Shaw's campaign slogan, 'The Sun Still Shines in Los Angeles', must have appeared unconvincing. The gossip and vilification of Shaw, spread with almost $100,000 of Clinton's money, won the day; Bowron triumphed by a margin of 232,427 to 122,692, and a similar margin passed the anti-picketing ordinance. Shocked middle-class suburban voters had been the bedrock of Bowron's support and Shaw became the first mayor of a major American city to be successfully recalled.[19]

The successful reformers have largely written the political history of Los Angeles and they portray the CIVIC campaign against Shaw and the 1938 election as an unambiguous triumph of Good versus Evil. The careers of Clinton and Bowron are usually described in totally uncritical and eulogistic terms. The 1934 grand jury was 'honest' and 'independent', even though Bowron had misused his position to pack it with his political fellow travellers. Clinton was described by a national magazine as a 'racket-buster' in the Dewey mould even though, far from upholding the law, he illegally tapped telephones and conspired with criminal elements to advance his political cause. His investigators included Baron Lawson, who was later charged with handling protection in the black district, and James Utley, a pimp, extortionist and narcotics peddler who became one of the city's leading racketeers. In 1942 the *Los Angeles Times* revealed that Utley had contributed $3,800 to one of Clinton's later campaigns. The most interesting historical distortion, however, is that of the character of Harry Raymond, the victim of the bomb blast, who had been Clinton's chief investigator and adviser. Raymond is usually briefly described as a 'private investigator' and 'former peace officer', although he was much more than that. He had been fired as Police Chief of both Venice and San Diego for extortion, and had been involved in the police-protected vice scandals of a previous Los Angeles administration. It seems probable, therefore, that Raymond was acting more out of self-interest than in the cause of Good Government in aiding Clinton's efforts to overthrow Shaw's administration.[20]

Immediately after the 1938 election the city tried and convicted Joe Shaw, the Mayor's brother, of civil service fraud. In November and December 1939 a series of articles in *Liberty* magazine cited this conviction as further proof of the justice of the recall of Mayor Shaw. The articles heaped praise on Bowron and Clinton, and castigated the Shaw administration as the most corrupt in history. Further court action, however, exonerated the Shaw family. In 1941 the State Supreme Court overturned Joe Shaw's conviction and implied that the reformers' chief witness was the guilty party, and the following year

Frank Shaw sued *Liberty* for libel and settled out of court for an estimated $50,000 and a public apology—both rarities in American journalistic history. *Liberty* agreed to this settlement after Clinton, who was the chief source of the articles, left the city during the trial to join the army as a 42-year-old private.[21]

In 1938, however, the public had been convinced of Shaw's corruption without any evidence and had effectively finished his political career. Bowron remained Mayor until 1953 and, as we shall see, railed ineffectively against vice, organized crime and police corruption throughout his long tenure. If the criterion for the recall of American mayors was the amount of corruption uncovered in Shaw's administration, recalled mayors would have been the rule rather than the exception. On this criterion the citizens of Los Angeles should have recalled most of Shaw's predecessors and his successor, Bowron himself. The difference was that Clinton and Bowron had orchestrated a dirty campaign which united moral crusaders with the business community. Despite every effort Shaw had not been found to be personally corrupt, nor was his administration riddled with corruption to the extent claimed by the reformers. He was merely the loser in a bitter political struggle and just one of many scapegoats in the country's perennial struggle to enforce the vice laws.

Clifford Clinton's final successful campaign was the defeat of District Attorney Buron Fitts in the 1940 election, and Clinton again used his radio programme on station KEHF to devastating effect. Four times daily during the campaign thinly disguised episodes from Fitts's life were broadcast which portrayed the District Attorney as a drunken philanderer and shattered his public image as a conservative, moralistic prohibitionist. Fitts was also accused of using his office to prosecute his political enemies and protect Hollywood personalities such as Howard Hughes. Hughes had been involved in a fatal traffic accident but had not had to face trial; during the campaign it was damagingly revealed that Hughes had given Fitts the lavish present of several horses. The key issue, however, as in 1938, was the inability to control vice, and Clinton's candidate, John Dockweiler, won the November election by the substantial margin of 262,000 votes.[22]

During his four years as District Attorney Dockweiler made no genuine attempt to combat vice in Los Angeles County; the only important development was that Bugsy Siegel, the New York gangster, tried to batter his way into control of local bookmaking. It was later revealed that Siegel had contributed $30,000 to Dockweiler's campaign, which helps to explain the District Attorney's leniency when he took over a case in which Siegel and an associate, Frank Carbo, were charged with the murder of a Brooklyn gangster, Harry Greenberg. Dockweiler delayed the case time and again and explained that he wanted to save the taxpayers the cost of an expensive trial. The case against Siegel was finally dropped after the leading witness for the prosecution, Abe Reles, fell or was pushed out of the sixth-floor window of a Coney Island hotel.[23]

During the anti-Shaw campaign Clinton had alternated charges that vice in Los Angeles was centrally controlled by 'politico-racketeers' with warnings that 'Eastern Gangsters' were about to invade the city. The experience of the most famous of these intruders, Bugsy Siegel, indicates, firstly, that the reformers did not actively oppose this invasion and, secondly, that vice in Los Angeles could not be centrally controlled in the way Clinton had charged. Siegel had arrived in Los Angeles in 1937 intending to organize the numbers racket and bookmaking but had gone broke in the process, constantly frustrated by too many law enforcement agencies overlapping each other in Los Angeles City and County. The city police, the sheriff's deputies in the county, and various district attorneys' offices, all had to be taken care of. Over all of these were the State's Attorney-General officers who could move and demand tribute anywhere in the state of California. By the 1940s Siegel was reduced to borrowing large sums of money from his Hollywood film-star friends, who were foolish enough to lend it to him but not foolish enough to ask for it back.[24] Vice protection by police and politicians had existed under Shaw as it had since the laws which defined vice were enacted in Los Angeles, but Clinton's alleged centralized organization was impossible in the city's particularly decentralized government. Frank Shaw was an easy scapegoat for much more dispersed and complex criminal networks.

Mayor Bowron actively pursued an anti-vice crusade in the early years of his administration. Slot and pinball machines were banished from the city, and prostitutes and bookmakers harassed more than usual. The city's new police board sometimes let their zeal and prudery go to extremes. A Health Department film about venereal disease was refused a showing and there was pressure to deny entry to nightclubs and bars to unescorted women, and women wearing slacks. The police were also directed to be suspicious of anyone wearing sneakers at night. In 1941 an opponent in the mayoralty campaign accused Bowron of over-reacting against vice, and using police raids on beer parlours and 'penny-ante' poker games to gain publicity.[25] The Mayor, however, had little difficulty with such criticism. A majority of voters accepted his claim that the administration 'had broken the most powerful ring that ever had an American city in its grip'.[26]

Bowron even joined other officials in a crusade against gambling at sea. Gambling ship operators had established floating casinos a few miles off the Los Angeles coast. Advertisements appeared in the city newspapers, on radio and even by sky-writing, encouraging people to enjoy 'All the thrills of Biarritz, Monte Carlo and Cannes' and 'Action as you like it'. The ships were anchored three miles out at sea, just far enough, in theory, to be safe from local and state anti-gambling laws. The most luxurious of the ships was the *Rex*, opened by former rumrunner Tony Cornero in 1938, and equipped with 300 slot machines, a bingo parlour that would seat 500 people, six roulette wheels, eight dice tables and a Chinese lottery. In one week 30,000 eager citizens took advantage of the opportunity to gamble openly, lining up for blocks to get ferried out to the *Rex* by water taxi. Bowron's own campaign against the ships was ineffectual but he travelled up to the state capital of Sacramento and persuaded the State Attorney-General, Earl Warren, to take steps to eliminate the moral menace. Warren's tactic was to serve the ships with nuisance abatement orders. The ships, the orders read, 'induced people to lead idle and dissolute lives . . .'. When the ship owners ignored the orders, Warren ordered raids. The *Texas*, the *Showboat* and the *Tango* were seized on the afternoon of 2 August 1939. Slots and tables were ripped out, some to be illegally dumped at sea. The *Rex*'s crew, however, fought off Warren's men with fire hoses and baseball bats. Cornero remained on board, surrounded by a flotilla of state vessels, and shouted his defiance to reporters, 'If I go off, it'll be in a box'. He gave up after nine days on the pretext that he needed a haircut, 'and the only thing I haven't got on board is a barber'. He carried on fighting his case through the courts but without luck. And, just to make sure, Californian authorities pressured Congress in 1948 to pass a law that prohibited gambling in US coastal waters. If Angelenos insisted on gambling they now had to travel further to do it legally.[27]

Bowron's period of intense vice crusading did succeed in making gambling less accessible in Los Angeles. It became more secretive and dependent on regular custom built up over the years.

Some gambling operators moved across city lines into more amenable county territory, and others, such as Guy McAfee, Tudor Scherer and notably Bugsy Siegel, decided to go legitimate and buy casinos in Las Vegas, Nevada, an easy drive from Los Angeles.

In 1931 the mainly desert state of Nevada decided to legalize gambling and prostitution. Development was at first slow. The early casinos were slow to shed the trappings of illegality—shadowy, smoky rooms reached through discreet entranceways. Las Vegas remained for over a decade little more than it had been before legalization, a stopping-off place where travellers could drink, gamble and visit prostitutes before setting off. However, because it was close to Los Angeles, Las Vagas took off during the 1940s to become the more successful of several Nevadan 'sin cities'.

Bugsy Siegel was one of the first to see the potential profitability of a haven of legalized gambling in an affluent but constrained America. When he visited Las Vegas he saw beyond the low-key gambling houses of his competitors and began the transformation of the city into the 'Entertainment Capital of the World', with the dazzle to attract not only the 'high rollers' on card, dice and roulette games but the millions of low-stake players on which American casino gambling depends. Siegel put all the money he could raise into building the lavish Flamingo Hotel, the first of many massive luxury hotels which made the reputation of the Las Vagas Strip. Siegel succeeded in building the hotel during wartime by paying extortionate black-market prices. The Flamingo opened on 26 December 1946 with a guest list of Hollywood film stars and an entertainment bill headed by Jimmy Durante.

The following June, Siegel's entrepreneurial innovation ended when he was shot dead in the wealthy Los Angeles suburb of Beverly Hills, thus becoming another unsolved gang murder statistic.[28]

After an uncertain beginning the Flamingo turned a handsome profit. In the following decade professional criminals from Cleveland, Chicago, Minneapolis and the East Coast poured money into additional luxury casinos and profited from the loose state control of the gambling industry during the 1950s. The new out-of-state owners and operators had naturally come from the big city crime networks because these were the people who knew the business of gambling. Unfortunately for the tax man, many also soon learnt the business of 'skimming'. Only those who count up the money in casinos can know how much has been taken in and they can be persuaded or ordered to divert substantial amounts before the final total is arrived at. Only honest and diligent state regulation can minimize this practice, and this has come slowly to Nevadan authorities.

Post-war affluence enabled millions of Americans every year to travel to Las Vegas for the opportunity to gamble senselessly in all-night sessions encouraged by cheap or free liquor provided by enterprising hotel managements. The situation therefore encouraged Nevadan gambling interests to back politicians such as Bowron, who were pledged to try and enforce the prohibition of gambling in the big cities.

Despite Mayor Bowron's efforts and the departure of some criminal interests, there was still a tremendous demand for vice in Los Angeles, and this demand increased during the disruption and prosperity which accompanied the Second World War. As well as being the centre of the nation's film industry, Los Angeles was a major port and a centre of the expanding aircraft and defence industries. The city was therefore overflowing with military personnel and contract workers and off-duty priorities were liquor, gambling and women. Although Bowron had purged the police force of some of the more notoriously corrupt officers, adjustments were made behind the scenes and new groups collected the protection money.

Bowron was re-elected in 1941, 1945 and 1949, exploiting his reputation for honesty and the apathy of the electorate; for example, it took just 16 per cent of the registered voters to return him in 1945.[29] The breaking of inhibitions during wartime and the burgeoning post-war Californian economy made Los Angeles a particularly fruitful place to engage in criminal enterprise, while Bowron's only response to organized crime was to issue warnings about an imminent invasion by 'Eastern Gangsters'. In 1948 and 1949, however, a series of scandals came into prominence, embarrassed Bowron's city administration as well as state and county authorities, and showed that electing a reform mayor was no answer to organized crime.

The first scandal to break concerned an attempt by former Los Angeles policemen, working for State Attorney-General Fred Howser, to organize the state for protected gambling. The estimated 'licence fee' for punchboards alone was $500,000 monthly. The pay-off schedule allotted 25 per cent to the collector, 25 per cent to local law enforcement personnel, and 50 per cent to headquarters at the Biltmore Hotel in Los Angeles. The California Crime Commission exposed the operation, but only Wiley Cadell, an ex-Los Angeles vice-squad detective, was tried and convicted. Howser was heavily implicated but managed to escape prosecution. His term as State Attorney-General had not been noted for activity that damaged certain vice interests. The investigators he sent to incidents reported to him were frequently those whose names had been mentioned as being personally involved, and when cases were brought to trial the full power and authority of the Attorney-General's office was regularly and openly devoted to the defence. Howser also refused to block the use of Western Union facilities by the bookmakers' racing wire service. (See pp. 115–116 for a fuller explanation of the racing-news wire service in the United States.) The crime commission did succeed in discrediting Howser and he was returned to private practice in the 1950 state elections.[30]

The next major scandal revealed the selective law enforcement of Los Angeles County. The Sheriff and the District Attorney shared responsibility for vice law enforcement in the county districts, and both maintained vice squads ostensibly for this purpose. Both squads actually existed to extort money from criminal enterprises. The fact that vice was restricted to small zones kept voters happy in outlying areas and they rarely failed to return incumbent officials. Early in 1949, however, a raid by city vice-squad detective James Fisk on a large bookmaker's at 1747 East Florence Avenue, county territory, upset the established protective arrangements.[31]

Fisk's raid uncovered the fact that the company using these premises, the Guarantee Finance Corporation (GFC), financed the operations of more than 160 bookmakers. The Sheriff's vice squad knew of the operation but declined to take any action and demanded an end to city police activities in the county's jurisdiction. The Californian Crime Commission then became involved in the case and revealed that the GFC did $7 million annual business in gambling, and paid as much as $450,000 of that in protection to state and county officials. The Crime Commission criticized Sheriff Eugene Biscailuz and vice-squad commander Captain Carl Pearson for their reluctance to prosecute the case. As in the first scandal only one conviction resulted. Captain Al Guasti, also from the vice squad, was sentenced to two years' imprisonment for perjury, after denying in court the existence of a letter from the telephone company which had informed on GFC's operations. The Crime Commission also revealed how easy it was for high-ranking police officers to make large profits on small investments. Guasti, for example, had purchased a liquor licence for $525 and straightaway sold it for $12,000.[32]

In the wake of this scandal the Crime Commission revealed a memo written by Captain Pearson to a sergeant in charge of a raiding party. Pearson directed him to:

Make your raids specifically at 10 o'clock. At that time the gambling tables will be covered. Observe the girl show and then leave. During that time, there will be no gambling conducted so your officers will not be embarrassed.[33]

Arrest statistics had, however, to be compiled and the Crime Commission also showed how this obstacle to gambling was removed. Policemen arriving at the jails with arrested bookmakers were met by lawyers with completed writs of habeas corpus. These 'quickie writs', the Crime Commission's report explained, were supplied by 'a small coterie of lawyers, bailbonders, and judges'. Judge William McKay, for example, had once issued three writs within thirty minutes, while experienced judges suggested that it should take at least two hours to obtain one writ.[34]

Sergeant Fisk's raid on the GFC and the revelations of the Crime Commission had struck a fine opening note for Fletcher Bowron's 1949 re-election campaign. They gave the impression of the city administration's honesty and incorruptibility in contrast to the county's chicanery and corruption. Bowron campaigned 'on the record' and asserted that he had protected the city from 'Eastern gangsters'. In one speech he claimed:

We have met the onslaught of gangsterism. It was planned in New York and Chicago and westward to take over this city . . . We have saved a decent police force and a fine civil service.[35]

Bowron was thus presenting himself as a bulwark against an invasion by an unspecified, mysterious conspiracy which was alien to Los Angeles, a very convenient scapegoat for the shortcomings of his own administration.

The newspapers supported the Mayor and the *Daily News*, in particular, urged its readers to defeat the 'gambling ring' and vote for the 'honest government' of Bowron. The day after the election, in which Bowron duly triumphed in another low poll, the *Daily News* broke a story about another scandal, this time in Bowron's city police force. The newspaper had known of corruption in the police force for over a year but had not printed anything that might have embarrassed the Mayor before the election. Mainly as a result of the *News's* revelations, which concerned the protection of a call girl and brothel operation by Sergeant E.V. Jackson of the city's vice squad, the grand jury was obliged to begin an investigation of vice and corruption. The jury had also been aware of police corruption before the election.[36]

The jury revealed that the rise of a street-walker called Brenda Allen to become the coordinator of hundreds of other prostitutes needed only the permission of the vice squad. This gave the newspapers an abundance of spicy stories but only concerned a relatively minor source of graft. The jury did little probing into bookmaking where the major source of corruption lay and its investigations only led to the resignations, suspensions, demotions, and indictments without convictions which were customary in the wake of police scandals. The local Press were reluctant to dig too deep into the city's affairs and criticize Bowron's administration since, in 1946, they had been exempted from a tax on all commercial and professional transactions and probably feared a change in their status.

More, however, was revealed by two nationally known journalists, Carey

McWilliams and Florabel Muir. First Muir accused George Bowman, head of the city's gangster squad, of shaking down Mickey Cohen, one of Bugsy Siegel's former henchmen. She wrote that Cohen had paid $30,000 to Bowman and his squad for the recovery of transcripts of recordings that the squad had made in his home. Cohen had battered and bribed his way to a position of dominance in the gambling world of Los Angeles, collecting enormous tribute from hundreds of individual bookies, as well as the large horse parlours and gambling houses. On 20 July 1949, soon after the shakedown, Cohen survived a spectacular attempt on his life; as his party left a restaurant in the early hours a volley of gunfire was fired off from the other side of the street. One of his close associates was killed and Cohen and several others were wounded, including one bodyguard provided by State Attorney-General Fred Howser for undisclosed reasons.[37]

Carey McWilliams charged in the *Nation* that there had been an 'almost complete fix' of law enforcement agencies and newspapers, which blocked efforts to clear up the mess and, in particular, to examine Cohen's relationship with the police. 'Fix' in this case was not simply synonymous with bribery but with a network of alliances and commitments and obligations, 'all mutually reinforcing, of such a nature as to work an almost complete paralysis of law enforcement'.

The underlying cause of the mess was hypocritical state gambling legislation. The only legal way to bet on the result of a horse race in California was through the *pari mutel* machines at the licensed tracks. As in New York, corrupt state officials had a financial stake in the tracks and thus worked to preserve their betting monopoly. Any drives either to close down the tracks or legalize off-track bookmaking were easily neutralized. Without Santa Anita and the other licensed tracks, McWilliams argued:

> the wire services would not be interested in California; without the wire services there could be no domination of bookmaking by gangsters; as long as there are people too poor or two busy to go to the tracks, there will be bookies, for the bookies democratize gambling. Therefore everyone is 'fixed' for everyone is morally implicated in the situation which creates Mickey Cohens and corrupts police departments and does strange things to the press.[38]

Bowron's reaction to the police scandals was to complain that he had no way of knowing what went on in the city, which was probably accurate but a far cry from the campaign image he had fostered as a bulwark against vice, corruption and Eastern gangsterism. Although his administration was tarnished in the eyes of the voters, he survived a hasty and poorly financed recall campaign in November 1950, which he characteristically charged was the work of Chicago gangsters. Bowron finally met defeat in 1953, in an election fought on an unrelated public-housing issue.

Mayor Bowron's simple approach to vice and organized crime was based entirely on hoping for better law enforcement and ultimately proved counter-productive. His attempts to enforce the prohibition of gambling and prostitution did not prevent the enrichment of the corrupt networks which controlled and operated such activities in Los Angeles, but did help to provide a substantial market for frustrated gamblers in Las Vegas. Bowron's efforts were representative of the country's continued attempt to impose morality after the repeal of Prohibition. His response to the failure of this attempt was also representative—he looked around for someone to blame, in his case, they were 'Eastern gangsters'. Other politicians, law enforcement personnel and journalists sought a more convincingly elaborate explanation. In doing so they did not overestimate the intelligence of the public.

Every US city made its own particular response to the problem of vice and gambling law enforcement, but none found an answer to the unlimited opportunities for illegal enterprise that the morality laws offered. The stability of organized crime operations and the amount of centralized control within cities varied from place to place and depended primarily on the continuity of party rule and the type of city government.

The sporadic responses to organized crime were generally no more than highly publicized and politicized campaigns which ultimately failed. The crime and corruption issue was simply exploited in local political power struggles. The main achievement of Dewey, Courtney, Bowron and other 'crime crusaders' had been to gather votes from a gullible public who believed that the answer to organized crime was to install such honest and energetic individuals in public office. The newspapers helped engineer public compliance by reducing the question of organized crime to a simplistic battle of Good versus Evil; 'crusading' mayors and 'fearless, racket-busting' district attorneys against 'corrupt, political machines' and criminal 'big shots'. In effect the voters were led to believe that the installation of the right public officials of itself would put an end to organized crime. In every case I have examined this optimistic, partial and often hypocritical approach to the problem of organized crime was tried and found wanting. Organized crime survived the defeat of corrupt politicians because more corrupt politicians simply took their place. The imprisonment of important criminals had little effect other than to destabilize conditions and sometimes cause bouts of competitive blood-letting amongst gangsters. Organized crime only requires a demand for illegal goods and services to exist and any vacuums created by imprisonment or assassination are soon filled. Periods when visible law enforcement increased simply came and went.

8 Post-war perfidy

After the lean years of the 1930s the Second World War provided an immense boost to illegal as well as legal businesses. More people were employed and earning good wages, rationing and war production cut back on available consumer goods, an increasing amount of money became available to spend on prohibited goods and services, and the profitability of vice increased.

Gambling, in particular, enjoyed a wartime and a post-war boom. Gallup polls indicated that 45 per cent of the population gambled in 1945 and this rose to 57 per cent in 1950, in spite of the fact that practically all of the states had laws prohibiting gambling. Off-track bookmaking and slot-machine gambling flourished in most cities, bookmakers made arrangements to operate in factories, offices, building sites and on the waterfront, slot-machine distributors ensured that thousands of private clubs and lodges gave their members the opportunity to play on what were known as 'devil machines' to moral crusaders and 'one-arm bandits' to everyone else. Illegal casinos operated in many areas around the country, notably northern Kentucky, Hot Springs (Arkansas), Saratoga (New York), northern New Jersey and greater New Orleans. In southern Louisiana the law was held in such contempt that Celestin F. Rowley, Sheriff of St Bernard Parish, adjoining New Orleans, complained bitterly that the Press notoriety of Jefferson County and its Sheriff, Frank Clancy, was drawing business away from his own wide-open parish. *Newsweek* magazine quoted the indignant Rowley as saying, 'I'm thinking of taking out some ads, Sheriff Clancy is getting too much damned publicity for the joints in Jefferson'.[1]

An article in *Life* surveyed the gambling situation across the whole country and found that:

> In any city where gambling exists . . . the police department knows the addresses and owners of every joint in town. The reason the joints stay open is always just one thing: graft, paid either to the police, the city officials or the political machines, and in some cases all three. The United States is full of policemen, sheriffs and prosecuting attorneys who have built mansions, bought yachts or loaded their safe deposits boxes to bursting.[2]

Journalists had a field day exposing an endless string of gambling corruption scandals and speculating on who were the 'Mr Bigs' behind the scenes. Ed Reid, for example, of the Brooklyn *Eagle*, produced an influential eight-article series, in December 1949, in which he detailed the extent of gambling in Brooklyn and claimed that the crime bosses were even 'infecting our school children with the gambling fever'. Reid's 'Mr Big' turned out to be Harry Gross, a bookmaker who paid off $1 million a year in 'ice' money to the police and was later convicted by Brooklyn District Attorney, Miles McDonald.[3]

The favourite 'Mr Big' of the time, however, was Frank Costello, a New York gambling entrepreneur with investments in several semi-legitimate operations in other parts of the country. The newspapers promoted him to 'Prime Minister of the Underworld' or 'America's No. 1 Mystery Man'. By the late 1940s the exaggerated and sometimes ludicrous claims about Costello's power and influence included: immense political pull in Kansas City, Los Angeles, New Orleans as well as in New York, where he undoubtedly had some (see p. 67); the power to 'order' the assassination of Bugsy Siegel in 1947; key involvement in the movie extortion plot of the Chicago syndicate (see p. 79); and such complete domination of rackets in the eastern United States that he took a cut from all. Convincing evidence for such statements was never produced.[4]

Despite the hysteria of the popular press, in many ways gambling in post-war America resembled the liquor situation during Prohibition. Gambling was a popular and socially approved pastime, and the fact that it was illegal only succeeded in enriching corrupt politicians, policemen and criminal entrepreneurs. The fact that the gambling laws, like the dry laws, were plainly not being enforced produced some calls for liberalization and regulation, so that tax revenue would replace illegal enrichment. Proposals for the legalization of gambling in various forms were put before the state legislatures of Arizona, California, Florida, Idaho, Illinois, Louisiana, Minnesota, Montana and New York during the immediate post-war period. These proposals failed partly because the state legislatures were still dominated by the Protestant culture of rural America which regarded gambling as sinful, but more because the proponents of legalized gambling lacked the immense financial support that pushed through the repeal of the Prohibition amendment. Repeal had been financed by important manufacturing and business interests, disillusioned about the promised economic benefits of Prohibition, and pre-Volstead brewers and distillers, eager to profit legally again.

In contrast, established legal gambling interests, such as the licensed race tracks and the Nevada casinos, would face unwanted competition if gambling was an accepted and generally available pastime. Illegal gambling interests also had no interest in changing the situation, with little to gain and much taxable income to lose if gambling were legalized. Business interests were either uninterested, or accepted the anti-gambling arguments of the Citizens' Crime Commission movement which had gained strength in the post-war years. The essence of these arguments was that the laws prohibiting gambling were right and necessary not only because gambling was immoral but also for sound business reasons. Virgil Peterson, the influential head of the Chicago

Crime Commission, reflected a common theme and echoed an old Prohibition argument when he stressed that 'gambling withdraws money from the
regular channels of trade vital to the well-being of a nation or a community'.
Gambling, in other words, was bad for business; ways had to be found to
enforce the gambling laws.[5]

Because of the strength of the opposition and despite the popularity of the
pastime it took a brave politician publicly to favour legalizing gambling. In
1950, for example, Mayor William O'Dwyer of New York, well aware that
gambling enforcement was a hopeless and corrupting task, urged the state
legislature to legalize gambling on sporting events. He was immediately
attacked from every side: newspaper editorials, religious and business
organizations, and even, as noted before (see p. 66), Governor Dewey
himself castigated the Mayor for such an immoral idea.[6] Given the torrent of
abuse that greeted O'Dwyer's suggestion, it is not surprising that most city
executives preferred a passive approach to the gambling laws; gambling
arrest statistics were compiled with the minimum of disruption to protected
gambling operations.

Mayor deLesseps S. Morrison of New Orleans was a far more expedient
and, as it turned out, influential politician than O'Dwyer. He had been
elected in 1946 after a campaign that was on two levels. The first was that of a
holy crusade against the incumbent Mayor Robert Maestri and his corrupt
political machine. Morrison's opening statement was:

> I accept the call of my fellow citizens to lead the fight against dictatorship in our
> city. Common decency and real democracy must and will be restored to the
> people of New Orleans.
>   This is a battle of the masses against the few in the corrupt political clique that
> holds our city in an iron grip. New Orleans now stands in the shadow of vicious
> gangster rule, a rule made possible by the consent and co-operation of the corrupt
> leaders of the present city machine.
>   The returning solider finds in our city the same conditions that brought about
> the terrible war we have just won. He has seen ·his fill of dictatorship, gang-
> sterism, corruption and the destruction of progress and morale. He is now
> determined, as are now the majority of our citizens, to remove these evil
> influences through the medium of the ballot.[7]

Morrison's pledges to end vice and corruption secured him the support of
the religious and women's organizations; the most publicized image of the
campaign was a demonstration of women in support of Morrison, brandish-
ing brooms as a symbol of the sweeping-out of corruption. Morrison also
promised industrial expansion to secure business support and made glowing
references to returning soldiers to get the support of the veteran's associations. His dynamism and campaign organization stood in stark contrast to the
slow and inarticulate Maestri and he won by 4,372 ballots in a total vote of
133,708.[8]

The other side of Morrison's campaign was not revealed for several years
but was just as necessary for victory as the first. Morrison knew that his

prospects of winning the election were remote if he threatened an important part of the city's economy—vice. New Orleans had been a centre for vice long before the state of Louisiana became part of the United States in 1803 and the city's prostitution and gambling interests still met a massive demand from residents as well as the seamen, tourists and businessmen who constantly passed through the city. Brothels flourished, particularly in the famous French Quarter, and taxi drivers often made more money by pimping and bringing custom to the houses than in regular fares. Gambling was wide open in every form, lotteries, slots, racing handbooks and casinos. Morrison visited many brothels and gambling houses to assure them that they would be allowed to continue in operation after his election. Henry Muller, a pimp and brothel operator, also testified that he had campaigned aggressively for Morrison, ordering his prostitutes to 'talk up Morrison with the trade', and had made substantial contributions to Morrison's campaign fund.[9]

As one final reassurance to the vice interests, Morrison held a special meeting in the early hours of election day, 22 January 1946, at a hall on Esplanade Avenue. At the meeting were representatives of all the city's vice element, prostitutes, taxi drivers, gamblers, nightclub owners and racketeers. Morrison was quoted as telling them:

> I know how you people make your living and I assure you I will do nothing to stop you from continuing if I am elected Mayor. I am not a silk-stocking candidate and I do not try to ever change things, so vote for me and here's to bigger and better things.[10]

In the following years Morrison acquired a crime-busting reputation in the local and national newspapers solely through the efforts of his third-choice Police Chief, Adair Watters. Watters made a rare attempt to enforce the gambling and vice laws in New Orleans and made life difficult for the policemen who organized graft collections. Morrison forced Watters to resign in February 1949, replaced him with the more amenable Joseph Scheuering, who allowed the old graft system to return, and brushed aside any criticism. However, in the run-up to the 1950 elections Morrison's crime-busting reputation began to look shaky as the normally compliant local press ran some critical articles about Morrison's police force. The *Item*, for example, charged that the police were once again being systematically paid off and that the operations of brothels, lotteries and handbooks was wide-open.[11]

Morrison's initial response to these changes was complete denial. He stressed that the police were doing a good job and that the city was free of vice, crime and corruption. 'There is no possibility', he said, 'of the return of slots, books or lotteries'.[12] While sticking to this patently false position, Morrison began to use his presidency of the American Municipal Association (AMA) to divert attention away from the shortcomings of law enforcement in New Orleans. The AMA provided a national platform for Morrison's new ideas about organized crime. In a speech in Chicago, Morrison urged the

federal government to investigate the political activities of Frank Costello of
New York, 'the reputed leader of a nationwide gambling syndicate', and
continued:

> A national and international syndicate, which is reportedly headed by Costello, is
> attempting to seize power in key cities in the nation . . . A few years ago they
> occupied behind-the-scenes positions of power in Chicago, Los Angeles, New
> Orleans, Miami and other cities. Good government administration has kicked
> them over the municipal borders. Now they are trying to bring their operations,
> power and influence back into key cities.[13]

Morrison was cynically capitalizing on Costello's notoriety and his own
mythical reputation as being a foe of the New York gambling operator.
Costello's connection with New Orleans was that in 1934 he and his partner
Phil Kastel had removed their slot machines away from New York's axe-
swinging Mayor, La Guardia, down to New Orleans at the invitation, as
Costello later testified, of Huey Long, then the notoriously corrupt Governor
of Louisiana. In 1947, Police Chief Watters also began destroying the
valuable machines, this time by machine-gunning. Although at the time
Morrison had actively opposed the destruction, by 1949 he was loudly
claiming that he had chased the Costello-Kastel syndicate out of the city.

In the same Chicago speech Morrison claimed, for the benefit of the New
Orleans newspapers, that Costello had given immense financial support to his
opponents in the forthcoming elections. The Costello syndicate, in other
words, might take over if he were not re-elected. Morrison won the 1950
elections comfortably and had thus, like Mayor Bowron in Los Angeles,
successfully exploited people's fears about distant and nebulous conspiracies
to distract attention from corruption in his own administration.

Morrison continued his nationwide 'crusade' against organized crime after
his re-election and pressure from him, in particular, provoked a response by
the federal government. Attorney-General Howard McGrath agreed to hold a
conference of mayors and law enforcement officials, which Morrison used as
a platform for his organized crime ideas. McGrath's opening address expressed the official attitude towards gambling:

> In organized gambling, we are dealing with the biggest illicit traffic since
> Prohibition. Everywhere the pattern is the same—struggling and double-
> crossing to eliminate competitors for the right to cheat the public. The racket
> produces nothing. It contributes nothing to society but trouble.
>   . . . Businessmen's associations are concerned with not only the numbers
> racket, but with bookmaking, slot machines, punchboards and all forms of
> lotteries. They find that in communities where the business of gambling openly
> flourishes, the clientele of the legitimate businesses are not paying their bills and
> are dissipating their earnings.
>   I need not dwell on the demoralizing effect upon our children, who are
> everywhere bombarded, by sight and by hearing, with the temptations of gaming
> and lotteries.
>   I think the time is ripe for the drive for public support through press, radio,

motion pictures, civic clubs, business leaders, churches, schools, labor unions, and every form of decent organization. The stage is set for you to capture the popular imagination in a stirring campaign to crush organized crime in your communities.[14]

After McGrath, Morrison again boasted about his administration's ousting of Frank Costello's slot machines, and stated that two groups, the Costello syndicate and the Chicago syndicate, ran the wire service and the slot-machine racket across the whole country. These two groups were, according to Morrison, 'the root of the whole evil' of organized crime in America, whose

> wealth, power, scope of operations, and influence have recently grown to gigantic and alarming proportions. It is an ugly, vicious, un-American picture of systematic law violation, huge profits, corruption of public officials who can be bought—and operations outside the jurisdiction of those who cannot be purchased.

Morrison added that the Costello and Chicago groups worked with others in a 'loose confederation of mutual respect, co-operation, allocated territories and huge profits'.[15]

The Mayor presented these views along with a ten-point plan of action against organized crime. In addition to legislation dealing with slot machines and the wire service, Morrison's programme called for easier access by municipal officials to FBI and Internal Revenue information (presumably easier access for corrupt as well as honest municipal officials) as well as a 'co-ordinated masterplan of action' against nationwide rackets by the Attorney-General's office. Most significantly, Morrison's programme endorsed Senator Kefauver's bill for a Congressional investigation of interstate crime, which was then being referred to the Senate Judiciary Committee and in danger of being discarded. The publicity generated by the Attorney-General's conference and by Morrison's speech, in particular, helped rescue Kefauver's bill from oblivion. As we shall see, Kefauver later returned the favour.

Morrison's speech was followed at the conference by one from Mayor Fletcher Bowron of Los Angeles supporting the main features of the ten-point plan. Federal assistance was needed because, as Bowron pleaded:

> This thing is so large and it is Nationwide. This is no fiction about organized crime—it is a reality, and it extends from one end of the Nation to the other. In some respects, it is in its organizations rather loosely coordinated, and yet there are certain definite persons who give the orders and who make the policy. The thing is too big.[16]

Local authorities were simply unable to cope. Bowron also supported Kefauver's proposed national investigation.

The two mayors had hit upon a way to absolve themselves from responsibility for gambling-related organized crime and corruption in their cities. Other local government officials followed their example. Morrison and Bowron had been among the first to articulate an analysis that dominated policy-making for the next two decades. Organized crime was 'un-American' and simply 'too big' for local authorities to deal with. The morality laws could not be tampered with. Legalization of gambling, in particular, was out of the question; that would be a capitulation to powerful and alien criminal interests whatever label was used for the benefit of an unsophisticated public. The only solution was increased federal commitment, involving the enactment of more laws and the establishment of a federal law enforcement capacity that was capable of succeeding where local authorities had failed. By some means people had to be prevented from indulging in the activities that filled the coffers of the 'underworld'.

The first task of this new phase of America's moral crusade was to persuade people of the correctness of the above approach. As Edmund Brown, District Attorney of San Francisco, told the conference, '. . . we should find some new way to use modern propaganda to get a natural psychology against gambling'.[17] Part III describes how this new way was found and developed, and how a scapegoat explanation conditioned the country's response to gambling and organized crime. The inevitable result of this dishonest approach was that organized crime activities continued to prosper as the country grew richer.

Part III   Distracting from failure, 1945–

Newspeak was designed not to extend but to diminish the range of thought, and this purpose was indirectly assisted by cutting the choice of words down to a minimum.

George Orwell, *Nineteen Eighty-Four*, 1949

The Mafia is history's greatest threat to morality.

Ed Reid, *Mafia*, 1952

The Mafia v. America

Cover of *Time* magazine, 1969

9 Blaming aliens

Scapegoat explanations for the problems of the United States have long enjoyed a widespread acceptance among the population, particularly those which blamed newly arrived immigrants. In 1857, for example, fears about the impact of different cultures and religions were voiced by a New York State committee which concluded:

> As a surety we must, as a people, act upon this foreign element, or it will act upon us. Like the vast Atlantic, we must decompose and cleanse the impurities which rush into our midst, or like the inland lake, we will receive the poison into our whole nation system.[1]

Throughout the nineteenth century lawless disorder in the cities was most often blamed on the Irish-Americans. As one politician put it: 'If they did not lie, steal, cheat, rob and murder, get drunk, perjure themselves, quarrel and fight, they would be almost as good as other nations'.[2] As noted in the Introduction the same kind of ignorant ethnic prejudice was used by the moral crusaders to achieve their legislative successes.

Blaming aliens was also a useful distraction from the brazen greed of nineteenth-century politics. In 1888 James Bryce described proceedings in the New York and Pennsylvanian legislatures as 'such a Witches' Sabbath of jobbing, bribing, thieving and prostitution of legislative power to private interest as the world has seldom seen'.[3] Congress itself was concisely summed up by Mark Twain as the only 'distinctly native American criminal class'. Venal politicians faced the unpleasant prospect of exposure if they resisted the movement to make virtue a statutory duty. The expedient thing to do was to go along and join in with the clamour against the alien poison—the undisciplined hordes of people and the sinister rings which were corrupting an otherwise pure system.

During Prohibition, when the drys saw their law was being nullified they drew attention to conspiracies abroad in order to explain the failure of Prohibition at home. As the historian Andrew Sinclair noted:

> It was an old trick, recommended by Machiavelli . . . The dry leaders said that the greater part of the liquor in the country came from foreign rumrunners and conspirators overseas, who were attacking the global prohibition revolution by trying to wreck it in the country of its birth.[4]

The drys, however, soon became a discredited minority; fewer people were prepared to believe them. During Prohibition ethnic stereotyping and alien conspiracy theories temporarily went out of fashion as explanations for crime. In part this was because bootlegging was indisputably the main criminal enterprise and not many thirsty Americans could consider bootleggers to be un-American. Al Capone, Dutch Schultz, Legs Diamond and the rest were simply gangsters, never alien intruders or members of ethnically exclusive conspiracies.

For a time after Prohibition the perception of organized crime in America as an American phenomenon persisted. In 1935 Martin Mooney published a conspiracy interpretation entitled *Crime Incorporated*, which was an all-American conglomerate. When a criminal conspiracy with nationwide implications was uncovered in Brooklyn at the end of the 1930s it was labelled 'Murder Inc.', and no writer tried to pretend that it was other than a multi-ethnic group of United States' citizens.[5]

Racist bigotry, however, was not far beneath the surface. Westbrook Pegler, a national newspaper columnist, wrote in 1940:

> extortion was a native Italian peculiarity or vice as characteristic as garlic. Racketeering formerly known as black-handling, is not a native American trait but was imported from Sicily and Naples . . .

and added, on another occasion, that 'The Italian character will always wear the scar of shame like the squalor's mouth of the underworld'.[6]

The following year the United States entered the Second World War. This, and the fact that the country was fighting Italy helped to fan the nativist xenophobia that spawns ethnic stereotypes and alien conspiracy interpretations. In the immediate post-war years early century images of Sicilians and Italians as 'death-bound assassins' and 'Black Hand' extortionists were refashioned into a catch-all explanation of the country's organized crime problems; something now called the 'Mafia' had taken over! It is also worth noting that American revulsion at German atrocities against the Jews ensured that no Jewish conspiracy theory could have been sold to the public at this time although one could have undoubtedly been concocted.

Alien conspiracy theories were rife during the post-war period. Many people believed that a communist conspiracy, emanating from the USSR, was plotting to take over the country's government. Communism and organized crime were the two main preoccupations of post-war America and both proved to be sensational issues that enabled ambitious young senators to get their names before the public. On 5 January 1950, Senator Estes Kefauver of Tennessee introduced Senate Resolution 202, which called for an investigation into crime in inter-state commerce. At the same time Senator Joseph McCarthy of Wisconsin was looking for a dramatic issue on which to bolster his candidacy for re-election in 1952. Initially he wanted crime, making an abortive effort to have the Special Investigations Committee, on which he served, assume principal responsibility for any organized crime investigation. This effort failed and Kefauver was named chairman of the Special Committee to Investigate Organized Crime in Interstate Commerce on 11 May 1950. McCarthy had already found the issue to which he gave his name. In February he announced the discovery of a large but imprecise number of Communists making foreign policy for the Democratic administration.[7]

The beliefs that both communist and organized crime activities in the United States were directed by alien forces ran parallel after the war. Both were false issues which substituted scaremongering and distortion for intelligent analysis. Both beliefs appealed to ignorance and prejudice, and both inevitably led to a diminution of civil liberties and were entirely negative in their effects, the chief of which was an all-pervasive mental paralysis.

Kefauver's five-man committee was made up of himself, two fellow Democrats, Herbert O'Conor of Maryland and Lester C. Hunt of Wyoming, and two Republicans, Alexander Wiley of Wisconsin and Charles W. Tobey of New Hampshire. Of these, Kefauver and Tobey made the most political capital out of the hearings which as they progressed captured the attention of the nation. The hearings were a huge press and above all television event.

Kefauver decided to concentrate the work of the committee on gambling because, as he explained, the activity supplied substantial money for corruption of public officials and no federal laws controlled inter-state gambling activity. The main work of the committee, therefore, revolved around national racing-news wire services and gambling operators, notably Frank Costello, with widespread investments. Investigating committees, as historian William Moore pointed out, do little real investigating. Rather they dramatize a particular perspective on a problem and place the prestige of a Senate body behind a chosen point of view.[8] In effect the committee's goal was to reduce the complexities of organized crime to a simple Good versus Evil equation. The evidence uncovered by the hearings was only incidental to the committee's conclusions, which had been decided upon before the hearings began. Traditional American morality, and the argument that gambling was detrimental to business, ensured that the committee's conclusions would be against the legalization of gambling, and two main influences combined to convince the committee that the mysterious Mafia controlled organized crime in the United States.

Although the committee was mainly concerned with gambling, the first of these influences was Harold Anslinger, head of the Federal Bureau of Narcotics (FBN), who dominated his agency in much the same way as J. Edgar Hoover dominated the FBI. Anslinger took a criminal rather than a medical approach to the problem of drug addiction; an approach that was being seriously challenged for the first time in the post-war years not only by doctors and academics but by professionals within the law enforcement community. The influential Californian Crime Commission came to this conclusion in 1950:

> As long as there is an abundant world supply of illegal narcotics it necessarily follows that vigorous and efficient enforcement of the narcotics laws will merely result in raising the price of narcotics locally thus increasing the possibility for fabulous profits to those who are able to engage in the traffic even for a brief time. The experience in California and in all other parts of the United States in recent years should suggest serious doubt as to whether the narcotics traffic can ever be stopped by the mere prohibition of the possession and traffic of narcotics. Experience has indicated that instead of limiting ourselves to a single line on the problem which takes the form of attempting to prevent the evil by destroying the sources of supply we would do well to consider the possibility of supplementing our efforts with a second line of attack designed to destroy the demand.
>
> The motivation of the narcotics traffic is strictly economic. It exists only as long as the narcotics peddler is able to demand a high price from the addict. If the addict could register, and as a matter of medical treatment could receive at low cost his narcotics dosage from carefully supervised dispensary the traffic in illegal narcotics would vanish overnight. It would disappear because it would no longer be worthwhile financially to bring illegal narcotics into the country which could not be profitably sold in competition with a medical clinic.

The Commision noted that England and other European countries did not have narcotics problems to compare with those of the United States despite 'the super-abundance of the world supply', and recommended further study of drug-control policies which prevented 'the development of a narcotics traffic by undercutting the profits of the peddler'.[9] This approach, however, called into question the very existence of Anslinger's organization and he ensured that no such study was undertaken.

Anslinger had no answer to rational arguments. Instead he developed self-serving distractions; one was to blame aliens for America's drug problems. Through statements and disclosures to the Press and by appearances before Senate committees, beginning with Kefauver's, Anslinger and his agents propagated the idea that the Mafia super-criminal organization controlled both the worldwide drug traffic and the core of organized crime activity in the United States. The Bureau could, therefore, justify the importance of its task, and explain its lack of success without having to inquire more deeply into the problem of addiction itself. Just as anti-gambling campaigners asserted that legalization would be a capitulation to criminal interests, Anslinger used similar arguments to justify calls for yet more penalties against drug users and traffickers. The only result of this approach has been, as the Californian Crime Commission warned, to increase 'the possibility for fabulous profits to those who are able to engage in the traffic even for a brief time'. Some historians have also suggested that Anslinger's scare stories about the Mafia helped increase his Bureau's budgetary appropriations, and that he had learnt a lesson from Hoover's headline-grabbing exploits and organizational empire-building in the 1930s.[10]

To make certain that the Kefauver Committee came to conclusions that were acceptable to the FBN, Anslinger lent them one of his top agents, George White. In the early months of the investigation, White was particularly influential, briefing the committee's members and counsel on what questions to ask. His help was frequently acknowledged and he was referred to as 'one of the great experts on the Mafia'.[11]

The committee's funds were limited and Kefauver expressed his gratitude to the FBN after the hearings:

> Our greatest help in tracking down the trail of the Mafia came from the Federal Bureau of Narcotics . . . Because of the Mafia's dominance in the dope trade, the Narcotics Bureau has become the leading authority on this sinister organization.[12]

Anslinger and his agents, however, had not been at all convincing on the subject of the Mafia in the public hearings. When, for example, the committee's chief counsel, Rudolph Halley, pressed Anslinger on his concept of the 'underworld' structure he got the following response:

> ANSLINGER. I would say that all of the members of this combine are very well acquainted with everybody else throughout the country. The fellows in New York, Florida, California, all know each other. Seizing their telephone lists, they are all on there, you find. It is interlaced and intertwined.
> HALLEY. Do the activities in one part of the country occur as a result of instructions given in other parts of the country?
> ANSLINGER. No; I do not think it works on that basis. In some sections it is pretty well organized in that particular way, but I wouldn't say that one section of the country controls another section.
> HALLEY. Do they confer together?
> ANSLINGER. They confer together, oh yes; talk to each other, deal with each other.
> HALLEY. They confine their dealings pretty well to the family; is that correct?
> ANSLINGER. That has been our experience. They have off-shoots. They have associates in other rackets. They make connections for persons outside of their own combine.[13]

Anslinger, the chief federal government sponsor of the Mafia concept, did not use the term Mafia in his testimony, which itself gave little support to the contention that organized crime was dominated by a nationwide and centralized criminal organization.

One of Anslinger's agents, Claude Follmer, tried to be more specific during the Kansas City hearings. Halley asked him how the Mafia operated and Follmer replied:

> My understanding is that they don't have written rules or by-laws, but they have a sort of understanding that once you are a member you can't withdraw. You are always a lifetime member. Their code is that if you double-cross another member of the organization there is only one penalty, and that is death.

Follmer went on to explain that there was an 'inner circle' and an 'outer circle' of the Mafia. The inner circle was composed of men who were rewarded for 'special duty they have performed in the past' or 'through their standing prior to their coming into the organization'. They got the most lucrative rackets. The outer circle, according to agent Follmer, was 'just the run-of-the-mill type, the ones who do the heavy work and the rough things'.[14]

Halley asked whether the inner circle made the decisions and Follmer replied: 'Yes. They are supposed to have an international head in Palermo, and through him the various heads in other countries are designated'. Through the New York head, state or city leaders were appointed in the United States. Follmer then explained how he knew all this: 'I have heard several of these fellows testify at various times and I have seen transcripts'. The committee listened to this agent with respect and Kefauver quoted him at length in this book on the hearings. Not surprisingly, Kefauver also reached the conclusion he was intended to reach:

> While it is heartening to learn that the federal government has a bureau which is alive to the danger presented by this criminal organization, it was discouraging to find that the Federal Bureau of Narcotics is sadly undermanned. I strongly favour increased appropriations to give this bureau more manpower with which to carry on the fight against the Mafia-dominated narcotics traffic.[5]

The work of two journalists constituted the other main influence on the committee's Mafia conclusions. Jack Lait and Lee Mortimer, columnists on the New York tabloid, the *Daily Mirror*, produced a series of best-selling books beginning with *New York Confidential* in 1948, the more successful *Chicago Confidential* in 1950, *Washington Confidential* in 1951, and *U.S.A. Confidential* in 1952. *Chicago Confidential* was the first book to string together anecdotes about Italian gangsters and claim that this proved the existence of the Mafia super-criminal organization. Lait and Mortimer, therefore, were the first in a long line of literary entrepreneurs to profit from the gullibility of the public in matters relating to organized crime. Kefauver read *Chicago Confidential* while he was preparing his investigation into organized crime, and was impressed enough to arrange meetings and dinner engagements with Mortimer, and to flatter the author on the floor of the Senate, in book advertisement and in a testimonial letter to the publisher, William Randolph Hearst.[16]

The *Confidential* books feature the two main preoccupations of post-war America—communism and organized crime—in an amalgam of racial and political bigotry. The only evidence they provide about the American Mafia indicates that the concept originated in the paranoid imagination of reactionaries. The Mafia, according to Mortimer and Lait, is

> the super-government which now has tentacles reaching into the Cabinet and the White House itself, almost every state capital, huge Wall Street interests, and connections in Canada, Greece, China and Outer Mongolia, and even through the Iron Curtain into Soviet Russia.

The organization is 'run from above, with reigning headquarters in Italy and American headquarters in New York'.[17] It 'controls all sin' and 'practically all crime in the United States',[18] and is

> an international conspiracy, as potent as that other international conspiracy, Communism, and as dirty and dangerous, with its great wealth and the same policy—to conquer everything and take over everything, with no scruples as to how.[19]

They explained the absence of Sicilian names in the Washington DC police files in this way:

> Vice, crime, gambling and narcotics and, to a lesser extent contraband liquor, are farmed out by franchise to a cohesive local mob which deals with and pays tribute to national headquarters.[20]

Lucky Luciano and Frank Costello were named as the 'Mr Bigs' of the Mafia. Luciano was 'the richest man in Italy' who 'pays off half the government and most of the cops'.[21] Costello merely ran the Eastern seaboard of the United States, as well as Louisiana and 'the entire slot machine industry . . .'.[22]

Having demonstrated the existence of the Mafia by assertion, the authors used the same historical methods to explain the attractions of Marxism:

> Marxism came into Russia on a wave of free love. In countries which have not yet been engulfed dreary men and pimply women are brought into the fold with promises of purple and unconventional delights . . . Judging from the looks and odour of most revolutionists, we prefer to remain capitalists . . . Negro men get first choice of white women . . . The Red bed-battalion is also committed to romancing unioneers in sensitive industries.[23]

Any public official of remotely liberal persuasions was abused. The Supreme Court Justice, Felix Frankfurter, was 'the evil genius of the socialistic revolution, godfather of Acheson and Hiss and the whole host of appeasers, left wingers, welfare staters, do-gooders and queer intellectuals . . . arrogant, self-centred, a Pink Napoleon'. Fiorello La Guardia was described as 'strident, greasy and pharisaical' and 'New York's pink little stink weed' who was on close 'personal and financial terms with the Mafia'.

Among the other ridiculous claims Lait and Mortimer made were that there were '300,000 school age dope addicts',[24] and that great growth of the 'plague' of narcotics addiction had been 'parallel to the spread of Communism in our country'.[25] 'Organized gangsters' combined with 'Communists and pinks' were working 'to turn Americans into addicts'.[26] America's youth was 'unbridled, hopped up, sex-crazy and perverted',[27] and all 'weed heads' were 'cop haters, carrying a fierce resentment against the conventional forces of society'.[28] The authors showed racist and sexual fears and hatreds throughout the four books. Communist women always used their sexual favours to convert 'darkies' and children to the party line, and black

Americans were regarded as 'soft converts' which had to be 'imbued by practical demonstration with the complete equality of all comrades'.[29] Most women in the books were 'nymphomaniacs' or 'bare babes', all homosexuals were 'faggots', 'fairies' and 'perverts'. Lait and Mortimer were representative of an intolerant and hysterical period in United States history; they succeeded because they were only telling millions of Americans what they wanted to hear.

The *New York Times* literary critics reviewed the *Confidential* books respectfully. *New York Confidential* was described as 'this sprightly book' and the authors compared to O. Henry. *Chicago Confidential* was a 'shocking social document' and the reviewer of *U.S.A. Confidential* opened by noting that 'Lait and Mortimer have been dropping lighted firecrackers down the nation's sewers for some time and by now quite a crowd has gathered to watch the excitement'.[30]

To a man like Kefauver himself, who came from a small-town background, and was naïve about crime and vice in the big cities, the easy explanations of big city reporters like Lait and Mortimer must have seemed convincing. The committee's interpretation of organized crime, as expounded in the Third Interim Report, was no more than a more temperate version of the conspiracy theory of the two journalists. Both were based purely on assertion, and neither could see organized crime as something that had developed inside the United States and was thus essentially an internal, domestic problem. The committee's conclusions traced the history of the Sicilian Mafia and its implantation into America:

> The various drives against the Mafia in Sicily which were made by Italian governments from the 1870s down to Mussolini's time, were . . . largely ineffective in destroying the Mafia. However, these drives had the effect of causing large numbers of Mafia members to migrate to the New World and many of them came to this country . . . The Mafia became established in New Orleans and other cities. Moreover, like many underworld organizations, it grew rich and powerful during Prohibition in the sale and distribution of alcoholic beverages. In addition both during Prohibition and since that time this organization has entered every racket promising easy money. Narcotics, pinball machines, slot machines, gambling in every form and description are some of its major activities at the present time.

To support its case the committee's report then recounted some drug trafficking stories provided by the Narcotics Bureau and made these frequently quoted conclusions:

> 1. There is a Nationwide crime syndicate known as the Mafia, whose tentacles are found in many large cities. It has international ramifications which appear most clearly in connection with the narcotics traffic.
> 2. Its leaders are usually found in control of the most lucrative rackets of their cities.
> 3. There are indications of a centralized direction and control of these rackets, but leadership appears to be in a group rather than in a single individual.

4. The Mafia is the cement that helps bind the Costello-Adonis-Lansky syndicate of New York and the Accardo-Guzik-Fiscetti syndicate of Chicago as well as smaller criminal gangs and individuals criminals throughout the country. These groups have kept in touch with Luciano since his deportation from this country.

5. The domination of the Mafia is based fundamentally on 'muscle' and 'murder'. The Mafia is a secret conspiracy against law and order which will ruthlessly eliminate anyone who stands in the way of its success in the criminal enterprises it chooses. It will destroy anyone who betrays its secrets. It will use any means available—political influence, bribery, intimidation, etc.—to defeat any attempts on the part of law enforcement to touch its top figures or to interfere with its operations.[31]

Despite a great deal of hopeful effort, no evidence had been produced at the hearings to support this view of a centralized Sicilian organization dominating organized crime in the United States. Lait and Mortimer were right when they dismissed the report as 'practically a plagiarism of *Chicago Confidential* and *Washington Confidential*'.[32] The committee attached a great deal of significance to the above-mentioned assertions of Anslinger and his agents and expressed incredulity when Italian racketeers denied they were in an organization called the Mafia. These, if they testified at all and did not plead the 5th Amendment, were constantly prodded, probed and encouraged by committee members and counsel to admit that they were in the Mafia, but none did so. The Third Interim Report was reduced to describing Phil D'Andrea of Chicago as a 'notable exception'. D'Andrea had testified that the Mafia 'was freely discussed in his home when he was a child'. The report did not, however, explain what an Italian immigrant family's talk about a criminal organization in the old country had to do with American organized crime. D'Andrea was in fact putting the Mafia back into the context in which it belonged—Sicilian peasant society.[33]

Contrary to its Mafia conclusions, the committee found men of several ethnic groups at the head of criminal syndicates around the nation, and frequent contact and cooperation between different ethnic groups. The ethnic origins of the suspected syndicate figures called before the committee were fairly equally divided between Irish, Jewish and Italian. Even in the committee's own choice of the two most powerful syndicates in the country—the Costello-Adonis-Lansky syndicate of New York and the Accardo-Guzik-Fiscetti syndicate of Chicago—which were supposedly bound together by the Mafia 'cement', Meyer Lansky and Jacob Guzik were Jewish, and Frank Costello, Joe Adonis and Charles Fiscetti originated from mainland Italy. Presumably Tony Accardo represented the Sicilian 'cement'. The networks of illegal activities that the committee described cut across ethnic designations and always depended on official sanction. The evidence the committee uncovered showed that gambling operators in differemt parts of the country had sometimes combined in joint ventures, in the same way as businessmen everywhere, and had made a lot of money for themselves and for public officials. The committee could not accept the fact that gambling was popular and that its illegality therefore made it a popular source of graft for public officials who were not really concerned who ran operations. As Frank Costello explained before the hearings, 'I don't operate anywhere I am not invited'.[34]

When the committee's conclusions were published in mid-1951 the Press and the academic community with only a few exceptions, failed to point out the almost complete absence of evidence and logic in the committee's Mafia interpretation of organized crime and, in fact, confirmed large sections of the public in a belief that the committee had proved the existence of the Mafia. In the wake of the hearings sensational journalists and publishers enjoyed a field day explaining and enlarging upon the committee's work. Gangster movies, television programmes and works of fiction dramatized versions of the same theme, and academic and legal experts joined in echoing the committee's conclusions.[35]

The Kefauver Committee's prestigious backing of an alien conspiracy theory developed by the FBN and the likes of Jack Lait and Lee Mortimer was a decisive stage in the process by which the knowledge that some Italian-American racketeers had become rich and powerful in some cities, and had contact with racketeers in other cities, became distorted into something far more mysterious and menacing. A frame of reference was established which we shall return to in Chapter 11.

The Kefauver Committee's hearings were televised and sensationalized between May 1950 and May 1951. The committee attracted immense attention and support, but accomplished little in the way of legislative action. It did little intelligent investigation of the causes and conditions of organized crime and concentrated on dramatizing the opinions of certain anti-gambling pressure groups, in addition to those of Anslinger, Lait and Mortimer. The entire thrust of the proceedings was directed towards providing the public with scapegoats to protect the country's morality legislation. The next chapter describes this.

10 The Kefauver Crime Show

The Kefauver Committee's main task had been to investigate illegal gambling around the country and, during the first few months of hearings especially, it attempted to demonstrate the existence of centralized control of the racing-news wire service by former members of the Capone gang in Chicago.

In its reports the committee traced the history of the wire service from 1936, the year Moses Annenberg's National News Service began the lucrative business of instantaneous communication of racing information (see p. 35). The legality of the purpose and methods of the Annenberg organization was not at first challenged, and by the end of its first year of operating the service covered the entire country. From the beginning the process of consolidation was accompanied by violence, murder and growing political and police corruption.

In 1939 Annenberg was indicted on tax evasion charges. He had declared and paid tax on a profit of $7 million in 1936, but had actually made an additional $13 million in that year. He had also broken anti-monopoly laws because his organization had owned most of the regional outlets of the service, which in turn selectively sold it to bookmakers. Because of his tax difficulties Annenberg ceased operations on 16 November 1939, leaving the lucrative racing information business up for grabs.

The vacuum created by Annenberg's abdication was soon filled by James Ragen and Arthur McBride, former managers of the old organization. They pieced the organization together, renamed it Continental Press, and through subterfuge concealed their ownership of the distributors. The Ragen-McBride outfit was soon violently competing with a rival service, Trans-American, which was controlled by former Capone gangsters, Jacob Guzik, Tony Accardo and Murray Humphries. (Guzik was Jewish-American, Accardo was Italian-American and Humphries was Welsh-American, indicating that the Chicago syndicate was a lot less ethnically exclusive than Congress.) On 24 June 1946, Ragen, of Continental, was murdered in Chicago, and warfare between the two organizations continued in different parts of the country for several months, during which time neither made any money. In May 1947, the two groups came to an understanding: McBride's son Eddie was left in charge of Continental, which once again became America's chief source of racing information, and the Guzik distributorship received special rates.[1]

In its Third Interim Report, published in 1951, the Kefauver Committee stated that:

> It is clear that in many cities across the country the Capone affiliates and the Mafia are now in control of the distribution of racing wire news with the resultant source of enormous profits and power of bookmaking.[2]

For the committee the wire service was the key to organized crime in America, the country's 'Public Enemy Number One'.[3]

However, according to William Moore's most thorough examination of the Kefauver Committee, the hearings had not shown how extensive the influence of Guzik, Accardo and Humphries really was on Continental, or indeed how much influence Continental actually had over subdistributors and bookmaking operations in Chicago and other parts of the country. In fact the committee's own evidence about first Annenberg and then Ragan and McBride had revealed that attempts to impose centralized national control were fraught with difficulties, and that the illegal bookmaking business was much more decentralized.[4] The committee's study of the wire service and gambling in general did indicate inter-state links, but the evidence in every city visited showed clearly that local police and government policy was the important determinant of the extent of gambling.

Kefauver himself recognized this. At the same time that his committee was busy 'proving' a centralized, alien conspiracy, he made a more accurate analysis of organized crime that found a decentralized American phenomenon:

> The Federal Government could not reach the roots of organized crime. They lie deep in the every day administration and functioning of the criminal law in the self-governing units of our country; our cities, towns, counties and states. No matter how organized crime may proliferate through the interstate facilities and operations, in the last analysis, it lives by violation of local and state laws, by the ability to flout local enforcement of criminal justice and to form corrupt, profitable alliances with local public servants, civic employees, municipal or state officials.[5]

Unfortunately it was not politicially sensible to repeat this insight too often during the 1950s. Too many public servants and journalists wanted to blame aliens.

Numerous 'corrupt, profitable alliances' were revealed during the hearings. The committee found that the assets of public officials often bore no relation to their salaries. Sheriff James Sullivan of Dade County, Florida, increased his net worth from $2,500 to over $90,000 during his five-year term. At the same hearings in Miami, Sheriff Walter Clark of Broward County disclosed that he owned a substantial interest in the Broward Novelty Company, which operated an illegal slot-machine business. The Gross income of this company between 1945 and 1947 was more than $1 million.[6]

While Sheriffs Sullivan and Clark had been less than forthcoming about their assets, the testimony of Sheriff Frank Clancy of Jefferson County, Louisiana, however, was so ridiculously disingenuous that it provided the Kefauver Committee with the kind of publicity it needed to arouse national interest in its hearings. A Kefauver aide described Clancy's testimony as 'the best one-man show to date'. Sheriff Clancy had at first refused to answer the committee's questions, but relented when threatened with contempt charges. He testified in Washington, DC, on 8 February 1951.

Clancy explained that judicious betting was the reason why his annual income of '$20,000 or better' was three times that of his annual salary. He offered the Senators the following advice:

> You cannot play every horse and win . . . If you play the first races, you stay there and get hooked and try to get out. If you play the last races, you get a winner, you go home.

Clancy tolerated gambling in his parish not because of graft but because the gambling casinos provided work for hundreds of 'underprivileged and old people who could not get work any place else'. Clancy's performance gave Senator Tobey his first chance to express righteous indignation before the television cameras:

> It is a revealing and disgusting thing . . . that a man like you can continue in office . . . simply cannot sit and listen to what I call political vermin.[7]

As the hearings progressed and captured public attention Tobey's moral outbursts tended to get longer and more frequent.

During his testimony Clancy made it clear that gambling establishments operated only at his discretion. He thanked Tobey for his remarks and noted 'I think it will help me make Jefferson a better place'. Clancy gave the committee his word of honour that he would close up gambling in his parish and break off his connections with the gamblers. Clancy telephoned his office from Washington and by 6 p.m. it was reported back to him that the Jefferson gambling establishments were closed. He told newspaper reporters that the 'lid was on tight', and promised it would stay on. A cartoon in the New Orleans *Times-Picayune* suggested a more plausible outcome. It showed Clancy proclaiming 'Gambling prohibited forever!' and a citizen asking a racketeer, 'What's the odds on that one?' Gambling in Jefferson County was simply put on a more discreet basis.[8]

The committee showed in every city it visited that police corruption was always a condition for successful organized crime. In Philadelphia a former policeman, Michael McDonald, testified that the payment of protection money to police in the lower echelon totalled more than $150,000 a month, and he said that his own captain had been reported to be getting $1,000 a month. McDonald declared that the police were discouraged from arresting numbers runners and that if they persisted in doing so, they were moved to beats where there were none. The Third Interim Report concluded that:

> The general picture given by McDonald indicated that there is a tie-up between the politico-gambler-police triumvirate in Philadelphia which permits these operations to continue with the token 'convenience arrests' that are characteristic of the same kind of operations in other cities.[9]

In Philadelphia the enforcement of the vice laws was the responsibility of police precincts where the offences took place, and specialized vice squads had not been set up. The committee chose Los Angeles as an example of the 'vice squad pattern' which they described as a device 'used in many cities where the rackets thrive', and in which

> The police department bosses set up a vice squad composed of a chosen few directly accountable to them. They instruct the remaining law enforcement officers to stay away from gambling and vice and to channel any complaints to the vice squad for action or, in most cases, inaction. By this device, a small clique frequently controls the collection of protection pay-offs. It directs police activity against operations that conflict with those who are 'in' or those slow to recognize their responsibilities to purchase 'official tolerance' to operate.[10]

The pattern of crime and corruption in the city of New Orleans was not revealed by the committee, and the evidence suggests that the reasons for this were political.

As noted before (see p. 100), Mayor deLesseps Morrison had been instrumental in getting Kefauver's investigation established. Morrison was among the first to expound views that came to represent orthodox thinking on organized crime in the 1950s, after the Kefauver Committee had endorsed them. Two groups, the Costello syndicate and the Chicago syndicate were the 'root of the whole evil' of organized crime in America because they ran the slot-machine industry and the racing-news wire service. Morrison claimed that he had shown the way by driving both groups out of his city. Strict enforcement by local officials with more federal support was the answer. Gambling prohibition laws were right and necessary because, as Morrison told a meeting of mayors in Los Angeles, 'The bookies make their living off the $2 sucker'.[11]

While Morrison was expounding his views on organized crime on the national stage, a long series of local crime, vice and police graft scandals was beginning. On 1 January 1950, Robert Dunn, a wealthy tourist from Nashville, died in a French Quarter bar after being given a 'Mickey Finn' or knockout drop in his drink. The story did not feature in the newspapers until March because, according to losing mayoralty candidate Alvin Cobb, a 'police and political silencer' had been put on the case until after the January elections. In March, however, the murder caused an uproar, and both the Press and community leaders attacked the growing lawlessness of the French Quarter. The *States*, on 24 March, voiced fears about the effects of such stories on the city's vital tourist trade:

> These stories are carried by the major press associations nationwide . . . They are
> a simple warning to all visitors to stay away from New Orleans . . . The places in
> the French Quarter need cleaning up . . . The Quarter harbours racketeers,
> macers, bums, killers, thieves and procurers.

The following week the same paper criticized Morrison's 'bland' statement
that 'the city that care forgot, based on "Mickey Finns" and "cat girls", is a
thing of the past'.[12]

Morrison responded to the criticism by setting up a citizens' committee to
investigate crime in the French Quarter. The committee's superficial
recommendations were soon enacted as local ordinances. One new ordinance,
for example, required taxi drivers to stand within arm's length of their cabs
between 6 p.m. and 6 a.m., thus preventing them, it was hoped, from
soliciting trade for prostitutes. The police also began the usual flurry of
activity against vice, making a number of token arrests.[13]

The Mayor received a most welcome respite from the French Quarter
controversies in January 1951, when the New Orleans hearings of the
Kefauver Committee were held. The hearings were the first to be televised
and aroused immense interest. Reportedly the city's streets buzzed about
little else, and 1,300 letters reached the television broadcasting station within
three days of the hearings.[14] Morrison used this opportunity to give his
crime-crusading reputation a much needed boost and the committee sat back
and let him, ignoring a wad of information that their investigators had
collected.

In his opening remarks Morrison described the role of the American
Municipal Association in the formation of the committee, and discussed
crime in New Orleans, claiming that,

> with some justifiable pride, we say that in New Orleans today we have achieved
> the greatest degree of law enforcement against gambling and related rackets
> within recent memory.

He then reiterated his version of the history of organized crime:

> The Costello axis, operating in a loose coalition of mutual interest with the heirs
> of Al Capone in Chicago, became a powerful, monopolistic combination of
> anti-social interests which constitutes a definite menace to the various levels of
> government.

In conclusion he particularly pleased the committee, which had a strong
anti-gambling bias, by speaking of the benefits that his tough stance had
brought to the city:

> There were people back in 1946 who thought that the elimination of gambling in
> the city would destroy our tourist business. May I say how wrong the past five

years have proven these people to be? Instead of decreasing, the tourist business in New Orleans has increased by leaps and bounds, and so has all the other general business in the city limits . . . My conclusion is that the elimination of gambling from our city limits has not lost us any tourists; but a healthier, progressive, law-abiding community, we believe, has brought us many more.

After his contribution Morrison answered some docile questions from the committee who then praised and thanked him.[15]

The committee had chosen to ignore evidence that contradicted everything the Mayor had said. It was commonly known that the city was as tolerant of illegal gambling and commercialized sex as it always had been. Not long before the hearings, for example, a correspondent for *Life* magazine had found 443 bookmaking establishments within the city limits, each paying a minimum of $24 a week for police protection. It was also widely suspected that Gasper Gulotta, a bar owner whose support and friendship Morrison openly acknowledged, was the official collector of police graft in the French Quarter. Despite this Morrison appointed Gulotta to the worthless investigatory committee mentioned earlier.[16] But more damningly the Kefauver Committee ignored detailed evidence about Morrison that their own investigators had collected. The committee knew that Morrison was especially close to Henry Mills and Osmond Litolff, controllers of the city's lucrative illegal lottery business. They knew also that Superintendent Watters, not Morrison, was responsible for the city's brief period of effective law enforcement, and that Morrison had effectively nullified Watters's achievement in cleaning up the police department. A six-page memo prepared for the committee's use summarized the expedient reality behind Morrison's crime-busting image, including such details as Morrison asking Watters to ease the enforcement of the gambling laws against the Mills-Litolff syndicate because they contributed handsomely at election time, and Morrison's proposal to Watters that handbooks should continue in operation, but more discreetly.

Two important members of Morrison's political machine also featured in the memo:

Blair Lancaster, who is Third Ward leader and was on the City Attorney's payroll, represents the pinball association. Through his influence the Police Department makes certain that only those machines of the operators belonging to the association can receive permits. Incidentally all the machines in New Orleans pay off. Lou Scanlon, another ward leader, was head of the mayoralty permit fund. This is a private slush fund of the Mayor's, which he can spend at will with no accounting. Its revenues are obtained principally from tax on coin operated devices.

The memo concluded:

Morrison attempted to dominate and control the Police Department, as well as all law enforcement, by insisting that members of the Police Department be transfered and promoted at the whims of the ward politicians, causing an embarrassing and untenable position for Superintendent Watters. He eventually resigned and was succeeded by the present Superintendent Scheuering.

This Superintendent and the Assistant Superintendent are both extremely co-operative to the suggestions and demands of the ward politicians. Some of the ward politicians are actively connected in gambling interests.[17]

When Senator Kefauver published his own account of the hearings in his book, *Crime in America*, he omitted all mention of Watters and credited Morrison with destroying the Chicago racing wire service operation in the city and stymieing the 'Costello-Kastel slot machine empire'.[18] In fact, as Kefauver's investigators made clear, Watters was solely responsible for all police action against gambling, and acted inspite of, not because of, Mayor Morrison. The conclusion is inescapable that Morrison's crime-crusading image was not publicly undermined by the committee because, firstly, it needed a success story, however phoney, in the enforcement of the gambling laws and, secondly, because Morrison was a political ally of Kefauver and thus got the benefit of a great deal of doubt.

The impact of the Kefauver Committee hearings was immeasurably increased by the fact that the proceedings were televised in several cities, beginning with New Orleans and finishing with a 'grand finale' in New York, which had overtaken Chicago as the nation's crime capital in the eyes of the Press. In eight days of public hearings in New York City during March 1951 the Senate Crime Investigating Committee became, in Kefauver's words, 'a national phenomenon'. The hour-by-hour television coverage of the proceedings, relayed to other large cities, reached an estimated audience of between twenty and thirty million. The New York newspapers were full of stories of neglected housework, deserted cinemas and department stores, and Consolidated Edison had to add an extra generator to supply power for all the television sets being used. One Broadway theatre operator told the *New York Times* that the hearings were hitting his business 'It's a lucky thing the crime show is going to close soon'. As one of the first real-life dramas to be shown on the small screen, interest in it exceeded baseball's annual World Series, and its occurrence was later said to mark television's coming of age in America.[19]

In retrospect the New York hearings can be seen as a historical drama in another sense: every aspect of the response to organized crime since the repeal of Prohibition was on show to the massive and over-credulous television audience. On show, firstly, was the rigid determination to persevere with unenforceable laws and blindly resist alternative approaches to vice based on control and regulation. Having thus been presented with an unsolvable problem, on show, secondly, was the necessity to provide scapegoats for the public by pointing to alien conspiracies and individually corrupt, or allegedly corrupt, politicians. On show, finally, was exploitation of the crime issue as a career vehicle for ambitious and opportunistic politicians.

Rudolph Halley emerged as the dominant personality of these hearings, and the senators merely played a supporting role to their Chief Counsel. Halley had made sure he was thoroughly prepared for New York, labouring up to eighteen hours daily for forty days before the hearings in order to unearth material on which to base his questions. To help his investigation he enlisted the assistance of newspaper reporters, narcotics agents, lawyers and judges, and received special assistance from the offices of Frank Hogan and Miles McDonald, District Attorneys of Manhattan and Brooklyn respectively. Halley's closest advisor, however, was Louis Yavner, formerly a commissioner of investigation under La Guardia, steeped in New York City politics and passionately devoted to the late Mayor. Yavner's influence, and Halley's own political ambitions, gave a distinctly partisan air to the New York proceedings, which manifested chiefly when Halley successfully and publicly discredited William O'Dwyer, Democratic Mayor of New York until the year before the hearings, when he was appointed US Ambassador to Mexico.[20] Halley made the supposed ties between O'Dwyer and Frank Costello, the gambling entrepreneur, the keystone of the hearings and had obviously seen the public interest potential of linking such twin symbols of Irish politician and Italian mobster.

The first days of the hearings were devoted to setting the scene for a dramatic climax. The vast extent of gambling in New York City was soon established. District Attorney Miles McDonald of Brooklyn and his assistant, Jules Helfand, outlined for the committee the magnitude of gambling operations and the accompanying police corruption that they were currently uncovering. Helfand estimated that an absolute minimum of $300 million a year was bet with bookmakers alone. One bookmaker, Harry Gross, whom they had recently convicted, had taken in $20 million in a year and admitted to paying police officials $1 million annually in 'ice' payments for protection. Helfand also described the inter-state tie-up of gamblers in New York, who phoned their bets to New Jersey wire rooms, operated in many instances by New York gamblers. McDonald reiterated that no large-scale gambling operation could be conducted without the knowledge and consent of at least the plain-clothes detectives charged with the enforcement of the gambling laws. He estimated that a weekly charge of about $250,000 was normal practice. The Gross case had also revealed that policemen had been tapping the telephones of bookmakers, not to gather evidence against them, but to ensure that no bookmaking was done except by those who paid-off.[21]

In the course of his testimony Helfand had briefly mentioned that drugs had been sold outside some schools and colleges in New York. Senator Tobey used this peg on which to hang one of his longest moral outbursts and effectively ended the day's hearings, thus preventing any intelligent discussion of Helfand's testimony:

What bothers me most about your splendid testimony this afternoon is your allusion to the conditions of the school children of Brooklyn, where they are corrupted by these emissaries of evil, these ambassadors of evil, and they begin to think that these things are justified and right and that these things are the norm in America, and they grow up to the stage of adolescence and then become young men and women, and then they have a family life, and this family life has a lower standard of morals, and a lower standard of citizenship . . .

What we must have—and you will pardon me for saying this, because I mean it in all sincerity—what we need is a revival of the application of the life and teaching of the Master of Men, so that we who grope will have a feeling of fellowship and understanding for our fellow man, and until that consciousness of virtue lives in America, lives in America again, I worry about America's future. Do you agree?

After securing the assent of McDonald and Helfand, Tobey proceeded to quote a poem of John Whittier which he wanted to 'submit for the record and to the people on radio and television':

> But solution there is none
> Save in the rule of Christ alone.

There is the answer. When the hearts of men and women are touched, when they take their inspiration from the Master of Men, and then we will have a righteous and a new America, and we will have in this nation a nation in which 'dwelleth righteousness,' and, before God, it is high time.[22]

The speech was so remote from the bulk of the day's testimony that many people believed that Tobey had been talking about betting cards distributed to schoolchildren. Nevertheless, spectators applauded and the day was ended on an appropriate note of moral outrage.

On the following days an impressive array of top crime figures was set before the television viewers who 'gawked', as one pundit put it, 'like a country boy looking at a painted woman for the first time'.[23] Big names such as Joe Adonis, Albert Anastasia, Meyer Lansky, Frank Erickson and Willie Moretti testified but understandably gave little away; most pleaded the 5th Amendment and refused to answer questions on the grounds that it would tend to incriminate them. Moretti, described in the committee's report as 'one of New Jersey's gambling overlords', was certainly loquacious and at times threatened to make a mockery of the proceedings. For example, when Halley attempted to use Moretti's friendship and acquaintance with gamblers and racketeers in other parts of the country as illustration of the 'complex network of interlocking and intertwined relationships' that constituted the Mafia, he sparked off the following exchange:

HALLEY. Well, are these people we have been talking about, like Rocco Fiscetti and Frank Milano and Joe Adonis and several of the others, what you would call rackets boys? I mean aren't they fellows who were in the rackets?
MORETTI. Well I don't know if you would call it rackets.

HALLEY. How would you put it?

MORETTI. Jeez, everything is a racket today.

HALLEY. Well what do you mean by that?

MORETTI. Everybody has a racket of their own.

HALLEY. Well, some of them are lawful and some are not. Are these fellows in the gambling racket? Would you call it that way?

MORETTI. If you want to call it a racket call the race track a racket, too; that's legitimate, isn't it?

HALLEY. Well, we are talking about illegitimate rackets. Let us confine it to illegitimate rackets.

MORETTI. The stock market is a racket too.

HALLEY. Well, it is legal, is it not?

MORETTI. Well, why not make everything legal; let the Government control it?

And when Halley asked whether he was a member of the Mafia, Moretti answered with another question: 'What do you mean by a member, carry a card with Mafia on it?' Halley failed to answer and tried to restore some dignity to the proceedings. At the end of his testimony Moretti was thanked by Senator Tobey who remarked that it was 'rather refreshing to find a witness as frank as this'. Moretti responded by inviting the committee to his seaside home if ever they felt like it.[24]

In the wake of the Kefauver hearings newspapers printed stories about Moretti having lost his sanity. John Selser, an attorney who had represented Moretti, told a New Jersey Legislative Committee much later that he, too, had been willing to accept the story that Moretti's mind had been affected until he read the Kefauver testimony. Then he concluded that Moretti was 'mentally capable—more so than his examiners'.[25]

On 13 March, Frank Costello, like Moretti, chose to answer the committee's questions. Before the questioning began his attorney, George Wolf, read a statement by Costello attacking the many newspaper charges, based on a 1 March 1951 interim report by the committee, in which Costello was named as the head of one of the two major crime syndicates that were supposed to be dominating the nation's crime. The statement asked for evidence and 'the right to publicly reply to your evidence or construe your surmises'. But Halley intended to present Costello as, in the words of the intrim report, 'the most influential underworld leader in America', and evidence did not come into it—the Chief Counsel simply had to confirm people in their prejudices. Halley's task was made more simple by Costello's objection to having his face filmed. The committee told the television people to avoid Costello's face and instead the viewers saw the gambler's nervous, sometimes twitching hands, which, combined with the hoarse, whispering voice of a man who had had a throat operation, must have suggested immense conspiratorial power.

Halley took him through his early bootlegging days, his financial 'net worth', and his gambling and political connections without ascertaining anything that was not already known. Costello was a rich man, with far-flung gambling investments, and had previously been a power in Manhattan's Democratic political organization, Tammany Hall. The Chief Counsel, however, looked convincing in his devastating use of his only weapons, innuendo and guilt through association. Halley tried to show Costello as the dominant figure of an Eastern crime syndicate which paralleled the Chicago syndicate and was bound to it with the Mafia 'cement'. The evidence presented by Halley during his cross-examination of Costello was unconvincing; he showed only that Costello had been in contact for years with a number of other gambling figures in the New York area, including partnerships in casinos with Adonis and Lansky. To reveal that Costello was top of a national chain of command Halley resorted to 'evidence' collected from a tap on the gambler's telephone. Halley referred to one conversation in which Willie Moretti had called Costello 'Chief'. Costello replied that he used the same expression himself. Halley later referred to another occasion when Phil Kastel, then operating in New Orleans had said 'O.K. Frank' several times. Costello had no real answer to that. After the hearings Halley admitted that he had failed 'to dig out the most fascinating crime story of all—that of the Mafia criminal super-government in America'.[27]

Accepting that his efforts to uncover the national conspiracy had failed, Halley directed the entire thrust of the final days' proceedings towards the local politics of the previous decade, and against one man, the recently departed Mayor of New York, William O'Dwyer. Political opportunism overcame all pretence that the Kefauver Commitee was only interested in the inter-state aspects of crime.

Before examining the O'Dwyer interrogation, a biographical sketch of the former Mayor is necessary. O'Dwyer's career showed how, with hard work and loyalty, a young man could climb within the old-style political machine. Born in 1890, O'Dwyer had left his native Ireland for America in 1910. He worked as a labourer and bartender in New York until 1917 when he joined the city police force as a patrolman. He studied law in his spare time, made the right political contacts in the Brooklyn Democratic party and by the 1930s had become first a city magistrate and then a judge. In 1939 he was elected Brooklyn District Attorney.

Even as a magistrate during the early 1930s O'Dwyer's liberal attitude towards personal behaviour made him a thorn in the flesh of moral crusaders. In Coney Island a moral campaign over bathing suits had developed when some men began to lower shoulder straps or otherwise expose their chests to widen the area of suntan. It had become fashionable among magistrates to denounce such practices as vicious and sentence offenders to up to ten days in prison. One magistrate revealed that he was being severe for the sake of the children, to protect them from indecency. When O'Dwyer took his turn at Coney Island court he threw all such cases out and the controversy was at an end.[28]

Like every other New York politicians in the 1930s and 1940s O'Dwyer comes out badly in matters relating to the waterfront. During the late 1930s John Harlan Amen was conducting a Dewey-type probe of the Brooklyn waterfront rackets. In April 1949, O'Dwyer convinced Amen to hand over all his files, testimony and exhibits so that he could prosecute an extortion racket involving six Brooklyn locals of the International Longshoreman's Association. The following month O'Dwyer allegedly ordered a discontinuance of the entire waterfront investigation.[29]

Within a few days of the ending of the waterfront investigations O'Dwyer began a series of prosecutions that revealed that a ring of hired killers, emanating from Brooklyn, had operated through the entire country. Gory and sensational details, plus the conspiratorial implications, ensured that the Press had a field day, and they immediately dubbed the killers 'Murder Inc'. These investigations, handled mainly by O'Dwyer's assistant, Burton Turkus, were based largely on the information of one of the murderers, Abe 'Kid Twist' Reles. Prosecutions resulted in the execution of several minor racketeers and eventually, in 1944, that of Lepke Buchalter, the most important New York industrial racketeer during the 1930s. O'Dwyer had also boasted that he had 'the perfect murder case' against another well-known gangster, Albert Anastasia, but this case was ruined when Reles fell, or was pushed, out of a Coney Island hotel window in November 1941. The six policemen who were guarding Reles claimed that they had been asleep when it happened, and O'Dwyer, later, defended them and their supervisor, Frank Bals, in a departmental investigation.[30]

In 1942 O'Dwyer resigned his office to join the Army as a special investigator. There he rose to the rank of Brigadier-General through his work uncovering fraud and mismanagement in the production and delivery of Army supplies. In 1945 he returned to New York politics to run for Mayor. In O'Dwyer's absence from the District Attorney's office, Governor Dewey had appointed Republican George Beldock to fill O'Dwyer's unexpired term. During the 1945 campaign Beldock launched a grand jury investigation into O'Dwyer's handling of the 'Murder Inc.' investigations. In a presentment, issued just before the election, Beldock's grand jury charged that while prosecuting lesser figures in the murder ring, O'Dwyer 'abandoned, neglected or pigeonholed' cases against waterfront boss, Albert Anastasia, Joe Adonis and other alleged heads of the conspiracy. The presentment dwelt on the circumstances surrounding the mysterious fall of Abe Reles and O'Dwyer's defence of the sleeping policemen.[31]

O'Dwyer angrily counter-charged that the grand jury presentments were politically motivated, and won the election comfortably. After the election, the presiding judge of the Brooklyn Court ordered the presentment expunged from the record on the grounds that it was indeed politically motivated. Subsequently, Beldock, seeking bi-partisan support for a judicial election, explained that none of his findings reflected on 'the personal integrity and honesty' of O'Dwyer and that his statements, made in the midst of an election campaign, had been 'heated and intemperate'.[32]

O'Dwyer was a popular Mayor and was re-elected in 1949 with another large majority. He was, however, constantly attacked by the anti-gambling lobby. Apart from the above-mentioned furore over his proposals to legalize some forms of gambling (see pp. 66 and 97), there were continual calls for stricter enforcement of the gambling laws. O'Dwyer's reply was that there were 'more serious things for police to do than hunt bookmakers', adding that he wanted word from the public before spending 'millions to have cops chasing bookmakers all over town'.[33] In late 1949, O'Dwyer came into conflict with Miles McDonald, the District Attorney who had defeated Beldock in the 1945 elections. McDonald had launched an inquiry into gambling and police corruption (see pp. 96 and 122) and O'Dwyer reacted impetuously. He angrily defended the police department, and labelled McDonald's investigation a 'witch hunt'. The following year O'Dwyer, who had only reluctantly accepted renomination for Mayor, accepted the post as Ambassador to Mexico. He agreed to return to New York for the Kefauver hearings without hesitation, in sharp contrast to Governor Dewey, who refused to come down to the city from nearby Albany and testify.[34] O'Dwyer could not have realized that his pro-gambling views made it essential for the committee to discredit him.

At the hearings, before O'Dwyer's appearance, Halley had already begun to establish guilt by association by repeatedly connecting O'Dwyer's name with crime figures. O'Dwyer's association with Irving Sherman, for example, was emphasized. Sherman had been Halley's first choice as 'Mr Big' in the city. Halley later said of Sherman: 'We banked on him a lot. In fact, at one time, Irving Sherman was our number one New York objective'. Sherman, however, left town before the hearings and all that could be established about him was that he had a '33 per cent share in a ladies coat business', and was well known in gambling circles. Despite failing to establish Sherman's importance in the criminal underworld, Halley spent a great deal of time with different witnesses establishing the fact that Sherman and O'Dwyer knew each other and that Sherman had helped O'Dwyer's 1945 mayoralty campaign. All of this was known before the hearings and O'Dwyer had never denied his association with Sherman.[35]

In his questioning of Charles Lipsky, a Republican city politician, Halley betrayed his desperation to link O'Dwyer's name with gangsters. He asked Lipsky about Frank Quayle, whom O'Dwyer had appointed Fire Department Commissioner:

HALLEY. Quayle is a good friend of O'Dwyer, is he not?
LIPSKY. Who?
HALLEY. Quayle?
LIPSKY. Yes.
HALLEY. In fact, he had been an old friend of Joe Adonis, hadn't he?
LIPSKY. Who?
HALLEY. Quayle.
LIPSKY. I don't know what you mean by 'friend'. He is a pretty high-grade fellow, in my estimation, and I can't say that I would classify Mr Quayle as a good friend of Joe Adonis.

Halley then had to concentrate on establishing that Quayle had eaten in Joe Adonis's restaurant, the implication being that this should have disqualified him from serving in O'Dwyer's administration. The only purpose of this type of exercise was to juxtapose O'Dwyer's name with gangsters.[36]

Halley's main intention however, was to link O'Dwyer's name with Frank Costello's, and to do so he built on speculation which had its origins in the late 1940s. The former actor, Robert Montgomery, had launched a campaign which demanded that the Justice Department deport Costello. During the 1949 mayoralty campaign, Clendenin Ryan, an eccentric millionaire who had sponsored Montgomery's campaign, lashed out at a supposed 'Costellodwyer' partnership. The evidence for this rested on a meeting between the two at Costello's apartment in 1942. Halley questioned Costello at length about this meeting and dwelt on the fact that there were Tammany Hall politicians present. Costello maintained that this was the only occasion he had met O'Dwyer, and that O'Dwyer had come to ask him some questions on Army business.[37]

O'Dwyer appeared before the committee for the first time on 16 March, and began with a prepared statement in which he gave his views on the development of organized crime since Prohibition. In this statement, and in his replies to the committee's questions, O'Dwyer expressed common-sense views which were totally unacceptable to the committee's self-righteousness and its ethnic conspiracy interpretation, designed to protect and strengthen the country's morality legislation.

O'Dwyer began by attacking the imposition of Prohibition, which he said bred racketeering, corruption and a disrespect for law:

> Let's thoroughly understand that Prohibition was jammed down the throats of the people by a few legislators and a few supporters. Let's accept what is now obvious: that Prohibition was not respected as a law by the majority of the people.[38]

When Halley noted at a later point that his administration had not suppressed gambling, O'Dwyer impatiently pointed out that:

> as long as you have 15 million people that want to bet, and as long as you have got $20 million as your own report shows, changing hands through bets on horse races throughout the country, and as long as you have got wires, State lines, information sheets, racing sheets and newspapers giving publicity, full publicity, giving full information to that 15 million, you have got something that is not entirely local.[39]

O'Dwyer also stated that at the beginning of his term as Mayor he had sought to democratize the procedures of Tammany Hall and rid it of gambler and gangster influences. He acknowledged his failure to do so and gave the reason why: 'It doesn't matter whether it is a banker, a businessman or a gangster, his pocketbook is always atractive'.[40] O'Dwyer's frank statement about the Manhattan organization could be applied to American politics in general, as the Kefauver Committee itself showed. Money buys power, and it doesn't always matter whether the money is 'clean' or 'dirty'.

In twelve months of hearings about 1,000 carefully chosen witnesses had appeared before the committee. The intention was always to provide evidence or support for the interpretation of organized crime that the committee had already chosen. The interpretation that suited the moral certainties of the Senators was that gambling was immoral, bad for business, and controlled by an evil ethnic conspiracy. The very thought of legalization was out of the question. No witness was allowed to shake the hold of the committee's anti-gambling bias and there was no room for balanced consideration and reporting of different arguments. O'Dwyer's interpretation was based on logic, evidence and the experience of running the largest and most complex city in America; but if the Senators had allowed such an interpretation to gain popular acceptance it would have meant dismantling the morality legislation. The committee did not argue with O'Dwyer's views, even though they directly contradicted the committee's naïve, simplistic analysis. Instead Halley discredited O'Dwyer.

Halley, in an interview with Lester Velie of *Collier's Magazine* immediately after the hearings, revealed his battle plan for the O'Dwyer interrogation:

> We were probing a man's motives, his state of mind—before millions of people. Why was O'Dwyer in Frank Costello's apartment? Why did he associate with that underworld character, Irving Sherman? Why didn't he close up gambling in New York? Motives. Motives.[41]

In other words, Halley intended firstly to prove O'Dwyer's guilt by association with Sherman and Costello and secondly to blame him for not closing up gambling in New York. Halley was probing O'Dwyer's 'motives' for doing nothing that could be proved to be criminal. Association was not a crime, and no mayor in New York's history had closed up gambling. It was trial by innuendo and proved to be devastatingly effective, at least in the eyes of the Press.

When Halley began to ask questions, many of them referring to events a dozen years earlier, O'Dwyer appeared stunned by the extent of counsel's preparation. Because his answers lacked the studied detail of Halley's questions, and because he invariably tended to blame subordinates or political enemies for his inconsistencies, O'Dwyer's answers seemed evasive or quarrelsome. Aided by copies of the 1945 Beldock Grand Jury reports obtained through a court order, Halley quizzed O'Dwyer in great detail about the alleged sabotage by O'Dwyer's office of Amen's waterfront investigation, the failure to prosecute Adonis and Anastasia, and his defence of the sleeping policemen after the death of Abe Reles.[42]

O'Dwyer reminded the committee that the Beldock Grand Jury presentment had been issued 'as a campaign document by the Republican candidate for District Attorney', and that also, in such cases, a grand jury is 'just putty in the hands of a District Attorney' who is able to 'twist it to any purpose'. He denied that he had sabotaged Amen's waterfront investigation and had, in fact, defended it when Mayor La Guardia wanted to end it. He had not ordered a discontinuance of the waterfront extortion cases in 1940 but had shelved them in favour of the 'Murder Inc.' cases because his office had a small staff and limited resources. He pointed out that 'organized murder is worse than organized extortion'. He had no case against Adonis, and his case against Anastasia had gone out of the window with Reles. He repeated his defence of the sleeping policemen. Whatever mistakes had been made, he argued, resulted from his preoccupation with the 'Murder Inc.' cases and from actions taken in the District Attorney's office after he had taken leave of absence to joint the Army in June 1942.[43]

Halley then turned to O'Dwyer's alleged association with Frank Costello and Irving Sherman. O'Dwyer said that he had made contact with both in relation to his work as an Army investigator. He testified that he had gone to Frank Costello's apartment in 1942 to question hime about a rumour relating to a contract for war materials and had found a cocktail party in progress, with Tammany leader Michael Kennedy and several lesser political figures as guests. O'Dwyer denied that he had ever done political favours for either Costello or Sherman and repeated that he tried to reform Tammany. Senator Tobey's characteristic reaction to the testimony about the visit to Costello's apartment was:

> It almost seems to me that you should say 'Unclean, unclean,' as the old Romans practiced it, and that you should leave him alone as they do a leper. But you trot up to him and do business with him.[44]

In effect Tobey was saying that investigators should not come into contact with suspected criminals. The committee, with its pro-La Guardia stance, had not pointed out that Costello had been playing politics in Manhattan during the entire twelve years of La Guardia's tenure.

Halley turned the final part of the New York hearings into an inquest into why O'Dwyer had not closed down gambling in the city. O'Dwyer admitted that bookmaking was a problem in New York, but argued that he had done everything in this power to cope with an impossible situation, by appointing the best men he knew to head the Police Department and by ordering John J. Murtagh, Commissioner of Investigations, to conduct a study of bookmaking and police corruption. When Halley persisted in implying that O'Dwyer was to blame for the great extent of bookmaking in the city, the Ambassador replied that the Mayor of a city of eight million people had the reponsibility of 'dealing with hundreds of millions of dollars worth of construction, housing, health and all the things that go to run a city', and that law enforcement was chiefly the responsibility of the police and the district attorneys. O'Dwyer pointed out that the absence of federal laws and law enforcement in the field of bookmaking made local enforcement virtually impossible. Murtagh's study had found that the wire-service rooms essential to gambling in New York had actually moved over the Hudson River to New Jersey in the early 1940s. Murtagh testified that in 1947 he had supplied New Jersey officials with information on a large number of wire-service rooms in their state and claimed that this information was ignored until three years later.[45]

Both O'Dwyer and Murtagh stressed that the illegality of gambling was counter-productive and tended to corrupt the police. O'Dwyer said that 'whenever you have gambling and it is illegal, and you have policemen, you have the danger of corruption'. Murtagh added: 'When you put cops to work enforcing the gambling laws, there is a certain percentage of them that tend to go sour. Unquestionably'. The committee's attitude and response to such statements was calculated to leave no doubt that they felt that O'Dwyer's administration had been negligent in the fight against organized crime.[46]

O'Dwyer's testimony was completed on the morning of the final day of the hearings, but Halley's stage management continued until the very end. First, the chairman of the New York Anti-Crime Committee, Spruille Braden, read a long statement in which he referred to Tobey's 'eloquent and impassioned plea for a spiritual and religious revival in this country if crime and corruption are to be exterminated (see pp. 122–123), and added his own comments about the threat of 'communism and Russian expansionism' and the 'breakdown in morality today, especially in Government'. Tobey returned the compliment by noting that Braden's paper was 'something that breathes the spirit that will save America' and finishing with an exhortation:

We must concentrate ourselves to a great cause and sing in the old battle hymn of Onward Christian Soldiers, go out and redeem this old world of ours.[47]

The climax of the hearings was, however, the testimony of John Crane, head of the Fireman's Union, who claimed he had personally handed Mayor O'Dwyer $10,000 for a political campaign. There was no opportunity for O'Dwyer to cross-examine Crane and the charge was not proved in a latter investigation. *Time* magazine indicated the sole reason for Crane's appearance and sensational charge was that it 'touched off the bangup ending the audience had been waiting for'. Halley had, indeed, provided a good show for the television viewers. As Ollie Crawford of the *Philadelphia Inquirer* commented: 'The Roman's were right—there's no show like watching people thrown to the lions'.[48]

The committee's final judgement on O'Dwyer came in the Third Interim Report:

Neither O'Dwyer nor his appointees took any effective action against the top echelon of the gambling, narcotics, waterfront, murder or bookmaking rackets. In fact, his actions impeded promising investigations of such rackets. His defence of public officials who were derelict in their duties, and his actions in investigations of corruption, and his failure to follow up concrete evidence of organized crime, particularly in the case of Murder Inc., and the waterfront, have contributed to the growth of organized crime, racketeering and gangsterism in New York City.[49]

The report, drafted chiefly by Halley and Kefauver, thus put the blame for organized crime in New York squarely on O'Dwyer's shoulders. However, even had the committee produced conclusive evidence of O'Dwyer's corruption, instead of innuendo, the charge of individual responsibility for the growth of organized crime would be absurd. No New York politician had solved the conditions on the waterfront or put a stop to gambling. Brooklyn District Attorney, Miles McDonald, though excessively praised by the committee for the conviction of a bookmaker, had not solved one waterfront murder and, in fact, was a regular guest at Joe Ryan's annual get-together of gangsters, politicians and corrupt businessmen (see p. 64). In contrast O'Dwyer, as Brooklyn District Attorney, had broken up a crime ring which, in Kefauver's words, was responsible 'for the execution of between 120 and 130 persons throughout the country'.[50]

At one point the committee demonstrated the extent of gambling in New York City by producing figures for the circulation of racing sheets which gave information that was only relevant to gamblers. Although La Guardia had the reputation of being an anti-gambling mayor, some forty million of these sheets were sold annually in his final years in office. By the end of O'Dwyer's tenure this figure had dropped to thirty million. The committee's logic, however, was that because O'Dwyer was in favour of legalizing some forms of gambling he was somehow more responsible for the extent of gambling in the city than La Guardia had been before him.[51]

In every city it visited the Kefauver Committee's limited staff and resources had required it to seek help from local pressure groups and political interests and, for the sake of simplicity, the committee tended to take sides in local political struggles. The inconsistency and distortion caused by this approach is illustrated by comparing the treatment received by O'Dwyer to that received by Mayor Morrison of New Orleans. The committee's investigators had gone to New Orleans and found out in short order: that Morrison was a close associate of Gasper Gulotta, representative of the Bourbon Street vice interests, and of Henry Mills, the city's main illegal lottery operator; and that Morrison had forced the resignation of his Superintendent of Police, Adair Watters, because he had been overzealous in the enforcement of the gambling laws. The evidence used to discredit O'Dwyer was far less conclusive; and yet the committee's questioning of Morrison was as docile as the following exchange suggests:

KEFAUVER. Mayor Morrison, in general, as I understand your testimony, I feel that you and your Police Department made a substantial effort to eliminate organized criminality and gambling in the city of New Orleans. Is that correct?
MORRISON. That is correct.[52]

The New Orleans hearings bolstered Morrison's image as a crime crusader at a time when it was in danger of being exposed as fraudulent. Morrison remained his city's top politician for a decade after the committee's visit, while, at the time of the New York hearings, O'Dwyer was finished in New York politics and discrediting him was worthless. The difference in their treatment can only be explained by the fact that Morrison was a political ally of the committee, and had recently and expediently become an outspoken critic of gambling, while O'Dwyer was the nation's best-known advocate of legalizing gambling, and thus a ready-made target for Chief Counsel Rudolph Halley, who had political ambitions of his own in New York.

Even after the New York hearings had finished the Senate committee continued to pursue O'Dwyer. Senator Tobey had received an anonymous postcard during the New York hearings concerning a mysterious million-dollar cheque in O'Dwyer's name that had circulated between New York and the Ambassador's residence in Mexico City. Since O'Dwyer had constantly stressed his poverty, and none of his attackers had been able to prove his acceptance of graft, this lead was taken seriously by the committee. The new chairman of the committee, Senator O'Conor, dispatched an investigator to Mexico City to inquire about the cheque, and several New York newspapers got hold of the story. A few days later, the State Department explained that the bank transaction did not involve O'Dwyer personally at all, but had merely been the first instalment on Mexican lend-lease repayments. Not surprisingly, O'Dwyer was furious at this embarrassing blunder by the committee.[53]

The architect of the New York hearings, Rudolph Halley, emerged as the new hero of the city's political reform movement. At the end of 1951 he demonstrated the continued impact of the hearings by winning the presidency of the New York City Council without the support of the two main parties. Halley's political rise, however, ended in 1953 with an unsuccessful bid to become Mayor; he had, predictably, exploited the law-and-order issue and promised to end street crime in New York. By suggestion and repetition, not proof, his charges linking Frank Costello and O'Dwyer gained a high level of public acceptance. In Costello and O'Dwyer and talk of the mysterious Mafia he had provided scapegoats for the problem of organized crime, and diverted attention away from re-examining the laws and law enforcement O'Dwyer himself later summed up the importance of Halley's conduct of the New York hearings; Halley had 'laid the groundwork for national acceptance of McCarthyism'.[54]

Boosted by the favourable public response to his chairmanship of the crime committee, Senator Kefauver campaigned for the presidency of the United States. By the end of 1951 opinion polls put him second to President Truman as the Democratic choice in the 1952 elections. Campaigning in a coonskin hat, symbolizing his senatorial victory against Tennessee bossism, he won a series of sensational primary victories. At the Democratic convention, however, he was passed over in favour of Governor Adlai Stevenson of Illinois. In 1956 Kefauver made a second bid for the presidential nomination but was again frustrated by Stevenson. He did get the party's vice-presidential nomination but the Democrats were anyway heavily defeated in the second Eisenhower landslide. After this election Kefauver returned to the Senate and the chairmanship of the Senate Subcommittee on Antitrust and Monopoly, from which he launched important investigations into price fixing and economic concentration in the steel, automobile and drug industries. Here he made the most significant contributions of his career. Hearings were in progress when, Kefauver, drained by years of almost constant campaigning and committee work, died of a heart attack in 1963 at the age of 60.[55]

Apart from getting organized crime accepted as a national problem, however, the Kefauver Committee's legislative and educative accomplishments were very limited. The committee made twenty-two recommendations to combat the giant conspiracy it claimed to have uncovered. These included a number of complicated acts tightening up the existing gambling legislation, the establishment of a Federal Crime Commission, imposition of heavier penalties for narcotics violations, and proposals related to regulation of immigration and deportation. Some administrative changes in the Justice Department and the Bureau of Internal Revenue followed the committee's suggestions, but most of the proposals for new legislation generated little enthusiasm in Congress and passed into oblivion.[56]

The committee's key recommendation was the passage of a bill completely outlawing inter-state transmission of gambling information, intended to curb the racing-news wire service. The bill was endorsed by Attorney-General Howard McGrath, who optimistically stated at the hearings that 'the delay that is provided in this Bill would, in our opinion, sound the death knell of illegal betting'. The bill failed to get through Congress despite McGrath's enthusiasm.[57]

In 1951 Congress, while refusing to pass the committee's gambling recommendations, did approve a wagering tax bill despite opposition from Kefauver. By this measure Congress was hoping to hurt gambling operators: first, directly through a 10 per cent tax on gross receipts; and second, through a registration requirement that would expose those registered to harassment from local law enforcement. The law was treated with contempt. In 1960–1, for example, three wagering stamps were sold in New York City while 2,600 bookmakers were arrested twice or more.[58]

The Kefauver Committee strongly recommended that the federal government take 'affirmative action to rid our shores of alien criminals who have become members of predatory criminal groups'—a predictable response since the committee considered organized crime to be an alien intrusion. The Bureau of Naturalization and Immigration began proceedings against many of the Italian-American suspected criminals named in the hearings. Joe Adonis was the most notable gangster to follow Lucky Luciano into exile. However, deporting suspected drug traffickers was not a very intelligent approach to America's drug problems. Luciano, Adonis and other former bootleggers had the connections, capital and inclination to help organize international networks for the production, shipment and distribution of drugs, heroin in particular. For most of the 1950s the government tried to deport Frank Costello, without success. Costello's case was aided by the Italian government's reluctance to take in yet another American-bred criminal.[59]

The Kefauver Committee had recommended that, while federal agencies could not be a substitute for state and local enforcement in dealing with organized crime, the federal government must provide leadership and guidance, establish additional techniques for maximum coordination of law enforcement agencies, take a positive approach in using its power to fight organized crime, and seek legislation when its powers were insufficient. In effect the committee was arguing the case for increased federal involvement in the enforcement of the gambling and drug laws; although the committee's own proposals in this regard were shelved, they had set an important process in motion. The federal government was dragged further and further into the hopeless and corrupting task of enforcing laws prohibiting certain activities involving cash transactions between willing parties.

The committee's final recommendations were optimistic entreaties to the American people. The voting public had to express 'an affirmative desire for the elimination of organized criminal operations and official corruption through the continued exercise of the vote' and pay careful attention 'to the efficiency and honesty of the men whom they employ to govern them'.[60] Throughout the hearings the committee had applauded apparent local successes in the fight against organized crime and castigated apparent corrupt or passive public officials who allowed vice in their jurisdictions. However, as shown in Part II, the voting public in New York, Los Angeles and New Orleans had already installed officials, in Mayors La Guardia, Bowron and Morrison, whom the committee approved of, without the desired effect of putting an end to protected, organized crime activities. Not even the most genuine of officials who claimed they were honest and efficient could resolve the basic dilemma of enforcing morality: prohibition laws were relatively easy and immensely profitable to exploit.

The Kefauver Committee's last words were:

Ultimate success in the war against crime depends on the uplifting of standards of public and private morality, a rededication to basic spiritual values, which will entail righteous indignation over crime and corruption. To this end, the committee looks with confidence to the great force of religion and morality as applied in all phases of life and to sound education of the generations which follow.[61]

The committee, having reduced the complexities of organized crime to a Good versus Evil equation, thus could only echo Senator Tobey and produce answers that were appropriate to the rural, small-town society of nineteenth-century America. These answers were not based on reality but wishful thinking. Calls for 'righteous indignation' have regularly been used to block other approaches to difficult problems and the committee's 'righteous indignation' had successfully ruled out other approaches to the problem of organized crime.

The only major federal legislative reverse suffered by America's moral crusaders had been in 1933 when the Prohibition of alcohol was repealed. Significantly this followed the Wickersham Commission's Report in 1931, which presented impartially collected evidence about the enforcement of the Volstead Act and reported the arguments of both wets and drys. The wets argued that Prohibition was a failure which deprived governments of revenue and enriched corrupt individuals and eventually won the battle. However, the Kefauver Committee did not consider other approaches to the prohibition of gambling and simply manipulated the evidence in order to find scapegoats among nebulous alien conspiracies and individual politicians. In doing so the committee were repeating the tactics of earlier moral crusades. In 1910 a critic of the moral crusaders had expressed his dislike of the practice 'of piling up recitals of filth and iniquity . . . and then . . . running to Congress for more legislation'.[62] In 1950–1, the members of Congress themselves piled up the equivalent tales of 'filth' and 'iniquity' with the sole intention of safeguarding the country's attempt to impose morality by tightening up enforcement of the existing legislation. The propaganda of the Kefauver Committee seriously impeded any other approach to the problem of organized crime.

11   Prolonging and crusade

The Kefauver Committee had helped to propagate a message that dominated public and professional opinion for the next twenty years. Organized crime was portrayed as the work of an alien conspiracy, corrupting or overwhelming public officials, and poisoning the country's morality. The only solution was increased federal involvement in gambling and drug law enforcement, complementing diligent and honest effort by state and local authorities. With effective gambling and drug prohibition, it was thought that citizens would no longer fill the 'coffers' of the Mafia. Variations of this message were repeated in virtually every means of mass-media communication—newspapers, books, radio, television and films. Events were distorted, even invented, to fit an alien conspiracy theory that the public were very willing to believe in. The theory was wrong and the policy based on it was counter-productive, sustaining rather than suppressing high levels of crime and corruption. This chapter describes how and why the American people were misled.

The federal agency which benefited most from the Kefauver Committee hearings was, predictably, the Narcotics Bureau, which had been so influential in the committee's conclusions about the Mafia. The Bureau's indispensability was firmly established and its budget would never again be cut. Commissioner Harold Anslinger continued to steer public opinion, as well as state and federal lawmakers, in the direction he wanted: more laws and more repressive powers; drug addiction in the United States was to be a police problem not a medical problem, draconian sentences would deter both use and sale. Federal legislation passed in 1951 sharply increased penalties for drug offenders, both users and suppliers. And in 1956 the peak of federal punitive action against drugs was reached when sentences for some offences were raised to five years on the first conviction, and the death penalty could be imposed for selling heroin to anyone under 18 years old.[1]

According to Anslinger and his agents, the main peril faced by the country were foreign conspiracies. Journalists were fed many stories about the FBN standing alone in brave defiance not only of the Mafia but the People's Republic of China. The intention of both was to speed up the moral degeneration of the United States. Anslinger himself co-authored a book published in 1954 which claimed that most of the illegal drug supply was grown and processed in communist China, from where it was spread 'with cold deliberation' to free countries, notably the United States. Drug trafficking, it was said, provided China with dollars for war, and weakened the health and moral fibre of its enemies. No credible evidence was ever produced to support such charges although they were often repeated as proven in the Press. In fact, research since the 1950s has indicated that America's friends in Asia, such as the Chinese Nationalists, Thais and Burmese, were behind the bulk of the drug traffic.[2]

Anslinger also claimed to have the name and address of virtually every drug addict in the entire United States and few people doubted his word. The Bureau was thus able to claim success in the war on drugs when the numbers went down. In 1962, for example, the *New York Times* reported that there was 'statistical evidence that the small and highly professional Bureau of Narcotics has done much to cut down the use of illicit drugs' and continued:

> The incidence of narcotics addiction in the United States today is estimated at one in 4,000 as compared with one in 2,100 in 1950, the peak of a brief post-war resurgence of drug addiction.
>
> The decline coincides with two control measures enacted by Congress, the Boggs Act of 1952 [sic] and the Narcotics Control Act of 1956. Both increased sharply the penalties for illegal possession and sale of narcotics.[3]

Anslinger's statisticians manufactured these estimates and it is therefore hardly surprising that they reflected well on his agency. The reality was that draconian laws had failed to deter drug traffickers from exploiting the richest market in the world, and that high-level operators had little to fear from an agency that was later revealed to be the reverse of 'highly professional'.

During Anslinger's tenure thousands of drug users and sellers did serve long sentences in federal and state institutions, most for selling minute quantities of drugs to informants or under-cover agents. The majority of those convicted were black and Hispanic-Americans, unable to afford lawyers capable of invoking constitutional safeguards as to forced confessions, entrapment and illegal search and seizure. A representative case was that of Gilbert Zaragoza, a 21-year-old Mexican-American, who was trapped selling heroin to a 17-year-old addict–informer for the FBN. Zaragoza was prosecuted under the 1956 sale-to-minors section which allowed for the death penalty upon conviction. The jury refused to recommend death and so the judge sentenced him to a life sentence with no chance of parole. Zaragoza's was the first of many thirty-, forty- and fifty-year sentences imposed in the following years on the lowest level of drug offenders.[4] Most agents were incapable or unwilling to attack those higher up the drug supply hierarchy. Low-level arrrest and conviction statistics were the easiest to compile.

Zaragoza was himself an addict who had to sell drugs to pay for his own habit. His treatment contrasts with that of another and much more famous addict, whose story is told by Anslinger in a book called *The Murderers* which he co-authored in 1962. 'This addict', Anslinger wrote, was one of the most influential members of the Congress of the United States. He headed one of the powerful committees of Congress. His decisions and statements helped to shape and direct the destiny of the United States and the free world.

Anslinger learnt that this leader was a morphine addict who had no intention of fighting his habit:

> It was a delicate moment in world affairs. The situation presented by the morphine-addicted lawmaker presented a precarious problem. There was imminent danger that the facts would become known and there was no doubt that they would be used to the fullest in the propaganda machines of our enemies. Such a scandal could do incalculable harm to the United States and the free world.

Commissioner Anslinger then admitted that he helped the legislator obtain regular supplies of morphine to prevent him going 'to the pushers'. The addict was later revealed to be America's other famous post-war conspiracy theorist, Senator Joe McCarthy.[5]

In recent years it has also been revealed that Anslinger and his agents were even more directly involved in the Cold War. Studies of documents released under the Freedom of Information Act by John Marks and other writers have detailed the FBN's involvement with CIA efforts to develop mind manipulation with drugs for interrogation purposes. During the paranoid early 1950s the CIA, fearing that the Communists were getting ahead of them, intensified their research into behaviour control. Anslinger cooperated and supplied the services of some of his agents plus 30 grams of heroin and 11 pounds of marijuana for research purposes. A CIA document noted that heroin 'can be useful in reverse because of the stresses produced when . . . withdrawn from those addicted'. In 1953 project MKULTRA began to explore the potential of a newly invented hallucinogen, LSD. In one experiment, Frank Olson, a researcher employed by the CIA, was spiked and subsequently leapt from a tenth-floor window, in circumstances that were covered up for twenty-two years, until 1975.

With Anslinger's explicit permission, the aforementioned George White (see p. 109) was seconded from the FBN on a part-time basis to set up safe houses for drug experiments. In 1955 White took over the running of the FBN's office in San Francisco and one of the CIA's most bizarre programmes. The San Francisco safe house was a plush apartment, decorated in the style of a film-set bordello and wired for sound. Drugs were served up to unwary victims in food, drinks and cigarettes in crude efforts to elicit information. Most of White's subjects were addicts, small-time dealers or prostitutes, who would be unlikely to complain if they found out what was being done to them or who could be blackmailed into compliance. White would also hire prostitutes to pick up men in bars, bring them back to the apartment, spike their drinks and take them into the bedroom. White would then watch the proceedings through a two-way mirror. As the various branches of the CIA obtained or developed new chemicals, they were taken to White for such clandestine testing. This type of programme was not ended by the CIA until 1966, when it was realized that the results did little to replace traditional spycraft, advanced electronic technology and interrogation techniques of the heavy-handed policeman.

Unlike his CIA counterparts White loved publicity. He had once worked for a newspaper and knew how to get reporters to write favourably about him. He continually talked up his arrests and, like Anslinger, the Mafia conspiracy theory. Many crime writers have acknowledged their debt to the FBN's 'Agent Extraordinary', as did the Treasury Department which awarded him their highest decoration—the Gold Medal for Exceptional Services. But, as John Marks has written, George White lived with extreme personal contradictions:

> As could be expected of a narcotics agent, he violently opposed drugs. Yet he died largely because his beloved alcohol had destroyed his liver. He had tried everything else, from marijuana to LSD . . . He was a law-enforcement official who regularly violated the law. Indeed the CIA turned to him because of his willingness to use the power of his office to ride roughshod over the rights of others—in the name of 'national security', when he tested LSD for the Agency, in the name of stamping out drug abuse, for the Narcotics Bureau . . .

After he retired he wrote his own epitaph for his role with the CIA, only half in jest. He wrote in a letter to a former colleague: 'Where else could a red-blooded American boy lie, kill, cheat, steel, rape and pillage with the sanction and blessing of the All-Highest?'[6]

Numerous lies and distortions about drugs can be attributed directly or indirectly to Harry Anslinger and his agents. Nothing, however, was more fraudulent than the image he cultivated for his agency. FBN agents in countless books and articles were portrayed as tough, dedicated and efficient professionals guarding against Mafia or communist plots to poison America. This image was not challenged until after Anslinger retired in 1962. But in 1968 Attorney-General Ramsey Clark revealed 'significant corruption' in the New York office of the FBN, by far the agency's largest. The corruption, Clark said, included 'illegally selling and buying drugs, retaining contraband for personal use and sale, taking money allocated for informants and failing to enforce laws'.[7]

Andrew Tartaglino, the inspector responsible for the investigation, later revealed more details in testimony before Congress:

> Corruption and questionable procedure were commonplace. Agents were engaged in illicit activities that included accepting bribes from all levels of traffickers, selling confiscated drugs and firearms, looting of searched apartments, providing tipoffs to suspects and defendants, and threatening the lives of fellow agents who dared to expose them.
> There was complete breakdown of discipline and administrative management

in that office. We found, for instance, that the file cabinet containing the names and payments to all the informants in the New York region was normally unlocked and located in an area that made it readily accessible to anyone who cared to inspect the file. Not surprisingly, the office was experiencing an unusually large number of informant homicides.

Tartaglino also stated that between February 1959 and early 1961 there were three separate incidents of federal narcotics agents receiving overdoses of heroin, none of which were investigated. One of the agents died. Reliable information was developed that all three agents received their overdoses because they attempted to extort money from traffickers who already had an 'arrangement' with other corrupt agents in the New York office.[8]

Eventually almost every agent in the New York office was fired, forced to resign, transferred or convicted, and this constituted about one-third of the agency's total manpower—a staggering proportion. Most were veterans appointed during Anslinger's time.

There is no doubt that Anslinger's agency was the most thoroughly corrupt, repressive and inept federal agency since the Prohibition Bureau of the 1920s. The Prohibition Bureau's honesty and efficiency had, however, been improved towards the end of its life; the Narcotics Bureau was so rotten that it had to be abolished and replaced by a totally new agency in the Department of Justice.

Anslinger spread his gospel nationally and internationally—many countries now tragically, uselessly and corruptly pursue drug control policies which he pioneered. Largely because of his efforts the United States had draconian powers to deter the use of marijuana, cocaine and the opiates. But as we shall see in the final part of the book, these powers failed to deter—from the 1960s the demand for illegal drugs increased, as did the hysteria, as did also the potential for organized criminal activity.

The strengthening of 'public and private morality', which the Kefauver Committee frequently said was essential to combat organized crime, did not happen. As the country got richer during the 1950s individual entrepreneurs, syndicates and corrupt public officials maintained the public's supply of illegal goods and services.

Prostitution remained widespread and came in a variety of packages. Streetwalkers concentrated in the slum and downtown areas of cities, rendering service in cars, back-alleys and in the sleazier hotels. Higher-class prostitution was more discreet and much more expensive. In most cities prospective customers could telephone 'call-girls', operating from comfortable apartments, and luxurious whorehouses in the tradition of New Orleans could still be found in parts of the country. Some anxious-to-please firms even provided girls for out-of-town buyers as a matter of course, with the burgeoning PR departments acting as procurers. The girls were chosen for their discretion and received as much as $500 a trick. Accountants saw to it that their fees were tax-deductible. A sociological study of this business practice was subtitled 'The Pimp in the Grey Flannel Suit'.[9]

Gambling, however, was still America's most popular and profitable illegal activity. Casinos in Hot Springs (Arkansas), Newport/Covington (Kentucky), Cicero (Illinois) and Beaumont (Kansas) continued to flourish during the 1950s. The take for the 1959 season in Hot Springs, for example, was reportedly $100 million, and there had been no gambling arrest there for over two decades. In many cities hotel porters, desk clerks and taxi-cab drivers would steer out-of-town businessmen to the regular high-stakes poker games, where as much as $100,000 changed hands every night. Slot-machine manufacturers, notably Bally, churned out new machines by the thousands for a domestic market which, apart from Nevada, was not supposed to exist. Numbers players could place their daily wagers at any police-approved spot—news-stands, luncheonettes, poolrooms and grocery stores. The Kefauver Committee exposure forced the Continental Press wire service to close down, but bookmakers were not unduly inconvenienced. They could get odds from companies such as Athletic Productions Inc. of Minneapolis, which catered to some 10,000 clients but could not be closed down because it simply sold information. The Delaware Sports Service also dealt in information, in this case race results at the rate of 1,300 in ten minutes. Layoff betting services continued to operate out of Newport and Covington in Kentucky, long after they were exposed by the Kefauver Committee. In the Northeast, demand for these services became so great that in New York City a separate system was established that operated from hotels and nightclubs, usually one step ahead of the law. In all, billions of tax-free dollars went to gambling operators. Millions of Americans continued to take their chances on the result of a wager, and the fact that they were bucking a moral crusade did not concern them.[10]

Gambling entrepreneurs prospered by supplying a demand that was obviously growing. The nation's most significant operator during these years was Meyer Lansky, a former New York bootlegger and partner of the late Bugsy Siegel (see pp. 89–90). After Prohibition Lansky had invested in numerous legal, semi-legal and illegal gambling enterprises in different parts of the country. In the 1950s he exploited a close and corrupt relationship with Cuban dictator Fulgencio Batista to develop Havana as a 'sin city' for American vacationers and frustrated 'high rollers'. With other notables, such as Phil Kastel, Moe Dalitz, Santo Trafficante and many more, Lansky promoted numerous plush casinos until Fidel Castro helped bring about Batista's downfall in 1959 and American gangsters were no longer welcome. Lansky and his friends then moved operations over to the British-run Bahamas.

Lansky also retained very profitable rackets within the United States. An indication of the extent of these was given in January 1973 when several of his associates pleaded guilty to entering into a conspiracy in 1960 to conceal Lansky's continuing financial interest in the La Vegas Flamingo, and to conceal true casino receipts by understating $4.5 million annually from 1960 and 1967, for a total figure of $36 million. Credit had been extended to junketeers who would repay IOUs which were not entered on casino records. As gambling historians Jerome Skolnick and John Dombrink have related, Lansky was credited with the development and refinement of skimming and the processing of untaxed revenue through Swiss banks which opened the way for Lansky's investment of millions of dollars in US real estate. Lansky never stood trial on the charges because the federal judge found that 'this elderly and seriously ill defendant will never be well enough to undergo the rigors of the trial of this complex case'. Lansky died five years later at the age of 79, leaving a fortune that probably no other gangster has approached.[11]

Back in the 1950s the conditions that enabled innumerable gambling operators to profit had not been affected by changes in local policing. In many cities police departments were reorganized with the intention of increasing efficiency and decreasing political interference. This was thought to be the prescription that would end the lax and corrupt enforcement of the vice laws. By the end of the decade most departments were fairly well insulated from political meddling and the control of vice had been transferred from the ordinary patrolman to special squads. However, these changes did not have the desired effect of better law enforcement. The massive size of many police departments and their lack of accountability prevented the easy detection of corrupt activities. Pimps, prostitutes, narcotics dealers and gamblers simply dealt directly with the squads without the need for ward politicians as intermediaries.

The lack of accountability to local people showed up in the selectivity of gambling arrests. In the late 1950s, for example, Judge David W. Williams charged that the Los Angeles police made about 90 per cent of their gambling arrests in the black community, which was the home of only a tenth of the city's population and the host of only a fraction of its illegal games. The only defense offered by the Los Angeles Board of Police Commissioners was that things were much the same in other cities.[12] There is little doubt that the heavy-handed and selective enforcement of the laws against gambling, prostitution and drugs contributed to the tensions between the police and the black community and helped ignite the 1960s riots. There is also little doubt that had such methods been employed against the 'respectable' professionals and businessmen who gambled there would have been outrage not seen since the time the country had tried to suppress alcohol. State laws and local ordinances would have been rapidly reconsidered.

Instead the failure of local law enforcement to enforce laws which tried to prohibit cash transactions between willing parties was perceived to be the fault of a national conspiracy of Italian-Americans. The only solution seriously contemplated was increased federal involvement. By the end of the 1960s the federal government's law enforcement capacity had been substantially increased and Congress had passed a body of legislation which, as one commentator put it, 'at the very least . . . constitutes a great leap toward a police state'.[13] The next section explains the rationale behind bringing back significant federal enforcement of the morality legislation for the first time since the repeal of Prohibition.

As an easy explanation for the country's organized crime problems the Mafia could not be beaten, particularly after the concept had been given a veneer of respectability by the Kefauver Committee. It continued to be fostered by a string of tabloid journalists in the tradition of Jack Lait and Lee Mortimer. These two characteristically cashed in on the interest aroused by the committee by bringing out *U.S.A. Confidential* in 1952 in which the Mafia was 'the nucleus on which all organized vice, crime and corruption, not only in the U.S. but all over the world, has been built'.[14]

Lait and Mortimer had produced a formula that unreflective journalists the world over have since turned to when writing about US organized crime. The trick was to describe briefly how a secret criminal brotherhood developed in feudal Sicily, was transplanted to urban America at the end of the nineteenth century, and then took over organized crime operations in the entire country. As 'proof' all editors required were unrelated anecdotes about Italian-American gangsters, mainly from New York, with the narrative enlivened by words like 'godfather', 'tentacles', and most essentially 'omerta'. 'Omerta' was, according to Lait and Mortimer, 'the secret and unwritten' code of silence of the Mafia. Every member lived in 'mortal fear' of violating this code.[15] Numerous other writers followed their lead and inserted paragraphs about 'omerta' in their work, thus justifying assertions that otherwise would appear quite ridiculous. Who could contradict them if the Mafia's code of silence could not be violated?

After the excitement caused by the Kefauver hearings was over, Lait and Mortimer concentrated on furthering the cause of Joe McCarthy, and trying to end the careers of anyone who opposed the views of the senator from Wisconsin. The first book-length development of their alien-conspiracy thesis was by Ed Reid in 1952. In *Mafia*, the conspiracy was 'history's greatest threat to morality', and was 'the principal fount of all crime in the world, controlling vice, gambling, the smuggling and sale of dope, and other sources of evil'.[16] In 1959 came Frederick Sondern's *Brotherhood of Evil* which was endorsed by Commissioner of Narcotics, Harry Anslinger. In the foreword, Anslinger stated:

> We are engaged in a war against organized crime which involves the whole nation; in a war against an army of subtle and defiant men whose power and wickedness have grown steadily throughout the last decade . . . The core of this army are the Mafiosi.[17]

Literally hundreds of newspaper and magazine articles repeated the same theme, reflecting the law enforcement perspective on the problem of organized crime. The Mafia provided bureaucrats and politicians with an easy-to-communicate threat to the nation. The answer to this threat of course was more police and more laws to legitimize new means of control. In particular, gambling had to be suppressed. Until the 1970s gambling was always described as the financial mainstay or 'lifeblood' of the Mafia, the 'Treasure Chest of the Underworld'. 'If you scratch the professional operator of gambling ventures', wrote Ted Posten of the New York *Post*, 'you will find the narcotics peddler, the loan shark, the dice game operator, the murderer'.[18]

The knowledge that some Italian-American gangsters had become rich and powerful in their own cities, and had contact with other gangsters in other cities, was distorted into something far more mysterious and menacing. By the end of the 1960s the constant repetition of the Mafia label in the Press, in films and on television and the best-selling work of fiction producers such as Mickey Spillane and Mario Puzo ensured that most Americans had a conception of something called the Mafia as a monolithic, ethnically exclusive, strictly disciplined secret society, based on weird rituals, commanding the absolute obedience of its members and controlling all organized crime. Mafia and organized crime became virtually synonymous.[19] A 1971 Harris poll showed that 78 per cent of the American public accepted this alien conspiracy version of organized crime. Meanwhile, even if the public now believed that the Mafia lurked behind every neighbourhood bookie, prostitute and drug dealer, they continued to purchase prohibited goods and services.

The existence of the American Mafia as a centralized organization dominating organized crime could never be proven but incidents and revelations involving Italian-American gangsters continued to be distorted, thus keeping the idea alive.

In 1957 a convention of suspected Italian-American racketeers was disrupted by state police at Apalachin, New York. No useful information resulted from this action, but the fact that a few of the sixty-odd conventioneers came from as far afield as Florida and California added a much-needed boost to the alien-conspiracy theory as interest had been dwindling. Gangsters from different cities had been getting together since at least May 1929, when Atlantic City political and gambling boss, Enoch Johnson hosted a get-together of numerous East Coast bootleggers. These included Al Capone, Frank Nitti, Jake Guzik, Frank McErlane and Joe Saltis from Chicago, Meyer Lansky, Frank Costello, Lucky Luciano and Dutch Schultz from New York, and Max Hoff, Sam Lazar and Charles Schwartz from Philadelphia. This multi-ethnic convention was well organized and not disturbed by the police, nor doubtless were other multi-ethnic gangster conventions after 1929. The fact that Joseph Barbara, host at Apalachin, could not organize a barbecued steak dinner proved to many writers that his guests controlled organized crime in America. The most credible account of the Apalachin gathering was by Serrell Hillman of *Time* magazine. The guests were not part of a tightly knit syndicate, but instead a loose 'trade association' of criminals in various cities and areas, who ran their own shows in their own fields but had matters of mutual interest to take up.[20]

In 1963 public interest in a Mafia-like conspiracy was again rekindled when Senator John L. McClellan's Senate Permanent Subcommittee on Investigations held televised hearings before which Joseph Valachi revealed he was part of what was now called 'Cosa Nostra' or 'Our Thing'. This odd change of name was necessary partly because Valachi's family had come to America from Naples and not Sicily, home of the Mafia, and partly because it gave J. Edgar Hoover, who had consistently refused to credit Mafia conspiracy theories, a chance of a volte-face without too many people noticing. Before, Hoover had successfully kept the FBI out of the futile task of gambling law enforcement. But from 1963 on he chose to go along with the consensus of law enforcement opinion: organized crime was an alien conspiracy and gambling was this conspiracy's main source of income; therefore the FBI had to go into action against gambling.[21]

The man most responsible for bringing about this consensus and Hoover's conversion was Attorney-General Robert Kennedy. Kennedy had made his reputation as counsel for an earlier McClellan committee investigating industrial racketeering, but gambling was his primary concern as Attorney-General. 'Corruption and racketeering, financed largely by gambling', he wrote in 1962, 'are weakening the vitality and strength of the nation'. The following year he told Congress that gambling was one of the principal sources of revenue for the 'organized underworld', which he said could be called 'Mafia', 'Cosa Nostra' or 'the mob'; the name was for him, 'a matter of semantics'. This multi-named 'private government' was in charge of 'organized lawlessness' in the United States, 'with an annual income of billions, resting on a base of human suffering and moral corruption'. His term as Attorney-General was noted for a concerted federal drive against gambling and his own strong opposition to any moves to legalize this 'baleful influence', which he said, 'was weakening the vitality and strength of the nation'. A number of anti-gambling statutes were pushed through Congress including the prohibition of the inter-state transportation of wagering information or paraphernalia, and inter-state travel with intent to engage in certain unlawful activities, one of which was gambling. The Department of Justice and the Internal Revenue also went on the offensive, arresting hundreds of gamblers in a series of raids. But Kennedy and other influential members of the law enforcement community realized that more laws and more police manpower were required. The Valachi show was put on to mobilize support.[22]

The McClellan Subcommittee concluded from Valachi's testimony that a criminal structure had emerged from a New York gang power struggle in 1930–1. This structure was based on military levels of authority and organized into entities called 'families'. There were five such families in New York City, and equivalents all over the country, linked into a national crime syndicate by a commission of approximately twelve members 'who decide policy, settle disputes, and regulate territorial operations'. The main sources of income for the Cosa Nostra were specified as illegal gambling and trafficking in narcotics. Murder was the main instrument of organizational control and the conspiracy had a code of absolute obedience and authority, reinforced by an initiation ceremony based on blood, fire, gun and knife.[23]

Robert Kennedy claimed that Valachi had provided the 'biggest single intelligence breakthrough yet in combating organized crime and racketeering in the United States',[24] and a new rush of books and articles started repeating, embellishing and changing Valachi's words. Valachi's qualifications for such a comprehensive analysis of organized crime in the United States were that he had been a getaway driver for a burglary ring in the 1920s, a mercenary in the New York gang war of 1930–1, and from then until his conviction for drug smuggling in 1960 no more than a criminal odd-jobs man around New York with connections to the syndicate run by Vito Genovese. His criminal career was not in the least well organized and his 'singing' produced no convictions. Although Valachi had never claimed any expertise on the national scene his limited knowledge of crime in the New York area was used to explain the structure of organized crime throughout the entire country.

Valachi's stories were accepted as factual even though he believed and repeated on oath 'anything' he heard in conversation 'here and there' with his fellow criminals. His evidence was not corroborated on any essential point and was anyway frequently inconsistent. It also contradicted many of the conclusions that the subcommittee drew from it. For example, membership of Cosa Nostra was said to confer benefits such as a share in its illicit gains and protection in times of trouble. But Valachi's testimony made it clear that he got nothing from crime other than what he took for himself and that he got no protection when he needed it.

Cosa Nostra was also said to require the total obedience of its members, yet Valachi testified that he was just one of many who took part in the drugs business even after being told not to by the bosses—'Because', as he explained, 'of moneymaking, the profit of it'. In 1968 Gordon Hawkins wrote an article which rendered Valachi's testimony much less credible; but, by then, it was too late. 'The Canary that Sang' had confirmed many old prejudices and misconceptions. Inconsistencies and contradictions did not matter. Valachi's testimony had been successfully distorted to fit political and bureaucratic needs.[25]

In the short term the Valachi hearings successfully helped justify Robert Kennedy's strategy to expand the national government's capacity to fight organized crime. When Kennedy became Attorney-General in 1961 the national government had twenty-six investigative units at work on the domestic crime scene. The Organized Crime and Racketeering Section of the Department of Justice had been set up in 1954 to coordinate the efforts of these units but was poorly staffed and got minimal cooperation especially from the FBI. Kennedy quadrupled the Organized Crime Section in size to over forty attorneys and encouraged its lawyers to target suspected racketeers. Convictions of racketeers by the federal government steadily increased from nineteen in 1960, ninety-six in 1961, 101 in 1962, 373 in 1963 and 677 in

1964. Gambling, being the 'principal source' of organized crime revenue, was a specific target. Information services such as Delaware Sports and Athletic Productions Inc. were closed down. The Biloxi, Missouri and Newport/Covington, Kentucky layoff centres were put out of operation. Slot machines were destroyed in Kentucky and pressure was put on the Arkansas state government to end casino gambling in Hot Springs.[26]

J. Edgar Hoover claimed that the Valachi testimony merely corroborated what the FBI already knew and began to repeat what was becoming the conventional wisdom about organized crime. In 1966, for example, he told a House Appropriations subcommittee that:

> La Cosa Nostra is the largest organization of the criminal underworld in this country, very closely organized and strictly disciplined. They have committed almost every crime under the sun . . . La Cosa Nostra is a criminal fraternity whose membership is Italian either by birth or national origin, and it has been found to control major racket activities in many of our larger metropolitan areas . . .

Hoover's words were quoted by the 1967 report of President Lyndon Johnson's Commission on Law Enforcement and the Administration of Justice to substantiate the report's own assertion that:

> the core of organized crime in the United States consists of 24 groups operating criminal cartels in large cities across the Nation. Their membership is exclusively Italian, they are in frequent communication with each other, and their smooth functioning is insured by a national body of overseers.

The Commission's report emphasized that gambling was the greatest source of revenue for organized crime, followed by loan sharking, narcotics, the infiltration of legitimate businesses, and labour racketeering. It recommended a complete package of laws to combat the Cosa Nostra's subversion of 'the very decency and integrity that are the most cherished attributes of a free society'.[27]

The conception of organized crime as an alien and united entity was vital. It could then be plausibly presented as many-faced, calculating and relentlessly probing for weak spots in the armour of American morality. Morality had to be protected from this alien threat. Aliens were corrupting the police; therefore the police had to be given more power. Compromise such as a reconsideration of the laws governing gambling and drug taking was out of the question—the only answer was increased law enforcement capacity and more laws to ensure the swift and effective capture of gambling operators and drug traffickers behind whom the Mafia was always lurking. (The Cosa Nostra label did not catch on with most journalists and fiction writers, but federal officials still use it.)

The message got across to the people who mattered, the legislators. By the end of the 1960s members of Congress were convinced enough by the Mafia supposed 'threat to the nation' to enact a series of measures long sought after by the federal law enforcement and intelligence community. Organized crime control provisions in the 1968 and 1970 omnibus crime control acts included: special grand juries; wider witness-immunity provisions for compelling reluctant testimony; extended sentences for persons convicted in organized crime cases; and the use of wiretapping and eavesdropping evidence in federal cases. The measures gave the same kind of head-hunting powers to federal police and prosecutors that Thomas E. Dewey had used to such superficial effect against organized crime in the 1930s on a local level. They inevitably tipped the balance away from such civil liberties as the right to privacy and protection from unreasonable search and seizure, and towards stronger policing powers. These laws and concurrent anti-drug legislation had a great potential for abuse. However, their potential for genuine and effective organized crime control was minimal because the conditions which fostered endemic crime and corruption in the United States persisted. The new control measures were, as constitutional scholar Leonard Levy put it, 'a salvo of fragmentation grenades that missed their targets and exploded against the Bill of Rights'.[28]

Among the 1970 measures were a series of bills that extended federal jurisdiction over gambling offenses even further. Federal prosecutors could now bring cases against gambling operations involving more than five persons and involving either thirty continuous days of operation or $2,000 per day in wagering. The FBI and the Department of Justice were then able to begin an aggressive anti-gambling campaign in many cities and finally, or so many writers thought, attack organized crime where it hurts—in the pocket. Organized Crime Strike Forces, recruited from different agencies, were set up in seventeen cities and initially put most of their resources into investigations of illegal gambling—around 60 per cent of strike force time was taken up with the effort.[29]

Wiretapping became standard procedure, and some prosecutors seemed to become more interested in justifying wiretaps than in controlling crime. In 1970 former Attorney-General Ramsay Clark put the opposing case forcefully. He pointed out that between the late 1950s and 1965 hundreds of man-years of FBI agent time had been wasted listening to the most trivial conversations or nothing at all and that in 1967 and 1968, without the use of any electronic surveillance, FBI convictions of organized crime and racketeering figures were several times higher than during any year before 1965. An agent could be investigating crime instead of spending eight-hour shifts sitting with a pair of headphones waiting for a suspect conversation. Clark thought that effective safeguards against misuse were unlikely and noted the known instances of police tapping bookies to determine what the pay-off should be for not shutting down the operation. He continued:

> The decision of whom to wiretap is necessarily selective. There is not world enough or time with present methods to overhear more than a few. The choice lends itself to persecution. Who is unpopular? Whom would we like to get? . . .

There have been repeated allegations [these allegations were later confirmed as true] that the FBI placed bugs in hotel rooms occupied by Dr Martin Luther King, Jr., and subsequently played the tapes of conversations . . . for various editors, Senators and opinion makers . . . A free society cannot endure where such police tactics are permitted. Today they may be used only against political enemies or unpopular persons. Tomorrow you may be the victim. Whoever the subject, the practice is intolerable.[30]

By the mid-1970s the strike forces' effort against gambling had subsided with little accomplished for all the enormous surveillance expense. Relatively few prison sentences resulted and those that did were short. In 1982 a former strike force chief told the *Wall Street Journal* that gambling cases had become something to keep the statistics up: 'We would investigate a couple of low grade bookmakers, call them organized crime figures and go after them'.[31]

The FBI similarly did not distinguish itself with its new weapons to fight 'the principal bank roll' of the Mafia. The most celebrated gambling case involving the FBI began sensationally on 6 May 1971. More than 400 federal agents and local police took part in a Michigan operation which resulted in 151 people being arrested, including sixteen Detroit police officers. They were charged with being involved in a $15 million-a-year gambling operation. The dragnet had been carried out in thirty-seven Michigan cities. Attorney General John Mitchell announced that this police action was the largest in the nation's history involving gambling. J. Edgar Hoover also crowed about this 'massive blow' against 'the underworld'. The case, however, fell apart in court. In 1974 charges against all 151 defendants were dropped when a federal court judge ruled that the government had obtained information through illegal wiretaps.[32] With corruption at local level and ineptitude at federal level the débâcle is representative of the country's crusade against gambling.

While politicians and law enforcement officials were clamouring for action against the monolithic Italian conspiracy which was thought to be controlling organized crime, some of the many thousands of conspiracies which actually do constitute successful organized crime were unravelling. Nor surprisingly they involved politicians and law enforcement officials.

A large part of the organization of gambling in New York City began to be revealed in the late 1960s. In 1966 a police officer named Frank Serpico was invited to join a gambling 'pad': a group of officers in a plain-clothes gambling squad who were paid off by gamblers. Serpico refused to join, as he had refused similar offers in the past. When he reported the existence of the pad to Captain Philip Foran, he was told that 'By the time it's all over, they'll find you face down in the East River'. Serpico then tried, successively, to interest the commander of the police area in which he worked, the First Deputy Police Commissioner, the mayor's assistant for police matters, and the Commissioner of Investigation. Unhappy with the lack of response,

Serpico took his information to the *New York Times* which began publishing a series of articles in April 1970.

The newspaper's stories, written by David Burnham, found other officers to support Serpico's allegations and concluded that bookmaking and policy play were the main sources of highly systematic corruption in the police department:

> New York gamblers maintain an intimate and financially rewarding relationship with many policemen that at times perverts law enforcement into a system of 'licensing' the city's vast gambling industry.

Each plain-clothes unit had a regular monthly meeting to decide which gamblers to take on and which to drop; those who had become 'too hot' were dropped. Charges to gamblers were based on their take. The policemen interviewed reported that while the basic graft collectors were plain-clothesmen, the payments circulated up through the department to inspectors and lieutenants. The basic payment to corrupt plain-clothesmen from gamblers was about $800 to $1,000 a month, with lieutenants sometimes getting double. Some got much more. 'You really are limited only by your own initiative', one detective said, 'Like you go out and make your own scores. I heard one guy openly boasting that he made $60,000 in the past two years'. Law enforcement had been replaced by regulation of crime. As one numbers operator later testified: 'You can't work numbers in Harlem unless you pay. If you don't pay, you go to jail . . . You go to jail on a frame if you don't pay'.

In response to the *New York Times* stories Mayor John Lindsay appointed a Commission to investigate the allegations, chaired by former Assistant District Attorney, William Knapp. In October 1971, when the Knapp Commission held its public hearings, the extent of police corruption began to be publicly disclosed. The hearings destroyed the popular police argument that corruption was limited to a few 'rotten apples' in an otherwise healthy barrel. While the police union president labelled the Knapp Commission evidence 'a tale concocted in a whorehouse', testimony and tape-recorded evidence provided conclusive documentation of highly organized corruption in almost every area of the police department. Most graft derived from the prohibitions of gambling, prostitution and drugs.[33] As August Vollmer had warned back in the 1930s, the policeman's duty was to protect society from criminals, not try to control morality which would turn out to be counter-productive.

Frank Serpico, the idealistic young officer who refused to go along with a well-established system, was shot on 3 February 1971 on a drugs raid, in what appeared to be a set-up. He survived but thought it advisable to leave the force and the country.[34]

The New York corruption scandals continued for several years (see p. 184) and revelations in such cities as Chicago, Indianapolis, Albany, Philadelphia and Washington, DC, indicated that conditions were similar throughout the country.[35]

The role of higher-level officials was also occasionally visible. A study of the small city of Reading, Pennsylvania was made by John A. Gardiner and published in 1970. In it he describes the relationship between political influence and gambling corruption. The non-enforcement of the gambling laws was achieved through campaign contributions to help ensure the election of tolerant officials and regular pay-offs to those elected as well as to the police department. During one prolonged period the mayor had appointed a police chief who shared the graft with him, while a city councilman kept the books for the rackets boss. In Johnstown, also in Pennsylvania, a similar situation existed between the mayor and his police department. Any gamblers who refused to pay off were harassed by raids, while those who cooperated were warned in advance of a 'crackdown'.[36]

Seattle was the subject of insightful research by William Chambliss. He found that the people who ran the organizations that supplied gambling, drugs, prostitution and pornography were members of the business, political and law enforcement communities—not simply members of a criminal society. Seattle's crime network included police officers, politicians and racketeering businessmen, and relied on coercion or cooptation to continue the profitability of the system. Usually intimidation was enough to keep people in line but Chambliss noted fifteen deaths between 1955 and 1969 which were suspiciously convenient for the network. Eric Tandlin, for example, had developed extensive knowledge of the network's operations in his job as county auditor for the city. Unexpectedly he lost his job to the brother-in-law of the chief of police. Soon after he began drinking heavily and talking. One evening he met a reporter who promised to put him in touch with someone from the attorney general's office. On the following night he was found drowned in the bay. The coroner, who was the brother-in-law of one of the leading network members, could be relied on to diagnose all such deaths as 'accidental'.

The network was disrupted in 1971 when fifty-four public officials were indicted on charges of bribery, corruption and misuse of office. They included the former county prosecutor, the former chief of police, the president of the city council, the county sheriff, the undersheriff, the head of the county jail, and a former sheriff. Most of those indicted were exonerated, or the charges dropped. In the end only two former high-ranking police officials were convicted on charges of conspiracy to promote and allow gambling, bribery, extortion, blackmail and liquor law violations through a system of police payoffs. Since most of Seattle's illegal operations continued after the case, Chambliss concluded that a new, even more discreet network shared the profits of illegal enterprises. The faces changed but the system went on.[37]

In addition to the systematic illegal enrichment of those in positions of power and influence, the hopelessness of trying to prevent gambling cash transactions between willing parties was slowly becoming more obvious. The discrepancy between numbers arrested and numbers convicted began to be noticed. In 1969 New York State made 2,096 arrests for felonious gambling, the most serious charge, which led to 281 indictments, fifteen convictions and just one jail term. In 1970 Philadelphia police made 4,720 gambling arrests; 517 people were convicted. Five of these went to jail and the remainder paid fines averaging $100 each. In 1973–4 police in Cook County, Illinois were effective enough to make 15,000 gambling arrests, but ineffective enough to secure only five indictments. Many more Americans began to realize that police and court time could be better spent. The 1976 National Gambling Commission surveyed the corruption and wasted effort involved in gambling law enforcement and concluded: 'Contradictory gambling policies and lack of resources combine to make effective gambling law enforcement an impossible task under present conditions.' The Commission also addressed the problem that ruling politicians and law enforcement personnel had avoided addressing for decades: 'How can any law which prohibits what 80 per cent of the people approve of be enforced?'[38] Pompous lectures about the evils of gambling, delusions about alien conspiracies, and deceptive claims for the potential of anti-gambling measures could no longer halt a re-examination of policy by many state and local authorities.

By the middle of the 1970s the trend towards decriminalization and legalization of gambling was well established. There were 1,394 gambling arrests in New York City in 1975 as compared to 11,467 in 1965, and legal off-track bookmaking had been available since 1970. Numerous other cities and states have since followed suit and legalized various forms of gambling; now only four states totally prohibit gambling. Forty-five states allow some form of bingo or charitable gambling, thirty-three states permit *pari mutuel* betting at horse tracks, dog tracks or Jai Alai, twenty-one states and Washington, DC operate lotteries, eight states have card rooms and two have casino gambling. In 1976 New Jersey had joined Nevada by legalizing casino gambling in Atlantic City after an expensive referendum campaign. Objections to gambling on moral and social grounds were overcome by state and local governments' pressing need for additional revenue and the attraction of a relatively painless source of such funds. Religious groups, once in the vanguard of the anti-gambling movement, are now some of the major beneficiaries of legalization, sponsoring bingo and other games for cash prizes.[39] Complaints about the immorality of gambling are now no longer taken seriously.

The country's inconsistent attitude towards gambling, however, still enriches numerous illegal operators. For example, while legal opportunities to bet on horses have multiplied in recent years, it remains mostly illegal to bet on the results of immensely popular sports such as football, basketball, baseball and boxing where top events attract huge television audiences and the greatest gambling action. National television companies have hired commentators such as Jimmy the Greek and Pete Axthelm to increase interest in betting by explaining odds and other technicalities, even though legal sports betting is restricted to four states. Telephone technology now permits betting transactions to be made easily and with little fear of law enforcement interference. As gambling historian Jerome Skolnick told President Reagan's Commission on Organized Crime (henceforth referred to as the Kaufman Commission as its chairman was Judge Irving R. Kaufman) in 1985, anybody 'who can't find a bookmaker in this society has to be regarded as mentally deficient'.[40]

The experience of most states with legal lotteries has been mainly positive, with millions of dollars of profits being used for a variety of socially useful purposes such as education and transportation. Control is possible and abuses can be checked. An elaborate attempt to rig the result of the Pennsylvanian lottery was uncovered in 1983. Two officials were convicted of perjury and theft in connection with a televised drawing that was fixed by injecting liquid weight into numbered table-tennis balls so that only two of the ten could be blown up a plastic tube by a machine that selected the winning number.[41] But on the whole cheating is difficult and corruption scandals are rare.

Legal lotteries did not end the long tradition of illegal numbers games in US cities. Since the advent of lotteries, numbers racketeers have kept most of their customers by increasing pay-offs, offering door-to-door service and allowing people to play for as little as 25 cents a day. Often the state's number is also used for the illegal games and operators thus take advantage of the televised drawings to increase interest. Evidence about numbers in New York indicates that black-, Hispanic- and Italian-Americans racketeers run separate and lucrative operations, and no monopoly situation has been discovered in any city for any one ethnic group. Murders, beatings and destruction of property still characterize competition for territories and markets.[42]

Technology is producing ever more ways of parting people from their money and video gaming machines are an important new addition to games of chance. At the Kaufman Commission hearings, Lieutenant Robert Gaugler of New Jersey State Police underlined the enormous profitability of electronic poker machines which in most jurisdictions are still classed as illegal slot machines. One investigation revealed a net profit of $500,000 from five machines alone in a fifteen-month period. He also explained that the owner of the machine can determine how much was paid out by the machine possessor by inserting a personal code and thus can be reasonably assured of not being cheated. In September 1983, the small Nebraskan town of Bellevue was the first, outside of Atlantic City and Nevada, to install such devices legitimately for tax revenue purposes. Within fifteen months the machines had helped the city wipe out a $500,000 deficit and produce a $1.9 million surplus. The revenue was set aside for a mini-van for the elderly, 10,000 books for the library, a third firehouse, and an assortment of environmental improvements plus a cut in property taxes. The town's publicity, however, reactivated moral-crusading elements in the state, and the machines were closed down by order of the state authorities. Most of the United States will probably slowly come round to legitimizing a type of gambling which is apparently possible to regulate effectively. In the meantime the machines are proliferating anyway, under the control of racketeers.[43]

Most illegal gambling operations are decentralized and restricted in scope, but some racketeers obviously succeed more than others in the acquisition of money, power and influence. Meyer Lansky was one, of course; José Miguel Battle Sr. is another. Battle's rise to prominence was detailed by Kaufman Commission investigator Anthony Lombardi. Battle was born in Cuba in 1929; as a young man he became a vice cop in Havana and later served in Batista's army. With Batista's downfall he left for the United States and there was trained by the CIA for the 1961 Bay of Pigs invasion attempt, along with other anti-Castro Cubans. 'After the failure of the invasion force', Lombardi continued;

> Battle was made a lieutenant in the U.S. Army by an Act of Congress, then returned to the Miami area and became deeply involved in the establishment of this country's first Cuban-controlled gambling operation. His organization has grown steadily with the migration of Cubans to other areas of the country. Battle is noted for his organizational genius and toughness, but his empire expanded initially, mainly through police and political corruption. Battle moved to Union City, New Jersey, in the late 1960s and established his gambling operation in the Northeast, with the help of traditional organized crime members, such as Joseph 'Bayonne Joe' Zicarelli and Santo Trafficante . . .

Battle's organization expanded mainly by taking over existing policy operations by means of homicides and arsons. By the early 1970s the Battle group was making an annual net profit of at least $45 million from New York City gambling operations alone.

Despite legal difficulties throughout the 1970s involving gambling racketeering, weapons and conspiracy to murder charges, Battle continued to flourish, and stayed mainly out of jail, serving only a total of thirty-one months. He moved operations back to Florida in 1982 and Investigator Lombardi 'conservatively' valued his 'Corporation' 'at an estimated several hundred million dollars, with an endless, substantial cash inflow'. Lombardi named a number of Battle-controlled companies and added that the 'Corporation' owned and/or controlled interests in domestic and foreign financial institutions, and had large real estate holdings. Millions of dollars in illegal revenues were laundered through financial institutions and the Puerto Rican Lottery. Lombardi expressed the hope that the exposure would help law enforcement bring Battle and his organization to justice.[44] If that happens, however, there is every likelihood that other racketeers will fill the vacuum created in the traditional way. The illegal policy games taken over by Battle were vulnerable to violent competition precisely because they were illegal and therefore without recourse to police protection.

Legal casino gambling in the United States still has its own racketeering problems. A tightening up of accounting regulations and internal control mechanisms has not ended skimming of casino profits by hidden owners, especially in Las Vegas. The Stardust was involved in two major skimming scandals, in 1976 and 1983. Hidden owners of the Aladdin were convicted in Detroit in 1979. Known racketeers systematically skimmed from the Tropicana in the late 1970s. And in 1985 the Kaufman Commission were able to listen to tapes of a casino executive, Carl Thomas, teaching top Kansas City gangsters, Nick and Carl Civella and Carl De Luna, how to skim. Before the 1970s, however, the practice was probably much more rife.[45]

The racketeering problems of Atlantic City are not primarily the threat of large-scale tax evasion. The links between gangsters and the current management and ownership of the casinos are remote, but gangster participation and control of the city's service industries and labour unions is significant. Competition for the city's lucrative peripheral businesses is the likely motive for the recent upsurge in gangster slayings in nearby areas. Angelo Bruno, reputedly the top Italian-American racketeer in Philadelphia, was shot dead in March 1980; his successor Philip Testa and several others met similar fates. In December 1980, prominent Atlantic City union leader, John McCullogh, was also murdered, at a time when he was attempting to organize casino security guards. According to Kaufman Commission testimony, the current 'on-site power for organized crime in Atlantic City' is Nicky Scarfo, who claims to control all unions in the city.[46]

An independent study of Atlantic City's problems does not lay the blame on gambling for this situation, 'but rather a pattern of business that gives potential access to organized crime'. Criminal control of the type of periphery business involved such as cigarette-vending machines, liquor distribution, trucking and laundry has a long history in many United States cities. 'Casino gambling in Atlantic City', according to the study, 'may present nothing more than an enlargement of the market, a sudden boomtown bonanza for vendors, both corrupt and otherwise'.[47] The bloodshed suggests that this bonanza is being fought over in the time-honoured American tradition.

The crusade which prohibited gambling in most parts of the United States produced nothing positive. Instead of eliminating gambling, it perversely fostered glamour, excitement and mass appeal that is much less apparent in countries which pursued rational policies based on regulation and control. The US anti-gambling laws created an immense market, with no legal suppliers, and thus stimulated the illegal entry of suppliers to meet the high demand. Opportunities to profit from protection of or extortion from gambling suppliers were eagerly accepted by innumerable public officials. Often the authorities controlled illegal gambling to a great extent, exploiting bookies and policy operators, and keeping the bulk of the profits for themselves. But with ineffectual and corrupted enforcement there were also opportunities for the more ruthless and violent criminal individuals and organizations to reach positions of power and influence. Either way the demand for gambling was met.

There is now no question that economic pressures will ensure that the process of gambling legalization will continue. The moral arguments against gambling convince fewer and fewer people, and law enforcers, having got the intrusive powers they demanded to fight the 'Mafia-controlled gambling business', are now no longer very interested. But the legalization process is slow and the federal government seems reluctant to say anything logical or coherent on the subject and fails to provide a lead. The 'police arrests numbers' game is still played, but without effort or enthusiasm. Gambling law enforcement continues only as a niggling inconvenience in most states.

Since the end of alcohol prohibition, many Americans have pleaded for a policy towards gambling based on regulation and control. They wanted to limit gambling-related crime and corruption and devote some of gambling's enormous profits to legitimate public needs. Instead the logic of their arguments was countered with moral indignation or the Mafia distraction. The re-examination of the anti-gambling laws was delayed until the often proposed solution of increased federal involvement was shown to be worthless. The process of legalization was too slow to prevent gangsters and corrupt public officials continuing to exploit the ineffectual laws and too late to allow for a smooth transition to a policy of effective regulation and control. For a long time gambling will remain a criminal industry in the United States.

The era of gambling prohibition is at an end, but myths and misrepresentation of fact concerning Italian-American organized crime persist, and it is necessary to return to this subject.

There is no doubt that Italian-American syndicates have been prominent in US organized crime since the Prohibition years. The dispute is over the identification of organized crime almost exclusively with Italian-Americans and the suggestion that organized crime is some sort of alien transplant onto an otherwise pure political and economic system. Many unreflective people in every part of the world, not just in America, believe that something called the Mafia runs organized crime in the United States as a result of the twenty-year campaign of misinformation already described and a single work of fiction published in 1969 which put the law enforcement perspective into its most digestible form yet.

The writer of *The Godfather*, Mario Puzo, was an Italian-American and to many this somehow confirmed that he knew what he was talking about. In fact, on his own admission and like the vast majority of Italian-Americans, he had never met 'a real honest-to-god gangster', and wrote the book entirely from research.[48] The research was obviously much influenced by the Kefauver hearings and the Valachi testimony which, as we have already seen, were exercises in crude distortion.

Puzo's publishers hyped the book as an inside look at 'the violence-infested society of the Mafia . . .' and it enjoyed immediate critical and popular success. Most reviewers thought it was real. Fred Cook, for example, who was a well-known organized crime 'historian', wrote that Puzo had brought home the reality of Mafia power 'more vividly and realistically than the drier stuff of fact ever can'. Nor surprisingly, law enforcement officials approved of the book, even in some cases by placing it on recommended reading lists in organized crime control training manuals.[49]

The novel was on the *New York Times* best-seller list for sixty-seven weeks and sold just as impressively in overseas markets. The film of the book was even more successful, breaking numerous box-office records and enriching its producers, but in the process fixing misleading images about Amercian organized crime for many years to come. An Irish-American, William V. Shannon, Described the film's exploitation of Catholic rituals and Italian customs as 'part of the biggest cultural ripoff that any commercial promoters have gotten away with in years'. 'The Godfather', he continued, 'stereotypes Italian-Americans as gangsters or as the half-admiring, half-fearful pawns of gangsters. The authentic details of how a bride receives money gifts at a wedding or how spaghetti is cooked only give credibility to that central lie about Italian-Americans'.[50] Most people, however, were more interested in putting visual images to what they already believed as true.

A kind of Godfather industry has since developed with innumerable cheaper versions of the same themes turned out in every form of media communication—even Superman and Batman waged war on the Mafia in the August 1970 issue of *World's Finest Comics*—and with by-products ranging from Godfather sweatshirts and car stickers to pizza franchises.[51] Mafia mythology had taken a firm grip on people's imagination, the fictional creation of the likes of Jack Lait and Lee Mortimer had finally been given almost universal credibility by constant repetition of an image.

The aforementioned Fred Cook also cashed in in the wake of the Godfather and brought out a history entitled *Mafia*! with the following endorsement by Mario Puzo on the cover: 'Reads like a novel—but it's true . . . terrific'. Cook did little more than rewrite old speculation. For example, part of his account of Lucky Luciano's career reads as follows:

> Across the nation, in precisely timed executions, some forty of the old 'Moustache Pete' contingent were murdered. It was a purge made possible only by the executive genius of Lucky Luciano, and it was carried out with an efficency and ruthlessness that would have done credit to a Stalin or a Hitler.
> The face of the American underworld had been changed, literally overnight. The Mafia had been Americanized . . .

Cook called this nationwide purge 'a sweeping and historic and bloody changing of the guard', carried out by Lucky Luciano 'in just twenty-four hours' in order to bring 'a new orderliness to the American underworld'. It was a remarkably similar account to the one by Richard 'Dixie' Davis already mentioned (see pp. 00 and 00), although Davis had suggested that '90 guineas' had been slaughtered. Joe Valachi had been questioned about this alleged purge day by the McClellan Committee and said that he thought about 'four or five' men had been killed. Cook and most other writers, including academics, seem to have picked numbers between Davis's and Valachi's estimates quite arbitrarily, without of course naming Luciano's alleged victims.[52]

The existence of the American Mafia as a centralized organization dominating organized crime was never proved and the concept has been discarded by all commentators who do not selectively examine the past. Even the federal perspective on organized crime now recognizes and stresses that organized crime is not restricted to one ethnic group. However, continued distortion of real incidents and revelations keep an adaptation of the Mafia concept alive and useful for a variety of cynical motives.

The most notable Italian-American racketeer of the early 1970s was Joseph Colombo Sr., not for his criminal success or power, but because he orchestrated probably the most counter-productive anti-defamation campaign in the country's history. Colombo was under increasing legal pressure, particularly from the federal authorities, and faced tax evasion, perjury and gambling charges. When his son was also arrested on charges of conspiracy to melt silver coins into more valuable ingots, Colombo's reaction was to organize a picket of FBI headquarters and help to form a militant pressure group called the Italian-American Civil Rights League in order to protest against what he thought was unreasonable and selective harassment of Italian-Americans. The League soon attracted over 40,000 paid-up supporters and belatedly tried to do what the Jewish Anti-Defamation League had been doing for Jews for decades, that is, protect them from ethnic slurs and stereotyping. However, Colombo's complaints about persecution and the claims of some of his supporters that the Mafia did not exist appeared ridiculous to those who knew or suspected his criminal activities and connections. The FBI made its opinions clear by publicizing stories about Colombo's 200-strong 'Mafia family' and its various rackets in Brooklyn. Colombo's crusade came to an abrupt end on 28 June 1971, when a black gunman shot him in the head less than an hour before a large League rally was due to begin at Columbus Circle in New York. The assailant was immediately killed by Colombo's bodyguards. Colombo himself survived but was paralysed and unable to organize either crime or ethnic pride any longer. The circumstances of his death confirmed people's suspicions and discredited any progress the League had made. Colombo's self-interested use of the League backfired, but the crudity of the effort does not support exaggerated notions of Mafia power. More discreet, sophisticated and powerful gangsters, notably Meyer Lansky, had been far more successful in helping to ensure that their own ethnic groups were not stereotyped as prone to crime and threats to the nation.[53]

A succession of Italian-American gangsters have been slain in New York since the early 1970s, often in spectacular 'gangland' style. All the shootings were followed by examples of what Jack Newfield was to call 'The Myth of Godfather Journalism', ill-informed speculation about who ordered the hits and who benefited by rising up the Mafia hierarchy. Newfield was writing in

July 1979 after the shooting of Carmine Galante, a drug trafficker, and described most Mafia reporting as 'consumer fraud' with the need to 'name new godfathers with the frequency of new Miss Subways' and an over-reliance on clipping files and leaks from law enforcement agencies. The agencies' motive to exaggerate was 'bigger budgets derived from greater publicity', but their knowledge of organized crime was in fact very limited, as reflected in their inability to solve any of the assassinations or control any of the activities. Newfield pointed out that the Mafia as the coherent, hierarchical corporation portrayed in most articles was journalistic myth-making.[54]

A similar point was made by James Fratiano, the most famous Italian-American informer of recent years. Fratiano had been a successful hit-man but an unsuccessful criminal entrepreneur; he was a member of the small and weak Los Angeles 'Mafia' family. He did, however, help produce a much superior conviction rate to Valachi and other informers, testifying against three New York gangsters, one Los Angeles gangster and Rudy Tham, an important San Francisco Teamster official. Fratiano thought that most Mafia journalism was a joke and he poured scorn on the presentation of the Mafia as a tightly knit national organization controlling organized crime. In an interview with crime writer Ovid Demaris, Fratiano revealed what he thought of a May 1977 article in *Time* magazine. The article was entitled 'The Mafia—Big, Bad and Booming', and began with a brief description of the organization and its chain of command:

> The Mafia is overseen nationally by the commission, a dozen or so dons who, usually, but not always, defer to the dominant boss in New York because he controls the most men and rackets.

The story contended that the Mafia was in a state of unrest since the death of 'Don Carlo Gambino', the 'capo di tutti capi' or 'boss-of-all-bosses', who had brought a measure of peace to the nation's Mafia families 'through guile, diplomacy and strong-arm discipline'. Fratiano's only reaction to this was, 'How they liked this boss-of-all-bosses bullshit'.

The article, in the customary way, then 'supported' its assertions with a list of Italian-American gangsters including Tony Spilotro, one of Fratiano's associates. Spilotro, according to *Time*, controlled loan-sharking, prostitution and narcotics along the Las Vagas Strip, and the assertion was supported with a quote from an unnamed Justice Department official. Fratiano's first-hand knowledge of Spilotro was different:

> Spilotro was nothing but a strong-arm errand boy. The thought that he could control loansharking, prostitution and narcotics along the Strip was mind-boggling. It would be like trying to control three tidal waves with a machine gun.[55]

Contradictory and ignorant 'Godfather' journalism is the rule rather than the exception—'mind-boggling' assertions are common both in print and in television documentaries. Examples are legion, especially across the Atlantic. The *Guardian*, for example, regularly publishes stories and articles that are garbled versions of Jack Lait and Lee Mortimer's original formula. Key words and phrases like 'omerta', 'vendettas', 'blood oaths of allegiance' and 'tentacles' are turned out to gratify the expectations of editors and readers alike and 'prove' that the Mafia controls organized crime in America.[56] It is very likely that this idea of the Mafia will survive, justified only by lazy references to an unexamined past.

There have been and still are strong links between Sicilian and Italian-American gangsters, but US power and US policy have influenced Sicilian organized crime development far more than the reverse process. Under Mussolini, Sicily's mafiosi had little power and influence. After the Second World War, US Army agents helped indigenous mafiosi back into positions of power as bulwarks against communism. After that, US drug control policy has had the most influence on Sicilian and southern Italian organized crime development. This policy ensured that the United States constituted the largest and richest market for heroin in the world. During the 1950s and 1960s it is probably that French exporters were the dominant suppliers of this market, but by the late 1970s cooperation between Sicilian exporters and Italian-American importers had become immensely profitable. According to an Italian sociologist, Pino Arlacchi:

> One Sicilian finance group linked to the mafia possesses a fortune estimated to exceed a thousand million dollars. Investigations carried out under the new Italian anti-mafia legislation are bringing to light almost unheard-of concentrations of wealth: an obscure mafia entrepreneur from a little town near Palermo turns out to have accumulated a personal fortune of some two hundred and fifty million dollars, and still larger amounts are being discovered in the course of investigations in northern Italy.[57]

But, as the following chapters will show, Sicilian and Italian gangsters were not the only foreign nationals to benefit from US drug control policy.

Organized crime in the United States is not the result of an alien intrusion. In reality, as the journalist Hank Messick has pointed out, it 'is so intermingled, so interwoven with the political and economic life of the United States that to simplify it is to be dishonest'.[58] The idea of the all-powerful Mafia was a dishonest concept sold to the American public to prolong the moral crusade and distract from the reality of US organized crime. Within the United States, American gangsters, American police and American politicians have always run organized crime. Organized crime would have flourished if no Italians or Sicilians had ever entered the country. The idea that one ethnically exclusive organization could control organized crime in such a huge and disparate country is as absurd and racist as the idea propagated before the Second World War that a Jewish conspiracy controlled world capitalism.

More than twenty Italian-American crime syndicates exist and participate in an environment that is peculiarly conducive to crime. They will continue either to operate separately or compete or cooperate on occasion. They will also continue to be collectively called the Mafia and be much overrated.

Numerous powerful and not-so-powerful Italian-American gangsters have come and gone. This is hardly surprising since around 7 per cent of the United States population are of Italian extraction; other large population groups have a proportionate share of the organized crime pie. The history of Italian-American organized crime has been more notable for savage struggle against each other and other groups than for the mutual enrichment, discipline and codes of absolute obedience described in most accounts. Criminal syndicates are powerful in the United States and they are often based on such unifying factors as religion, kinship, ethnicity and prison experience, just as racially exclusive, old-school or masonic networks exist in other businesses. They are necessarily secretive, all have 'omerta-like' codes; criminal activity is not something that is intelligent to talk about. Organized crime in the United States mirrors the country itself in that it is composed of every major ethnic group, including white Anglo-Saxons. The endless speculation about the Mafia merely distracted attention away from defects in the political, economic and legal systems, defects which provided unmatched opportunities for plain greed.

The alien conspiracy interpretation of organized crime had no positive results; the laws and policy based on it continue to foster rather than combat organized crime. The only beneficiaries have been: literary entrepreneurs and lazy journalists who used the Mafia peg to concoct sex and violence formula fiction or on which to hang otherwise routine crime stories; members of non-Italian crime syndicates, who attracted much less attention from the authorities; and grafting public officials who could explain their helplessness against the country's scope for illegal enrichment. The Mafia was an easy-to-communicate 'threat to the nation' which required more laws to legitimize new means of control, primarily against gambling.

Economic forces, however, proved stronger than moral forces and the era of gambling prohibition was nearing its end in the early 1970s. But as one aspect of the crusade was petering out, another took its place. The final phase of the country's moral crusade is against illicit drug use. It has all the absurdities, violence, corruption and injustice of previous crusades; it has been spread to other countries and it promises to run and run, defying all rationality.

Part IV The final phase: drugs, crime and politics, 1960–

Why should persons in authority wish to keep the dope peddler in business and the illicit-drug racket in possession of its billion-dollar income? It will be obvious, I think, that this is the significant question at issue . . . If we, the representatives of the people, are to continue to let our narcotics authorities conduct themselves in a manner tantamount to upholding and in effect supporting the billion-dollar drug racket, we should at least be able to explain to our constituents why we do so.

Congressman John Coffee, 1938

No one in authority doubts that the business of filling the vast and varied illicit drugs shopping list of modern America has taken on the dimensions of a major industry, dwarfing many legitimate ones in terms of gross sales and net profits and leaving a destructive trail of crime, violence and official corruption wherever it appears.

Arnold Trebach, 1982

If I were asked what I thought was the greatest government scam perpetrated upon the American public, I would unhesitatingly name our so-called war on dope. It is a fraud on at least three counts; it cannot succeed, it will continue to suck billions out of the national Treasury, and it will swell the ranks of bureacratic enforcers and line the pockets of corrupt cops and politicians.

Sidney Harris, 1985

12 Expansion

US drug control policy has changed since the early 1960s. Education, treatment and rehabilitation programmes were added to the policy of bare repression of drug use and sale. But there was no fundamental break with the essence of past policy, which was based on the irrational moral righteousness of early twentieth-century America. The old illusion that a drug-free country could be achieved with relentless enforcement persisted. Pragmatic approaches to recreational drug use and the problems associated with addiction were discredited or neglected. Instead the law enforcement approach to personal drug use was consolidated and expanded to a capacity never dreamed of for the much larger task of eliminating the liquor traffic in the 1920s. The policy was not only an exercise in futility but dangerously counter-productive, fostering and sustaining crime, violence and official corruption. This chapter describes how the problem of drugs was turned into a major disaster.

Harry J. Anslinger held his position as head of the Federal Bureau of Narcotics (FBN) until 1962. For three decades he had used his agency as a propaganda vehicle to strengthen the complex of federal, state and local laws which prohibited the importation, manufacture, sale and possession of certain drugs without the need for a Constitutional Amendment. Anslinger often stated that his approach to drug control was: 'Get rid of drugs, pushers and users. Period'.[1] But the provision made for this absurd panacea was insignificant. His own agency was a small group of low-paid, unprofessional and often corrupt agents—numbering around 300 for the entire United States and worldwide assignments. On 5 July 1962, President John F. Kennedy accepted Anslinger's resignation. The ineptitude and corruption of his agency was not revealed for several years but it soon became clear that it had made no significant impact on the drug trade itself (see pp. 140–141).

The Kennedy administration's interest in the drug issue had been minimal like its predecessors'. After Anslinger's departure a series of White House conferences, panels and commissions signified a new involvement which, according to drug law historian Rufus King, was motivated by practical political instinct. King plausibly argued that the Kennedy administration's interest in drugs increased when a dangerous political opponent, Richard Nixon, began to exploit the issue in the 1962 election campaign for the governorship of California. One of Nixon's main charges against incumbent

Governor Edmund Brown was that Brown was 'soft on dope peddlers'. In response the White House came to the aid of their Democratic ally by promising firm federal action and, in particular, giving Brown a national forum to repudiate Nixon's charges. A few days before the election at a White House conference on 'narcotics and drug abuse', Brown was able to boast about his 'grim war on narcotics' and to claim that California had 'turned the tide' on drug addition with a tough policy of quarantine for addicts and stiff penalties for any who possessed or sold drugs. Boosted by the conference publicity and the administration's support on other issues, Brown returned to California to win the election. Nixon had been deprived of a potentially damaging issue and, in addition, of a power base for future presidential ambitions.[2]

Whether or not White House interest was politically motivated, the period does mark the beginning of much greater presidential involvement in an issue which now had the potential to win or lose elections. In January 1963, President Kennedy appointed a new Advisory Commission on Narcotic and Drug Abuse to plan a course of action for the federal government. On 1 November the commission's report was issued, recommending more resources for a better balanced drug-control policy, more emphasis on research, education and treatment, and an increased enforcement capacity. Subsequently, the country's increasing wealth meant that both sides could be funded for expansion, but social and political developments hardened the commitment to a punitive approach to the drug problem.

John F. Kennedy's term of office was abruptly terminated on 23 November 1963, when he was shot and killed in Dallas, Texas. The Kennedy assassination highlighted a violence and instability in the United States that became increasingly obvious as the nation plunged into a period of social upheaval. Black ghettos in New York, Los Angeles and other cities spontaneously erupted into riots. Many young Americans protested loudly as the nation became embroiled in the war in South East Asia. Alarming reports in the Press or on television spoke of crime waves and disorder. There was a widespread feeling that the country was becoming lawless—crime, violence and rebellion were seen as getting out of control. There was a need to find something to blame for these problems and, as the 1960s progressed, drugs became a favourite scapegoat. The use of drugs was an easy way to explain the rise in violent crime and theft in the cities and also the growing disaffection of many young, white Americans.

Politicians increased and exploited the fear of drugs, especially heroin. Nelson Rockefeller was the first to prove that creating panic about heroin addiction could be politically profitable when he campaigned successfully for re-election as Governor of New York in 1966. By skilfully using the Press, Rockefeller managed to convince many voters that nearly all crime in New York was committed by heroin addicts. He spoke of heroin as an infectious disease—an epidemic which threatened the lives of innocent children—and addicts as menaces who threatened the lives and properties of citizens. The problem was successfully distorted and exaggerated with dishonest statistics; Rockefeller won a mandate to produce a draconian 'solution' (see pp. 184–185) and in the process gave himself the tough law-and-order image that was necessary to advance in Republican national politics.[3]

Marijuana, however, was the drug that reflected a generational conflict of unprecedented intensity. Before the 1960s black and Hispanic Americans were virtually the only users. Now, as Patrick Anderson put it, 'it was young white Americans, with their long hair and dirty talk, who had become the foreigners, the alien culture, the threat to respectable America'.[4] There was an unbridgeable gap between the millions of new users and their critical elders. Critics claimed that marijuana caused idleness, hedonism and sexual promiscuity; users thought that this was part of the attraction. Critics claimed that marijuana was addictive or inexorably led to addiction to 'hard' drugs; users were sceptical and the vast majority did not become addicted to anything. Critics saw marijuana as a challenge to cherished American values; users, many alienated by the Vietnam war, agreed.

Efforts to suppress marijuana increased more dramatically than with any other drug. Thousands of people were arrested, usually for merely possessing the drug. In 1965, there were 18,815 marijuana arrests, 31 per cent of a drug arrest total of 60,500. In 1967, there were 61,843 marijuana arrests, 50 per cent of a total that had doubled to 121,500, and this trend continued.[5] At a time of political unrest the potential for abuse was recognized by FBI Director, J. Edgar Hoover. In a 1968 memo to all FBI field offices, Hoover wrote: 'Since the use of marijuana and other narcotics is widespread among members of the New Left, you should be alert to opportunities to have them arrested by local authorities on drug charges'.[6]

Apart from marijuana's increasing popularity, the drug arrest totals were being inflated by 1965 legislation which criminalized whole new areas of drug activity. In that year, Congress passed the Drug Abuse Control Amendments, which placed police controls on barbiturates, amphetamines and hallucinogens. Before, medical control over these drugs was thought to be more appropriate and effective. Even Harry Anslinger thought so, and had warned Congress against extending the field of battle beyond all hope of government victory. The act was soon profitably exploited, either clandestinely by professional and amateur chemists, or from diversion from licit channels. The percentage markup in profits for amphetamines made in Mexico, for example, was sixty times the cost of the material and naturally encouraged diversion to illicit traffickers. John Pekkanen suggested in his book, *The American Connection*, that the sales boom experienced by Strasenburg-Penwalt, a US drug manufacturer, was, to say the least, suspicious. The company had a plant in Mexico, where its amphetamine sales jumped from 3.3 million pills in 1969 to 17.6 million in 1971.[7]

The administration of Lyndon B. Johnson was also responsible for a radical restructuring and strengthening of federal drug law enforcement. In

1965, the FBN, located in the Treasury Department, was forced to share responsibility for drug control with the Bureau of Drug Abuse Control (BDAC), located in the Department of Health, Education and Welfare. BDAC was still trying to establish itself when, in 1968, it was disbanded and reorganized, with the FBN, into the Bureau of Narcotics and Dangerous Drugs (BNDD)—a new Justice Department agency. The move was against the advice of Johnson's Attorney General and head of the Department of Justice, Ramsey Clark, who felt that drug control and regulation should be transferred completely to the Department of Health, Education and Welfare so that policy could develop with flexibility and better medical and scientific orientation. Instead, President Johnson, believing that such an approach might lead to charges of 'softness' against the drugs 'menace', created his new 'gangbusting' agency—the BNDD. Clark has since also revealed that Johnson had first asked him to try to persuade FBI Director Hoover to take over drug jurisdiction. Clark refused even to attempt the impossible—knowing that Hoover would not allow his agents near the hopeless and corrupting task of drug prohibition.[8]

On 7 February 1968, the President sent a message to Congress warning of the 'powders and pills' that 'threaten our nation's health, vitality and self-respect' and claiming that the reorganization would

> serve notice to the pusher and the peddler that their criminal acts must stop, No matter how well-organized they are, we will be better organized. No matter how well they have concealed their activities, we will root them out . . .[9]

Few in Congress were informed enough or brave enough to oppose the reorganization and drug control became the duty of the Department of Justice for the first time. In the process the number of federal drug enforcement agents was more than doubled to over 700. The first major task of the BNDD was to investigate corruption in its predecessor organization (see p. 140) and the new agency recognized, from the beginning, a clear need to police itself.

Giving drug control to Justice Department 'gangbusters', at a time when a more rational policy option was open to him, was one of President Johnson's last significant actions. In March 1968 he decided not to campaign for re-election—pulling out of a potentially tough fight for the Democratic nomination

The two main contestants in the 1968 presidential race were Vice-President Hubert Humphrey and Richard Nixon who had ended a period of political obscurity by winning the Republican nomination. Neither candidate wished to make the Vietnam war the central issue of the campaign, frustrating many Americans who thought the war was the country's paramount problem. Nixon's campaign strategy was designed to play down the war by repeating disingenous statements about a 'secret plan' to end the war which would be jeopardized if he had to say any more, since negotiations were, supposedly, already under way. Instead his campaign was aimed squarely at the 'average American' or the 'silent majority'—the millions of Americans concerned and confused by the disruptive social changes of the preceding years. His campaign managers banked on a backlash against rising crime rates, anti-war protest, campus disorders, black militancy and moral permissiveness. An election newsletter, for example, made the following appeal to the hearts—if not the heads—of the electorate:

You're old enough to remember the real America—if you can remember when you never dreamed your country could lose. When you left the front door open . . . When a girl was a girl. When a boy was a boy . . . When you didn't feel embarrassed to say this was the best damn country in the world. When socialist was a dirty word. When liberal wasn't. When a nickel was worth 5 cents and you could buy a magazine, or a good cigar, or a 12 ounce Pepsi, or a big ice cream cone with choc sprinkles, or a beer . . . When taxes were only a nuisance. When the poor were too proud to take charity. When you weren't afraid to go out at night . . . When you knew the law meant justice, and you felt a little shiver of awe at the sight of a policeman . . . When the flag was a sacred symbol . . . When a man who went wrong was blamed, not his mother's nursing habits or his father's income. When everyone knew the difference between right and wrong, even Harvard professors . . . When people still had the capacity for indignation. When you considered yourself lucky to have a good job. When you were proud to have one . . . When college kids swallowed goldfish, not acid. [Acid was the slang term for LSD, a hallucinogen which became fashionable in the late 1960s]. When America was the land of the free, the home of the brave.[10]

Television commercials were more sophisticated. One showed a nervous middle-aged woman walking down the street on a dark, wet night with the following commentary:

Crimes of violence in the United States have almost doubled in recent years . . . today a violent crime is committed every sixty seconds . . . a robbery every two and a half minutes . . . a mugging every six minutes . . . a murder every 43 minutes . . . and it will get worse unless we take the offensive.[11]

At every opportunity Nixon himself repeated this theme and even managed to pin the blame for widespread disorder on Attorney General Ramsey Clark. At election rallies he solemnly pledged to 'restore order and respect for law in this country' by appointing a new Attorney General. Nixon hardly touched the drugs issue during the campaign but once in power it became his great crusade.

The election victory of November 1968 was narrow and Nixon needed to maintain his 'law-and-order' constituency to win re-election in 1972. Results had to be produced, otherwise the tough talk and promises to restore law and order might backfire.

The administration initially had no idea how to deliver on its promises to restore law and order and reduce crime on the streets. It had no jurisdiction, constitutionally and historically such crimes were the responsibilities of the cities and the states. However, the federal government did have the power to combat the drug traffic and a cynical strategy was devised: inflate the drug problem, blame crime on drugs, and then give the impression of firm executive action by waging war on drugs. According to Edward J. Epstein, who has written an account of the Nixon years based on interviews with top administration officials, the strategy that justified a massive expansion of drug law enforcement was to persuade Americans that their lives and the lives of their children were threatended by a rampant 'epidemic' of drug addiction. Americans would then support draconian measures to produce results.[12] As Nixon's Domestic Advisor, John Ehrlichman, later testified, parents worry and '. . . narcotics suppression is a very sexy political issue. It usually has high media visibility'.[13]

Nixon's former law partner, John Mitchell, was appointed the new Attorney General and, soon after taking office, introduced the first phase of the war on drugs:

> The battle against narcotics is an integral part of the Administration's anti-street crime program. A narcotics addict may need $70 or $80 a day to satisfy his habit. Thus, he turns to robbery, mugging and burglary in order to obtain money. It was recently estimated that in New York City alone $2 billion a year is stolen by narcotics addicts and that a substantial proportion of violent crimes are committed by narcotics addicts.
>
> . . .persons who live in ghetto areas, which have substantial numbers of narcotics addicts, literally bar the doors of the apartments at night. They are attacked in broad daylight on the streets. They are terrorized by the knowledge that the heroin addict who needs a fix will commit the most vicious crime in order to obtain a TV set for resale for a few dollars. Even our high school children are beginning to use hard narcotics . . .[14]

Mitchell and other government spokesmen based their arguments on dishonest estimates. When a reputable economist, Max Singer, examined them, he found that the figures implied that addicts stole almost ten times as much as was estimated actually to have been stolen annually in New York City.[15] But accuracy was not necessary for Mitchell and the rest; creating a climate of fear was.

Such misinformation went unchallenged by the news media. As Epstein has demonstrated, White House press releases were abridged and printed by the newspapers or spoken on television almost verbatim. If any journalists had pressed government officials about the method they used for estimating the number of drug addicts, or the cost of their daily habit, they would have quickly found out that the officials' certainty and assurance was a bluff. They had no way of knowing the number of addicts, made no distinction between addicts and occasional users, and, in effect, made up the numbers to support drastic measures. Journalists failed to challenge the figures because multimillion numbers provided dramatic news while the lack of credible data did not. And so when the number of heroin addicts escalated from 69,000 in 1969 to 322,000 in 1970, and to 560,000 in 1971, few were sceptical. More spoke of the sensational heroin 'epidemic' without realizing that the same 1969 data were used for all three estimates. The higher numbers were arrived at by using different statistical formulus rather than discovering new addicts.[16]

The White House even persuaded the entertainments media to back the campaign. Television producers of crime shows of the 'Hawaii Five-O' type began to add anti-drug messages to their formulas. As Epstein suggested, the image of glassy-eye fiends compulsively driven to commit violent crimes was established for most Americans. The campaign to inflate the fear of drugs had succeeded. Even in parts of the country which did not have an illegal drug problem, people now felt threatened by the spreading epidemic. The Nixonites distorted and exaggerated the drug problem even though they knew—from information from their own agencies—that the problem did not compare in extent or severity with the problems of alcoholism, mental illness or road deaths.[17] Drugs, however, in Ehrlichman's words had 'high media visibility'.

In July 1969, the President restated the themes of the crusade and then outlined a ten-point programme of action. In a speech to Congress he first warned that the abuse of drugs had grown from 'essentially a local police problem' into a 'serious national threat to the personal health and safety of millions of Americans'. He said that the number of addicts had grown to where it had to be estimated in hundreds of thousands, that several million college students had at least experimented with marijuana, hashish, LSD, amphetamines or barbiturates, and continued:

It is doubtful that an American parent can send a son or daughter to college today without exposing the young man or woman to drug abuse. Parents must be concerned about the availability and use of such drugs in our high schools and junior high schools.
    The habit of the narcotics addict is not only a threat to himself, but a threat to the community where he lives. Narcotics have been cited as a primary cause of the enormous increase in street crimes over the last decade . . .

The President then stated that addicts reduce themselves to any offences, any degradations to acquire drugs and mentioned 'street robberies, prostitution, even the enticing of others into addiction to drugs'.

'Society', he concluded, 'has few judgements too severe, few penalties too harsh for the men who make their livelihood in the narcotics traffic'. The measures he proposed for congressional support were: more international cooperation, a 'major new effort' by the Bureau of Customs, comprehensive new federal and state laws, suppression of domestic trafficking with 'action task forces', 'no-knock' warrants and heavier penalties, more education, research, rehabilitation, and better liaison with local enforcers.[18]

The first sign of the administration's international effort came in September 1969, when an attempt was made to curb the importation of illegal drugs from Mexico. In Operation Intercept nearly 2,000 agents of the Bureau of Customs and the Immigration and Naturalization Service worked around the clock along the 2,500 miles of the United States–Mexico border stopping and searching over two million people within the first week. The effect was an immense traffic jam, harm to business and tourism on both sides of the border, and tension between the two countries. A negligible amount of drug contraband—mainly marijuana—was seized during the operation and it was called off after three weeks. A new approach was begun and the administration gave the Mexican government $1 million to 'eradicate' poppy and marijuana fields.[19]

More expensive international intervention began in 1971. Turkey was thought to be the major source of heroin and was vulnerable to diplomatic pressure because of its dependence on massive US economic and military aid. The Turkish government therefore agreed to ban all opium-growing for a three-year period in return for a payment of $35 million—intended to assist the development of alternative crops to replace opium. Little of the money reached the tens of thousands of farmers who lost income because of the ban and by 1974 the Turks had found the policy to be unworkable and lifted the ban.[20] Any vacuum in the US heroin market during the years of the Turkish ban was filled by Mexican and South East Asian heroin.

Nixon's administration more than doubled the corps of narcotics control officers assigned to United States embassies and missions abroad and their numbers have since continued to expand.[21] Anslinger's effort to spread the gospel of US drug-control policy around the world was intensified at great expense. Other countries were bullied or persuaded to make futile, often cynical, drug-control gestures on America's behalf. Americans continued to pay the top prices for their products and the effort only revealed that processable plants grow everywhere and that foreign drug enforcers accept bribes just as enthusiastically as their counterparts in the United States. Drug control remains the justification for US intervention into the affairs of other countries.

Domestically the Nixon administration's main legislative achievement was to secure the passing of a complicated statute which restated what was already in federal laws. The Comprehensive Drug Abuse Control Act of 1970 pulled together everything Congress had done in the drug field since opium-smoking curbs in 1887. The law gave the Department of Justice an array of powers over licit and illicit drugs covering possession, sale and trafficking. Drug offenders faced severe sanctions including life for those engaged in a 'continuing criminal enterprise' or who qualify as a 'dangerous special drug offender'. Treasury funds were to be made available to enforcement agents to hire informants, pay for incriminating information, and make purchases of contraband substances. Agents were also given the power to seize on sight any property they thought was contraband or forfeitable, and execute search warrants at any time of the day or night, with a new 'no-knock' procedure if a judge had authorized it. To limit these new powers to the control of drugs,

Congress felt obliged to add a disclaimer into the definition of 'controlled substance': 'The term does not include distilled spirits, wine, malt beverages or tobacco'.[22]

The act was passed without difficulty. Few legislators dared to appear 'soft' on drugs and point out the dangers inherent in its policing provisions. The hysteria about drugs was at its peak and in such circumstances politicians follow the paths of least resistance. Something had to be done because, as Senator Thomas Dodd put it: 'people are watching us. The hoodlums are watching us. The dope peddlers are watching us. They all want to know if we mean business'.[23]

Nixon stated that his intention was to 'tighten the noose around the necks of drug peddlers, and thereby loosen the noose around the necks of drug users'.[24] For this the BNDD was given more men and ever larger budget appropriations. At its formation in 1968 the agency had 615 agents and a $14 million budget. The number of agents then increased from 760 in 1969 to 900 in 1970 and 1,150 in 1971. By 1973 the BNDD had 1,586 agents operating within the United States alone and a budget of $74 million.[25] The quality but not the quantity of the agency's arrests improved. There had been a shift in emphasis away from the FBN's high volume of mainly insignificant arrests; as Director John Ingersoll put it, 'from the addict, abuser and small-time street peddler to the important illicit traffickers and illegal supply sources'.[26]

The White House was not content with the BNDD's new tactics. The war on drugs had to have an impact at local level where voters would notice it. Having tried and failed to persuade Ingersoll to reverse his policy of quality arrests, the administration created a new agency under its direct control—the Office of Drug Abuse Law Enforcement (ODALE), to be headed by Customs Chief Myles Ambrose. ODALE was intended to dramatize Nixon's war on drugs by concentrating on lower levels of heroin distribution networks and piling up arrest statistics. Its strike forces were generously funded with 'buy money' to purchase drugs and pay informants and for numerous 'undercover' operations. A 'Heroin Hotline' was set up in April 1972 to encourage informers. With the authority of 'no-knock' warrants ODALE agents could strike any time against virtually anyone selected as a target. Targets tended to be street addicts who traded in drugs to pay for their own habits.[27]

The federal government's drug budget appropriations were multiplied during the Nixon years, from around $14 million in 1968 to $200 million in 1973. The expansion of treatment and prevention programmes matched, for the first time, the expansion of drug law enforcement capacity in the hope of reducing the demand for illegal drugs and thereby street crime. The administration reasoned that if addicts were supplied with methodone—a heroin substitute and just as addicting—they would not need to steal to pay inflated black-market prices for their habits. Methodone was put forward as the answer to drug-related street crime and even to the problem of heroin addiction itself. From 1971 methodone maintenance clinics proliferated and tens of thousands of doses of an addictive drug were dispensed daily, undermining yet more of the logic behind the war on drugs.

Methodone did not turn out to be any solution to America's drug problems, although undoubtedly it has helped some people. Neither street crime nor the demand for heroin were significantly affected and many methodone patients simply traded their prescribed drugs for other drugs or money. A relatively high number of deaths from an overdose combination of methodone with other drugs was noticed within a few years and heroin addicts continued to break the law to pay for their drug of preference and to use methodone only as a last resort.[28]

Before the 1972 presidential election, however, the methodone programmes still held promise. With the international initiatives, sponsorship of tough legislation and expanded law enforcement capacity, the public had been given the impression of firm executive action against the menace of drugs and few opportunities were missed to remind them of this action. In the preceding March the President claimed that the 'corner had been turned' on addiction, pointing to a decreasing rate of increase that the statisticians had turned out. In another speech he pledged that the fight would go on: 'We must have no budget cuts in waging total war on public enemy number 1'. In September Nixon found scapegoats for continuing drug use and trafficking. he attacked 'permissive' judges whose leniency left a 'weak link' in the country's efforts to 'rid the streets of the pushers of hard drugs'. No names or specific documentation for his attack were mentioned at the time or later. Finally, in October, his Attorney General, Richard Kleindienst, went back to the impending victory theme and claimed that the 'crime wave which shocked us in the 1960s is now under control and America once again is becoming a safe and lawful society'.[29]

Nixon's rival in the election, Senator George McGovern, was successfully identified with a 'soft' attitude to drugs and crime, and in November 1972 the President was re-elected by an overwhelming margin. His war on drugs had achieved its primary purpose and Nixon's tough law-and-order image was maintained. The tawdry realities behind the image were, for the time being, still concealed.

Nixon's creation, ODALE, along with state and local drug squads, pursued a campaign against drugs of unprecedented hostility and intensity and one immediate effect was that scores of innocent Americans were subjected to mistaken, violent and often illegal raids and harassment:

— On 24 April 1972 local and federal police moved in on the mountain retreat of 24-year-old Dirk Dickenson near Eureka, California, to seize what their informants had told them was a 'giant lab' producing drugs. Arriving on foot with dogs, the agents, who were not in uniform and did not identify themselves, assaulted the cabin with rifles and hand guns.

Mr Dickenson ran towards the woods, apparently baffled and frightened. He was shot in the back as he fled and died later. No 'giant lab' was found.

— On 24 May 1972 at 3 a.m. in Norfolk, Virginia, Mrs Lillian Davidson heard someone breaking into her house. The someone began to batter down her locked bedroom door. She grabbed a .32 caliber revolver and shot through the door. Twenty-two-year-old patrolman Lewis Hurst was wounded and died minutes later.

— On 23 January 1973 three off-duty Philadelphia patrolmen were drinking in a bar when another patron told them that they could find drugs at a nearby house. The three men went to the house on Wiota street, ransacked it and beat-up three occupants. Not finding any drugs, they forced a passer-by into the house and beat him up as well. Then the original bar patron took the officers to another house where they beat up three more occupants without producing any drugs. These policemen were suspended and arrested.

— On the night of 23 April 1973 there were ODALE raids on the homes of Herbert Giglotto and Donald Askew in Collinsville, Illinois. Mr Giglotto and his wife were asleep when more than fifteen roughly dressed men broke down two doors, handcuffed and then held the couple at gun-point. They then emptied drawers and closets, shattered pottery, threw a television set on the floor and shouted obscenities at the couple. A half-hour later a similar event occurred across town at the home of Mr Donald Askew. In both cases the raiders were at the wrong address, they had no search or arrest warrants and did not identify themselves until well into the raids.

Often the raids were characterized by shoddy or non-existent pre-raid investigation. The strong-arm tactics were justified by ODALE chief, Myles Ambrose:

> This is dirty, scummy work. You see these vermin selling drugs and what they do to people and our cities and you get sickened and angry and perhaps you take your hostilities and frustrations out on some guy's bookcase. It's not right. But how are you going to prevent it?[30]

ODALE ceased to exist in July 1973 when it was swallowed up in another reorganization. The Attorney-General at the time, William Saxbe, conceded that the ODALE effort had caused more problems than it solved. The Heroin Hotline had already been wound up. Of 33,313 calls received in the first three months, agents deemed 28,079 of them useless—obscene calls, pranks or simply heavy breathing. Most of the remainder were thought to be sincere but of no immediate use. Only 113 calls provided any leads at all and even these produced only one seizure and four arrests. The first four months of Hotline's operation cost $260,000 and resulted in the total seizure of 2 grams of adulterated heroin which, even using the street–values of drug enforcement agents, only amounted to $2 worth.[31]

In July 1973 the Drug Enforcement Administration (DEA) was created by the presidential fiat of Richard Nixon to take over the functions of the BNDD, ODALE and the narcotics intelligence programmes of other agencies in a move described by a top BNDD official as 'the old reorganization shell game'—the cannibalizing of enforcement agencies and the creation of new bureaucratic titles. By 1975 the new agency had a staff of more than 4,000, about half of whom were investigators, and it possessed, in Rufus King's words, 'every armament and prerogative that could conceivably be conferred on a peacetime domestic agency'. It did, however, lose its 'no-knock' authority when Congress finally took account of the numerous cases of mistaken entry and frequent tragic consequences.[32]

Out of the many thousands of drug raids and arrests during these years, an unknown number were politically motivated. There is no doubt, however, that there was considerable federal, state and local persecution of the underground press on the basis of the drug laws and also that police agencies often found it convenient to arrest politically active youths either by finding or 'planting' drugs on them. Two cases attracted some attention in the early 1970s. John Sinclair, a poet and leader of the radical White Panther Party in Michigan, received a ten-year prison sentence for lighting a marijuana cigarette while two undercover police intelligence officers had him under surveillance for his political activities. Lee Otis Johnson, a black militant and anti-war organizer at Texas Southern University, got thirty years for giving a marijuana cigarette to an undercover officer who had posed as his friend.[33]

Whether Nixon's war on drugs even produced the 'decreasing rate of increase' claimed by the administration is arguable because, for all the hard work of government statisticians, estimates about private activities are always arbitrary and prone to distortion. However, there is no doubt that the United States remained by far the richest market for drugs in the world and that the expansion of drug enforcement capacity and anti-drug rhetoric was primarily a show for the voters and an exercise of expedient hypocrisy. As Nixon's Chief Domestic Affairs Advisor, John Ehrlichman, candidly told a Senate committee in 1975:

> We can consolidate, we can reorganize, we can budget and you can put up a lot of money. You can hire a lot more agents and put them out there. It is going to be marginal . . .
> I think there is a genuine question of hypocrisy in all of this, as to whether the Federal Government, the people in the Federal Government aren't just kidding themselves and kidding the people when they say we have mounted a massive war on narcotics when they know darned well that the massive war that they have mounted on narcotics is only going to be effective at the margins.[34]

Better documented than the political abuse of the new drug laws and enforcement capacity is the abuse of the Organized Crime Control Act which, as we have already seen (see p. 148), was passed by legislators who were profoundly ignorant about the realities of organized crime. The inherent dangers within this 1970 law received no more than cursory attention from congressmen, who knew that opposing the bill and appearing 'soft on crime' at such a feverish time would be committing political suicide during an election year. Some who voted for the bill might have expected the courts to check the worst abuses but most simply supinely obeyed the wishes of the Nixon–Mitchell Justice Department.[35]

Among the many measures which constituted the Act were two which affected the grand jury process. One centralized control over federal grand jury work in Washington, allowing the Justice Department to by-pass local US attorneys and set up special grand juries whenever and wherever the Attorney-General pleased. The other changed the rules governing the immunity of witnesses, and enabled the government to immunize witnesses any time it wanted, as opposed to the sparing and carefully delineated use of immunity powers before. This so-called 'use' immunity gave great scope to resourceful prosecutors to undermine the Fifth Amendment self-incrimination rights of numerous witnesses. Additionally, uncooperative witnesses could be jailed for civil contempt during the lengthy periods in which grand juries were sitting, and many were.

Armed with such new powers the Justice Department began a grand jury offensive that had little or nothing to do with organized crime but much to do with hurting the political enemies of the Nixon administration.[36]

A documented list was later compiled to show that the Nixon administration had abused the grand jury process in the following ways: to frighten citizens from political activity; to discredit 'non-mainstream' groups; to disrupt legal dissent; to embarrass political rivals; to assist management in a strike situation; to punish witnesses for exercising their Fifth Amendment rights; to hide the failures of law enforcement agencies; to disrupt personal lives by unwarranted geographical removal; to disrupt the news-gathering process; to cover up official wrongdoing; to break the attorney–client privilege; to bring accused persons to trial on insufficient evidence; to entice the commission of perjury; finally, to gather domestic political intelligence.[37]

One of many cases which illustrate the last-mentioned and most significant abuse happened in Tucson, Arizona in 1970 during an investigation of the alleged purchase of dynamite by a young man who drove a car registered to a woman in Los Angeles. Months of surveillance of the woman revealed not much more than that she lived in a commune of five people. But on the strength of this the prosecutor asked one of the woman's friends the following question:

Tell the grand jury, please, where you were employed during the year 1970, by whom you were employed during the year 1970, how long you have been so employed and what the amount of remuneration for your employment has been during the year 1970.

> Tell the grand jury every place you went after you returned to your apartment
> from Cuba, every city you visited, with whom and by what means of trans-
> portation you travelled and who you visited at all of the places you went during
> the times of your travels after you left your apartment in Ann Arbor, Michigan,
> in May of 1970.
>
> I want you to describe for the grand jury every occasion during the year 1970,
> when you have been in contact with, attended meetings which were conducted
> by, or attended by, or been to any place when any individual spoke whom you
> knew to be associated with or affiliated with Students for a Democratic Society,
> the Weathermen, the Communist Party or any other organization advocating
> revolutionary overthrow of the United States, describing for the grand jury when
> these incidents occurred, where they occurred, who was present and what was
> said by all persons there and what you did at the time that you were in these
> meetings, groups, associations or conversations.

On principle she refused to answer, as did all five of the witnesses. They were
jailed for contempt for the seven-month remainder of the grand jury's life and
finally capitulated when faced with imprisonment for the eighteen-month
term of a new grand jury which, they thought, could be repeated *ad infinitum*.
They answered a few questions about the dynamite purchase in which they
were not involved and countless questions of the type transcribed above. The
information, without much doubt, was disseminated around the government's intelligence community.[38]

Representative John Conyers testified in 1976 that it was clear that
'radicals, supporters of unpopular causes, ethnic groups and organizations,
civil rights organizations . . ., and people who are suspected of being
sympathetic to any of the above are all the people who are regularly
victimized by the grand jury' and also noted that:

> in case after case . . . Justice Department officials have used the grand jury to
> railroad—the only word that adequately describes a situation where there are no
> accusers, accused or evidence—their enemies and irritants behind bars. The
> Nixon administration pioneered this stratagem . . .

He was echoing a similar point made by Senator Edward Kennedy three
years earlier:

> we have witnessed the birth of a new breed of political animal—the kangaroo
> grand jury—spawned in a dark corner of the Department of Justice, nourished
> by an Administration bent on twisting law enforcement to serve its own political
> ends, a dangerous modern form of Star Chamber secret inquisition that is
> trampling the rights of American citizens from coast to coast . . .

Kennedy had put the blame for the many abuses partly on Congress for
failing to recognize 'the sinister potential abuses lurking beneath the innocu-
ous surface of the 1970 law', and partly on the Justice Department 'for lulling
Congress not only with excessive protestations of the need for this new Act as
a law and order tool, but also with equally excessive and wholly unfulfilled
promises of good behaviour if only the Act would pass . . .'.[39]

Ironically, the country's founding fathers had retained the grand jury process in the Constitution as a safeguard against malicious and oppressive prosecution and a shield for people who might be politically persecuted or prosecuted. But between 1970 and 1974, in particular, grand juries, along with the increased wiretapping and eavesdropping powers, became quite clearly part of the government's armoury against dissent.[40] The 1970 Organized Crime Control Act was, in sum, a malevolent piece of legislation which failed to make a noticeable impact on the problem it was enacted to correct, the level of organized crime activity in the United States, but succeeded, with other laws, in opening up the potential for a very sophisticated police state—in a country which most citizens believe to be the 'land of the free'.

From the beginning of 1973 Americans gradually came to realize that they had bestowed an armoury of repressive crime-control laws on people who were themselves criminally inclined. Almost as soon as President Nixon had been inaugurated for his second term there began an avalanche of revelations and disclosures of criminal activity by top officials indicating a visible level of federal government corruption with no parallel since the Prohibition years.

Nixon's most immediate enemies were not radicals but mainstream opposition politicians and it was a short step to use covert intelligence mechanisms against Democratic politicians—either to discredit them or to find out their campaign strategy. The bungled attempt to install wiretaps at the Democratic National Committee headquarters in the Watergate hotel in June 1972 was merely the extension of existing practices and the tip of an iceberg of abuse.[41] 'The subsequent concealment', according to John Conyers' comments to the House Committee on the Judiciary, 'was intended not merely to protect the White House from its complicity in the Watergate incident itself, but to avoid disclosure of the entire train of illegal and abusive conduct that characterized the Nixon presidency', which Conyers proceeded to summarize:

> obstruction of justice, perjury and subordination of perjury, offers of executive clemency, attempts to influence a federal judge, destruction of evidence, disclosure of secret grand jury proceedings, withholding information of criminal activity, impounding of Congressional appropriations, wilful tax evasion, possible bribery in connection with the ITT antitrust and milk support decisions, and interference with the lawful activities of the CIA, FBI, IRS, Special Prosecutor, House Banking and Currency Committee, Senate Select Committee on Presidential Campaign Activities, and finally, the House Judiciary Committee. In these ways, the President sought to avert disclosure of a seamless web of illegality and impropriety.[42]

In August 1974 Nixon resigned, faced with the certainty of an impeachment vote in the Senate, and relinquished his office to Vice-President Gerald Ford. Ford had replaced Spiro T. Agnew a few months before, after Agnew had resigned over tax evasion and kickback revelations. Subsequently, several key Nixon officials were tried and convicted of Watergate-related offences, notably Chief Domestic Affairs Advisor John Ehrlichman, who served eighteen months in prison for perjury and conspiracy, White House Chief of Staff Bob Halderman, who served the same sentence for perjury and obstruction of justice, and former Attorney-General John Mitchell who served nineteen months for his role in the cover-up. Nixon himself was pardoned by his successor.[43]

In order to be elected in November 1968 Richard Nixon had repeatedly told the American people that he was going to restore order and respect for the law. By November 1973 he was trying to reassure them that he was 'not a crook', but by then fewer people were believing him.[44] He was forced to resign when he could no longer cover up the fact that an administration pledged to fight crime had directed massive burglary, sabotage, spying and campaign fund illegalities.

The final irony of the Nixon years was that a commission that he himself had appointed to study corruption gave the most appropriate epitaph for his crime control policies. As long as official corruption flourished, the commission concluded,

> . . . the war against crime will be perceived by many as a war of the powerful against the powerless, 'law and order' will be a hypocritical rallying cry, and 'equal justice under law' will be an empty phrase.[45]

Only Nixon and his administration were discredited by Watergate, not his politically useful 'hard line' against drugs and whatever the government chose to define as 'organized crime'.

In the aftermath of Watergate there was only moderate reform of the crime-control laws and minimal re-examination of US drug-control policy which, in essence, remains today the one established by the Watergate conspirators: aggressive domestic and international enforcement efforts to reduce the supply of illegal drugs, education and methodone-based treatment programmes attempting to reduce demand, the emphasis being primarily on the former because 'gangbusting' remained the most politically useful charade. Drug enforcement, however, has always been characterized more by corruption and futility than success. The multiplication of drug seizures and arrests could only partly obscure this reality. The next section looks at the case of New York and describes firstly how the expansion of drug law enforcement was accompanied by an expansion of corruption, and secondly how the nation's toughest drug law was also the nation's most futile.

Drug deals involve cash transactions between willing parties; the best evidence is lacking—no injured citizen complains to the police and serves as a witness. The police therefore develop cases through informers and covert methods, then make arrests, seize evidence and interrogate. The police control the situation totally until a case reaches the courts since they alone decide whether an offense has been committed and whether they have a legal case against the suspect. The potential for corruption is always present.

Despite the federal government's increasing involvement in drug control, the main responsibility for drug law enforcement remained with the cities. Responding to political demands for action, most city drug squads also expanded in size, most notably in New York, the nation's largest city and the one with the largest drug problem.

The Narcotics Division of the New York Police Department more than doubled during the 1960s so that by the end of the decade more than 500 detectives directed enforcement activity. At the beginning of 1970 Police Commissioner Howard Leary reflected the change of emphasis in the country's moral crusade by announcing a shift of 200 men from gambling law enforcement to anti-narcotics work and requesting 2,000 more to add to his 32,000-man force because, as he said, 'You have to protect people against narcotics in spite of what they think or what they want to do or their feelings toward it. It's something very much like a contagious disease'. All the department's 'energy and effort' should be directed at control of the drug problem but, Commissioner Leary added, he needed more manpower to do this effectively by making 'arrests, arrests, arrests'.[46]

The early results of Leary's new offensive seemed impressive: drug arrests rose from 27,000 in 1968 to 72,000 in 1970, but the reality behind the statistics soon became too blatant to be hidden any longer. The Knapp Commission, in particular, scrutinized police drug-enforcement methods in unprecedented detail. Their investigators found that arrest quotas were largely made up of the same addicts, users and low-level pushers brought in time and again. Ploys to counter Constitutional safeguards and secure convictions were routine. Unreasonable searches and seizures, for example, should make evidence inadmissible. But if police testified that they had seen defendants dropping heroin on the ground, a search became 'reasonable' and a seizure admissible as evidence. The commission thought that this kind of evidence was too frequent to be credible; too many suspects were dropping drugs on the floor whenever a policeman was in sight. In hundreds of other cases policemen had testified that they had seen drugs on defendants' floors and sofas because doors had been left open. This meant that policemen could go in and make an ostensibly legitimate arrest. But the idea that drug dealers left quite so many doors open in inner-city areas again strained the commission's credulity.[47]

In the course of its investigations the commission became familiar with many other corrupt police practices including:

Keeping money and/or narcotics confiscated at the time of an arrest or raid.
Selling narcotics to addict-informants in exchange for stolen goods.
Passing on confiscated drugs to police informants for sale to addicts.
'Flaking', or planting narcotics on an arrested person in order to have evidence of a law violation.
'Padding', or adding to the quantity of narcotics found on an arrested person in order to upgrade an arrest.
Storing narcotics, needles and other drug paraphernalia in police lockers.

Illegally tapping suspects' telephones to obtain incriminating evidence to be used either in making cases against the suspects, or to blackmail them.
Purporting to guarantee freedom from police wiretaps for a monthly service charge.
Accepting money or narcotics from suspected narcotics law violators as payment for the disclosure of official information.
Accepting money for registering as police informants persons who were in fact giving no information and falsely attributing leads and arrests to them, so that their 'cooperation' with the police may win them amnesty for prior misconduct.
Financing heroin transactions.

These were typical patterns. The commission also learnt of individual instances of corrupt conduct:

Determining the purity and strength of unfamiliar drugs they had seized by giving small quantities to addict-informants to test on themselves.
Introducing potential customers to narcotics pushers.
Revealing the identity of a government informant to narcotics criminals.
Kidnapping critical witnesses at the time of trial to prevent them from testifying.
Providing armed protection for narcotics dealers.
Offering to obtain 'hit men' to kill potential witnesses.[48]

Soon after the Knapp Commission had completed its report more scandals revealed that the most successful drug squad in the NYPD was also the most corrupt. The Special Investigating Unit (SIU) was an elite squad of detectives that could trace its origins from a much-publicized drugs case known as 'The French Connection', on which a best-selling book by Robin Moore and two award-winning films were based.

In October 1961 two detectives, Eddie Egan and Sonny Grosso, stumbled upon a ring that imported heroin, processed in France. Egan and Grosso were backed up by a small squad of the best detectives available which became the SIU. Eventually these detectives arrested several important drug traffickers and seized 97 pounds of heroin—the largest street seizure up to that time. It was thought that a major source of supply had been seriously curtailed and that these ends justified some unorthodox police procedures including illegal wiretapping and thuggery. Robin Moore represented the case as 'the most crucial single victory to date in the ceaseless, frustrating war against the import of vicious narcotics into our country', and claimed that the case was leading to 'the progressive breakdown of Mafia investment and proprietorship in the United States narcotics market', despite the fact that it was a sophisticated French smuggling ring that had been disrupted.[49]

Although people flocked to see the exciting, first-filmed account of the case in 1971, it was to be rendered a worthless exercise. In December 1972 the new Police Commissioner, Patrick Murphy, disclosed that 57 pounds of the French Connection heroin had been stolen from the property clerk's office. Two-thirds of the largest drugs seizure therefore ended up in the New York market anyway. The following February, Murphy concluded from further investigations that about one-fifth of all the heroin and cocaine seized by the New York police between January 1961 and December 1972 had also been stolen—398 pounds to which he gave a street value of $73 million. The thieves were never found but it was thought that they were a relatively small group of policemen who were aware of the drug cases involving large seizures. Also not in the book or the two films relating to the case was the fact that Eddie Egan was fired from the New York Police Department for failing to deliver narcotics evidence to the property clerk upon completion of court hearings.[50]

The integrity and effectiveness of the SIU had not been in doubt at the end of the 1960s. It was a small group of about seventy detectives who, according to former New York police officer, David Durk, seized more heroin and other drugs in 1970 than were seized by all Customs, Border Patrol and federal narcotics agents working throughout the country.[51] SIU detectives had city-wide jurisdiction, chose their own targets, and made their own decisions as to whether or not to enforce the law.

Many of the detectives had a lavish lifestyle and an income far exceeding their official income. Some even carried self-addressed, stamped envelopes with them for making 'night deposits' in mailboxes soon after seizing large sums of money. In his book, *The Pleasant Avenue Connection*, Durk detailed how money, jewellery and drugs were stolen from drug dealers and then shared out between lieutenants, sergeants and detectives, how cases were fixed for a price, and how the unit had become a kind of 'heroin brokerage' in which cases were made to regulate competition by taking out unprotected dealers.[52]

In February 1971 this lucrative world began to come apart. In that month Detective Robert Leuci began a series of meetings with Nicholas Scoppetta, a lawyer with the Knapp Commission, and disclosed that he had direct and hearsay evidence of widespread corruption at every stage of the criminal justice system—from assistant district attorneys who routinely told detectives how to perjure themselves and lawyers who offered as much as $15,000 to detectives to fix cases, to the judges at the very top. Leuci was persuaded to go under-cover in the pursuit of evidence that would stand up in court and to wear a recording device attached to his body while talking to lawyers, prosecutors, private investigators, bail bondsmen, drug traffickers and his detective colleagues. Leuci had wanted to prove that to focus only on corrupt policemen, as the Knapp Commission was doing, was to see only a small part of the picture. He was prepared to help convict corrupt police officers but he intended to work primarily against higher-level and better-paid criminals within the criminal justice system. He had not intended to work against his friends and partners in the SIU.[53]

Inevitably the cases against policemen proved to be the easiest to make. Fifty-two out of the seventy-odd SIU detectives were convicted of various corrupt practices , two committed suicide, while Leuci and most of the rest served as the pardoned witnesses.[54] For years top police officials had been explaining away instances of corruption as 'rotten apples' in otherwise sound barrels; after the New York police scandals fewer people believed them.

In 1972 a Special Prosecutor, Maurice Nadjari, was appointed to find out how high the corruption went in the criminal justice system—a difficult task since bribes, deals and favours take place behind closed doors and between allies and willing partners. Therefore to test out the integrity of the system, Nadjari's agents worked under-cover, used wiretaps and recording devices, and even staged a mock robbery. Judges and politicians were thus subjected to the same methods routinely used to arrest and convict less well-connected people. By the end of the first eighteen months of his investigation Nadjari had indicted a number of high-ranking public officials and won a string of major courtroom victories, including the conviction of a district attorney. But by the end of 1975 many of his most impressive investigations had begun to disintegrate under harsh legal tests imposed by the appeals courts. Convictions were reversed, indictments were dismissed. Nadjari charged that the closer he got to the hard core of corruption—'the small band of franchised corruptors who manipulate all of us'—the more he was abused and pressured to resign. In the end no judges, district attorneys, or prominent people targeted by Nadjari's agents finished up behind bars, although the prosecutor had used the 'same tools and means of law enforcement' as in 'investigations and prosecutions of killers, robbers, rapists and drug pushers'. The only difference was that Nadjari's targets had power. Nadjari was removed as Special Prosecutor on 29 June 1976.[55]

Robert Leuci stayed with the police force for a few years after the final trial of his SIU partners but, shunned by fellow officers, he took early retirement in July 1981.[56] The corruption he had helped to expose in New York was not unique; other cities have experienced similar scandals and it is a subject we shall return to in the final chapter.

Corruption was only one reason why the drug laws did not work; others were revealed by a Drug Abuse Council study of the effects of New York's 1973 drug laws which were the legislative culmination of Governor Rockefeller's cynical anti-drug posturing (see pp. 166–167). The new legislation ensured a minimum fifteen year jail sentence for heroin dealers selling an ounce or more, or possessing more than two. Lesser quantities attracted lesser minimum penalties, but anyone selling heroin could be jailed for life. Convicted dealers were subject to formal surveillance by parole officers for the rest of their life—in other words, the draconian 'solution' that Rockefeller had long called for.

The legislation was intended to frighten dealers, deter addicts from continuing their habits, and prevent hardened offenders from selling by locking them up for long periods of time. But, as the study made clear, the desired deterrance and increased conviction rate did not happen. After the passage of the new laws the chances of arrest of the average dealer remained minimal, but the courts still became congested since many more defendants opted for trial and many more defense counsels used delaying tactics. Just before the new laws were implemented, imprisoned drug offenders and drug enforcement officers had been interviewed in another study. The researchers found a cynical attitude towards a criminal justice system that was incapable of supporting existing, let alone more stringent, laws. A grossly overloaded system could no more deter than the one it replaced. And so, by all major indicators, heroin use, addiction and trafficking remained as great or greater in New York City and State in the years following Rockefeller's law. For this result and for the problems of court congestion the government had spent around $32 million of taxpayers' money. 'It is implausible', concluded the Drug Abuse Council report, that basic social problems 'can be effectively solved by the criminal law'.[57]

Although the propaganda behind the expansion of drug enforcement activity emphasized the devastation of heroin addiction and scapegoated the drug for increased street crime, the bulk of actual enforcement capacity was directed against marijuana—a drug which a Nixon-appointed commission (see p. 197) had stressed was not addictive and did not promote crime. There was a tremendous upsurge of marijuana arrests from the mid-1960s. In 1965 there had been 18,815 marijuana arrests, 31.1 per cent of the total drug arrests; in 1967, 61,843 marijuana arrests, 50.9 per cent of the total; by 1974 there were 445,000 marijuana arrests, virtually 70 per cent of the total.[58] The overwhelming majority of these arrests were for possessing, not selling, the drug. Marijuana was the drug of choice of millions of Americans and therefore bringing charges for possession of small amounts of the drug was the easiest way for local police, in particular, to meet arrest quotas. Blacks, Hispanics and hippies made up the numbers; 'respectable' users tended to be safe from arrest.

From the early 1970s there was a strong movement to relax the marijuana laws. The National Organization for the Reform of Marijuana Laws (NORML) was set up to represent users and to try and educate America into understanding that although it was unwise to abuse any drug the answer was not attempted repression and mass imprisonments. NORML and sympathetic journalists sought to publicize some of the worst and most absurd aspects of the anti-marijuana policy.[59]

The first issue of NORML's newsletter, *The Leaflet*, came out in Autumn 1971. The lead article was an account of a Vietnam veteran in Ohio, with no previous arrest record, who had been sentenced to twenty to forty years in prison for being present when a friend sold marijuana to an undercover agent.

Equally irrational and harsh sentences were imposed in other states. In Texas, for example, about 700 young men were serving average sentences of about ten years. Thirty had sentences of thirty years or more, and thirteen had been sentenced to life. Half of the 700 marijuana prisoners were first offenders, a third were younger than 22, and many had been convicted for simple possession. Peter Trevino was a 20-year-old who was convicted for selling several ounces of marijuana. The judge, noting that he was an orphan, said, 'Son, we'll give you a home', and sentenced him to forty years.

Many of such sentences were eventually reduced or struck down as 'cruel and unusual punishment' but lives continued to be shattered by severe prison terms received under archaic regional marijuana laws. Jerry Mitchell, for example, from West Plains, Missouri, was introduced by a friend to a third party, to whom Mitchell sold some locally grown marijuana. Mitchell's friend was a drug informant and the purchaser was an undercover highway patrolman. Mitchell pleaded guilty to selling one-third of an ounce for five dollars; his lawyer reasoned that the court would take into account the fact that he was 19 with no arrest record and looked after his parents, both of whom were blind. In June 1976, Mitchell was sentenced to twelve years, later reduced to seven. Eve Wilson of Greenfield, Missouri, received a five-year sentence for selling her date, who turned out to be an undercover policeman, less than an ounce of marijuana. Roger Davis, probably the best-known case, was sentenced to forty years by a court in Wytheville, Virginia, for selling four ounces of marijuana to a police informant and possessing six more ounces in his home. He was first arrested in October 1973 and not paroled until the summer of 1984, after being refused a pardon by the Governor of Virginia, Charles Robb. The unusual severity of his sentence has been attributed to the fact that Davis was a black in a mainly white community who wore his hair long and married a white woman.[60]

Perhaps the saddest case, however, was that of Billy Nester, a young marijuana smoker from Pennsylvania. His parents found a marijuana cigarette in his room, informed the police and said that they wanted him arrested and sent to prison, if that was the only way to save him from drugs. Soon after Nester's arrival in prison he was gang-raped. Shortly afterwards he hanged himself. The case was featured on a nationally networked news programme, *60 Minutes*.[61]

The wrecking of many thousands of American lives by the drug laws is a tragedy compounded by the realization that a proportion of drug arrests are achieved through frame-ups and that only a few of these come to light. Between August 1973 and August 1974, for example, Detective Paul Lawrence made more than 100 drug arrests in the small town of St Albans in Vermont and organized one raid which was the biggest in the state's history. The townspeople welcomed this rounding up of 'dirty, long-haired, ragged youths' and applauded Lawrence's work. He was being considered to head a planned state-wide drug-enforcement agency, until it was discovered that he was framing his victims with drug evidence that he was providing himself. He had always operated alone and so there was never corroborating evidence of the alleged buys, and his activities only came to light when he tried to frame another undercover police officer. Robert Gensburg, the prosecutor in the Lawrence case, spoke of the personal impact of the frame-ups:

> Here's one kid who was mentally sound prior to this arrest and now has a history of two years in and out of mental hospitals. There's two or three cases of

marriages breaking up. Here's a letter from a girl whose family threw her out and would never believe her. Here's a guy who can't get meaningful work.

Even after Lawrence's conviction many townspeople still justified his methods as necessary to keep the hippies out. One former city councilman told a *New York Times* reporter:

I'm still in Lawrence's corner. Hell, I've got five children myself, and I've got to protect them. Everything was going on back then. They were jumping up and down on cars and ranting and raving. We've got to bring our children up with the fundamentals of Americanism and the fundamentals of our various religions.[62]

In August 1977 President Jimmy Carter became the first president to recommend a relaxation of criminal penalties for the non-medical use of drugs when he advocated the 'decriminalization' in federal law of the simple possession of up to one ounce of marijuana. He therefore backed a trend that was already occurring in some states. However, decriminalization only put marijuana in a position similar to that of alcohol during Prohibition; possession was legal but cultivation, sale and importation were not. By the end of the 1970s there were still over 400,000 marijuana arrests a year and this still constituted over 70 per cent of the total drug arrests.[63]

The Carter administration continued to fund marijuana crop-eradication programmes in Mexico, which utilized aerial spraying of cannabis fields with the herbicide paraquat. The herbicide is a potent poison which could produce fibrosis, a severe form of lung damage, if inhaled in marijuana smoke. In 1979 the potential health hazard was acknowledged by the government which withdrew US funds from the spraying programme.[64]

The scare that accompanied the spraying programme among users triggered significant growth in domestic production of marijuana and advanced horticultural techniques soon produced a hybrid, called sinsemilla, with many times the potency of imported varieties. Marijuana grows easily in every part of the United States, both indoors and outdoors, but the main growing areas are thought to be in California, Kentucky and Hawaii, followed by Oregon, North Carolina, Oklahoma, Tennessee, Arkansas, Florida, Georgia, Missouri, Kansas and South Carolina. It is now clearly established as one of the nation's most profitable cash crops, despite intensive eradication efforts.[65]

Despite the growth of home-grown produce, much of the marijuana consumed in the United States still comes from neighbouring countries such as Mexico and Colombia. The enormous popularity of marijuana makes smuggling it an attractive venture for large-scale operations. Up to the 1970s, marijuana trafficking was mainly an individual pursuit for private use and distribution to friends. By the end of the decade, federal agents were confiscating whole shiploads and planeloads of baled marijuana, while admitting that they were intercepting only a small fraction of the imports.[66]

Compared to heroin or cocaine, marijuana smuggling is a more difficult operation simply because of its relative bulk. The profit level is also much lower. However, the market for marijuana is so large and so well established that profitability is assured and the greater risk of apprehension is obviously thought worth taking.

Heroin, derived from the opium poppy, had to take a longer international trip before it reached the American market, at least until the 1970s when Mexican heroin appeared. As Roger Lewis has written, opium has long been a tempting cash crop for impoverished tribals peoples in South East and South West Asia: 'With its high price, high yield per acre, labour-intensive nature and inaccessibility on high, rugged, hard-to-control terrain . . . It is a low-bulk, high value, non-perishable commodity'. Eradication efforts are fiercely fought off. The peasant farmer, however, only receives a tiny fraction of what his crop will realize when converted into heroin: 'Value increases by a factor of anything from 125 per cent to 1,000 per cent in its transition from raw material to finished product'.[67] The truly astonishing profits go to the people who control the refining process, to those who ship the refined product to its market, and finally to those at the top of the consumer distribution system.

From the 1970s, however, much larger-scale and more lucrative trafficking operations involved cocaine, a drug which had re-emerged as popular and fashionable after decades of obscurity. Its use increased within all classes of Americans, but was most noticeable among athletes, entertainers and 'young, upwardly mobiles' in well-paid professions. The drug is a powerful stimulant and can be dangerous, dependency can develop and overdoses or accidents have sometimes been fatal. Much of the drug's glamour and mystique is related to its outlaw status, and its popularity has not been dented by sensational news media treatment of the dangers of excessive cocaine use.

The coca plant is a relatively easy crop to grow—hardy, disease-resistant and long-lived. The major, known growing areas are in sparsely-populated, inaccessible areas of South America. According to 1979 estimates, a peasant farmer could hope to realize $250 from the sale of 500 kilos of coca leaves in regions where the average monthly wage was around $50. This same amount—not taking account of the costs of refinement, smuggling and distribution—might realize $80,000 in the United States.[68]

The fastest and safest means of smuggling cocaine is by aeroplane. Pilots are paid enormous sums of money to take loads in small private aircraft. One pilot, for example, testifying before the Kaufman Commission in November 1984, stated that he and his associates had flown more than 250 plane-loads from South America without being caught. They found that the hardest part was what to do with the money.[69]

Larger quantities of cocaine and marijuana go by sea, most often by freighter to Caribbean and Bahamian islands close to the Coast of Florida, and then transferred to smaller, faster boats for the shorter journey, although such transfers can also be made anywhere along the Atlantic and Pacific coastlines. When chased by inferior Customs or Coastguard boats, the smugglers tend to emulate their rumrunning forefathers and win.[70]

Even small amounts of drug contraband has great value; thousands of dollars worth of heroin or cocaine can be smuggled into the country in containers the size of cigarette packets. There are countless devices: false petrol tanks in cars, false-bottomed suitcases, shipments of canned foods or any manufactured goods, even pregnancy cages worn by women who are not pregnant, or the hollowed-out heels of shoes. There is the so-called 'body-packing syndrome' where the courier swallows condoms or balloons full of cocaine or heroin. The most horrific means was reported in March 1985 when Customs agents in Miami discovered a dead baby which had been cut open, stuffed with cocaine and sewn shut.[71]

Smuggling organizations tend to restrict their operations to importation, leaving distribution within the United States to indigenous groups. No ethnically based monopoly in the drug business has ever existed. WASP-, Irish-, Jewish-, Italian- and other European Americans compete or cooperate with black-, Hispanic- and Asian-Americans to supply the market. There are many thousands of drug distribution and smuggling networks—decentralization characterizes the industry with a high turnover of personnel. Many sources of raw materials exist. Many organizations, large and small, buy and process the raw materials, import the product into the country, where it is sold to and processed and distributed at retail by a host of outlets. Although some operations have lasted for decades, organization in the drug business is largely spontaneous, with anyone free to enter it at any level if he or she has the money, the supplier and the ability to escape arrest or robbery. There does appear to have been a shift in recent years from small to large drug organizations. As enforcement increased it created competitive advantages for syndicates that had the skills, connections and capital to nullify enforcement with corruption and the manpower and firepower to resist theft and takeover bids.

The heroin and cocaine distribution structure tends to be pyramidal, similar to food distribution. All deal in consumer goods bought on a frequent basis, typically in small amounts for immediate consumption and have no need for special technology or equipment. There are relatively few suppliers at the top and thousands of retailers at the bottom. Drug distributors either sell their product to local wholesalers or transport large quantities to other cities for sale to regional wholesalers. Wholesalers divide the produce into pounds for sale to pound dealers, who further divide it into ounces for sale to ounce dealers and so on down the chain of distribution to the consumer. Adulteration with anything from powdered milk to talcum powder occurs at every stage. Lower-level heroin dealers are often addicted themselves and make minimal profits. The cocaine retail level tends to be an informal network of friends and acquaintances. Entrepreneurs need to insert themselves towards the top of the pyramid, buying cheap and selling dear, while minimizing such overheads as processing, transport and bribery.[72]

As the cocaine business boomed from the late 1960s, groups of Cuban exiles became particularly prominent and Hank Messick, Penny Lernoux and other writers have detailed the confusing mixture of violence, corruption and political expediency that accompanied their rise.

Soon after the 1959 Cuban revolution was deemed contrary to US interests, a large contingent of CIA agents was transferred down to Southern Florida to organize attempts to topple Fidel Castro. Around 2,000 anti-Castro Cuban exiles were trained in the arts of guerrilla warfare and terrorism, notably bomb-making and murder. The 1961 Bay of Pigs invasion ended in failure and humiliation, leaving survivors of the force with their grudge against Castro intact and, as already mentioned (see p. 155), the training to succeed as gangsters in their adopted country.

Since the 1960s scores of assassinations, kidnappings, bombings and extortion rackets, as well as blatant drug trafficking, have been excused as the acts of freedom-loving anti-Communists as the profits of crime supported an expansion of terrorist activities. Large sums of money derived from the drug trade sometimes supported the anti-Castro crusade but more often simply enriched numerous 'patriots', with traffickers moving into mansions equipped with elaborate security systems and every conceivable luxury.

In this confused and violent world Ricardo 'Monkey' Morales stood out. Morales had worked briefly as a secret agent for Castro before emigrating to the United States in 1960, where both the CIA and FBI employed him. While working for these agencies, Morales, on his own admission, was an enthusiastic participant in the assassination of Castro sympathizers and, in October 1976, in the bombing of an Air Cubana plane which resulted in seventy-three fatalities, including the entire Cuban national fencing team. Morales used his intelligence connections and local police corruption as protection from prosecution for these crimes and for a deep involvement in the drug trade. Morales' additional role as a police informer possibly accounts for his death in a Miami bar in 1982, after a gun battle.[73].

In New York the career of Frank Matthews was just as spectacular, but without the international political overtones. Matthews was a black American whose move as a young man from rural North Carolina to the big city signalled the beginning of a short but successful career. He found a base in the Bedford-Stuyvesant area of New York and, after employment in various numbers operations, decided that drugs offered greater potential. Around 1967 he made a direct contact with French heroin refiners and smugglers for his supplies, and therefore by-passed the Italian- and Jewish-American middlemen who had dominated the traffic for decades. For distribution he utilized an existing network of numbers sellers and collectors, after the raw materials had been 'cut' and 'bagged' in a number of fortified locations by employees working regular eight-hour shifts. Local police were probably paid off since there is no record of them disturbing Matthews's operations. By 1970 he had expanded, and his organization distributed much of the heroin in the larger East coast cities, with outlets in Clevelands, Detroit, Cincinnati, Chicago, Kansas City, Las Vegas and Los Angeles.

Matthews made no effort to hide his rapidly increasing wealth–buying expensive property and cars, turning up at championship boxing matches in floor-length sable or mink coats, and losing heavily and ostentatiously at Las Vegas roulette tables. He was arrested there by federal police on 1 January 1973 and indicted on numerous drug-related charges. While released on bail, he converted an estimated $20 million of his assets into cash and then disappeared.

A national and international manhunt followed with the DEA offering $20,000 in reward money for information about Matthews's whereabouts. One tip, as journalist Donald Goddard described it, mobilized a small army of police, state troopers, and federal agents in Syracuse, New York. 'After sealing off the area, an assault group armed with riot guns and automatic weapons filtered into a downtown rooming house and burst in suddenly on an eighty-year-old man watching television', whose name also happened to be Frank Matthews.[74] The real Frank Matthews, apparently, remains a fugitive after more than a decade.

White Anglo-Saxon Protestants, of course, have their share of gangsters and drug traffickers in the United States. This can be seen most clearly in the rise of outlaw motorcycle gangs since the Second World War, notably the Hell's Angels, who were the first national and international motor-cycle gang and always have been composed primarily of WASPs.

The Angels grew rapidly during the 1950s but declined almost to extinction by the mid-1960s. Around that time some of its leaders sought to revive the almost defunct movement by using methods perfected over the years by organized crime syndicates. They built up legal businesses with money gained through systematic criminal activity, often buying property to establish motor-cycle shops and taverns which could also be used to fence stolen parts and other merchandise and to distribute drugs. The Hell's Angels, operating primarily on the West and East coasts, have been joined by three major rival organizations: the Bandidos, operating largely in the South with some membership in the Northwest; the Outlaws, mainly on the Eastern side of the United States, as are the Pagans. Under these umbrella organizations there are now over 800 individual gangs, highly structured, tightly disciplined and very mobile. Some are particularly difficult to infiltrate by law-enforcement agencies since they require major crimes, such as rape or murder, as conditions of membership.

Drug trafficking, mainly in domestically manufactured methamphetamine and the hallucinogen PCP, has become the major source of income for many of these gangs. The Angels, for example, were found recently to be producing 'speed' from twelve clandestine methamphetamine laboratories in California; and, in central Ohio, one illicit laboratory was said to be producing enough illegal drugs to distribute throughout Ohio into California, West

Virginia, New York and New Jersey. Income derived from drugs can be supplemented by pimping, pornography, contract murders and robbery.

In recent years the federal agency most successful in prosecuting motor-cycle gang members has been the Bureau of Alcohol, Tobacco and Firearms (ATF). The ATF has been able to obtain scores of successful convictions against the most powerful gang members by focusing federal firearms and explosive laws on them, and then allowing other agencies to develop their own cases. However, Phillip C. McGuire, Associate Director of ATF's Law Enforcement Office, still emphasized in February 1985 that outlaw motor-cycle gangs were 'the largest and most well-armed criminal organizations in the country'.[75]

The Kaufman Commission, established by President Reagan in 1983 to investigate organized and drug-related crime in the United States, initially undertook to investigate the power and activities of motor-cycle gangs. They chose instead to highlight smaller, less well-armed and less violent Asian drug-trafficking syndicates in three days of New York hearings in October 1984, it still being obviously preferable to camouflage the fact that American gangsters are produced by American conditions, and to give the impression that somehow aliens are to blame.

Violence in the drug trade far exceeds anything experienced during the bootleg wars of the 1920s and is not confined to the big Northern cities. The motives are, however, generally the same—protecting territory or goods from rivals, discouraging, or retaliating for, betrayal to the authorities, or stealing drugs or money or both from other traffickers. Police estimated that over a hundred of Detroit's 690 homicides in 1971 were related to the heroin trade. In New York in 1981 there were 393 drug-related slayings, including 160 in which drug dealers were killed during robberies. From the mid-1970s the homicide rate in South Florida jumped more than 400 per cent in a few years mainly because of violence associated with the drug traffic. In 1980 there were 108 Florida killings where the motive could be related to the drug trade. In 1981 the Dade County medical examiner had to rent a refrigerated hamburger van to cope with the increase in corpses, and Miami has become one of the world's most dangerous cities. Californian cities have also witnessed several hundred street shootings and 'gang-style' murders. In Los Angeles around sixty-five drug-related slayings occurred in 1984 and the small city of Oakland saw forty more between January 1983 and October 1984.[76]

Drug-trafficking-related mass murders have also become increasingly common. On Easter Sunday 1972, Tyrone Palmer and four others were shot dead in a gun battle in a Philadelphian nightclub that also left twenty-six wounded. Palmer was Frank Matthews's main contact in Philadelphia.[77] In July 1977, four gunmen broke into a bungalow in Carol City, west of Miami, during a drug deal. They forced the owner, Livingston Stocker, and his seven companions down to the floor and then shot them. Six died. On 28 June 1978, five men were found dead in an office in Boston. Police said a dispute over drugs was the cause of the massacre. One was a former 'investigative reporter' for Boston television who was planning to write modern stories in the style of Damon Runyon.[78] In August 1982, three women were shot dead with machine guns in South Miami. There were no signs of forced entry or robbery; a one-pound package of cocaine was found in their apartment. The following month two young men and two young women were found stuffed in the trunk of a car. And in another incident, also related to drugs, four men were found shot in the back of the head.[79]

The expansion of enforcement to combat crimes which have no complainants has been necessarily accompanied by an increased need for police informants to secure convictions. Although the identity of these people is now better concealed than during the pre-1970 period in New York, when scores of federal police informants were murdered through the incompetence or corruption of the Federal Bureau of Narcotics (see p. 14), their lives are still precarious. The ultimate rebuke or warning for an informant took place on 15 April 1984. A team of professional hit-men walked into a flat in Brooklyn and shot dead two women and eight children, either holding them in chairs while shooting them in the head or propping them up afterwards. The flat was the home of Enrique Bermudez, a Puerto Rican who operated on the fringes of the drugs trade. In 1976 he pleaded guilty to selling half an ounce of cocaine to an undercover policeman. Under New York's stringent drug law, he could have received a life sentence. Instead he chose to cooperate with the authorities in return for a five-year term. He was paroled in 1981 and worked for the kind of cowboy taxi service sometimes used by drug traffickers. The deaths of his girlfriend and children, and the others, were probably either a warning or a rebuke for informing.[80]

Informing or 'snitching' has become an integral part of the drug-trafficking and enforcement world, with both small and large operators willing to implicate or testify against rivals or friends in exchange for shorter sentences. Donald Goddard has written about an informant system that suited both police and selected traffickers in New York during the 1960s and 1970s:

> As an alternative to bribery, snitching was the only effective means of dealing with straight cops and prosecutors, and as such, an accepted business practice. But it had to be used with discretion. The big operators usually covered themselves by means of bilateral treaties, one promising not to inform on another in return for the same consideration, and both would commonly unite to liquidate any lesser third party who threatened either one of them from below.[81]

Informing is still a precarious as well as treacherous business, however, as the case of Barry Seal shows. Seal was an aeroplane pilot who, by his own admission, had flown countless tons of cocaine from Colombia to the United States in the late 1970s before being convicted on charges involving conspiracy to distribute bootleg quaaludes (slang term for methaqualone tablets which belong to the depressant category) in 1983. He was sentenced to ten years but offered to work it off by doing undercover work for the DEA as an informant. In that role he worked for top Colombian drug smugglers such as

Pablo Escobar, Juan Ochoa and Carlos Lehder. He also helped entice the Prime Minister of the Turks and Caicos islands, Norman Saunders, to come to Miami to launder cocaine money and accept bribes in full view of video cameras. Saunders was convicted and sentenced to a long prison term. However, Seal, like many others, was working for himself while working for the government. In 1984 he was convicted in Louisiana on charges involving 200 kilos of cocaine and a list of money-laundering charges. The sentence he received was six months of 'community service' at a Salvation Army drug rehabilitation centre where, in the spring of 1986, he was machine-gunned to death by two men. This case leaves many questions unanswered, one being why was such an obvious target as Seal not protected by his government employers?[82]

The incentive for all the violence and treachery in the drug world is, of course, money and in recent years more has been revealed about what happens to this money after it has been collected.

Not only corrupt officials and ruthless gangsters benefit financially from the drug trade; ostensibly legitimate financial advisers and institutions have also prospered. Banks, most noticeably in Florida, have boomed by laundering vast amounts of cash generated through drug prohibition. In Miami so many drug-trade dollars have flowed through the city's branch of the Federal Reserve System that it has not needed to issue any new currency for some time and even exports used dollars to other Federal Reserve districts. Since 1970 the city has become an international banking centre, rivalling London and New York, and no one seriously disputes that dollars generated by the trade in marijuana and cocaine account for this rapid rise to prominence.[83]

As the drug trade expanded dealers amassed mountains of cash, primarily in small-denomination bills. This cash—often stuffed into carrier bags or cardboard boxes—was then brought to the banks and pushed through to the tellers. Bales of it were then fed into high-speed money counters or simply weighed. The totals were usually just under $10,000, since each bank by law must report cash deposits of more than this amount which might attract the attention of regulators. More recently, as *Business Week* has reported, the size of the launderers' deposits has tended to go down further and therefore be even less likely to be noticed. But teams of cash couriers can still deposit as much as $300,000 in a day. And couriers can be the least likely people; one group of grandmothers on the West Coast laundered more than $25 million before being noticed.[84]

The $10,000 currency transaction law itself has also been regularly subverted. Some bank officials take bribes and neglect to file the report forms. Some launders create accounts in the names of 'off-shore' shell corporations, so the forms can contain no useful information. A legal exemption from the form can also be obtained by launderers with the assurance to pretend they are a legitimate retail outfit with large cash-flows.

Once the money is deposited in the bank, launderers can transfer it into the accounts of more 'off-shore' shell corporations in such places as Switzerland, Hong Kong, Panama and Grand Cayman island. Once the money is off-shore, local bank-secrecy laws will usually defy attempts to trace it. Little will then prevent it supporting the most lavish life-styles and being invested in legitimate businesses with always the option to reinvest in the drug trade—the business with the highest rate of capital return of all.

It has become clear that banks are willing accomplices to all this, since they have much to gain and little to lose. Some have been found to launder money knowingly on a regular basis, earning up to 3 per cent in commissions on it and lending it out profitably at the same time. Also, drug money always goes into non-interest-bearing accounts or is changed into cashiers' cheques, which usually remain uncollected for months, providing banks with yet more incentive to turn a blind eye. And, despite numerous instances of active or passive bank complicity revealed in recent years, few, if any, bankers have received jail sentences.

Money-laundering drug dealers are only using mechanisms long familiar to large corporate concerns for the purposes of avoiding tax or maintaining 'slush' funds and to pioneering figures such as Meyer Lansky for 'cleaning' organized crime money. The relative ease of large-scale money-laundering is likely to persist since the international business community will probably stall efforts by authorities to penetrate bank secrecy laws and expose some of the shadier business practices.[85]

Since the late 1970s financial investigative task forces have been formed and have had a certain amount of success. Operation Greenback, a joint IRS, Customs Service and DEA effort, for example, targeted entire laundering networks of attorneys, accountants, money brokers, money couriers, and bankers, and documented $2.6 billion laundered through sixteen drug-trafficking organizations. By 1984, 164 people had been arrested. The most notable money-launderer Greenback turned up was a Colombian, Isaac Kattan. Kattan did business with four Miami banks: the Bank of Miami, the Great American Bank, the Northside Bank of Miami and the Popular Bank and Trust Company, depositing as much as $1 million each day. Raids on the banks revealed a number of irregularities: employees had been switching funds from one of the Kattan's accounts to another, pages of cash-deposit logs and some cashiers' cheques were missing, and employees assigned to count the rushes of cash sometimes complained that the bills were wet or smelly—as if they had been buried. An agent testified that on one occasion he heard Kattan apologize to a bank official for a suspicious-looking transaction. The bank official reassured him: 'Don't worry—the main thing now is to count the money'.[86]

Another case revealed that over a four-year period Eduardo Orozco and his associates deposited about $151 million in cash in eighteen bank and currency exchange accounts, before transferring it elsewhere within the United States or abroad. Orozco's customers were primarily Colombian cocaine dealers, but he also did some business with Sicilian heroin traffickers. In his 1983 trial the jury were convinced that Orozco was a financial institution in and of himself and was therefore required to file currency-transaction reports. Despite being careful never to deal directly with convicted drug dealers, Orozco was found to be 'aiding and abetting' in a conspiracy to violate drug laws and was sentenced to eight years in prison.[87] However, despite substantially increased efforts against money-laundering in recent years illustrated by such results, the authorities have only really succeeded in capturing a few middlemen and revealing something of the vast profitability of the drug trade. The root of the problem, as Senator William Proxmire has put it, is that 'Many banks are addicted to drug money, just as millions of Americans are addicted to drugs'.[88]

By 1980 many millions of Americans regularly or occasionally used illegal drugs. Each year more than half a million of them were arrested for drug offences—70 per cent for offences involving the most popular and least harmful drug, marijuana. Courts struggled to cope and prisons had become so congested that some were declared to constitute 'cruel and unusual punishment'. The opportunities for corruption, brutality and power abuse had been multiplied—all without affecting an immense trade in illegal substances beyond keeping prices inflated and profits high for smugglers, manufacturers and distributors and giving the competitive advantage to the most ruthless and best-connected criminal syndicates. Expanded drug enforcement still constituted no more than an acceptable level of risk to be taken with the prospect of fortunes to be made. One San Francisco policeman summed up the futility of the effort in 1983 when he told *Time*: 'All we can hope to do is prevent someone setting up a cocaine stand in Union Square'.[89]

Exploiting the fear of drugs had helped elect politicians and promote bureaucrats, but the hard-line 'solution' of expanded enforcement and severe penalties was counter-productive. Enforcement capacity was wasted trying to achieve the unachievable. The country became more lawless; corruption, betrayal, deception, chaos and terror have become an institutionalized part of the drug law enforcement world. The final chapter describes the perpetuation of a solution that exacerbated the problem of drugs.

13 Perpetuation

In 1973 an official report on drug use in America warned about the 'rapid institutionalization' of the 'drug abuse problem'. The National Commission on Marijuana and Drug Abuse, appointed by President Nixon in 1971, described how:

> The high degree of public concern has generated a shifting of large quantities of money, manpower and other resources at the federal, state and local levels to meet the problem and lessen the public concern. This response has created, in the short span of four years, a 'drug abuse industrial complex.'
>
> With spending at the federal level alone of upwards of one billion dollars annually, with a rapid growth in bureaucracy, with an almost compulsive spending on drug projects without benefit of evaluation or goal setting, the drug abuse industrial complex has firmly established itself as a fixture of government and society.
>
> The Commission is concerned that the underlying assumptions about the problem and the organizational response of the 'complex' may, rather than resolve or de-emotionalize the issue, tend to perpetuate it as an ongoing part of the American way of life. There is a real need to evaluate the present system to ensure that the government directs its efforts toward the achievement of success rather than the perpetuation of government activity.[1]

Later in the report, in a section entitled 'Perpetuating the Problem', the Commission elaborated upon this theme:

> Because of the intensity of the public concern and the emotionalism surrounding the topic of drugs, all levels of government have been pressured into action with little time for planning. The political pressures involved in this governmental effort have resulted in a concentration of public energy on the most immediate aspects of drug use and a reaction along the paths of least political resistance. The recent result has been the creation of ever larger bureacracies, ever increasing expenditures of monies, and an outpouring of publicity so that the public will know that 'something' is being done.
>
> Perhaps the major consequence of this *ad hoc* policy planning has been the creation, at the federal, state and community levels, of a vested interest in the perpetuation of the problem among those dispensing and receiving funds. Infrastructures are created, job descriptions are standardized, 'experts' are created and ways of doing business routinized and established along bureaucratic channels. During the last several years, drug programming has become a multi-billion dollar industry, one administering to its own needs as well as to

those of its drug-using clientele. In the course of well-meaning efforts to do something about drug use, this society may have inadvertently institutionalized it as a never-ending project.[2]

The Commission called for a new approach to drug use before it was too late. One that was coherent and flexible emphasized treatment rather than punishment for addiction, and stigmatized only those habits that threatened society.

The Nixon administration's reaction to the report was described as 'frosty'. No photographs were permitted when the Commission's chairman, Raymond Shafer, formally presented the report to the President; its major recommendations were ignored.[3]

Succeeding administrations also failed to heed the Commission's warnings. Since the report was issued, US drug control policy has been one of reacting to pressure, increasing expenditures, following the paths of least political resistance and giving the appearance that 'something' is being done. Much of the expenditure goes on disseminating information that perpetuates an irrational approach to drug use. The information is designed to, first, sustain the fear of all drugs—not just those that are addicting—and, second, to assure Americans that the government's response is right and needs supporting.

Government information agencies sustain the emphasis on law enforcement as the primary response to drug use. The largest agency, the National Institute on Drug Abuse (NIDA), for example, has been most notable in recent years for spreading alarmist and unscientific information about the danger of marijuana. These scares have helped to thwart a movement towards regulation and control and allow enforcement agencies to continue to fill their quotas with the easiest of drug arrests.

In addition, millions of American parents are encouraged to join or form groups which, effectively, are dedicated to the perpetuation of the drug-abuse industrial complex. At the beginning of the 1980s there were around 3,000 such organizations. These groups put pressure on their local lawmakers first, and then on their representatives in Congress. State and federal legislatures react by supplying more funding and expanded powers to the government information and enforcement agencies, which turn around and generate more fear to keep the cycle going.

In 1982 Laurence Gonzales published an update of the Shafer Commission's description of the drug-abuse industrial complex and likened it to:

an old-fashioned church in which the preacher—through threats of hell-fire and damnation—frightens the congregation into giving him money to build bigger churches in which to frighten them with hell-fire and damnation, all the while claiming to save their souls.[4]

The difference is that the preaching of the complex is made to appear rational even as the US drug-control effort becomes more visibly irrational as each year passes.

The Shafer Commission recommendations have been reversed; US drug policy remains incoherent and inflexible; punishment of offenders not treatment for addicts emphasized and drug habits which do not threaten society stigmatized. As a consequence America's lawless crusade is sustained. Bureaucratic empires are created and electoral advantage goes to the hardliners. Criminals and corrupt public officials continue to prosper as the law of the land is subordinated to the iron law of supply and demand. Recent government initiatives against drugs and organized crime have only sustained this situation.

In the 1980 presidential elections, no interest group fought harder for Republican candidate, Ronald Reagan, than the 'Religious Right'—a term which loosely describes the political wing of the country's numerous Protestant fundamentalist churches and sects. Millions of dollars and intense effort for Reagan's campaign came from activists organized under such headings as: Moral Majority Inc., Religious Roundtable, Christian Voice, Christian Voter's Victory Fund, Campus Crusade for Christ, and Christians for Reagan.[5] Using the latest communications techniques, these supported the former Governor of California as the man most likely to turn back what was seen as the country's dangerous slide into moral permissiveness, godlessness and sin and effect a cure based on 'traditional family values'.

In a slick, professional campaign, the incumbent, Jimmy Carter, was beaten comfortably, and Reagan took office in January 1981 with some dues to pay. The new President could not, of course, fulfil every 'moral majority' expectation. His powers were restricted to filling judicial vacancies with acceptably right-wing applicants and pressuring for anti-abortion and other 'pro-family' legislation. But, to give the impression of firm executive action in time for the re-election campaign, more visible activity was required. In the Nixon tradition, drugs were chosen as the issue to highlight the administration's commitment to America's moral regeneration. Soon after taking office Reagan warned that if action on drugs was not taken, the country was 'running the risk of losing a great part of a whole generation' and at his first major post-inauguration press conference he stressed that drug abuse was 'one of the gravest problems facing us internally in the United States'.[6]

To address this problem, the President announced, on 14 October 1982, an eight-point plan intended to 'end the drug menace and cripple organized crime'. First, he promised an extension of the South Florida Task Force, which had been established at the beginning of the year under the auspices of Vice-President George Bush: 145 customs agents, 101 FBI-DEA agents, and around sixty more from other agencies were given unprecedented access to military assistance in a campaign to stop drugs coming in through Florida. Smugglers were now faced with destroyers, fighter planes, E2-C Hawkeye radar planes, and Cobra helicopters and a balloon-shaped NORAD radar nicknamed 'Fat Albert' hovering 10,000 feet above Key West. The campaign had been visually impressive. The military hardware was photogenic and press and television cameras dutifully followed the Vice-President on his trips to inspect cocaine and marijuana hauls. In the short run the campaign had been judged a success. Reports of a 40 per cent increase in drug-related arrests and a doubling in seizures in South Florida were circulated and the President referred to these in his address.[7] He therefore announced the establishment of '12 additional task forces in key areas in the United States', to follow the South Florida example. The President believed that 'these task forces will allow us to mount an intensive and coordinated campaign against international and domestic drug trafficking and other organized criminal enterprises'.

Announcing the second point of the plan the President claimed that 'no weapon against organized crime has proved more effective or more important to law enforcement than the investigations carried on by the Kefauver Committee and the McClellan Committee in the 1950s', and he singled out federal informant Joseph Valachi's testimony in the 1960s. On the basis of this he announced the creation of a panel of 'distinguished Americans from diverse backgrounds and professions with practical experience in criminal justice and combating organized crime'. This nationwide investigation was to last for three years, 'analyse and debate the data it gathers', and 'hold public hearings on the findings'. Apart from legislative recommendations, the intention was 'to heighten public awareness and knowledge about the threat of organized crime and mobilize citizen support for its eradication'.

Third, the administration was to launch a fifty-states project 'that will enlist the nation's governors in bringing about needed criminal justice reforms'. This was necessary because, for example, 'without effective enforcement of local and state statutes against various kinds of racketeering like illegal gambling, this vital source of revenue for organized crime will never be dried up'.

The fourth and fifth points of the plan promised greater 'interagency and intergovernmental cooperation in the struggle against organized crime', and a new police training centre. The sixth was the promise of a new legislative offensive 'designed to win approval of reforms in criminal statutes dealing with bail, sentencing, criminal forfeiture, and exclusionary rule and labor racketeering that are essential in the fight against organized crime'. The seventh was a yearly report by the Attorney-General on 'the status of the fight against organized crime and organized criminal groups dealing in drugs'.

Finally, he committed 'millions of dollars' to be allocated 'for prison and jail facilities so that the mistake of releasing dangerous criminals because of overcrowded prisons will not be repeated'. 'The time has come', the President said, 'to cripple the power of the mob in America'.[8]

Reagan was repeating the theme of a radio address the previous week, when he said: 'Drugs are bad and we're going after them. We've taken down the surrender flag and run up the battle flag and we're going to win the war on drugs'. Drug traffickers 'can run but they can't hide'.[9] The following month he was filmed and photographed inspecting packages of confiscated cocaine at a Florida Air Force base where he claimed that the success of the South

Florida Task Force 'proves we have the will and resources to break up the organized criminal syndicates'.[10] The rhetoric went on endlessly repeating all the themes of America's moral crusade and the cynical assertions of a host of 'law-and-order' politicians. In sum, Reagan's plan was to attempt to seal the nation's borders, campaign aggressively against domestic production and trafficking, and highlight these efforts as the correct and only approach to the problem. The administration intended to replay Nixon's politically successful war on drugs.

The first part of Reagan's plan was implemented soon after the speech. Twelve special task forces were formed across the country; 900 new agents were recruited for the FBI, DEA and Customs, in addition to 200 new assistant US Attorneys and a support staff of 400 people. In 1983 the South Florida Task Force was expanded into the National Narcotics Border Interdiction System (NNBIS) also under the control of Vice-President Bush. With budget and staff diverted from other agencies, the intention of NNBIS was to coordinate the new effort to seal the nation's borders from drugs. Undercover operators of the CIA were also to be employed, and military surveillance was to be increased.[11] Without time for proper evaluation the 'success' of the South Florida Task Force had provided the justification for these new initiatives.

The tens of millions of dollars spent achieved little. Smugglers were perhaps inconvenienced and required to use more ingenuity but the new elaborate and expensive surveillance techniques did not stop drugs coming into the country.

By 1984 the failure to prevent smuggling by sea was, according to US District Court Judge Frederick B. Lacey, 'plain for all to see'. Lacey charged that the authorities had been overrun in their attempt to prevent shiploads of drugs from evading 'sieve-like' patrol barriers along the coasts. The truth of these remarks was confirmed by Commissioner William von Raab of the Customs Service when he acknowledged before a House subcommittee that few smugglers' boats were caught out of the several thousand a year involved in the trade. Plane smuggling was also virtually unaffected by the new effort. There were still numerous ways to evade surveillance, however sophisticated. One was mentioned by a pilot testifying before the Kaufman Commission in November 1984. He said that he used to land at commercial airports in the United States even when his plane's wings were packed with cocaine. He evaded all the military surveillance simply by filing a flight plan and flying in normally: 'There was lots of traffic and they never noticed us'.[12]

The failure of the effort was acknowledged by most authorities not connected with the White House. In 1984, Congress's General Accounting Office (GAO) concluded that drug availability was on the increase and that seizures only represented a small portion of the total supply. Los Angeles Police Chief, Daryl Gates, emphasized the point: 'The situation is totally out of hand. We're just shovelling sand against the tide'. Two years later many top local policemen were still admitting that the situation had not changed.

Los Angeles County Sheriff, Sherman Block, said in April 1986, for example: 'It's staggering. There's so much of it around that . . . large raids aren't unusual anymore. We are losing the war in spite of stepped up enforcement'.[13]

Even in South Florida, the focus of the administration's efforts, drugs were and are freely available. Miami continued to be the place for most cocaine deals and the main importation and distribution point in the United States.

The White House continued to make grandiose claims about the success of its anti-drug effort. In January 1984, for example, the Vice-President's office issued a press release asserting that NNBIS and the South Florida Task Force 'have captured almost 5 million pounds of marijuana . . . and 28,000 pounds of cocaine', but the figures were soon found to be spurious. In May, a memo on these figures from DEA Director Francis Mullen was leaked to the Press. Mullen said that his figures showed only two million pounds of marijuana and 8,000 pounds of cocaine, and protested that false credit was being claimed by NNBIS spokesmen. He then attacked the NNBIS/task force system as 'an intellectual fraud' that 'has made no material contribution' to the administration's enforcement effort.[14]

The following year Mullen's criticisms were confirmed by another GAO report which concluded that NNBIS, despite its enormous expense, had not played a significant role in interdicting drugs. One investigator was quoted as saying: 'NNBIS is a brilliant political stroke, but a lousy agency. Instead of helping to coordinate drug agencies working the borders, this agency has caused them to splinter'.[15] NNBIS, so far in its short and undistinguished history, has drained resources from other agencies, grossly inflated its accomplishments, and exacerbated—not coordinated—the nation's drug-control efforts, while the White House has continued to insist that the new initiatives were highly successful but needed more money to make them more successful.

Various excuses, such as poor equipment and lack of staff, have been made for the nation's overall inability to stem the flow of imported drugs, but the real reason is more fundamental. The total amount of all imports of all kinds that enter the United States each year by air or sea—even omitting goods imported in trucks and cars—is so vast that looking for small amounts of drug contraband is clearly an impossible task, however much money and manpower is put into the effort. The President should have heeded the warning he himself gave at his first press conference on 6 March 1981:

I've had people talk to me about increased efforts to head off the export into the United States of drugs from neighbouring nations. With borders like ours, that as the main method of halting the drug problem in America is virtually impossible: It's like carrying water in a sieve.

At the same press conference Reagan suggested that the approach he intended to take on drug-control policy would emphasize education, treatment and prevention, not law enforcement:

> It is my belief—firm belief—that the answer to the drug problem comes through winning over the users to the point that we take the customers away from the drugs . . . it's far more effective if you take the customers away than if you try to take the drugs away from those who want to be customers.[16]

The policy that emerged proved to be the reverse. After an initial freeze in spending, federal drug law enforcement received a massive boost in manpower and funding, while prevention and treatment programmes were underfinanced—surviving despite the Reagan administration's budget priorities, not because of them. Referring to Nancy Reagan's much-publicized campaign to warn children of the dangers of drug abuse, the *Drugs and Drug Abuse Education Newsletter* complained in 1983: 'The federal presence in the drug prevention and education arena has devolved to the president's wife hugging precocious children in privately-funded rehabilitation centers before banks of TV cameras'.[17]

Mrs Reagan had rapidly become the most visible part of the administration's anti-drug crusade, frequently appearing on television talk shows and singling out marijuana as the drug 'that is taking America captive'.[18] In 1984 alone she attended 110 anti-drug events and in April 1985 she entertained seventeen other presidential spouses from around the world in an event called the First Ladies' Conference on Drug Abuse. On this occasion when asked about her husband's proposed 40 per cent cut in federal funding for drug-abuse programmes, she replied: 'I'm speaking mother-to-mother today. I don't get into the other'.[19] Whatever her motives, and improving an initially unpopular image was undoubtedly one of them, the result was a caring face for an uncaring policy.

Before Reagan's October 1982 speech on policy, an important structural change in federal drug law enforcement had already taken place, announced by Attorney-General William French Smith at the beginning of the year. At a press conference French Smith took pains to praise the DEA, saying that it had 'done fine work at home and abroad' and 'accomplished a great deal'. The agency, however, had failed to make a substantial impact on the drug traffic and the Attorney-General also announced that it was to be relegated. From then on the FBI would take over much of the responsibility for combating the nation's 'most serious crime problem'. The DEA would continue to exist but in a subordinate role—in effect the troubled agency was to be placed under FBI supervision. The FBI's Director William Webster put it differently; his bureau was 'ready to lock arms with our colleagues at the Drug Enforcement Administration'.[20]

The growth of FBI drug law enforcement resources was substantial. From November 1983, over 875 agents were committed to this work and the FBI was investigating over 1,600 drug cases. More than 600 of these investigations were being conducted jointly with the DEA. The FBI had thus

become fully involved in drug law enforcement for the first time. The
bureau's architect, J. Edgar Hoover, had always opposed this, partly because
he feared that his agents might be corrupted by drug work involving large
amounts of cash. Hoover's fears have already been vindicated. FBI undercover agent, Dan Mitrione, pleaded guilty to charges of possessing and
distributing more than 90 pounds of cocaine and receiving $850,000 in bribes
and payoffs in March 1985.[21]

After the reorganization one of the first intentions was to change the image
of cocaine trafficking from that of a low-risk, high-capital-return enterprise.
It had become apparent that middle-class professional and businesspeople
were adding to their fortunes by trading in what had become a status symbol
among the affluent.

In 1982 local and federal officials announced a series of seizures and arrests
of middle-class and upper-income Americans who had no previous arrest
records.

— In September federal officials announced that businessmen, physicians,
  lawyers and bank officials were among the leaders of a ring that
  smuggled into the country 3,748 pounds of cocaine confiscated in March
  in Florida—the largest seizure up to that date. In another case, officials
  in Georgia accused a once-prominent local businessman and a former
  mayor of Clarkesville of smuggling 300 pounds of cocaine into the state.
— In August two employees of the Environmental Protection Agency were
  arrested for operating a thriving cocaine business in the Kluczynski
  Building in Chicago's Loop.
— In July a federal grand jury in Phoenix, Arizona, indicted 106 people,
  including businessmen and housewives, in nine states on charges of
  participating in an inter-state ring that netted some of the principals
  almost $400,000 a year.
— Finally, in June, a lawyer, a restaurant owner and three other businessmen were arrested in Islip, Long Island with around 600 pounds of
  cocaine, the potential retail value of which was around $200 million.

People were attracted by a large, fast, untaxed profit. As a DEA agent told
New York Times reporter Robert Lindsey, 2.2 pounds of cocaine sold for
$50,000–$60,000 on the black market and by the time it was sold at retail
level it brought in $300,000–$400,000 a pound. Ronald Cunningham, a
young Iowan involved in the Phoenix case, testified that he had gone into the
drug business with an investment of $500 and before long was earning more
than $300,000 a year.[22]

The showcase of the government's effort to dissuade people from making
such profits began with the arrest of car manufacturer John De Lorean at the
end of October 1982. The New York Daily News trumpeted, 'DE LOREAN
NABBED IN COAST COKE BUST'. Time magazine was more business-
like; De Lorean made the cover with the announcement, 'The Bottom Line
. . . BUSTED'. The manufacturer was charged with conspiring to acquire

220 pounds of cocaine in the expectation of making a $50 million profit. Federal agents described De Lorean as a man driven by the fear of his car company failing, who had turned to the lucrative drug trade as a means to save it.[23]

The arrest was the result of a six-month investigation, using undercover agents posing as drug distributors while clandestine cameras and microphones recorded both sight and sound. The operation involved the FBI, the DEA, investigators from U.S. Customs and local Los Angeles and Ventura police, and was said to exemplify the new spirit of cooperation among the often feuding agencies. As it turned out the case was an expensive débâcle.

In October 1983, American television viewers were shown the FBI video tapes of De Lorean apparently making a drug deal in a Californian hotel room and then being arrested. The tapes were shown by the CBS network despite efforts by the prosecutors to prevent their broadcast before the trial. In the tapes, the crucial scene was De Lorean apparently receiving a suitcase full of cocaine from a man and thanking him. At this point a second man walked into the room and said: 'Hi, John. We're the FBI. We're here to arrest you on narcotics law violations. Would you stand up, please?'[24]

The case against De Lorean almost collapsed in disarray with the court losing control over such vital evidence a few days before the trial was supposed to begin. There was a farcical struggle between the court and sex-magazine publisher Larry Flint over the source of a tape recording in which a government informer allegedly threatened to smash the head of De Lorean's five-year-old daughter if the deal fell through. Flint told the court that 'not even a hot lead enema' would make him reveal the source. In the event the date of the trial was put off until the following year.[25]

The jury in a Los Angeles court found De Lorean not guilty on all eight charges of cocaine smuggling in August 1984. The main defence lawyer, Howard Weitzman, said:

It should never happen again. The government did, in fact, create, choreograph, and set up John De Lorean and, in spite of lapses in his judgement, this was explained by the government when they said they knew he was desperate and they knew he was vulnerable.[26]

Weitzman had destroyed the government's case by, in effect, putting the government on trial. He put the chief prosecution witnesses through rigorous cross-examination and uncovered numerous examples of infringements of investigatory procedures by the agents and by the government's chief witness, a professional informant and convicted drug smuggler, James Hoffman. One agent, for example, who impersonated a dishonest banker admitted to rewriting some of his investigative notes. Another, who posed as a drug dealer, backdated forms that authorized the videotaping of two critical sessions involving De Lorean. And Hoffman, who was working for the government in order to reduce his own sentence, was quoted in court testimony as promising government officials: 'I am going to get John De Lorean for you guys'.[27]

After the verdict the Attorney-General William French Smith announced that the demise of the De Lorean 'sting' operation had not altered the government's faith in such schemes.[28] Targets can still be ensnared by agents disguised as criminals and manufacturing criminal opportunities, often involving informants who are practising criminals.

The main result of the case's great exposure therefore was probably to alert white-collar drug dealers to the dangers of dealing with strangers and to devise more sophisticated schemes to conceal the movement of their money through ostensibly legitimate front companies.

The government's motivation for the De Lorean case was probably the promise of great publicity to warn potential drug traffickers that they do face a chance of being caught. In the case of David Curry the motivation was probably more suspect.

In 1981 Curry, a sociologist and Vietnam war veteran, took a leave of absence from a position as Associate Professor at the University of South Alabama to help establish a veterans' centre in Mobile. His military service had left him deeply disillusioned but eager to help others who had been scarred by the war. He had been a counter-intelligence agent in Vietnam and when he returned he reacted against what he saw as a pattern of oppression in his own country by joining a number of radical and liberal causes. At different times he worked for Vietnam Veterans Against the War, civil and gay rights organizations, and a rape crisis centre before helping out at the veterans' centre in Mobile.

In November 1981, Curry was introduced by friends to Grady Gibson at another veterans' centre in Birmingham, Alabama. Gibson had spoken of his war-related problems: marital difficulties, lingering war guilt, periods of confusion and incapacitating headaches from a head wound sustained in Vietnam. These headaches, according to Gibson, could only be relieved with cocaine. In reality, Gibson was an under-cover agent of the Alabama Bureau of Investigation who had been assigned to infiltrate the centre and find out if the liberals and radicals amongst its staff were committing drug offences.

Shortly after meeting Curry, Gibson began pressuring him to provide him with small amounts of cocaine for his headaches. Curry refused several times, but was vulnerable to the ploy and later obtained some. No profit was involved and the total amount of cocaine came to less than an ounce. (The De Lorean case involved 220 pounds of cocaine and tens of millions of dollars.) In February 1982, the federal government closed down the centre and indicted Curry on three counts of possession of cocaine with intent to distribute. He was sentenced to thirty-four years in prison, although this sentence was subsequently reduced. An appeal was turned down in March 1984. Two other members of the centre's staff received similar sentences as a result of this particular 'sting' operation.[29]

The suppression of political dissent at the time of writing is of course not on the scale of the Vietnam war era: there is no need. But the drug laws, as the Curry case shows, and the organized crime-control laws, as the 'Sanctuary' cases show, give the government great potential for concealing the abuse of power, and, as an overwhelming weight of evidence shows, a negligible potential to control either drug use or organized crime. (From 1984, Reagan administration officials infiltrated church meetings and wiretapped church phones in Arizona and Texas to try and end the efforts of some churches to provide 'sanctuary' to Central American refugees. These refugees were primarily from El Salvador and Guatemala, countries whose regimes had the support of the US government despite much documented evidence of violent suppression of dissent. For a single set of indictments, 40,000 pages of secretly taped conversations involving priests, nuns and ministers were compiled, leading Steven Shapiro to conclude: 'This heavy-handed reaction speaks volumes about the administration's attitude towards human rights abroad and civil liberties at home'.)[30]

In the Reagan administration's war on drugs, an attempt was also made to stop American marijuana growers producing their increasingly profitable cash crops. The volume of stories detailing the extent of domestic production had become embarrassing. The White House therefore urged state authorities to conduct an aggressive eradication campaign. 'Hard-hitting' special strike forces were formed, capable of using helicopters and aeroplanes, and states could also call on the National Guard if required.

Initially the seizures seemed impressive. In Santa Barbara, California, police confiscated 1,000 high-grade marijuana plants in five fields, within eight miles of President Reagan's ranch. In Columbia, South Carolina, police burned and buried more than 4.5 acres of sinsemilla. But mistakes were inevitable. In Cochise County, Arizona, for example, one DEA operation involved a spotter plane and a squad of heavily armed local deputies. They ransacked a house, breaking things as they went, and held two young children at gunpoint, but turned up nothing.[31]

The campaign got increasingly militaristic and a 1984 Supreme Court decision was used to its fullest and beyond. In *Oliver v. United States*, the Court gave the police the right to search private property without a search warrant. The most visible results of the campaign came in California where various state and federal officials and agencies took part in the Campaign Against Marijuana Planting programme. By 1985 it became apparent that in case after case the CAMP programme had violated the constitutional rights of citizens whose only crime was to live in areas where it was suspected that marijuana was being grown:

— A CAMP team of about twenty-five armed officers surrounded the house of Judy Rolicheck, ordered her family out of the house with their hands up, and held the entire family at gunpoint for two and a half hours while conducting an identification check. One of the family dogs, which Mrs Rolicheck testified was standing still and barking, was shot and killed by a CAMP team member. The nearest marijuana field turned out to be 600 yards away on a neighbour's property.

— Rebecca West testified about how her friends and children were terrorized first by helicopters and then held at gunpoint while the agents conducted a fruitless search of her property.

— Two 12-year-old girls were chased by helicopters for about twenty minutes. When they hid under bushes the helicopters lifted up and waited for the girls to come into the open again.

These and numerous other cases were taken into account by a federal judge who found that:

> These helicopters are no longer just surveying open fields, but are deliberately looking into and invading people's homes and curtilage. Moreover, this prying is not limited to an occasional, casual peek during an overflight to a raid site, but is accomplished through sustained and repeated buzzings, hoverings, and dive bombings that at best disturb, and at worst terrorize, the hapless residents below.

A lawsuit filed by NORML and the Civil Liberties Monitoring Project resulted in an order by United States District Court Judge Robert Aguilar enjoining many of the worst abuses of the CAMP programme.[32]

Another part of the administration's programme involved the spraying of paraquat and other herbicides on marijuana crops. Spraying was started in several states; the DEA in Kentucky even sprayed a long-abandoned rope plantation.[33] But to date court action by NORML and others has restricted the amount of spraying for environmental and health reasons. The DEA continues to press for the chance to expose more Americans to dangerous chemicals. In May 1985, Acting Administrator John Lawn expressed his displeasure at the reluctance of the United States to implement an effective all-out eradication programme within its borders while it was urging Mexico to continue with its paraquat-spraying programmes. As Representative Daniel Lungren put it: 'I guess the word "hypocritical" comes up'.[34]

Although the Reagan administration's efforts have not stopped the growing of vast amounts of domestic marijuana, they did reveal how arbitrary were the estimates produced for the benefit of the media. A DEA report on crop eradication noted that in 1982 38 per cent more domestic marijuana was eradicated than was previously thought to exist. About 1,818 tons were destroyed, while the DEA had before confidently asserted that only 1,200 tons were under domestic cultivation. They therefore raised the estimate to 18,000 tons.[35]

There is no evidence to suggest that domestic cultivation on the whole has decreased as a result of the eradication campaigns. However, there is little doubt that indoor cultivation has increased in recent years. Massive barns and warehouses are used with sophisticated hydroponic systems, and a book called *Marijuana Grower's Handbook: Indoor Greenhouse Edition* has sold thousands of copies.[36]

As part of his eight-point plan, President Reagan had committed his administration to the allocation of millions more dollars for prison and jail facilities. Reagan stated that this programme 'will prove to be a highly effective attack on drug trafficking and the even larger problem of organized crime'.[37] In other words, the strategy was to build more prisons and then fill them with drug offenders.

Apart from its expense—Americans were already paying around $400 million to incarcerate marijuana offenders alone and the lowest average cost of one new prison cell was around $40,000—no approach could be more counter-productive. Overcrowding the prisons and locking up tens of thousands of drug offenders had already created many more and much bigger drug trafficking networks than it had disrupted.

Prisons in the United States are grotesque parodies of the worst parts of the cities—gangs struggle to gain or retain control over prostitution, protection and drug trafficking rackets in systems based on brutality, informants and staff corruption. Most of the gangs are organized along racial and ethnic lines and some like the Aryan Brotherhood, the Black Guerillas, the Mexican Mafia, the Texas Syndicate and Nuestra Familia have state-wide and even inter-state influence, trading in drugs and frequently eliminating competition on the outside as well as on the inside. California and Texas are at present the most affected states but the prison gang phenomenon is likely to increase nationally. Politicians and bureaucrats remain predictably reluctant to address a problem that is directly related to the great expansion of drug arrests and convictions which stretched penal institutions to breaking point from the late 1960s. Putting tens of thousands of young men in with career criminals has plainly only succeeded in multiplying a thousandfold the domestic and international connections required to profit from the trade in drugs. The policy of mass imprisonments for drug offences has helped to perpetuate—not suppress—the traffic.[38]

President Reagan's advisers were probably well aware that the October 1982 plan to 'cripple the power of the mob' had no realistic prospect of success and therefore a crime commission to maintain public support for prevailing organized crime policies was also thought necessary. On 28 July 1983, Reagan signed Executive Order 12435 and thus formally established the President's Commission on Organized Crime to be chaired by Judge Irving R. Kaufman and composed of eighteen other men and women, mainly from the law enforcement community.

The commission's stated intention was to investigate the power and activities of 'traditional organized crime' and 'emerging organized crime groups'. At the first hearing in November 1983 the nation's top law enforcement officers were invited to explain the federal perspective on the problem. The main speakers were Attorney-General William French Smith, FBI Director William Webster and DEA Administrator Francis Mullen and each identified 'traditional organized crime' exclusively with Italian-Americans or 'the La Cosa Nostra'. However, they all also made it clear that organized crime was not synonymous with any one group and stressed the importance of 'emerging groups', mentioning motor-cycle gangs, prison gangs and 'foreign-based' organizations. At the hearing no doubts were expressed about the essential correctness of the law enforcement approach to organized crime control based on long-term investigation, under-cover operations, informants, wiretaps and asset forfeiture. Successes against 'traditional organized crime' and the need to 'stay in front' of the emerging 'cartels' were emphasized throughout. It was made clear that drug trafficking was the most profitable organized crime activity and that this was the problem that most needed addressing.[39]

The commission, which was to last three years, initially undertook to investigate two of the most powerful 'emerging crime groups': outlaw motor-cycle gangs and prison gangs, but in the end failed to fulfil this commitment. Instead, in its October 1984 hearing, the commission chose to highlight 'Organized Crime of Asian Origin', although most federal officials would admit that Asian criminal organizations are very marginal relative to indigenous American groups. By making Asians their priority the commission was being conveniently myopic, continuing the tradition of blaming aliens for America's organized crime problems.[40]

After three years' selective investigation the commission's conclusions were predictably in line with those of the Reagan administration. On 3 March 1986, the report on narcotics trafficking was issued. 'The ultimate goal of the nation's drug policy', the commision stated, 'is the effective suppression of drug abuse in the United States'. To this end were the following recommendations:

The Attorney-General should direct 'the formulation of a long range national offensive against drug supply and demand, including long term funding proposals'.

The cost of this nation's anti-drug efforts can be subsidized to a great extent by the seizure and forfeiture of drug traffickers' assets. That portion of the Federal Government's asset forfeiture fund derived from drug cases should be devoted exclusively to anti-drug programs . . . '.

'A proper and realistic goal of our interdiction efforts should be the maintenance of persistent pressure on drug traffickers, both as a deterrent and as a symbol of national determination. Operational and policy decisions should reflect that measure of success and specifically reject any less realistic or effective goal.

Those states still without a statute permitting court-ordered electronic surveillance should immediately enact one, consistent with current technology.

Domestic drug law enforcement efforts directed at high-level trafficking groups should be supplemented by and integrated with enforcement efforts directed at lower-level trafficking groups and street-level drug activity . . .

To respond effectively to the drug problem, state and local jurisdictions will have to increase expenditures for such critical resources as prison facilities, increased manpower, and sophisticated equipment.

Uniform and rational sentencing for drug offenses is essential. Such a system should provide a sentence of probation and a fine for a first offense involving mere possession of drugs. The terms of probation should include a requirement to remain drug-free, to be verified, if necessary, through periodic drug testing. A second offense for possession of drugs should result in a jail sentence or mandatory treatment or fines or all three.

The President should direct the heads of all Federal agencies to formulate immediately clear policy statements, with implementing guidelines, including suitable drug testing programs, expressing the utter unacceptability of drug abuse by Federal employees. State and local governments and leaders in the private sector should support unequivocally a similar policy that any and all use of drugs is unacceptable. Government contracts should not be awarded to companies that fail to implement drug programs, including suitable drug testing. No Federal, state, or local government funds should go directly or indirectly to programs that counsel 'responsible' drug use or condone illicit drug use in any way. Laws in certain states which 'decriminalized' the possession of marijuana constitutes a form of such condonation, and should be reconsidered.[41]

In sum, the commission had concluded that the basic approach of the nation's drug enforcement programmes was sound, but needed a harder line on virtually all fronts. The only recommendation to cause much controversy was the call for a widespread national programme to test most working Americans for drug use, in effect to force most working Americans to submit to regular, observed urine tests. The tests require supervision because people might be tempted to bring in someone else's clean urine.

Soon after the report was issued, several members of the commission revealed that they had not been informed about the urine-testing recommendation although the report had been released under their names. Thomas McBride, for example, said that he first learned of the addition to the report from news accounts. Similarly, another commission member, Eugene Methvin, revealed that when he read in the newspaper the parts that caused all the furore he thought, 'Gee, did we recommend that?'[42]

At a news conference Judge Kaufman revealed why the recommendation had been made. He said that his commission's investigation of organized crime had convinced him that 'law enforcement has been tested to its utmost . . . but let's face it, it hasn't succeeded. So let's try something else. Let's try testing'. Attorney-General Edwin Meese also defended the plan as constitutional.[43].

The recommendation surprised many Americans but, as the *New Republic* pointed out, the country was much closer to universal urine-testing than was generally realized. One-quarter of all Fortune 500 companies, including IBM and General Motors, already administered urinalysis tests to applicants or current employees, and another 20 per cent had plans for similar programmes.

The results of such tests have frequently been found to be wrong. A Naval doctor, for example, almost lost his job after regularly testing positive for morphine. It was finally discovered that he was only a consumer of poppy-seed bagels. The magazine also revealed that around 9,000 Army employees had been wrongly dismissed in 1982 and 1983 for testing positive. The

Pentagon was trying to track them down to apologize for convicting them on faulty evidence including mixed-up samples. Drug-testing, apart from being undignified and intrusive, is also likely to reflect class bias. Supervisors, managers, lawyers, stockbrokers and politicians are not as powerless as schoolchildren, job applicants and ordinary workers and, if necessary, can protect their jobs and privacy through expensive court action.

The tests also unfairly discriminate against the least harmful drug, marijuana. Cocaine, heroin, PCP and other indisputably dangerous drugs vanish from the bloodstream in less than forty-eight hours, but THC, the active chemical in marijuana, remains there for weeks. Even being in the same room with one of the many millions of Americans who smoke marijuana can trigger false positive results.[44]

Soon after the Kaufman recommendation was announced the case against the practice of urine-testing was graphically illustrated. On 18 March 1986, a House subcommittee held televised hearings about making such tests mandatory for all federal workers. Rodney Smith, deputy executive director of the Kaufman Commission, was seated at the witness table when he was asked to take the test at the outset of the hearing by the chairman, Representative Gary Ackerman, who said, 'The chair will require you to go to the men's room under the direct observation of a male member of the subcommittee staff to urinate in this specimen bottle', as a three-inch plastic jar was placed on the witness table. Smith refused and angrily complained that he was being embarrassed. Ackerman noted that the commission staff member had eloquently proved the point that the subcommittee had set out to prove.[45]

A few months later President Reagan brushed aside any doubts about urine-testing and announced a new phase of the war against drugs. The administration's efforts to cut off the supply—having obviously failed—were to be supplemented by an assault on demand. Drug users were now to be targeted and, if caught, punished. With this in mind the President signed an executive order permitting the testing of more than a million civilian federal workers. As an encouragement Reagan himself had his own specimen examined by one of the machines and 'persuaded' seventy-eight top aides to contribute specimens. All this took place in the run-up to the November 1986 mid-term elections.[46]

The testing programmes have already produced sizeable profits for the manufacturers of urine-testing equipment and the owners of urine-testing laboratories—they can afford effective PR departments and well-paid lobbyists to spread their messages internationally. But they are not the answer to the problem of drugs, and organized humiliation is certainly no answer to organized, drug-related crime.

With its proposals for urine-testing the Kaufman Commission had successfully distracted attention away from serious discussion of the organized crime issue and, in particular, the counter-productive implications of the recommendations to imprison many more Americans for drug possession, as well as trafficking, offences. If the recommendations were implemented,

American prisons, even if multiplied, would still be grossly overcrowded. Since the only groups that would be likely to benefit from this situation would be the most ruthless and powerful prison-based gangs—through increased membership and revenues—the commission's decision not to investigate them becomes more understandable. The prison gangs are so clearly products of draconian drug laws that the Kaufman Commission would not want to advertise the phenomenon.

It had taken the Kaufman Commission three years to decide that in the face of failure what was needed was a perpetuation of government activity and, in particular, increased profits for the manufacturers of urine-testing equipment and owners of urine-testing laboratories. The commission's work was only really relevant as a justification for bankrupt policies.

Another aspect of organized crime avoided by the Kaufman Commission was the problem of corruption. The decades of making organized crime synonymous, first, with the Mafia alone, and more recently with the Mafia plus marginal 'emerging' groups, enabled the commission to exclude corruption from its vague definition of the problem without attracting criticism.

President Johnson's 1960s Crime Commission had also de-emphasized corruption but at least made the clear and honest statement that 'All available data indicate that organized crime flourishes only where it has corrupted local officials', and corruption has continued to characterize drug law enforcement and criminal justice well into the 1980s. The cities of Detroit, Chicago, Miami and Portland have all experienced major scandals in recent years, and countless individual transgressions have been uncovered in every type of community. The offences uncovered have a familiar ring: 'skimming' cash and drugs from seizures, pocketing money earmarked for informants, lying to obtain search warrants, committing perjury in court to obtain convictions, selling drugs and guns, accepting bribes and protecting drug syndicates. In 1982, for example, ten Chicago policemen were convicted after a lengthy trial on various drug-related charges including aiding and abetting a continuing criminal enterprise and extortion. The violations related to the defendants' three-year symbiotic relationship with two large drug distributorships in which the police officers received substantial sums of money, weapons and goods in exchange for warning the distributors of impending police raids, delivering drugs seized from other dealers to the favoured syndicates, and threatening competitors.[47]

Higher-level officials have also been prosecuted for drug-related corruption in recent years. In 1982 the sheriff, chief of police, a judge and others from Henry County, Georgia, were convicted of aiding and abetting smugglers when landing at an airstrip and 'providing an escort service' into Atlanta. Southern sheriffs, in particular, have been revealed to be as involved in drug trafficking as their predecessors were in bootlegging. Most notable is Sheriff Howard Leroy Hobbs of Harrison County, Mississippi, who was sentenced to twenty years in prison in May 1984 following a guilty plea to a variety of drug-related offences. Hobbs had been elected on a promise to crack down on drugs and corruption. Also in 1984, Frank Robin of the US Attorney's office in Houston, Texas, was sentenced to ten years for seeking $200,000 in exchange for leaking information to suspects in a major drugs case.

The DEA itself has not apparently had the problem of wholesale corruption on the scale of its predecessor, the FBN, but in August 1982 Jeffrey Scharlatt, an agent attached to the Miami office, became the first DEA agent to be indicted on charges of smuggling and distribution. Scharlatt was a top agent who a year earlier had helped direct an under-cover DEA operation code-named 'Grouper' that led to 155 indictments and 127 convictions. At the same time, however, it was charged that Scharlatt was smuggling marijuana, obstructing justice and accepting bribes. In 1984 another DEA agent, Harold Lawrence, was convicted of selling drugs and received a five-year sentence. Lawrence decided to supply the DEA's Internal Security Department with the names of three agents, who, he said, had sold up to $1 million of marijuana to smugglers in 1973. Subsequently all three, one a DEA agent, the others US Customs Service agents, resigned, but none could be prosecuted because the statute of limitations had expired. According to a Justice Department official, this affair was 'not a one-time incident, and many agents are concerned it has gone on and on and on'.

The temptation of easy money has consistently proved too strong to resist. The New York Police Department alone now has over 350 officers assigned full-time to anti-corruption duties but the problem of endemic corruption in drug enforcement persists no matter how many policemen are assigned to police themselves. Since 1917, when the first narcotics agent was caught and convicted for taking a large bribe, corruption has been more characteristic of drug law enforcement than success.[48]

This corruption is sometimes accompanied by brutality. In 1981, 1,124 people were arrested for offences involving marijuana in San Jacinto County, Texas. The county has a population of less than 7,000, yet the marijuana arrest total was more appropriate for a big city. After a federal court case it transpired that Sheriff James Parker had operated a 'marijuana trap' along the highway since 1977. When a vehicle came by that appeared might contain a marijuana user, the police would stop it on such pretexts as 'dim license-plate bulb' or 'smudged license plate' and proceed to search it. They stopped vehicles particularly if the occupants had long hair or if political bumper stickers were displayed. Ninety per cent of these cars were 'found' to contain marijuana. The 'offenders' were taken to the county jail, denied access to attorneys, coerced to plead guilty, pay fines, bail and tow-truck fees and then sent on their way. Witnesses described one of the methods used to coerce confessions. They were handcuffed to a table or chair and their faces wrapped tightly with a towel. Their heads were pulled back and water poured over the towel. Faced with suffocation, prisoners tended to confess to the alleged crimes.

According to the county treasurer the trap accounted for $300,000 per year for the county, over a fifth of all San Jacinto's revenues. It also enriched bail bondsmen and the tow-truck operators, one of which was owned by the sheriff's cousin. Local people were not arrested and therefore had nothing to complain about. In September 1983, Sheriff Parker and two of his deputies were convicted. Parker got a ten-year sentence.[49]

Torture is also involved in a recent New York police scandal. Several police officers from the 106th district in Queens were charged with routinely using electric 'stun-guns' to force black and Hispanic youths to confess to selling small amounts of marijuana, as well as a number of other offences including forcing suspects to swallow cocaine, threatening to kill them if they complained, confiscating drugs without properly recording them and even the sexual abuse of one youth. Two officers were eventually convicted, some others were fired, and many more were given different jobs in one of the city police's periodic administrative shakeups.[50]

Drug raids and arrests continue to produce tragedies. On 23 April 1981, for example, Oliver Bruce Moorer was asleep in his home in Saginaw, Michigan, at about three in the morning when police began a raid. The probable cause justifying the warrant for the raid was the word of an informant saying that marijuana had been smoked in Moorer's house. The precise details of what transpired are still uncertain, but police testified that Moorer shot at them and therefore they poured gunfire into his house for about four minutes; after a lull two more shots were fired, one of which killed Moorer. In the immediate aftermath of the gun battle an attempt was made by a paramedic to examine the body with advanced life-support equipment and heart monitor but he was denied entry into the house for some time. The search after the raid turned up 1.1 pounds of marijuana, cocaine residue and codeine (codeine is a proscribed drug in the United States). In May 1984 the city of Saginaw agreed to pay more than $350,000 to Moorer's widow. In the wake of the shooting a *Saginaw News* staff writer, Mike Beyer, conducted a thorough investigation of the city's drug law enforcement. He found that the methods used by the city's police endangered civil rights while producing negligible results at a high cost to the taxpayer.[51]

In 1985 the case of John Hicks was reported. Hicks was a 22-year-old Californian who was stopped by three Ventura County sheriff's deputies for speeding. He tried to hide a plastic bag with less than an ounce of marijuana inside it in his mouth and, according to the policemen, tried to swallow it when it was noticed. One of the deputies then tried to employ a 'hand-to-throat' restraint technique on Hicks so that the contraband could not be swallowed. Hicks choked to death. According to the coroner's report, marijuana was the killer.[52]

Police officers also die during operations. In August 1982, Kathleen Schaefer, an under-cover narcotics officer was shot and killed by a uniformed Houston police officer when she pulled out her gun to arrest three men from whom she had bought drugs. The uniformed police officer had been sent to assist her but apparently had not been given a description. 'He apparently just thought that she was the bad guy', was the explanation of a police official.[53]

Many more Americans have been killed in the process of drug law enforcement. The question was asked during Prohibition whether the death toll of 1,400 in liquor law enforcement was worthwhile since enforcement had not suppressed either the use of alcohol or the 'abuse' of alcohol. The same question can be asked about drug law enforcement because, for all the effort and rhetoric of politicians and bureaucrats, many millions of Americans continued to use and sometimes 'abuse' illicit drugs.

United States bureaucrats and politicians have succeeded in perpetuating many myths about drugs, but one of the most useful has been the idea that domestic drug problems are largely caused by the producer nations. Under the Reagan administration the United States has continued to persuade or bully other countries into attempting to stop their citizens supplying the richest market in the world. In 1984 and 1985, more than $100 million dollars were allotted to this task by the State Department. Much of this went on crop eradication or substitution programmes, and on spreading the gospel of US drug-control policy, which is held up as a model for other countries to follow.[54]

The international strategies show no sign at all of succeeding. Eradication, most often by spraying herbicides, always leaves peasant farmers worse off than before, apart from damaging the environment. In any case, substantial eradication has never been achieved in the remote growing areas where most opium and coca crops are cultivated. Crop substitution—whereby farmers are encouraged to grow alternative cash crops, such as sugar beet, coffee, or potatoes—has failed for economic and geographical reasons. Growers are often far away from markets for legitimate crops and the cash return does not compensate for the effort. Opium and coca, by contrast, are worthwhile crops even for the most exploited farmers. Transportation is no problem since it is usually arranged by the traffickers. As long as there is a market in the world and immense profits to be made, sites for cultivation will always be found. In 1985, for example, large opium crops were discovered in Florida.[55]

The failure of US international efforts was acknowledged by the 1984 Annual Report of the House Select Committee on Narcotics Abuse and Control. The report stated that:

> in most of the major producing countries, illicit narcotic production, manufac-ture and traffic has dramatically increased, such as in Pakistan, Afghanistan, Iran, Lebanon, Burma, Peru, Bolivia, Columbia, Jamaica and Belize, or stayed about the same as in Morocco, Thailand and Laos.

Even in Turkey and Mexico where US technical and financial assistance had 'raised the competence and capability' of the governments to 'address the drug control problem existing in their territory', the report noted, patronizingly, some 'deeply disquieting signs of retrogression'.[56] Arrogance had, however, so far dulled the committee's intelligence that although it acknowledged continued failure, it recommended an expansion of the same US policy...

The committee's other recommendations also combine ignorance with *naïveté*. one, for example, suggested that if Peru and Bolivia do not begin programmes to 'eliminate the practice of coca leaf chewing' then suspension of US aid 'must be considered'.[57] While the United States had failed to prevent millions of its citizens using coca in the far more potent form of cocaine, its representatives were telling foreign governments to eliminate an ancient part of native customs and diet in almost inaccessible mountain or forest regions. It is as bizarre as the South Americans demanding an end to tobacco, coffee or alcohol use in Washington, DC, but the difference is that the South Americans do not have the power to push prejudices on to other countries.

The cocaine traffic is now established as an important part of the economies of countries like Bolivia, Peru and Columbia. According to Rafael Otazo, Bolivia's chief enforcement officer, the trade in drugs produces billions of dollars annually and employs as many as 200,000 people in the cultivation and processing of coca plants. The millions of dollars of aid which US politicians often threaten to suspend, dwindle into insignificance compared to the value of the drug trade. 'No one', as Otazo put it, 'can resist those dollars'.[58]

When foreign governments comply with US demands and make genuine efforts to enforce anti-drug laws, the result is often disastrous as peasant farmers defend their livelihood and traffickers fight for their profits. In November 1984, twenty-one members of a Peruvian, but US-financed, anti-coca squad, were slaughtered near the town of Tingo Maria on the Huallaga River. In April 1986, five more policemen and a government lawyer were killed in another ambush. On 7 January 1986, around 17,000 coca-leaf farmers surrounded the camp of the Bolivian anti-drug police force known as the Leopards. The 245-man unit, also financed by the United States, was under siege for three days, as the farmers protested against the destruction of cocaine-paste factories and the rape of a local woman by two drunken policemen. A peaceful but probably temporary solution was reached. In 1984 Colombia stepped up its drug control efforts after persistent US pressure. Justice Minister Rodrigo Lara Bonilla and around 140 policemen were slain within a few months. In November 1985, drug traffickers in a southern Mexican village ambushed and killed twenty-one police officers. The officers had found a marijuana shipment.[59]

Socialist and communist governments are frequently scapegoated for US drug problems. Stories implicating officials and citizens of these governments are circulated with the minimum of substantiation to provoke outrage from the nation's conservative press. Vice-President Bush combined two scares in February 1985 when he said, 'communist Cuba and Nicaragua are definitely in bed with drug smugglers'.[60] President Reagan joined in on 18 March 1986 when he said on television that:

> Every American parent will be outraged to learn that top Nicaraguan government officials are deeply involved in drug trafficking. There is no crime to which the Sandinistas will not stoop. This is an outlaw regime.

He made the statement to support his request to Congress for $100 million in aid to the Nicaraguan 'Contra' rebels. His allegation was not confirmed by the DEA, which said that it had no information implicating top Nicaraguan officials, and that it does receive 'sporadic allegations concerning drug trafficking by Nicaraguan nationals', but that these allegations had not been confirmed. A senior official of the agency, noting that it had issued similar statements in the past, said that repeating it was 'as far as we can go to refute' President Reagan's remarks.[61]

To date Ronald Reagan has said nothing about an increasing mount of evidence linking Contras with drug trafficking. Jonathan Kwitny, writing in *The Nation*, summarized this evidence as follows:

> Some of the biggest drug dealers in the United States have allied themselves with the *contras* in the hope of avoiding prosecution by the Federal government. Some prominent *contra* leaders have eagerly accepted airplanes, logistical help and, almost certainly, cash from drug traffickers. Records of aircraft sales and maintenance show that the *contras* obtained a minimum of $350,000 from one drug smuggler alone. Interviews suggest that the total amount of drug money that has gone into the *contras*' coffers runs well into the millions. As the proceeds of illegal drug sales, all that money properly belongs to US taxpayers. Instead, it went to the *contras*, during a period when Congress forbade the Reagan administration to provide them, 'directly or indirectly', with any military aid.[62]

The Reagan administration's desire to discredit and defeat the Nicaraguan government had at least one more beneficiary, an important Colombian drug trafficker. Jorge Luis Ochoa Vasquez was described by the Kaufman Commission as in control of one of the 'most significant trafficking organizations in Colombia'—handling the finance and enforcement of the vastly profitable business of getting cocaine to United States citizens.[63] On 15 November 1984, Ochoa was arrested by Spanish police, and attempts were made to extradite him to the United States, where he faced drug-related charges. As reported by Martin Lee in *The Nation*, Ochoa held on to his freedom as a result of a botched covert operation by US authorities. As Lee summarized the case:

> According to his lawyers, DEA agents proposed a deal to Ochoa: if he would implicate Nicaragua's Sandinista government in cocaine trafficking, the United States would deliberately bungle the extradition request. But Ochoa insisted that he knew nothing of a Sandinista coke connection, and he spent twenty months in jail fighting deportation to the United States. In the end, the Spanish courts ruled

that the United States was seeking to use Ochoa as a 'political instrument' to discredit Nicaragua; the extradition request was denied and Ochoa was sent to Colombia instead.[64]

In August 1986 Ochoa walked away from a Colombian prison.

At the time of writing Ochoa is a free man, probably as a result of a combination of ineptitude and corruption within Colombia. Late in 1987 he was released from prison, despite assurances given to the United States by the Colombian government that he would remain in custody pending his extradition. This, according to the United States, was a shocking blow to international law enforcement', and the Colombians were accused of 'duplicity' for allowing the drug trafficker to go free. In view of their own botched attempt at duplicity, it seems churlish of the United States to berate another country for being more effectively duplicitous.[65]

Without doubt some communist citizens and officials have been involved in international drug trafficking but never on the same scale as the friends and allies of the United States. Properly substantiated evidence has implicated the anti-Castro Cubans, the war-lords of South East Asia, right-wing regimes in Central and South America, the Mujaheddin rebels in Afghanistan, as well as the Contra rebels in Nicaragua, in large-scale trafficking often with the tacit consent of the CIA. US politicians and officials tend to downplay the significance of such cases as factors contributing to the country's drug problems.[66]

The corruption of foreign government officials provides one more scapegoat for problems in the United States. In the view of two members of the 1984 House committee, Dante B. Fascell and Laurence J. Smith, for example, 'the major obstacle confronting the US anti-narcotics effort' in 'certain countries in the Caribbean and Latin America' is 'the endemic corruption embracing all levels of those governments'. Similar statements have been made by Reagan administration officials.[67]

Of course, many foreign officials will prefer taking money to taking risks on behalf of the US government—in Colombia alone some 300 officials were recently found to be in the pay of drug traffickers. But for US politicians and officials to castigate foreigners for doing the same as a never-ending stream of US politicians and officials have done is remarkably hypocritical.

Few Latin American countries have indigenous drug problems that compare with those of their wealthy neighbour. Most of their difficulties stem from the immense demand for drugs generated by US citizens, and the US interference that this justifies. US drug-control policy has finally succeeded in spreading a disease of violence, corruption and instability to its neighbours. However, within the United States, the tendency to blame foreigners for its domestic problems persists—a myopia which justifies the continuation of the bizarre and destructive attempt to achieve throughout the world something that has never been achieved in the United States itself with lavishly funded and sophisticated police forces or even in US prisons with an almost complete absence of civil liberties; that is, the prohibition of drugs.

Although until the 1970s the United States was the only important market for illegal drugs in the Western industrial world, other countries have since begun to experience similar problems. Many have been persuaded to base their response on the US model, on the illogical assumption that the country with the worst record of drug control has the most experience and therefore knows best. After decades of controlling drugs and drug addiction with as much success as can rationally be expected, the United Kingdom has been a notably supine example of this trend.

Like the United States, Britain has had drug control policies since the early part of the twentieth century. However, the British approach was not based on absolute prohibition, and no special effort was expended against habits which, although sometimes personally destructive, did not threaten the rest of society. The police were allowed to concentrate their activity combating crimes which did have complainants. Individual doctors cared for individual addicts, using professional judgement rather than state-imposed moral ideals, and this meant that they could prescribe heroin and morphine legally. People who did not have the will-power to give up their habits had the opportunity for normal and productive lives under medical supervision. The system was imperfect but crucially it did help to keep the black market in drugs small and not very profitable, in contrast to the vast clandestine commerce in the United States exploited by Arnold Rothstein and his successors. Smuggling heroin into Britain was simply not worth the risks for large networks to develop. British addicts were registered and could be counted in their hundreds; American addicts were unregistered and their total number could only be guessed at in the tens of thousands. British policies were envied all over the world by every expert not connected to the US drug enforcement community. However, things began to change.

During the 1960s more people, in particular more young people, began to use drugs for recreational purposes and, in addition, there was a small rise in the number of new cases of heroin addiction. Although the problems associated with this development were tiny by American standards, the trend was presented as catastrophic. The popular press turned out a litany of drug horror stories, accompanied by demands for a harder line against all illicit drug use.

Scapegoats were found in a few doctors, probably less than ten in number, who had prescribed excessive quantities of heroin to addicts. The addicts in turn had made extra cash by selling their surpluses. The government's over-reaction was to change fundamentally the British approach to heroin. From 1968 only a limited number of doctors, usually psychiatrists in treatment clinics, were allowed to prescribe heroin for addicts. They were to be licensed, not by the government ministry responsible for the provision of health care, but by the ministry responsible for law enforcement—the Home

Office. The conditions were created for a much larger black market as the clinics prescribed much less heroin than the general practitioners from whom they took over. Again on the American model there was a steady move away from maintenance with heroin to maintenance with methodone. Most addicts chose to attend the clinics as a last resort, preferring instead to pay inflated black-market prices. There was a large organized illicit traffic in heroin for the first time in Britain as smuggling and distribution networks soon realized the potential that a myopic government policy had given them.[68]

Cannabis, however, was the most popular illegal drug in Britain and from the mid-1960s there was unprecedented intense police activity against its use (cannabis is the generic name for Indian hemp while marijuana refers only to the leaves and not the resin of the plant. However, in America, the term marijuana is used universally for the drug cannabis). Thousands of convictions were obtained yearly for offences usually involving mere possession of the drug. Much expensive police and court time was absorbed without noticeably affecting the extent of the trade in cannabis, or for that matter other more destructive drugs. In fact it can be argued that more young people felt they had to try the substances that police activity and mass-media sensationalism had inadvertently glamorized.

Meanwhile new types of drug-related stories began to appear in the media; not just the familiar appalled reaction to the annual rise in the number of heroin addicts and the sordid devastation of their lives. Britain now had its own drug 'barons', 'czars' and 'Mr Bigs', and seizures were reported not in weight but in impressive 'estimated street values'. Less well noticed was the fact that the British police now had more 'rotten apples' who profited from rather than suppressed the drug traffic and that heavy-handed policing of the cannabis laws in particular had helped to spark off the first riots on the British mainland for decades.

As drug problems increased through the 1970s and into the 1980s, British politicians reacted in the same way as their American counterparts—some were righteously indignant, calculating that this would impress their more gullible constituents, but most quietly followed the paths of least resistance. Not one could say anything rational and appear 'soft' on drugs. The rhetoric of the hard-liners was remarkably close to the cynical utterances of Nelson Rockefeller, Richard Nixon and other American anti-drugs crusaders. In May 1985, for example, a House of Commons all-party home affairs committee issued a report based on the lessons they had learned from a ten-day 'fact-finding' trip to the United States. They declared war on drugs, warning that drug abuse was 'the most serious peacetime threat to our national well-being', and the committee's chairman, Sir Edward Gardner, added: 'Every son and daughter of every family in the country is at risk from this terrible epidemic'. President Nixon had declared war on drugs in July 1969 with electoral success rather than a genuine solution in mind. He had warned that drug abuse had become a 'serious national threat to the personal health and safety of millions of Americans', and had added that every son and daughter was at risk. The British Prime Minister, Margaret Thatcher, also followed American precedents to score political points in August 1985. Accompanied by press and television cameras, she visited the customs area at Heathrow airport, the 'front line' of the war against drugs and warned traffickers: 'We are after you. The pursuit will be relentless. We shall make your life not worth living'.[69]

The essence of the proposed 'new' British battle plan was intensified and more aggressive drug law enforcement, more intrusive practices and stiffer penalties for drug offenders. More police were transferred to anti-drug duties, squads were reorganized, intelligence centres were set up, 'hot-lines' were established for informers, more customs officers were paid to strip-search travellers, more companies bought machines to test the urine of employees, and new prisons were promised. All were strategies tried and found wanting in the United States because so long as there are profits to be made, manufacturers, smugglers and distributors will find ways to circumvent each new gimmick. These strategies, moreover, take resources away from the only approach that can reduce the demand for dangerous drugs—treatment and education, of course, but, more important, making policy that attacks the causes of social problems not the symptoms. But British politicians appear intent on reproducing counter-productive American 'solutions' to drug problems and British people are likely to suffer the consequences: more opportunities for successful organized crime and corruption while 'law and order' politicians preside over a society deteriorating into one of lawless disorder. As in the United States this will most probably justify a further investment in repression.

On the remote assumption that US efforts could prevent the cultivation of opium and coca in the world's most inaccessible areas or even the cultivation of marijuana within the country's own borders, the demand for illicit drugs would still be met by clandestine laboratories manufacturing stimulants, depressants and hallucinogens from commonly available industrial chemicals.

According to the Narcotics Intelligence Estimate for 1983, the illicit hallucinogenic situation had been dominated for the previous eight years by the powerful veterinary tranquillizer, PCP or 'Angel Dust'. Since there is no known diversion of PCP from licit channels, 'The entire supply of PCP to the illicit user population is manufactured in clandestine laboratories and is distributed by small, locally-oriented organizations and outlaw motorcycle gangs'. PCP is easily and cheaply manufactured but unpredictable and often dangerous. In 1983 there were over 6,000 hospital emergencies related to the drug and over 200 deaths. Owing to its bad reputation PCP has often been marketed in a fraudulent way, such as being sprinkled on marijuana to produce a more potent effect, and the awareness of such practices has even encouraged some parents to allow teenage children to grow their own marijuana and eliminate such risks.

The existence of one particularly lethal form of synthetic heroin, 'China White', was discovered in 1980. The *New York Times* reported that it was nearly eighty times stronger than morphine and that its potency had accounted for at least a dozen deaths. Like many synthetics it was easy to make but the problem was that its potency made it difficult to cut. Miscalculations result in almost instantaneous respiratory arrest.[70]

Another synthetic which recently attracted some notoriety is MPPP, an analogue of Demoral which is itself a synthetic opiate. The manufacture of MPPP often has an unwanted by-product, MPTP, and there have been many reports of users of such concoctions showing signs of Parkinson's disease, and sometimes becoming permanently crippled as a result.

As a result of raids on laboratories many chemists have been arrested in recent years but most escaped conviction since they had kept ahead of the law. Because the 1970 drug law required the government to define drugs by their precise chemical names, circumvention was quite easy. If miniscule amounts of new substances are attached to the analogues, legal chemicals could be produced. As fast as the government could add drugs to the Schedule of Controlled Substances, the chemists could come up with subtle and legal variants on the basic theme. Illegal PCP, for example, could become legal PCC, PCE or PHP, and the same procedure could produce legal amphetamine and methaqualone analogues.[71] At the time of writing the government had still not closed up these loopholes.

Synthetics have not as yet challenged natural products as the choice of most users, and foreign and domestic cultivation ensures that their demand is easily met. The potential for synthetics to compete, however, is great as old formulas are improved or as new formulas are discovered. And as Robert J. Robertson, state director of California's drug programmes, warned the Kaufman Commission in 1985: 'A single chemist can make enough ersatz heroin to supply all the addicts in the country with the drug', which he described as the 'wave of the future'.[72]

Jack Shafer concluded from his study of the new synthetic developments in the drug marketplace that: 'The net effect, tragic and ironic, of drug prohibition has been the creation of synthetic drugs that are more potent, dangerous and unpredictable that the drugs originally banned'.[72] The situation recalls one of the tragic ironies of alcohol prohibition.

In September 1985, the US Justice Department held a National Policing State-of-the-Art Conference in Phoenix, Arizona, for 200 leaders of American law enforcement. Thomas C. Kelly, deputy administrator of the DEA, told the conference that the Reagan administration had made great progress in the drug fight. As evidence he cited a 1984 national survey that showed a relative decline in marijuana use by high-school seniors. His complacency reflected a self-congratulatory theme in recent administration pronouncements on the drugs issue, but was immediately attacked by city police chiefs, closer to the sharp end of the problem. Los Angeles Police Chief Daryl Gates pointed out that the figures left out the 25 to 30 per cent of children who were 'dropping out'. Those, he said, 'are the kids who are committing the crimes most of which involve drugs'.[74]

Gates himself could hardly feel complacent over irrelevant figures which purported to show a decline in the number of young people still in the education system using marijuana regularly. In his city 'Rock Houses' run largely by violent youth gangs had become something of an institution, and were said to number around a thousand. The rock houses are heavily fortified homes or apartments with barred windows and reinforced half-inch steel doors, which dispense cocaine and other drugs. Money is pushed through a slot, drugs are pushed back. A single house could take in as much as $10,000 a day. In 1984 the police raided around 150 rock houses, with heavily armed squads using battering rams and dynamite to end sieges.[75]

According to local law enforcement agencies in Southern California, in 1984 there were over 420 street gangs in the Los Angeles Area alone, with an estimated total gang membership of from 40,000 to 50,000. The most notorious gang with the largest membership was called the Crips, whose members ranged from 14 to 25 years of age. Street-gang-related crimes in the Los Angeles area during 1983 consisted of 180 homicides, 2,869 felony assaults, 4,201 robberies, and 191 rapes. In 1984 the figures were: 212 homicides, 2,950 felony assaults, 3,600 robberies, and 194 rapes. One incident stood out in 1984. On 12 October, eleven youths were gunned down at a party, and five died in what was thought to be a drug-related, street-gang dispute.[76]

The phenomenon of young recruits to the drug trafficking industry is not limited to Los Angeles. In January 1984, DEA spokesmen announced that groups of Detroit children, some as young as 12 years old, could make as much as $2,000–$5,000 a week. A two-year investigation of Young Boys Inc., for example, revealed that the group employed 300 young people to sell $350,000 worth of heroin a week. As outlined by police and prosecutors' reports consulted by Howard Blum of the New York Times, Young Boys Inc. operated this way: the leaders of the gang would take raw heroin to a 'hookup' house where half a dozen people would, like an assembly line, mix the heroin with sugar and quinine.

The mix would be spooned into coin envelopes that would be stamped 'Murder one' or 'Rolls Royce', the street drugs' brand names. Bundles of these envelopes would be taken to locations, usually street corners or public housing projects, which were supervised by a 'top dog' who would distribute the envelopes to runners, the lowest paid and usually the youngest participants.

The runners would sell an envelope to an addict for $13. From this the organization would receive $10; the runner would get the other $3 as his fee. If the runner worked hard enough his fees could amount to hundreds of dollars a day.

The leaders of Young Boys Inc. were convicted but the authorities admitted that the members just joined other gangs. 'Except now', according to local DEA supervisor, Robert J. De Fauw, 'the kids who were runners at 12 are now 15 and working in supervisory positions. We're now going after 15-year-olds who are very experienced criminals'. De Fauw did not believe the situation of the streets was going to improve much:

> Our major problem is, how are we going to reach these kids? I mean, do you tell them to work in a warehouse at J.L. Hudson's for $45 a week when they're making $2,000 a week selling drugs on the street? They'll just laugh at you.[77]

The drug traffic has a never-ending source of recruits, because it is far more profitable than unemployment or dead-end jobs. It is not hard to see that the United States is still a prolific breeder of gangsters and that drug prohibition in particular offers a great deal of potential to the Capones and the Lanskys of the future. All those who have the savagery, shrewdness and luck to survive will continue to prosper.

The prohibition of drugs has done no more than foster crime, violence and corruption and continues to enrich corrupt police, prosecutors and judges as well as a multitude of growers, smugglers, manufacturers, distributors, gunmen and informants. The US government's attempt to suppress drug use has proved as counter-productive as the attempts to prohibit alcohol and gambling. The heart of the problem is that millions of Americans will never have their personal habits dictated by outdated laws and statutes.

The only response that the Reagan administration makes to the accumulating evidence of the disastrous effects of prohibition is to claim that there is no alternative. The present policy of selective enforcement is made to look potentially effective by the periodic arrests of traffickers or celebrities and the seizures of shipments measured in dishonest, but impressive 'street-value' figures. Successful investigations are, however, isolated and the harsh penalties for drug trafficking and possession have merely guaranteed excessively high prices and profits in the most accessible mass market in the world.

An avalanche of government propaganda has convinced the people of the United States in the wisdom of current policies. According to recent opinion polls, over 70 per cent are against the legalization of marijuana use. And, in November 1984, their representatives in Congress revealed that intolerance overrides all other considerations on the drugs issue when they voted by a 355–55 margin to defeat a proposal to permit doctors to prescribe heroin to relieve the pain of terminally ill cancer patients.[78]

The prohibition of drugs inflates prices and thus makes addicts steal to support their expensive habits. It leads to addicts risking overdose deaths from drugs of uncertain strength and purity, and risking infections with the use of dirty needles. AIDS, for example, is being spread among intravenous drug users at an alarming rate in the United States. In The Netherlands, where drug users can buy or exchange needles and syringes, there is an extremely limited incidence of AIDS among users.[79] But a hard-line approach to drugs in the United States persists even when all evidence shows that this approach maximizes the harm that drugs can do to society. This approach persists not because it can succeed, but because it wins votes or advances bureaucratic careers. Other approaches to the drug problem, based on regulation and control and recognition of the limits of the criminal sanction, are discounted for no other reason than that officials speculate that they might make things worse. There appears to be a grim determination to perpetuate a solution that has proved far worse than the original problem. Something is very wrong in the logic of a drugs policy that exacerbates crime and damage to society in every way.

Politicians, however, know that voters have short memories and can be easily reassured about the correctness of the government's position. In January 1986, President Reagan announced another plan to end organized crime—this time there were nine points—and stated that:

> Our goal is simple. We mean to cripple their organization, dry up their profits and put their members behind bars where they belong.
> They've had a free run for too long a time in this country.[79]

Something was apparently going to be done about it.

Epilogue

The underworld is desperately afraid. The structure of organized crime in the city is about to break up.

Thomas E. Dewey, 1937

Society, at last, is organized. With convictions like these, it's the mob that's coming apart.

New York Times, 24 November 1986, editorial on the convictions of Anthony 'Fat Tony' Salerno, Anthony 'Tony Ducks' Corallo and Carmine 'Junior' Persico.

The United States still faces the dilemma set by Walter Lippman in 1931:

Sooner or later the American people will have to make up their minds either to bring their legislative ideals down to a point where they square with human nature or they will have to establish an administrative despotism strong enough to start enforcing their moral ideals. They cannot much longer defy the devil with a wooden sword.[1]

Although repeal of Prohibition in 1933 squared one law with human nature, the effective enforcement of the remaining morality laws still required, in Lippman's words, 'the establishment of the most despotic and efficient government ever seen on earth', 'thousands and thousands of resolute and incorruptible inspectors, policemen, prosecutors, and judges', 'the expenditure of enormous sum of money', and finally 'the suspension of most civil rights'.[2] Since 1933 the process of squaring laws with human nature has been slow and constantly impeded by misleading fictions emanating from politicians, journalists, morality pressure groups and vested interests in the law-enforcement community.

At best the local crime and vice crusades examined in Part II were gestures. 'Crusading' mayors and 'fearless', 'racket-busting, district attorneys made headlines, gathered votes and inspired imitators while only superficially affecting the extent of crime and corruption. A combination of cynicism and apathy outweighed honesty and effectiveness and the country's post-war affluence guaranteed excessive profits for the corrupt networks which supplied the prohibited goods and services.

The failure of local efforts was somehow explained by invoking the notion of an all-powerful and nationwide conspiracy of aliens which was poisoning an otherwise pure economic and political system. There was a science-fiction quality about the Mafia interpretation which gripped the public's imagination but impaired rational decision-making. Instead of looking at the reasons for the success of so many criminal enterprises, analysts and commentators continued to distract the public with a bizarre explanation for the country's endemic organized crime problem. It was, however, an explanation which provided the rationale for ever-increasing law enforcement capacity and more and more laws to legitimate intrusive and coercive government practices. So far, this approach has shown more potential for abuse, in particular for suppressing political dissent, than for combating organized crime.

Federal organized crime control strategy has evolved from the perceived success of Thomas E. Dewey's tactics in 1930s Manhattan: close and prolonged surveillance and wire-tapping, inducements for criminals to become prosecution witnesses and convict their associates and laws which facilitate conspiracy convictions. A strategy which resembles, to repeat Benjamin Strolberg's analogy, that of a 'psychologist who builds a labyrinthian trap for rats, to learn whether or how soon they can get out of it'.[3]

Such strategy is guaranteed to produce short-term and publicity-laden successes in the war against crime. It promises success in public relations terms for policing agencies and continues to enhance the career prospects of ambitious prosecutors. Perhaps it might have succeeded if the field of conflict had not been widened by early twentieth-century moral crusaders. But the United States has chosen to pursue a crusade that has made, and continues to make, illegal enrichment too easy.

Many thousands of career criminals, from every American ethnic group, have taken full advantage of the attempt to impose morality on a population too diverse and too indulgent to be dictated to. The effort to control behaviour has backfired in America and helped to proliferate not just ethnic and multi-ethnic gangs, but also many thousands of public officials willing and able to take part in systematic and successful criminal activity. There are simply not enough honest and efficient public officials to make the labyrinthian-trap strategy work. The current level of enforcement capacity only succeeds in wasting law enforcement, criminal justice and prison resources trying to fulfil the dream of a vice-free America.

A constructive political response would resist finding scapegoats and misleading the public with confidently ignorant assertions and mounds of dishonest statistics, and would concentrate on trying to make the system work with more flexible and regulatory programmes, backed up if necessary by criminal sanctions. Persevering with unenforceable, crime-breeding and corrupting prohibitions only enables the most violent and best connected to flourish. The function of the criminal law should be, as John Stuart Mill wrote in 1859, 'to prevent harm to others'. Man's 'own good, either physical or moral, is not a sufficient warrant'.[4] But the reverse has been the case in the United States. In a cynical effort to protect the health and morality of

Americans, prohibition laws have caused immeasurably more damage to both.

US prohibition laws have not succeeded. Instead of solving the problems of excessive drinking, gambling and drug-taking, the laws themselves caused the devastation and termination of countless lives, exacerbated street crime, fostered successful organized crime, nullified or corrupted the law enforcement and criminal justice systems and reduced civil liberties. America's moral crusade had two faces. The rhetoric was righteous but the reality only highlighted an unlimited capacity for lies, hypocrisy, violence and illegal enrichment. The American people have been the victims of a successful double-cross.

Notes to chapters

Introduction

1. David R. Johnson, 'A Sinful Business: The Origins of Gambling Syndicates in the United States, 1840–1887', in David H. Bayley (ed.), *Police and Society*, Beverly Hills, Sage, 1977; Paul Boyer, *Urban Masses and Moral Order in America, 1820–1920*, Cambridge, Mass., Harvard University Press, 1978.
2. Comstock quoted in Gay Talese, *Thy Neighbour's Wife*, London, Pan, 1981, p. 58; *New Masses*, September 1915; see also David Pivar, *Purity Crusade*, Westport, Conn., Greenwood Press, 1973.
3. Clifford Roe, *Horrors of the White Slave Trade: The Mighty Crusade to Protect the Purity of Our Homes*, London (privately published), 1911, p. 319.
4. *San Jose Mercury*, 8 October 1881; see also Cheng-Tsu Wu, *Chink!: Anti-Chinese Prejudice in America*, San Francisco, Straight Arrow Books, 1973.
5. Quotes from Denise A. Herd, 'Prohibition, Racism and Class Politics in the Post-Reconstruction South', *Journal of Drug Issues*, Winter 1983, pp. 77–93.
6. David Musto, *The American Disease: Origins of Narcotic Control*, New Haven, Conn., Yale University Press, 1973, p. 245.
7. Denise A. Herd, op. cit.
8. *McClure's Magazine (34), 1909*; Dearborn *Independent's* quotes from Keith Sward, *The Legend of Henry Ford*, New York, Russell & Russell, 1968, p. 150, *The Outlook*, 16 August 1913, quoted in Salvatore J. LaGumina, *Wop!: A Documentary History of Anti-Italian Discrimination in the United States*, San Francisco, Straight Arrow Books, 1973, p. 98; see also Dwight Smith, *The Mafia Mystique*, New York, Basic Books, 1975, pp. 27–61.
9. Gay Talese, op. cit., p. 58; Andrew Sinclair, *Prohibition: The Era of Excess*, London, Faber & Faber, 1962, pp. 117–23.
10. Ruth Rosen, *The Lost Sisterhood: Prostitution in America, 1900–1920*, Baltimore, Johns Hopkins University Press, 1982, pp. 32, 33, 137, 172.
11. Commission on the Review of the National Policy Towards Gambling, *Gambling in America*, Washington, DC, 1976, Appendix 1, p. 106.
12. Quoted in Frederick Lewis Allen, *Only Yesterday*, New York, Bantam, 1959, p. 82.
13. Frank Browning and John Gerassi, *The American Way of Crime*, New York, G.P. Putnam's Sons, 1980, p. 467.
14. Sunday quoted in Herbert Asbury, *The Great Illusion: An Informal History of Prohibition*, New York, Doubleday & Co., 1950, pp. 145–6; *The Anti-Saloon Yearbook*, 1920.

1 Making Crime Pay

1. *New York Times*, 15 February 1925; *New York Times*, 5 April 1929; Andrew Sinclair, op. cit., pp. 249–56.

2. Charles Merz, *The Dry Decade*, Seattle, University of Washington Press, 1969, pp. 56–61.
3. Alcohol traffickers had been called bootleggers long before national Prohibition. The term probably derives from the illicit liquor trade in colonial times when smugglers often concealed liquor in their boots for sale to the Indians.
4. Hank Messick and Burt Goldblatt, *The Mobs and the Mafia*, London, Spring Books, 1972, p. 52; John Kobler, *Ardent Spirits*, New York, G.P. Putnam's Sons, 1973, pp. 316–21.
5. Pinchot quoted in Brain Inglis, *The Forbidden Game: A Social History of Drugs*, London, Hodder & Stoughton, 1975, p. 147.
6. John Kobler, *Capone*, London, Coronet, 1972, pp. 81–9.
7. *Chicago Tribune* quoted but not dated in James O'Donnell Bennett, 'Chicago Gangland', a pamphlett in the Wickersham Commission (officially known as the National Commission on Law Observance and Enforcement), Official Records Volume IV, pp. 349–405. The quote is on page 372.
8. Humbert Nelli, *The Business of Crime*, New York, Oxford University Press, 1976, pp. 164–65.
9. Thomas M. Coffey, *The Long Thirst*, London, Hamish Hamilton, 1976; Herman Feldman, *Prohibition: Its Economic and Industrial Aspects*, New York, D. Appleton & Co., 1927, pp. 67–9.
10. Mark Haller, 'Bootleggers and American Gambling, 1920–1950,' in Commission on the Review of the National Policy Towards Gambling, *Gambling in America*, Washington DC, 1976, Appendix 1, p. 115.
11. Kenneth Allsop, *The Bootleggers*, London, Arrow Books, 1970, p. 76; Craig Thompson and Raymond Allen, *Gang Rule in New York*, New York, The Dial Press, 1940.
12. Thomas A. Repetto, *The Blue Parade*, New York, Free Press, 1978, p. 279.
13. Association Against the Prohibition Amendment, 'Scandals of Prohibition Enforcement,' 1929 in Wickersham Commission, *Report on the Enforcement of the Prohibition Laws of the United States*, 71st Congress, 3rd Session, H.D. 722, Vol. 5, pp. 197–218; Herbert Asbury, *The Great Illusion: An Informal History of Prohibition*, New York, Doubleday & Co., 1950, pp. 176–85.
14. Samuel Hopkins Adams, *The Incredible Era: The Life and Times of Warren Gamaliel Harding*, New York, Capricorn Books, 1964, p. 339.
15. Herbert Asbury, op. cit., p. 185; Charles Merz, op. cit., pp. 140–45.
16. Association against the Prohibition Amendment, op. cit., p. 211.
17. Mabel Willebrandt, *The Inside of Prohibition*, Indianapolis, Bobbs-Merrill Co., 1929, p. 200.

2 The Dangers of Enforcement

1. La Guardia quoted in Herbert Asbury, op. cit., p. 210; Smith quoted in Charles E. Goshen, *Drink, Drugs and Do-Gooders*, London, Collier-Macmillan, 1973, p. 34.
2. Wickersham Commission, op. cit., Vol. 1, pp. 149–223; Association Against the Prohibition Amendment, *Reforming America with a Shotgun*, Washington, DC, 1929; Herbert Asbury, op. cit. pp. 166–7.
3. Smith Brookhart quoted in Wickersham Commission, op. cit., Vol. 5, p. 515.
4. *Chicago Tribune*, 12 July 1933.
5. ibid., 1 March 1929.
6. James Reed, 'The Pestilence of Fanaticism', *American Mercury*, May 1925, pp. 1–7.

7. Hofstadter quote from his introduction to Andrew Sinclair, op. cit., p. 10.
8. Quoted in John Kobler, *Ardent Spirits*, op. cit., pp. 285–6.
9. ibid., p. 285; Sean Dennis Cashman, *Prohibition*, New York, The Free Press, 1981, p. 48.
10. Wickersham Commission, op. cit., Vol. 5, p. 222–3.
11. R.A. Goldberg, *Hooded Empire: The Ku Klux Klan in Colorado*, Urbana, University of Illinois Press, 1981, pp. 30–107.

3 The Fall of Al Capone

1. John Kobler, *Capone*, op. cit., pp. 10–11.
2. Frederick Lewis Allen, *Only Yesterday*, New York, Bantam Books, 1929, pp. 185–6.
3. Quoted in Mary McKintosh, 'The Growth of Racketeering', *Economy and Society*, Vol. 2, November 1973.
4. Quoted in Andrew Sinclair, op. cit., p. 233.
5. Quoted in Andrew Sinclair's introduction to F.D. Pasley, *Al Capone*, London, Faber, 1966, p. 4.
6. Kenneth Allsop, op. cit., p. 40, 193–207.
7. *New York Times*, 15 February 1929.
8. Eliot Ness and Oscar Fraley, *The Untouchables*, London, Hodder, 1967.
9. John Kobler, *Capone*, op.cit., pp. 312–30.
10. Gus Tyler (ed.), *Organized Crime in America*, Detroit, University of Michigan Press, 1967, pp. 44–5.

4 The End of One Prohibition

1. Senator Robert F. Wagner of New York, a speech made in the Senate of the United States, 17 February 1931, reprinted in U.S.A. Constitutional Documents, *Repeal the Eighteenth Amendment*, Washington, DC, 1931.
2. Norman H. Clark, *Deliver Us from Evil*, New York, W.W. Norton, 1976, pp. 194–7.
3. ibid., pp. 196–201; David E. Kyvig, *Repealing National Prohibition*, Chicago, University of Chicago Press, 1979, p. 94; Raymond Fosdick and Albert L. Scott, *Towards Liquor Control*, New York, Harper & Brothers, 1933. John D. Rockefeller financed the research for this book and wrote the Foreword.
4. Keith Sward, *The Legend of Henry Ford*, New York, Russell & Russell, 1968, pp. 290–304, 399; Sean Dennis Cashman, op. cit., p. 168. Ford quoted in Larry Englemann, *Intemperance*, New York, The Free Press, 1979, pp. 176–7.
5. Quoted in Sinclair, op. cit., p. 368.
6. Quoted in Sinclair, op. cit., p. 413.
7. Lippmann quoted in Sinclair, op. cit., p. 377.
8. Wickersham Report, pp. 37–44.
9. Poem quoted in Frederick Lewis Allen, op. cit., p. 182.
10. David E. Kyvig, op. cit., pp. 178, 186.
11. V.O. Key, *Southern Politics*, New York, Vintage Books, 1949, p. 235.
12. Frank Browning and John Gerassi, *The American Way of Crime*, New York, G.P. Putnam's Sons, 1980, p. 368.
13. Raymond Fosdick, op. cit., p. 16.
14. Donald Dickson, 'Bureaucracy and Morality: An Organizational Perspective on a Moral Crusade', *Social Problems*, Vol. 16, 1968, pp. 143–56.

15. Anslinger testified before a Subcommittee on Finance, *Taxation of Marijuana*, 75th Congress, 1st Session, H.R. 6906, July 12, 1937.
16. Quoted in Stuart Hills, *Crime, Power and Morality*, London, Chandler, 1971, p. 70.
17. Donald Dickson, op. cit.; David Musto, *The American Disease, Origins of Narcotics Control*, New Haven, Conn., Yale University Press, 1973, pp. 210–15.
18. David Musto, op. cit., pp. 207–8.
19. Rufus King, *The Drug Hang-Up: America's Fifty Year Folly*, New York, W.W. Norton, 1972, p. 108.
20. For Rothstein's life, see Leo Katcher, *The Big Bankroll*, New York, Harper, 1958; Jenna Weissman Joselit, *Our Gang: Jewish Crime and the New York Jewish Community, 1900–1940*, Bloomington, Indiana University Press, 1983, pp. 11, 12, 96, 142–9; Daniel Bell, *The End of Ideology*, New York, The Free Press, 1960, p. 131; *New York Times*, 27 October 1963.
21. William Moore, *The Kefauver Committee and the Politics of Crime, 1950–1952*, Columbia, University of Missouri Press, 1974, pp. 18–19.
22. Humbert S. Nelli, *The Business of Crime*, New York, Oxford Univerity Press, 1976.
23. Sandford Ungar, *FBI*, New York, Atlantic, Little & Brown, 1975, pp. 72–82. The series of G-men films glorifying the FBI's early exploits is reviewed in Carlos Clarens, *Crime Movies*, New York, W.W. Norton, 1980, pp. 116–28.
24. Daniel Bell, op. cit., p. 143.
25. Dayton David McKean, *The Boss: The Hague Machine in Action*, Boston, Houghton Mifflin Co., 1940, pp. 48–9.
26. Atherton's report published in full in the *San Francisco Chronicle*, 17 March 1937.
27. August Vollmer, *The Police and Modern Society*, Berkeley, University of California Press, 1936, pp. 99–118.

5 New York's Gangbusters

1. For accounts of the Seabury investigations, see: Herbert Mitgang, *The Man Who Rode the Tiger*, Philadelphia, Lippincott, 1963; Alfred Connable and Edwin Silberfarb, *Tigers of Tammany*, New York, Holt, Rinehart & Winston, 1967; Polly Adler, *A House is not a Home*, London, Ace Books, 1957, pp. 121–3.
2. Alfred Connable, op. cit., pp. 283–4.
3. *New York Times*, 8 November 1933; Tony Scaduto, *Lucky Luciano*, London, Sphere, 1976, p. 111.
4. Quoted in Robert Caro, *The Power Broker: Robert Moses and the Fall of New York*, New York, Vintage, 1975, pp. 444–5.
5. L.M. Limpus, *Honest Cop*, New York, Dutton, 1939, for biography of Valentine. See also Charles Garrett, *The La Guardia Years*, New Brunswick, Rutgers University Press, 1961, pp. 159–60.
6. *New York Times*, 5 July 1935.
7. ibid., 21 January 1935.
8. ibid., 1 March 1935.
9. Kross quoted in Garrett, op. cit., p. 161; *Daily News* quoted in Adler, op. cit., pp. 174–5.
10. *New York Times*, 20 February 1936.
11. Alan Block, *East-Side—West-Side*, Cardiff, University College Cardiff, 1980, pp. 134–8; New York *World-Telegram*, 2 December 1933.
12. New York *Post*, 30 June 1935.

13. Quoted in Dwight Smith, *The Mafia Mystique*, London, Hutchinson, 1975, pp. 79.

14. This information comes from a memo entitled 'Rackets Investigation' and signed by Dewey's assistant, Frank Hogan, who later became Manhattan's District Attorney, in the *Thomas E. Dewey Papers*, Series 1: Early Career, Box 90, Folder 3, The Rush Rhees Library, University of Rochester, New York State.

15. Quoted in Scaduto, op. cit., p. 130.

16. ibid. pp. 130–45.

17. *Daily News*, 4 June 1936.

18. Transcript of Dewey's summing up in *Thomas E. Dewey Papers*, Box 90.

19. *New York Times*, 7 June 1936.

20. *Daily Mirror*, 8 June 1936.

21. *New York Times*, 9 June 1936.

22. Daniel Bell, op. cit., p. 131.

23. For an account of the career of Lepke Buchalter, see Andrew Tully, *Treasury Agent* (1958), excerpted in Gus Tyler, op. cit., pp. 205–13.

24. *Thomas E. Dewey Papers*, Box 90.

25. Richard Norton Smith, *Thomas E. Dewey and his Times*, New York, Simon & Shuster, 1982, pp. 251–62.

26. Benjamin Strolberg, 'Thomas E. Dewey, Self-Made Myth', *American Mercury*, June 1940, pp. 144–5.

27. Alfred Connable, op. cit., p. 290; *New York Times*, 31 October 1939.

28. Rupert Hughes, *The Story of Thomas E. Dewey*, New York, Grosset & Dunlap, 1944, pp. 179–85; Benjamin Strolberg, op. cit., p. 145.

29. Quoted in Rupert Hughes, op. cit., p. 282.

30. Barry Beyer, *Thomas E. Dewey: A Study in Political Leadership*, New York, Garland Publishing Inc., 1979, p. 212.

31. Richard 'Dixie' Davis, 'Things I Couldn't Tell Until Now', *Collier's*, July–August 1939.

32. Carlos Clarens, op. cit., pp. 156–9.

33. Rupert Hughes, op. cit., p. 308.

34. Woollcott Gibbs and John Bainbridge, 'St George and the Dragnet', *New Yorker*, 24 May 1940.

35. Benjamin Strolberg, op. cit., pp. 140–7.

36. *New York Times*, 1 March 1935.

37. *Daily News* article referred to in the *New York Times*, 21 June 1943.

38. Charles Garrett, op. cit., p. 162.

39. *New York Times*, 12 June 1945.

40. *Journal* quoted in Harold J. Anslinger and Will Oursler, *The Murderers: The Story of the Narcotics Gangs*, London, Arthur Barker Ltd., 1962, pp. 46–8.

41. For conflicting accounts of Luciano's release, see: Fred Cook, *Mafia!* London, Coronet, 1973, pp. 149–56; Leonard Katz, *Uncle Frank: The Biography of Frank Costello*, London, Star Books, 1973, pp. 151–2; Tony Scaduto, op. cit., pp. 157–65; Rodney Campbell, *The Luciano Project*, New York, McGraw-Hill, 1977.

42. Estes Kefauver, *Crime in America*, London, Victor Gollancz, 1952, p. 217; William Moore, op. cit., pp. 177–8.

43. Unless otherwise stated, the information about the Luciano release comes from a memo prepared for Senator Kefauver by George Martin of the *Scranton Times*, dated 19 August 1955 and filed in the *Estes Kefauver Papers*, University of Tennessee Library, Knoxville, Tennessee.

44. Joachim Joesten's *Dewey, Luciano and I*, Great Barrington, Mass., privately

published, 1954, was an answer to Sid Feder's *The Luciano Story*, New York, David McKay Co., 1954.

45. Tony Scaduto, op. cit., p. 176.
46. For post-war Italy, see Norman Lewis, *The Honoured Society*, Harmondsworth, Penguin, 1967; for anti-Castro conspiracy, see Arthur M. Schlesinger, Jr, *Robert Kennedy and His Times*, London, Futura Publications, 1978, pp. 519–21.
47. William Keating, *The Man Who Rocked The Boat*, London, Four Square, 1958, pp. 90–2.
48. Father Corridan testimony, US Congress, Senate Subcommittee of the Committee on Interstate and Foreign Commerce, *Hearings of the Waterfront Investigation*, Washington DC, 1953, pp. 469–70.
49. William Keating, op. cit., pp. 180–5.
50. Joe Ryan produced this letter to justify his activities before the Senate Subcommittee, op. cit., p. 478.
51. William Keating, op. cit., pp. 180–5.
52. Art Preis, *Labor's Giant Step*, New York, Pathfinder, 1972, p. 481.
53. William Keating, op. cit., p. 186; see also Frank Pearce, *Crimes of the Powerful*, London, Pluto Press, 1976, pp. 141–6; and Alan Block, 'On the Waterfront Revisited', *Contemporary Crises*, Vol. 6, 1982, pp. 373–96.
54. *New York Times*, 1 April 1949; Commission on the Review of National Policy Towards Gambling, *Gambling in America*, Washington DC, 1976, p. 766.
55. William Moore, op. cit., p. 177.
56. Estes Kefauver, op. cit., pp. 212–17.
57. Quoted in Leonard Katz, op. cit., p. 129.
58. *New York Times*, 26 October 1950.
59. William Keating, op. cit., p. 224.
60. ibid., p. 225.
61. ibid., p. 223.
62. Estes Kefauver, op. cit., p. 231.
63. William Keating, op. cit., p. 224.
64. New York *Post*, 4 March 1954.
65. Harriman quoted in Daniel P. Moynihan, 'The Private Government of Crime', in Bruce Cohen (ed.), *Crime in America*, Ithaca, F.E. Peacock Inc., 1970, pp. 320–8.
66. William Keating, op. cit., pp. 248–9.
67. Jack Anderson, *Confessions of a Muckraker*, New York, Random House, 1979, p. 299.
68. Barry Beyer, op. cit., p. 295.
69. Richard Norton Smith, op. cit., p. 643.
70. Benjamin Strolberg, op. cit., p. 141.

6 Chicago: Corrupt, and Content

1. Lincoln Steffens, *The Shame of the Cities*, New York, republished by Hill & Wang, 1963, p. 163.
2. Quoted in Kenneth Allsop, op. cit., p. 132.
3. Capone was talking to Genevieve Forbes of the *Chicago Tribune*, quoted in Paul Sann, *The Lawless Decade*, New York, Bonanza Books, 1957, p. 214.
4. John Kobler, *Capone* London, Coronet, 1973, p. 192.
5. Chicago *Daily Tribune*, 9 April 1931.
6. *Nation*, April 1931.
7. Kenneth Allsop, op. cit., p. 243.

8. John T. Flynn, 'These Our Rulers', *Colliers' Magazine*, 6 July, 1940; *Chicago News*, 16 January 1960.

9. Alex Gottried, *Boss Cermak*, Seattle, University of Washington Press, 1962, p. 320; Kenneth Allsop, op. cit., p. 306.

10. Kenneth Allsop, op. cit., p. 307.

11. John T. Flynn, op. cit.

12. Milton Mayer, 'The Case of Roger Touhy', in Albert Harper (ed.), *The Chicago Crime Book*, London, Tandem, 1967, p. 79.

13. ibid., p. 74.

14. From a memo on John Factor, prepared by Matthew Swift, investigator for the Chicago Crime Commission, dated 8 January 1981.

15. Roger Touhy and Ray Brennan, *The Stolen Years*, Cleveland, Pennington Press, 1959, p. 264.

16. John T. Flynn, op. cit.

17. ibid.

18. *New Republic*, 25 August 1952.

19. Virgil Peterson, *Barbarians in Our Midst*, Boston, Little, Brown & Co., 1952, p. 255.

20. ibid., pp. 190–2, 232–8.

21. For an account of the motion pictures racketeers case, see Malcolm Johnson, *Crime on the Labor Front*, 1950, excerpted in Gus Tyler, op. cit., pp. 197–205.

22. The first genuine investigation into Chicago industrial racketeering did not come until 1957 and the hearings of Senator McClellan's Committee to Investigate Improper Activities in the Labour and Management Field.

23. Roger Biles, *Big City Boss in Depression and War*, DeKalb, Northern Illinois University Press, 1984, pp. 67–70; Flynn, op. cit.

24. Ovid Demaris, *Captive City*, London, Sphere Books, 1971, p. 123.

25. Ibid., p. 122; Estes Kefauver, op. cit., pp. 55–7.

7 Los Angeles: City of Fallen Angels

1. George Mowry, *The Californian Progressives*, Berkeley, University of California Press, 1951; *Encyclopaedia Britannica*.

2. Robert Fogelson, *Big City Police*, Cambridge, Mass. Harvard University Press, 1977, p. 132.

3. Joseph Woods, *Progressivism and the Police*, Ph.D. thesis, UCLA, 1975, p. 313.

4. Fred Viebe, 'The Recall of Mayor Frank Shaw. A Revision', *California History*, Winter 1980/81, p. 293.

5. Quoted in ibid., p. 294.

6. *Los Angeles Times*, 22 May 1934.

7. Fred Viebe, op. cit., p. 295.

8. Rena M. Vale, 'A New Boss Takes Los Angeles', *American Mercury*, May 1941, p. 301.

9. Fred Viebe, op. cit., p. 296.

10. Joseph Woods, op. cit., p. 375.

11. Joseph Risnik, 'California Racket Buster', *American Magazine*, June 1938, p. 14.

12. Joseph Woods, op. cit., p. 356.

13. ibid., p. 372.

14. Fred Viebe, op. cit., p. 299.

15. Joseph Risnik, op. cit., p. 107.

16. Fred Viebe, op. cit., p. 299.

17. ibid., p. 300.
18. Joseph Woods, op. cit., p. 374.
19. Rena M. Vale, op. cit., pp. 299–301.
20. *Los Angeles Times*, 5 February 1942; Rena M. Vale, op. cit., p. 306.
21. Fred Viebe, op. cit., pp. 301–2.
22. Rena M. Vale, op. cit., p. 299; Fred Viebe, op. cit., p. 301; Joseph Woods, op. cit., p. 375.
23. Burton Turkus and Sid Feder, *Murder Inc.*, London, Victor Gollancz, 1952, pp. 187–9.
24. Dean Jennings, *We Only Kill Each Other*, Greenwich, Conn., Fawcett Publications, 1968.
25. John Bollens, *Samuel Yorty: Politics of a Constant Candidate*, Palisades, Grand B. Geyer, 1973.
26. Quoted in Robert Lane, *The Administration of Fletcher Bowron*, M.A. thesis, University of Southern California, 1954, p. 161.
27. Bruce Henstell, 'Now, *Those* Really Were 'Floating' Crap Games', *Los Angeles Magazine*, December 1978; 'Gambling Ships', *Life*, 19 August 1946.
28. Dean Jennings, op. cit.
29. Robert Lane, op. cit., p. 41.
30. US Congress, Senate Special Committee to Investigate Crime in Interstate Commerce (hereinafter called the Kefauver Committee), 82nd Congress, *Third Interim Report*, Washington, DC, 1951, pp. 95–6.
31. Joseph Woods, op. cit., p. 339.
32. ibid., p. 401.
33. *Third Interim Report*, op. cit., p. 96.
34. Joseph Woods, op. cit., p. 402.
35. Quoted in Joseph Woods, op. cit., p. 405.
36. ibid., pp. 405–10.
37. Florabel Muir, *Headline Happy!* New York, Holt, 1950, p. 247.
38. Carey McWilliams, 'The Big Fix in LA', *The Nation*, 20 August 1949.

8 Post-War Perfidy

1. Commission on the Review of the National Policy Towards Gambling, *Gambling in America*, Appendix I, p. 46, Rowley quoted in *Newsweek*, 17 February 1947.
2. Ernest Havemann, 'Gambling in the United States', *Life*, 19 June 1950.
3. Brooklyn *Eagle*, 11–22 December 1949.
4. William Moore, *The Kefauver Committee and the Politics of Crime*, Columbia, University of Missouri Press, 1974, pp. 32–3.
5. Virgil Peterson, *Gambling: Should it be legalized?* Springfield, Ill. Charles Thomas Publisher, 1945, quoted in *Gambling in America*, op. cit., Appendix IV, p. 55.
6. Norton Mockridge and R.H. Prall, *The Big Fix*, New York, Holt, 1954, p. 224.
7. New Orleans *States*, 8 December 1945.
8. Edward Haas, *deLesseps S. Morrision and the Image of Reform*, Baton Rouge, Louisiana State University Press, 1974, p. 39.
9. *Report of the Special Citizens' Investigating Committee* (SCIC), New Orleans, April 1954, Volume II, p. 13.
10. ibid. p. 28.
11. New Orleans *Item*, 26–30 May 1949.
12. *Times-Picayune*, 18 June 1949.
13. *Item*, 14 September 1949.

14. *The Attorney General's Conference on Organized Crime*, 15 February 1950, Washington DC, Department of Justice, 1950, p. 6.
15. ibid., pp. 26–7; *Item*, 15 February 1949.
16. ibid., p. 49.
17. ibid., p. 58.

9 Blaming Aliens

1. *Report of the Select Committee Appointed to Examine Tenement Houses in New York and Brooklyn*, 1857, quoted in Gus Tyler, op. cit., p. 417.
2. *Oswego Daily Times*, 19 October 1892, quoted in Luciano J. Ionizzo, *The Italian Americans*, Boston, Twayne Publications, 1980, p. 315.
3. James Bryce, *The American Commonwealth*, New York, Macmillan, 1928, Vol. II, pp. 156–167.
4. Andrew Sinclair, op. cit., p. 349.
5. Martin Mooney, *Crime Incorporated*, New York, Whittlesey House, 1935; Joseph Freeman, 'Murder Monopoly: The Inside Story of a Crime Trust', *The Nation*, 25 May 1940; Burton Turkus and Sid Feder, *Murder Inc.*, London, Victor Gollancz, 1952.
6. New York *World Telegram*, 4 June 1940 and 20 June 1940, quoted in Salvatore J. La Gumina (ed.), *Wop! A Documentary History of Anti-Italian Discrimination in the United States*, San Francisco, Straight Arrow Books, 1973, p. 256.
7. William Moore, op. cit., p. 44; Theodore Wilson, 'The Kefauver Committee, 1950', in Arthur M. Schlesinger Jr. (ed.), *Congress Investigates, 1792–1974*, New York, Chelsea House, 1975, pp. 351–83.
8. William Moore, op. cit., p. 75.
9. State of California, Special Crime Study Commission on Organized Crime, *Third Progress Report*, Sacramento, 31 January 1950, p. 100.
10. See, for example: Dwight Smith, *The Mafia Mystique*, London, Hutchinson, 1975; Rufus King, *The Drug Hang-Up: America's Fifty Year Folly*, New York, W.W. Norton, 1972; William Moore, 'The Kefauver Committee and Organized Crime', in J.M. Hawes (ed.), *Law and Order in American History*, London, Kennicut Press, 1979, p. 179.
11. Kefauver Committee, *Hearings*, Part 10, p. 501.
12. Estes Kefauver, *Crime in America*, London, Victor Gollancz, 1952, p. 28.
13. Kefauver Committee, *Hearings*, Anslinger Testimony, Part 2, pp. 95–6.
14. ibid., Follmer Testimony, Part 4, pp. 418–19.
15. Estes Kefauver, op. cit., p. 28.
16. William Moore, op. cit., p. 85.
17. Lee Mortimer and Jack Lait, *Chicago Confidential*, New York, Crown, 1951, 14th printing, pp. 176–7.
18. Lee Mortimer and Jack Lait, *U.S.A. Confidential*, New York, Crown, 1952, p. 15.
19. Lee Mortimer and Jack Lait, *Washington Confidential*, New York, Crown, 1951, 9th printing, p. 178.
20. ibid., p. 172.
21. Lee Mortimer and Jack Lait, *U.S.A. Confidential*, op. cit., p. 27.
22. Lee Mortimer and Jack Lait, *Chicago Confidential*, op. cit., p. 182.
23. Lee Mortimer and Jack Lait, *U.S.A. Confidential*, op. cit., p. 52.
24. Quotes taken from review of *U.S.A. Confidential* in the *New York Times*, 16 March 1952.
25. Lee Mortimer and Jack Lait, *Washington Confidential*, op. cit., p. 107.

26. Lee Mortimer and Jack Lait, *U.S.A. Confidential*, op. cit., p. 29.
27. ibid., p. ix.
28. Lee Mortimer and Jack Lait, *Washington Confidential*, op. cit., p. 117.
29. Lee Mortimer and Jack Lait, *Chicago Confidential*, op. cit., p. 45.
30. *New York Times*, 25 July 1948, 5 March 1950, 16 March 1952.
31. Kefauver Committee, *Third Interim Report*, Crown, New York, pp. 147–50.
32. Lee Mortimer and Jack Lait, *New York Confidential*, Crown, New York, op. cit., p. 220.
33. *Third Interim Report*, p. 149.
34. Costello quoted in US Congress, *House Report No. 1752*, 'Transmission of Gambling Information', 81st Congress, 2nd Session, Washington, DC, 1950, p. 27.
35. William Moore, op. cit., p. 134. Moore's book is indispensable to all students of the Kefauver Committee.

10   The Kefauver Crime Show

1. This account of the history of the racing-news wire service is based on William Moore, op. cit., pp. 74–113; see also the testimony of Warren J. Olney, Chief Counsel of the California Crime Commission, at the proceedings of the *Attorney General's Conference of District and County Attornies on Organized Crime*, Austin, Texas, 30–31 March 1951; Estes Kefauver, op. cit., p.40.
2. *Third Interim Report*, pp. 150–1.
3. Estes Kefauver, op. cit., pp. 39–40.
4. William Moore, op. cit., p. 113.
5. Estes Kefauver's Introduction to the Report on Organized Crime and Law Enforcement, submitted by the Bar Association Commission on Organized Crime, 1951.
6. *Third Interim Report*, pp. 30–7.
7. Estes Kefauver, op. cit., p. 146; Kefauver Committee, *Hearings, Clancy Testimony*, Part 8, pp. 369–423; Tobey Quoted in Estes Kefauver, op. cit., p. 146.
8. *Times-Picayune*, 10 February 1951; *Chattanooga News Free Press*, 9 February 1951.
9. *Third Interim Report*, p. 48.
10. ibid., pp. 95–6.
11. *Item*, 15 February 1949, 19 March 1949.
12. Letter from Alvin Cobb to Estes Kefauver, 21 April 1950, *Kefauver Papers*; *States*, 4 April 1950.
13. Edward Haas, op. cit., p. 182.
14. William Moore, op. cit., p. 165.
15. Kefauver Committee, *Hearings, Morrison Testimony*, Part 8, pp. 1–3.
16. Ernest Havemann, 'Gambling in the United States', *Life*, 19 June 1950; Edward Haas, op. cit., pp. 180–3.
17. Memo prepared for the Kefauver Committee, marked *deLesseps S. Morrison* in file for the Louisiana Crime Hearings, *Kefauver Papers*, University of Tennessee, Knoxville.
18. Estes Kefauver, op. cit., p. 140.
19. ibid., p. 218; *New York Times*, 20 March 1951.
20. Lester Velie, 'Rudolph Halley: How He Nailed America's Racketeers', *Colliers Magazine*, 19 May 1951.
21. *Third Interim Report*, p. 132; *Kefauver Committee Hearings*, Part 7, pp. 724–966.

22. Kefauver Committee, *Hearings*, Part 7, pp. 1039–40.
23. Quoted in Moore, op. cit., p. 184.
24. Kefauver Committee, *Hearings, Moretti Testimony*, Part 7, pp. 334, 348.
25. Quoted in Fred Cook, *Mafia!* London, Coronet, 1973, p. 179.
26. Quoted in Leonard Katz, *Uncle Frank*, London, Star Books, 1973, p. 166; *Third Interim Report*, p. 113; William Moore, op. cit., p. 189; *Newsweek*, 26 March 1951; Kefauver Committee, *Hearings, Costello Testimony*, Part 7, pp. 942–1019.
27. Lester Velie, op. cit.; letter from Kefauver to International Claims Commission 9 February 1951, *Kefauver Papers*; William Moore, op. cit., pp. 42–74.
28. Oliver Pilat, *Sodom by the Sea*, New York, Doubleday, Doran & Co., 1941, p. 310.
29. Norton Mockridge, op. cit., pp. 40–7.
30. Burton Turkus and Sid Feder, *Murder Inc.*, London, Victor Gollancz, 1952, pp. 302–19.
31. William Moore, op. cit., pp. 174–5.
32. Quoted by O'Dwyer in Kefauver Committee, *Hearings*, Part 7, p. 1525.
33. Quoted in George Walsh, *Public Enemies: The Mayor, the Mob and the Crime that Was*, New York, W.W. Norton, 1980, p. 169.
34. William Moore, op. cit., p. 176.
35. Kefauver Committee, *Hearings*, Part 7, pp. 527–39, 722–4, 839–43, 979, 1066–72.
36. Kefauver Committee, *Hearings, Lipsky Testimony*, Part 7, p. 843.
37. *Newsweek*, 21 November 1949, 6 February 1950; *Time*, 28 November 1949; Kefauver Committee, *Hearings, Costello Testimony*, Part 7, pp. 1017–18.
38. Kefauver Committee, *Hearings, O'Dwyer Testimony*, Part 7, p. 1326.
39. ibid., p. 1515.
40. ibid., p. 1536.
41. Lester Velie, op. cit.
42. Kefauver Committee, *Hearings, O'Dwyer Testimony*, Part 7, pp. 869–1580.
43. ibid.
44. ibid., p. 1368.
45. Kefauver Committee, *Hearings, Murtagh Testimony*, Part 7, p. 1410.
46. ibid., p. 1411.
47. Kefauver Committee, *Hearings*, Part 7, pp. 1603–6.
48. *Time*, 2 April 1951; Crawford quoted in William Moore, op. cit., p. 172.
49. *Third Interim Report*, p. 144.
50. Estes Kefauver, op. cit., p. 223.
51. Circulation of racing sheets in New York City: 1941 – 23,000,000; 1946 – 42,000,000; 1947 – 40,000,000; 1949 – 35,000,000; 1950 – 30,000,000. From Kefauver Committee, *Hearings*, Part 7, p. 1040.
52. Kefauver Committee, *Hearings, Morrison Testimony*, Part 8, p. 24.
53. William Moore, op. cit., p. 220.
54. Quoted in Norton Mockridge, op. cit., p. 272.
55. William Moore, op. cit., pp. 235–7.
56. *Third Interim Report*, pp. 5–20.
57. Kefauver Committee, *Hearings, McGrath Testimony*, Part 7, p. 516.
58. *Gambling in America*, op. cit., Appendix I, p. 54.
59. *Third Interim Report*, p. 6; Leonard Katz, op. cit., p. 206.
60. ibid., p. 187.
61. ibid., p. 188.
62. Quoted in Horace Silver (ed.), *The Crime-Control Establishment*, New Jersey, Prentice-Hall, 1974, p. 187.

11 Prolonging the Crusade

1. David Musto, *The American Disease: Origins of Narcotics Control*, Newhaven, Conn., Yale University Press, 1973, pp. 242.
2. *New York Times*, 11 April 1954, for review of Harold Anslinger and William F. Tompkins, *The Traffic in Narcotics*, New York, Funk and Wagnalls, 1953. The idea of a Chinese communist drug conspiracy persisted even after the Anslinger era. See, for example, *The Chinese Communist Plot to Drug the World*, published by the World Anti-Communist League, February 1972. This book showed photographs of opium plantations, which could have been taken anywhere in the world, and claimed that: 'These photographs offer indisputable proof that the Chinese Communists are engaged in narcotics trafficking, and it is hoped that this evidence will serve as a warning to the free world'. See also: Jerald W. Cloyd, *Drugs and Information Control*, Westport, Conn., Greenwich Press, 1982, for an account of the ideology behind the war on drugs.
3. *New York Times*, 9 July 1962.
4. Rufus King, op. cit., pp. 148–9.
5. Harold J. Anslinger and Will Oursler, *The Murderers*, London, Arthur Barker Ltd., 1962, pp. 172–3; Brian Fremantle, *The Fix: The Inside Story of the World Drugs Trade*, London, Michael Joseph, 1985, pp. 73–4.
6. John Marks, *The Search for the 'Manchurian Candidate': The CIA and Mind Control*, London, Allen Lane, 1979, pp. 20, 88–99, 101, 199, 220; A.W. Scheflin and E.N. Optom, *The Mind Manipulators*, London, Paddington Press, 1978, pp. 134–41.
7. Clark quoted in *New York Times*, 14 December 1968.
8. Tartaglino testimony from US Senate hearings before the Permanent Subcommittee on Investigations of the Committee on Government Operations, *Federal Drug Enforcement*, 94th Congress, 1st Session, 9, 10 and 11 June 1975, Part I, pp. 134–44.
9. William Manchester, *The Glory and the Dream: A Narrative History of America, 1932–1972*, London, Michael Joseph, 1975, p. 602; Sara Harris, *They Sell Sex: The Call Girls and Big Business*, New York, Crest, 1960.
10. *Gambling in America*, op. cit., Appendix I, p. 54.
11. Hank Messick, *Lansky*, London, Robert Hale, 1971; Jerome H. Skolnick, *House of Cards: Legalization and Control of Casino Gambling*, Boston, Little, Brown & Co., 1980, pp. 129–31.
12. Robert Fogelson, *Big City Police*, Cambridge, Mass., Harvard University Press, 1977, p. 256.
13. Richard Harris, *The Fear of Crime*, New York, Praeger, 1969, p. 14.
14. Jack Lait and Lee Mortimer, *U.S.A. Confidential*, New York, Crown, 1952, p. 182.
15. ibid., p. 9.
16. Ed Reid, *Mafia*, New York, Random House, 1952, p. 1.
17. Frederic Sondern, *Brotherhood of Evil: The Mafia*, London, Victor Gollancz, 1959.
18. Ted Posten, 'The Numbers Racket', excerpted in Gus Tyler, op. cit., quote from p. 270; the 'scratch a gambler' analysis of organized crime was stretched to a whole book by Fred Cook, *A Two-Dollar Bet Means Murder*, New York, Crown, 1962.
19. Dwight Smith, op. cit., p. 13; Arthur M. Schlesinger Jr., *Robert Kennedy and His Times*, London, Futura, 1979, p. 181.
20. John Kobler, *Capone*, op. cit., p. 246; Humbert Nelli, *The Business of Crime*, New York, Oxford University Press, 1976, p. 213; Daniel Bell, op. cit., p. 140;

New York Times, 15 November 1957, 27 November 1957, 10 November 1958, 28 February 1960, 29 November 1960.

21. *New York Times*, 6 August 1963, 28 September 1963, 2 October 1963, 3 October 1963.

22. Robert Kennedy, 'The Baleful Influence of Gambling', 1962 article reprinted in Robert D. Herman (ed.), *Gambling*, New York, Harper and Row, 1967; *Gambling in America*, op. cit., Appendix I, p. 63; *New York Times*, 26 September 1963.

23. Dwight Smith, op. cit., pp. 229–30.

24. Kennedy quoted in Peter Maas, *The Valachi Papers*, London, Panther, 1972, p. 9.

25. Valachi's testimony is extensively quoted in Gordon Hawkins, 'God and the Mafia', *The Public Interest*, Winter 1969, and Norval Mooris and Gordon Hawkins, *The Honest Politicians Guide to Crime Control*, Chicago, University of Chicago Press, 1970, pp. 203–35. 'The Canary that Sang' was the original title of Peter Maas's best-selling book, *The Valachi Papers*, op. cit.

26. *Gambling in America*, op. cit., Appendix I, p. 63.

27. President's Commission on Law Enforcement and the Administration of Justice, *The Challenge of Crime in a Free Society*, Washington, DC, 1967 pp. 448–9.

28. This and other discussions of organized crime control legislation relies heavily on Alan Block and William Chambliss, *Organizing Crime*, New York, Elsevier, 1981, pp. 194–211; Levy quoted in Sam Pizzigati, 'The Perverted Grand Juries', *Nation*, 19 June 1976.

29. Peter Reuter, 'Police Regulation of Illegal Gambling: Frustrations of Symbolic Enforcement', *The Annals of the American Academy*, July 1984, pp. 43–4.

30. Ramsey Clark, *Crime in America*, New York, Pocket Books, 1970, pp. 271–2.

31. *Wall Street Journal*, 16 March 1982.

32. *Gambling in America*, op. cit., Appendix I pp. 156–7; J. Edgar Hoover, 'Gambling and Corruption', *FBI Law Enforcement Bulletin*, August 1971.

33. David Burnham articles in *New York Times*, 25 April 1970, 26 April 1970, *The Knapp Commission Report on Police Corruption* New York, George Braziller, 1972.

34. Peter Maas, *Serpico*, London, Fontana, 1977.

35. *New York Times*, 28 January 1972, 17 March 1974.

36. John A. Gardiner and David Olson, 'Wincanton: The Politics of Corruption', in William J. Chambliss (ed.), *Crime and the Legal Process*, New York, McGraw-Hill, 1969; *Gambling in America*, op. cit., Appendix I p. 82; John A. Gardiner, *The Politics of Corruption: Organized Crime in an American City*, New York, Russell Sage, 1970.

37. William J. Chambliss, *On the Take: From Petty Crooks to Presidents*, Bloomington, Indiana University Press, 1978; Alan Block and William Chambliss, op. cit., pp. 96–114.

38. Jonathan Rubenstein, *City Police*, New York, Ballantine, 1973, p. 379; *Gambling in America*, op. cit., Final Report, p. 3.

39. 'Gambling Rage Out of Control', *U.S. News and World Report*, 30 May 1983.

40. President's Commission on Organized Crime (Kaufman Commission), *Hearing VII*, June 24–26, 1985, New York, *Jerome Skolnick testimony*, p. 36.

41. *U.S. News and World Report*, 30 May 1983.

42. *New York Times*, 26 June 1978; see also Peter Reuter, *Disorganized Crime*, Cambridge, Mass., MIT Press, 1983.

43. Kaufman Commission, *Hearing VII, Robert Gaugler Testimony*, pp. 76–80; *Philadelphia Inquirer*, 17 March 1985.

44. Kaufman Commission, *Hearing VII, Antony Lombardi Testimony*, pp. 101–20.

45. William Eadinton, 'The Casino Gaming Industry: A Study of Political Economy', *Annals of the American Academy*, July 1984, pp. 25–9; Kaufman Commission, op. cit., Skimming is not of course a practice restricted to casino gambling. It is not unusual for retail enterprises that operate in cash to keep two sets of books; one with artificially low revenues, which will be used for tax purposes, and another that allows the owner to keep track of how much the business is really making.
46. Kaufman Commission, *Hearing VII*, pp. 242–3.
47. George Sternlieb and James W. Hughes, *The Atlantic City Gamble: A Twentieth Century Fund Report*, Cambridge, Mass., Harvard University Press, 1983. pp. 132–153.
48. Mario Puzo, *The Godfather Papers*, London, Pan, 1972, p. 31.
49. Fred Cook quoted in Dwight Smith, op. cit., pp. 276–7
50. *New York Times*, 1 August 1972.
51. *New York Times*, 15 August 1971; Dwight Smith, op. cit., p. 302.
52. Fred Cook, op. cit., pp. 84–5; for a historian's account of the alleged purge, see Alan Block, *East-Side—West-Side*, University College Cardiff, 1980, pp. 3–9.
53. *New York Times*, 3 May 1971, 29 June 1971.
54. Jack Newfield, 'The Myth of Godfather Journalism', *The Village Voice*, 23 July 1979.
55. Ovid Demaris, *The Last Mafioso*, New York, Corgi, 1981, pp. 452–3.
56. *The Guardian*, 17 December 1984, 19 December 1985, 13 January 1986, 29 May 1986.
57. Pino Arlacchi, *Mafia Business: The Mafia Ethic and the Spirit of Capitalism*, London, Verso, 1986, p. 224.
58. Hank Messick, *Secret File*, New York, G.P. Putman's Sons, 1969, p. 11.

12 Expansion

1. Quoted in Anslinger's obituary notice, *New York Times*, 18 November 1975.
2. Rufus King, *The Drug Hang-up: America's Fifty Year Folly*, New York, W.W. Norton, 1972, pp. 232–8; *New York Times*, 28 September 1962.
3. Edward J. Epstein, *Agency of Fear, Opiates and Political Power in America*, New York, Putnam's 1977, pp. 34–45.
4. Patrick Anderson, *High in America: The True Story Behind NORML and the Politics of Marijuana*, New York, Viking Press, 1981, p. 55.
5. *FBI Uniform Crime Reports 1965–1983*.
6. Hoover's memo quoted in Patrick Andreson, op. cit., p. 54.
7. John Pekkanen, *The American Connection*, Chicago, Follett, 1974, reviewed in *New York Times*, 7 July 1974.
8. Ramsey Clark interviewed, 29 April 1985.
9. Johnson quoted in *New York Times*, 8 February 1968; Rufus King, op. cit., p. 301.
10. *Republican Congressional Committee Newsletter*, 2 September 1968.
11. This account of the Nixon administration's cynical war on drugs relies heavily on Epstein, op. cit. Television commercial quoted on p. 62.
12. ibid., pp. 63–71.
13. Ehrlichman testimony in *Federal Drug Enforcement*, Hearings before the Permanent Subcommittee on Investigations of the Committee on Government Operations, US Senate, 94th Congress, Second Session, July 27, 28, 29, 1976, Part 4, US Government Printing Office, Washington DC, 1976, p. 794.
14. Quoted in Rufus King, op. cit., p. 308.

15. Max Singer, 'The Vitality of Mythical Numbers', *The Public Interest*, Spring 1971.

16. Edward J. Epstein, op. cit., p. 174. Estimates of the number of heroin addicts stabilized from the mid-1970s at around half a million. The *1984 National Strategy for Prevention of Drug Abuse and Drug Trafficking* claimed 'a decline in new, young users and that present users are largely from a group of people who began using heroin during the "heroin epidemic" in the late 1960s and early 1970s'. This apparent marginal success in the war on drugs coincided with an election year.

17. Edward J. Epstein, op. cit., p. 293; Jeb Stuart Magruder, *One Man's Guide to Watergate*, London, Hodder & Stroughton, 1974, pp. 103–5; *New York Times*, 3 April 1970, 8 April 1970.

18. *New York Times*, 15 July 1969.

19. Albert Goldman, *Grass Roots*, New York, Harper & Row, 1979, p. 100; Richard C. Schroeder, *The Politics of Drugs*, Congressional Quarterly Inc., Washington, DC, 1980, p. 123; Lawrence A. Gooberman, *Operation Intercept: The Multiple Consequences of Public Policy*, New York, Pergamon Press Inc., 1974.

20. The Drug Abuse Council, *The Facts About 'Drug Abuse'*, New York, Free Press, 1980, p. 38; Richard Schroeder, op. cit., p. 130; The Editors and Staff of Newsday, *The Heroin Trail*, 1974, pp. 3–4; Brian Fremantle, op. cit., pp. 125–6.

21. Peter Grose, 'US Doubles Narcotics Corps Abroad', *New York Times*, 3 April 1970.

22. Arnold Trebach, *The Heroin Solution*, New Haven, Conn, Yale University Press, 1982, p. 237, Rufus King, op. cit., 307–22.

23. Quoted in *Newsweek*, 9 February 1970.

24. Quoted in *New York Times*, 18 June 1971.

25. Rufus King, op. cit., p. 311; *New York Times*, 25 June 1973.

26. Ingersoll quoted in The Drug Abuse Council, op. cit., p. 39.

27. Edward J. Epstein, op. cit., pp. 221–2; David Harris, 'An Inside Look at Federal Narcotics Enforcement: Three Ex-Agents Tell Their Story', *Rolling Stone*, 5 December 1974; The Drug Abuse Council, op. cit., p. 40.

28. Abraham S. Blumberg, 'Drug Control: Agenda for Repression', in Richard L. Rachin and Eugene H. Czajkoski (eds), *Drug Abuse Control*, Lexington, Mass, Lexington Books, 1975, p. 8.

29. Nixon quoted in *New York Times*, 21 March 1973; Kleindienst quoted in David J. Bellis, *Heroin and Politicians*, London, Greenwood Press, 1981, p. 72.

30. *New York Times*, 25 June 1973; Joe Eszterhas, *Nark!* San Francisco, Straight Arrow Books, 1974.

31. Saxbe quoted in 1974 Review of the Year; Edward J. Epstein, op. cit., p. 223.

32. John Finlator, *The Drugged Nation*, New York, Simon & Schuster, 1973, pp. 322–3; August Bequai, *Organized Crime*, Lexington, Mass., Lexington Books, 1979, p. 146; Rufus King, op. cit., p. 319.

33. Charles Goodell, *Political Prisoners in America*, New York, Random House, 1973, p. 199; see also Abe Peck, *Uncovering the Sixties: The Life and Times of the Underground Press*, New York, Pantheon, 1985.

34. Ehrlichman testimony in *Federal Drug Enforcement*, Hearings before the Permanent Subcommittee on Investigations of the Committee on Government Operations, US Senate, 94th Congress, Second Session, July 27, 28 and 29, 1976, Part 4, US Government Printing Office, Washington, DC, 1976, p. 804, op. cit., p. 804.

35. Richard Harris, *Freedom Spent*, Boston, Little Brown & Co., 1976, p. 410.

36. Frank J. Donner, *The Age of Surveillance*, New York, Knopf, 1980, p. 361; Sam Pizzigati, 'The Perverted Grand Juries', *The Nation*, 19 June 1976; Leroy D.

Clark, *The Grand Jury: The Use and Abuse of Political Power*, New York, Quadrangle, 1976.

37. Charles Goodell, op. cit., p. 233; Frank Donner, op. cit., p. 361.
38. Quoted in Donner, op. cit., pp. 363–4.
39. Conyers and Kennedy testified to the House Judiciary Subcommittee No. 1 during *Hearings on the Fort Worth Five and Grand Jury Abuse*, 1973, and this was added to House of Representatives, Committee on the Judiciary, Subcommittee on Immigration, Citizenship and International Law Hearings on H.J. Res 46, H.R. 1277 and Related Bills: Federal G.J., Washington, DC, Government Printing Office, 1976, pp. 344–56, 498–513.
40. Frank Donner, op. cit., p. 358; John Conyers testimony, op. cit., p. 354.
41. William Chambliss and Alan Block, op. cit.
42. John Conyers' testimony, op. cit.
43. The fate of the Watergate conspirators is summarized in *Newsweek*, 14 June 1982, and in Tom Passavanat and Conan Putnam, Watergate, Inc.: An Anniversary Audit', *Playboy*, June 1982.
44. Nixon speech at Walt Disney World, 17 November 1973.
45. *New York Times*, 19 August 1973.
46. *New York Times*, 27 February 1970.
47. *New York Times*, 6 April 1971; *The Knapp Commission Report on Police Corruption*, New York, George Braziller, 1972; Richard Kunnes, *The American Heroin Empire*, New York, Dodd, Mead & Co., 1972, pp. 80–2, 116–7; Abraham S. Blumberg, op. cit., p. 13.
48. *The Knapp Commission Report on Police Corruption*, op. cit., pp. 91–3.
49. Robin Moore, *The French Connection*, London, Hodder & Stoughton, 1969, p. 1.
50. *New York Times*, 1 February 1973, 19 November 1971, 3 December 1971, 4 December 1971.
51. David Durk and Ira Silverman, *The Pleasant Avenue Connection*, New York, Harper & Row, 1976, p. 33.
52. ibid., pp. 33–40.
53. Robert Daley, *Prince of the City*, London, Granada, 1980, pp. 30–1.
54. *New York Times*, 9 August 1981, 30 August 1981; Steve Chapple, *Outlaws in Babylon*, London, Angus & Robertson, 1985, p. 234.
55. *New York Times*, 2 December 1975, 24 December 1975, 28 December 1975, 27 March 1977, 28 March 1977.
56. *New York Times*, 9 August 1981.
57. *The Nation's Toughest Drug Law: Evaluating the New York Experience*, report published in the *PharmChem Newsletter*. December 1978.
58. *FBI Uniform Crime Reports*, 1965–83.
59. Patrick Anderson, op. cit., pp. 57, 70, 109.
60. *Rolling Stone*, 30 November 1978; *New York Times*, 12 January 1982; *Washington Post*, 25 May 1982; *High Times*, July 1984.
61. Patrick Anderson, op. cit., p. 166.
62. *New York Times*, 2 August 1976.
63. *FBI Uniform Crime Reports*, 1965–83.
64. Richard Schroeder, op. cit., p. 54; Albert Goldman, op. cit., p. 251; *New York Times*, 22 June 1979.
65. US General Accounting Office, Report to the Chairman, Subcommittee on Public Lands and National Parks, Committee on Interior and Insular Affairs, House of Representatives, *Additional Actions Taken to Control Marijuana Cultivation and Other Crimes on Federal Lands*, 28 November 1984; *Law Enforcement Efforts to Control Domestically Grown Marijuana*, 25 May 1984, see also Steve Chapple, op. cit.

66. Richard Schroeder, op. cit., pp. 54–5.
67. Anthony Henman, Roger Lewis and Tim Malyon, *Big Deal: The Politics of the Illicit Drugs Business*, London, Pluto, 1985, pp. 10–11.
68. Richard Schroeder, op. cit., p. 121.
70. Albert Goldman, op. cit.
71. *Las Vegas Review-Journal*, 29 March 1985.
72. Robert B. McBride, 'Business as Usual: Heroin Distribution in the United States', *Journal of Drug Issues*, Winter 1983; Steven Wisotsky, 'Exposing the War on Cocaine: The Futility and Destructiveness of Prohibition', *Wisconsin Law Review*, 1983.
73. Hank Messick, *Of Grass and Snow*, Englewood Cliffs, New Jersey, Prentice-Hall, 1979, pp. 52–4; Penny Lernoux, 'The Miami Connection', *Nation*, 18 February 1984.
74. Hank Messick, op. cit., pp. 24–36; Donald Goddard, *Easy Money*, New York, Farrar, 1978, p. 361.
75. McGuire quoted in *Narcotics Control Digest*, 20 February 1985, p. 5; *New York Times*, 4 July 1980, 22 February 1985, 3 May 1985, 20 July 1984.
76. *Detroit Free Press*, 30 March 1972; *New York Times*, 18 February 1983, 7 October 1984; Steven Wisotsky, op. cit., p. 1401; Penny Lernoux, op. cit.
77. Donald Goddard, op. cit., p. 167.
78. Hank Messick, op. cit., p. 143.
79. Steven Wisotski, op. cit., p. 1402.
80. *New York Times*, 15 April 1984; *Newsweek*, 30 April 1984.
81. Donald Goddard, op. cit., p. 164.
82. Mark Swain, 'Who killed Barry Seal?' *High Times*, June 1986.
83. Penny Lernoux, op. cit.,; Philip Mattera, *Off the Books: The Rise of the Underground Economy*, London, Pluto, 1985 pp. 55–61.
84. *Business Week*, 18 March 1985.
85. Anthony Henman, *et al.*, op. cit., pp. 2–3.
86. Penny Lernoux, op. cit.,; Kaufman Commission, *Interim Report to the President and the Attorney-General, The Cash Connection: Organized Crime, Financial Institutions, and Money Laundering* US Government Printing Office, Washington, DC, October 1984.
87. Kaufman Commission, ibid., pp. 35–9.
88. Quoted in Penny Lernoux, op. cit., p. 198.
89. *Time*, 11 April 1983.

13 Perpetuation

1. National Commission on Marijuana and Drug Abuse, *Drug Use in America: Problem in Perspective*, Washington DC, 1973, p. 3.
2. ibid., p. 27.
3. *New York Times*, 19 March 1973.
4. Laurence Gonzales, 'The War on Drugs: A Special Report', *Playboy*, April 1982.
5. Martin Amis, 'Out of the Pews, into the Polls, Amen', *Observer*, 21 September 1980.
6. *New York Times*, 7 March 1981.
7. *Newsweek*, 9 August 1982.
8. Reagan's speech printed in full in *Drug Enforcement*, Spring 1983; *New York Times*, 15 October 1982.

9. *Washington Post*, 5 October 1982; *Boston Globe*, 9 October 1982.
10. *The Morning Union*, 18 November 1982.
11. *Drugs and Drug Abuse Education Newsletter*, January 1983.
12. Lacey quoted in *The Star-Ledger*, 24 January 1984; *New York Times*, 2 August 1984; Joel Brinkley, 'Drug Smugglers Say Hard Part Is What To Do With The Money', *New York Times*, 29 November 1984.
13. Gates quoted in *US News and World Report*, 8 February 1984. Block quoted in *Narcotics Control Digest*, 16 April 1986.
14. *Drugs and Drug Abuse Education Newsletter*, April/May 1984.
15. ibid., June 1985.
16. *New York Times*, 7 March 1981.
17. *Drugs and Drug Abuse Education Newsletter*, January 1983.
18. Mrs Reagan's quotation taken from her foreword to the book, *Marijuana Alert*, by Peggy Mann, New York, McGraw-Hill, 1985; *New Republic*, 16 and 23 September 1985.
19. Mrs Reagan quoted in *Newsday*, 25 April 1985.
20. *New York Times*, 22 January 1982.
21. Kaufman Commission *Organized Crime: Federal Law Enforcement Perspective*, Record of Hearing 1, 29 November 1983, US Government Printing Office, Washington, DC, 1983, p. 140; *San Francisco Chronicle*, 15 March 1985; *New York Times*, 15 March 1985, 17 March 1985.
22. *New York Times*, 24 October 1982.
23. *Time*, 1 November 1982; *Guardian*, 21 October 1982.
24. *Guardian*, 25 October 1983.
25. *Guardian*, 1 December 1983.
26. *Guardian*, 17 August 1984.
27. *New York Times*, 17 August 1984.
28. *New York Times*, 19 August 1984.
29. John Sellers, 'Sweet Scam', *In These Times*, 2–8 March 1983; information also from the David Curry Defense Committee, 5500 S. Dorchester, Chicago, Illinois 60637.
30. Steven Shapiro, 'Nailing Sanctuary Givers', *Los Angeles Daily Journal*, 12 March 1985.
31. *High Times*, September 1983; *San Francisco Chronicle*, 1 October 1982.
32. United States District Court, Northern District of California, No. C–83–4047 RPA, 20 February 1985; decision also discussed in Jack Anderson, 'Peeping Toms in Helicopters', *San Francisco Chronicle*, 15 March 1985, and *The Leaflet*, February 1985.
33. *High Times*, December 1983.
34. Lungren quoted in *Narcotics Control Digest*, 15 May 1985.
35. *Washington Post*, 2 March 1983; see also Steve Chapple, op. cit.
36. Anthony Henman, *et al.*, op. cit., pp. 73–4.
37. See note 8.
38. For prison gangs, see David B. Kalnick, *The Inmate Economy*, Lexington, Mass., Lexington Books, 1980; *Sunday Times*, 22 January 1978; *High Times*, April 1981; *Washington Post*, 7 February 1982; *New York Times*, 20 January 1982; *Narcotics Control Digest*, 16 October 1985; *San Francisco Chronicle*, 18 March 1985; *New York Times*, 20 January 1986.
39. Kaufman Commission, *Hearing I, Organized Crime: Federal Law Enforcement Perspective*, 29 November 1983.
40. Kaufman Commission, *Hearing III, Asian Roots*, 23–25 October 1984.
41. *Curbing The Narcotics Traffic: Recommendations of the Organized Crime Commission*, reprinted in *Narcotics Control Digest*, 19 March 1986.
42. McBride and Methvin quoted in *New York Times*, 6 March 1986.

248 NOTES

43. Meese and Kaufman quoted in Joel Brinkley, 'Meese Supports Drug-Testing for U.S. Employees', *New York Times*, 5 March 1986.
44. *New Republic*, 31 March 1986.
45. *New York Times*, 19 March 1986.
46. *The Guardian*, 5 August 1986, 15 September 1986, 21 October 1986.
47. President's Commission on Law Enforcement and the Administration of Justice, *The Challenge of Crime in a Free Society*, Washington DC, 1967, p. 446; *High Times*, October 1981; *Drug Survival News*, August 1981; *Boston Globe*, 15 July 1981; *Los Angeles Times*, 24 May 1982; *New York Times*, 9 January 1986.
48. *U.S.A. Today*, 2 November 1982; *Narcotics Control Digest*, May 1984; *National Law Review*, 22 August 1983; *U.S. News and World* Report, 6 February 1984; *Washington Post*, 24 November 1982; *Washington Post*, 4 November 1982; *New York Times*, 28 August 1982; *New York Times*, 3 April 1986; *Narcotics Control Digest*, 12 June 1985, 30 October 1985, 16 October 1985, 19 March 1986.
49. *New York Times*, 15 September 1983; *High Times*, June 1983.
50. *New York Times*, 22 April 1985, 3 May 1985, 7 May 1985, 25 April 1985; *New York Post*, 23 April 1985; *Newsday*, 25 April 1985; *Guardian*.
51. *Saginaw News*, 24 June 1981, 14 March 1982, 3 May 1984.
52. *High Times*, March 1985.
53. *New York Times*, 19 August 1982.
54. Anthony Henman, *et al.*, op. cit., pp. 65–6.
55. *Narcotics Control Digest*, 18 September 1985.
56. US House of Representatives, Select Committee on Narcotics Abuse and Control, *Annual Report for the Year 1984*, 98th Congress, 2nd Session, Washington, DC, 1985, pp. 10–11.
57. ibid., pp. 18–21.
58. *The International Herald Tribune*, 25 January 1984.
59. *New Republic*, 15 April 1985; *The Guardian*, 4 November 1985; *New York Times*, 20 January 1986; *The Guardian*, 11 November 1986; *New Republic*, 3 February 1986; *Narcotics Control Digest*, 19 February 1986; *The Guardian*, 26 April 1986.
60. Bush quoted in the *Narcotics Control Digest*, 6 February 1985.
61. *New York Times*, 19 March 1986.
62. Jonathan Kwitny, 'Money, Drugs and the *Contras*', *The Nation*, 29 August 1987.
63. Kaufman Commission, *Report to the President and the Attorney General, America's Habit: Drug Abuse, Drug Trafficking, and Organized Crime*, US Government Printing Office, Washington, DC, March 1986, p. 101.
64. Martin A. Lee, 'How the Drug Czar Got Away', *The Nation*, 5 September 1987.
65. *The Independant*, 2 January 1988.
66. Penny Lernoux, op. cit.; Hank Messick, *Of Grass and Snow*, Englewood Cliffs, New Jersey, Prentice-Hall Inc., 1979; Alfred W. McCoy, *The Politics of Heroin in Southeast Asia*, 1984, op. cit.; *The Guardian*, 24 April 1986, 25 April 1986, 30 May 1986.
67. US House of Representatives, op. cit., p. 210; *Narcotics Control Digest*, 14 May 1986; *New York Times*, 17 July 1987.
68. For historical accounts of British drug control policy, see: Arnold Trebach, *The Heroin Solution*, New Haven, Conn. Yale University Press, 1982, and Jasper Woodcock, 'The Role of the Prescribing Clinic in the British Response of Drug Abuse', pamphlet from the Institute for the Study of Drug Dependence, 1984.
69. House of Commons, *Fifth Report from the Home Affairs Committee*, Session 1984–85, *Misuse of Hard Drugs (Interim Report)*, Her Majesty's Stationery Office, London, 15 May 1985; *The London Standard*, 20 June 1985, *The Guardian*, 24 May 1985, *The Guardian*, 10 August 1985.

70. *New York Times*, 21 December 1980.
71. *New York Times*, 22 February 1985; *Narcotics Control Digest*, 10 July 1985; *The Guardian*, 21 March 1986; Jack Shafer, 'The War on Drugs is Over. The Government has Lost', *Inquiry*, February 1984.
72. Robertson quoted in *New York Times*, 22 February 1985.
73. Jack Shafer, op. cit.
74. Gates quoted in *Narcotics Control Digest*, 2 October 1985.
75. *Observer*, 13 January 1985.
76. State of California, Department of Justice, *Organized Crime in California, 1984; The Annual Report to the Legislature*, Sacramento, Calif., 1985, pp. 29–30.
77. Howard Blum, 'U.S. Helps Detroit to Attack Drug Rings That Use Young', *New York Times*, 28 January 1984.
78. *Wall Street Journal*, 29 November 1984.
79. *Narcotics Control Digest*, 12 August 1987.
80. Reagan quoted in the *New York Times*, 8 January 1986.

Epilogue

1. Walter Lippmann, 'The Underworld as Servant', *Forum*, January and February 1931.
2. ibid.
3. Benjamin Strolberg, 'Thomas E. Dewey, Self-Made Myth', *American Mercury*, June 1940, p. 143.
4. John Stuart Mill, *On Liberty*, London, 1859.

Index